Elizabethan Silent Language

ELIZABETHAN

SILENT

LANGUAGE

Mary E. Hazard

UNIVERSITY OF NEBRASKA PRESS

Lincoln and London

Publication of this book was assisted by a grant from The Andrew W. Mellon Foundation.

∞

Library of Congress Cataloging-in-Publication Data
Hazard, Mary E.
Elizabethan silent language / Mary E. Hazard.
p.   cm.
Includes bibliographical references and index.
ISBN 0-8032-2397-8 (cl.: alk. paper)
1. England—Civilization—16th century. 2. Communication—Social
aspects—England—History—16th century. 3. Language and
culture—England—History—16th century. 4. Art and literature—England—History—
16th century. 5. Nonverbal communication—History—16th century. 6. Great
Britain—History—Elizabeth, 1558–1603. 7. Gesture—England—History—16th century.
8. Art, Renaissance—England. 9. Art, English. I. Title.
DA320.H286 2000
302.2'0942'09031—dc21   99-048632

For two who believed:
Martin Zuckerman,
Helpmate
and
Tom Canavan
Best of Deans
in
The Worst of Times

both of "whose merits tome-ward I do acknowledge,
in setting this hand free from the daily improvements of
a manuell trade, and giving it full liberty thus to express
the inclination of my mind, himself being the procurer
of my present state."
John Speed, *The Theatre of Great Britain*

CONTENTS

List of Illustrations ix

Acknowledgments xi

Abbreviations xiii

Introduction:
The Concept and Types of Silent Language I

PART I Line and Plane

1 Drawing the Line 23

2 Line as Intersection, Plane, and Idea 47

PART II Surface, Shape, and Substance

3 Surface, Color, and Texture as Superficial Comment 77

4 Shape and Substance as Matters of Weight 109

PART III Position, Gesture, Motion, and Duration

5 Place, Boundary, and Position 143

6   Motion, Measure, and Meaning   173

PART IV   Figure and Ground: Convention and Indeterminacy,
          Absence, and Silence

7   Ceremonial Departures
    and Indecorous Presentations   201

8   Absent/Presence, Present/Absence, Gesture,
    Silence, and the Uses of Indeterminacy   231

    Notes   267
    Works Cited   293
    Index   327

ILLUSTRATIONS

following page 140

1. Triangular Lodge, Rushton, north side; 1594–97
2. Franciscus Hogenberg (?). The Royal Exchange; 1566–68
3. Attributed to George Gower. *The Armada Portrait*; 1588(?)
4. Attributed to William Segar. *The Ermine Portrait*; 1585
5. Nicholas Hilliard. *George Clifford*; c. 1590
6. Marcus Gheeraerts the Younger. *The Ditchley Portrait*; c. 1592
7. Nicholas Hilliard. *Young Man among Roses*; c. 1587
8. Isaac Oliver. *Unknown Melancholy Young Man*; c. 1590–95
9. *The Shepheard Buss*; c. 1596
10. Hieronimo Custodis. *Frances Clinton*; 1589
11. Attributed to Marcus Gheeraerts the Younger. *The Rainbow Portrait*; c.1600
12. Antonio Mor. *Sir Henry Lee*; 1568
13. Jean de Beauchesne. *A booke containing divers sortes of hands*; 1571
14. Hardwick Hall
15. Wollaton Hall
16. Rothwell Market House
17. Lyveden New Bield
18. Quentin Massys the Younger. *The Sieve Portrait*; c. 1580–83

19. Crispin van de Passe I. *Queen Elizabeth*; 1596
20. John Case. *Sphaera civitatis*; 1588
21. *Queen Elizabeth as Europa*
22. Artist unknown. *Memorial Portrait of Sir Henry Unton*; c. 1596
23. R[ichard] H[aydocke], trans. *A Tracte Containing the Artes . . .*
24. Philip de Marnix, Elizabeth as Venus; 1580
25. Elizabeth mediates peace; 1587
26. Assistance to the United Provinces; 1585
27. Protestants supported in Belgium; 1587
28. Recovery from smallpox; 1572
29. The Phoenix Badge; 1574
30. *Dangers Averted*; 1589
31. Defeat of the Spanish Armada; 1589
32. The Gates of Honour

ACKNOWLEDGMENTS

THIS BOOK HAS BEEN SO LONG in its gestation that its end scarcely recalls its conception: "The forme to the fynisment foldes ful selden." Over these many years, a number of institutions and individuals have given me support that must have seemed gratuitous. To these, I am grateful. Two of the most constant appear as dedicatees. Among the most supportive institutions were Drexel University, for several study grants and travel funds that made it possible for me to have both the time and the money for research at home and abroad; the National Endowment for the Humanities, which granted me funds for a summer of visits to Elizabethan great houses; the American Council of Learned Societies, which generously funded a year of research in Europe.

Countless libraries have welcomed my intrusions and graciously given of their services. The staff of Drexel University, especially Richard Binder and the interlibrary loan facility, have been patient beyond professional call. I have tracked rare materials through the collections of the Bodleian Library, the British Library, the College of Arms, the Folger Shakespeare Library, the Koninklijke Bibliotheek in The Hague, the Library of Congress, the Newberry Library, the University of Pennsylvania, the Victoria and Albert Museum, and the Warburg Institute. I am deeply indebted to their staffs.

The professional critiques and friendly encouragement of Frances Hodes and Elizabeth McCutcheon have heartened me over many years. These pages are not the manuscript that either read, but my book has benefited from their comments on the Ur-version. Finally, without the help of a long series of graduate assistants at Drexel University, I should myself have forgotten the "forme" of my project, granted a heavy load of courses unrelated to it. Two readers of my manuscript for the University of Nebraska Press have offered helpful corrections and suggestions that I have attempted to incorporate into this palimpsest, and to them and the beleaguered staff of the Press, too, I am grateful.

To all of these, I owe whatever "fynisment" unfolds here.

ABBREVIATIONS

BL	British Library
CSPD	*Calendar of State Papers, Domestic*
CSPF	*Calendar of State Papers, Foreign*
CSPV	*Calendar of State Papers, Venetian*
EETS	Early English Text Society
ELH	*English Literary History*
HMC	Historical Manuscripts Commission
HMSO	His [or Her] Majesty's Stationery Office
PMLA	*Papers of the Modern Language Association*
SEL	*Studies in English Literature*
TSLL	*Texas Studies in Literature and Language*

Elizabethan Silent Language

INTRODUCTION

The Concept and Types of Silent Language

There was speech in their dumbness,
language in their very gesture.
Shakespeare, *The Winter's Tale* 5.2.13–14

In dumb significants proclaim your thoughts.
Shakespeare, *Henry VI, part 1* 2.4.26

O learn to read what silent love hath writ:
To hear with eyes belongs to love's fine wit.
Shakespeare, Sonnet 23

TO APPROACH A CULTURE remembered for its literature through its silent language must seem misdirected if not downright perverse. Still, the vehicles for the expression of silent language—such as the visual arts, material artifacts, costume, gesture, protocol, and procession—also form the subject, the object, and the vehicle for the written word. The association between the two modes of language, literary and silent, is close, if not inseparable. Understanding the silent language of the Elizabethan Renaissance illuminates the literature of the period that produced the works of Sidney, Spenser, and Shakespeare. The need for analysis of the written word has long been recognized, and has indeed been paramount in studies of the period. Investigation of silent language has more narrowly focused on the separate vehicles for expression; analysis of it as a system that supported and supplemented written and oral language has been largely neglected. Yet in countless ways, a synthesis of that kind can enrich reading. Consider, for example, the language of portrait as support and supplement for the written word, that "Faerie Queen" of poem and drama, the image of Queen Elizabeth.

The icon is familiar but the resemblance is remote. The image of Queen Elizabeth I as she appears on her portraits is well known: the stiff posture, the expressionless and ageless mask, the elaborate clothing, the panoply of jewels and fabrics—the fairy queen of courtier and poet, and today the best-known image of the most prominent historical figure of her time. Descriptions by her contemporaries, on the other hand, put a different face upon the image, one that appears on only a couple of graphic images of the queen, one corresponding more closely to the wicked witch of stereotypical tale, and one that perhaps represents the image of Elizabeth as she is imagined by unsympathetic readers of early modern history. She is described as having a hooked nose, but she does not appear in profile on canvas. She is described as having blackened teeth, but her portraits are unsmiling. She was reputed to wear a wig, so not even the color of her hair as it appears on the portraits would be of help in identifying her if observed in dishabille. Yet the extant portraits of Elizabeth are presumably official portraits in the sense that they were permitted to circulate after Elizabeth and her ministers had made efforts to destroy unseemly portraits, to control production of any others, and to establish an approved pattern for future images. Perhaps most incongruous is the language of the draft proclamation that would have controlled production of the portraits: it prescribes that some skillful painter shall be appointed to take a "natural" likeness of the queen.[1] Yet on some later portraits, she appears younger than on earlier ones. The most natural or realistic part of her portraits, in fact, is the representation of her gowns. Worn even by another lady, Elizabeth's gowns would be recognized. There is a serious cognitive dissonance between the verbal and nonverbal data available to scholars studying the period. So would there have been in Elizabeth's own day. The literal and nonverbal languages sometimes confirm, sometimes supplement, and sometimes contradict each other.

Modern effort to decode Elizabethan language is complicated by differences in vocabulary and syntax between modern and earlier usage. To understand the intention of the use of material objects of the period often requires an exercise no less tortuous than to disentangle the sense of the queen's speeches. As compared with the voluminous critical commentary devoted to Elizabethan literature as canon and as transgression, the material context of the literature has received relatively little analysis. The shape and size of a cup, the architectural fabric of a country house, the ornament of a gown, even the constituents of a menu—a patron's or a consumer's selection of physical substance itself involved a meaningful choice from prescriptions significantly made, often harshly imposed, by outside agents. The user's intentions were further shaped by political, religious, socioeconomic, or aesthetic constraints, whether self-imposed or responsive to the expectations or limitations of an audience. Although constraints upon nonverbal communication in most cases continue to operate today, historical differences are critical to understanding a culture. They may seem irrelevant to appreciation of the art and literature, but these differences are material witness to the cultural matrix or context of a work of art—and often to the meaning of the artifact or text itself. At least, ignorance of the material context leaves the modern audience unaware of the weight of much detail; at worst, it leaves them unreceptive to significant thematic intention.

The portraits of Elizabeth I, for instance, convey another kind of information and express another aesthetic sensibility than is expected from modern official portraits. Taken as a group, they tell more about the nature of Elizabethan portraiture than they do about the physical nature of Elizabeth I. The jewels she wears, the elaboration of her costume, the rigidity of her posture and gestures, the emblematic settings, the timeless mask that substitutes for her natural features—all of these reveal different information than would the realistic likeness painted in order to satisfy modern expectations of what is now described as a "natural" portrait, to say nothing of a photographic image. To the modern eye, Elizabethan artificial pictorial devices convey information not only of a different kind, but also usually in a larger quantity, through a greater variety of modes, and of a culturally more significant nature, than would a naturalistic portrait. This is not to say that the modern state portrait is without its own artificiality, but rather that pictorial devices and aesthetic intentions have changed. The excrescence of ornament and rigidity of pose that represented magnificent power to an Elizabethan would strike the modern Western viewer as signs of an unacceptably overbearing and coldly inaccessible personality. These variant responses exemplify how separate properties and attributes figure as parts of a larger system of silent communication, a whole network of wordless or extraverbal signification that figures against a ground of changing expectation.

To tease out the significance of the portraits of Elizabeth is to draw out but one thread from a huge knotted skein. Not only graphic images, but also architecture, the decorative arts, pageants, protocol, and even silence itself could convey threat, reprimand, or praise—as well as other, more complex meanings that defy categorization. The more ephemeral the form of communication, the greater the challenge to recover it. In many cases, recovery is impossible: the material world of the lower social classes was by nature, custom, and by economic and legal constraint a world rendered ephemeral. The objects of this world were often made of less durable substance, they were subject to daily hard use, they were disregarded by contemporary observers and, until recently, by modern historians as well. Inevitably, the material world of Elizabethan culture is largely accessible to modern investigation only through the precious object that caught the attention of the early commentator, the later conservator, and the modern curator. Thus the silent language of the period, like the literary medium of the time, expresses most directly the culture of the gentry and the upper classes. Glimpses of the impressions, reactions, imitations, and vernacular expressions of the lower classes reflect the values and forms of the upper classes, but with the proviso that judgment is based only on what has survived.

Even efforts to record and to interpret the silent language of the upper classes are hampered by the confines of what has survived, but there are other restrictions as well, such as the ephemeral nature of the media that conveyed that language. Most elusive are the uses of time, space, and motion as media of communication—the abrogation of a traditional holiday, the adjustment of conventional seating arrangements, the departure from an anticipated choreography of an event. Yet these changes reflect either an impulse or a conscious decision based upon a perceived need for new schematization. It is impossible to recover or to reconstruct the whole system of extraverbal and silent language, but contemporary discourse does uncover many particulars whose configuration sketches the outlines of the larger scheme.

That a type of silent language—or languages—did exist is apparent in the artifacts that often inscribe a significance beyond modern comprehension; sometimes literature and historical accounts of the period decode the elusive meaning of the nonverbal. Elizabethan literature is, however, more familiar than the artifacts that comprised the material culture of the day, if only because so little of the material survives in pristine condition. Occasionally, but rarely, a writer will name the concept of a silent language or allude to it as a resource. Thomas Wilson concludes his *Arte of Rhetorique* (1553) with the observation that "the gesture of man, is the speache of his bodie" (1:436–37). In a book he first published near the end of the reign of Elizabeth, Thomas Wright uses a number of figures that depend upon the analogy between spoken and nonverbal language. In *The Passions of the Minde in Generall,* Wright describes one's changing facial expression as "a silent speech," and at another point as "a silent voice." On a broader scale of comparison, he recognizes action as "either a certaine visible eloquence, or an eloque[n]ce of the bodei, or a comely grace in deliuering conceits, or an external image of an internall minde, or a shadow of affections, or three springs which flowe from one fountaine, called *vox, vultus, vita,* voice, countenance, life" (C7^r; M8^v). In his copy of the English translation of Guazzo's *Civile Conuersation,* Gabriel Harvey underscored, as follows, the figure of silent-gesture-as-speech in Guazzo's recommendation that one "keepe a certaine *maiestie in the iesture,* which *speaketh as it were* by vsing silence" (H4^r). Much Elizabethan discourse about manners and movement derives from Italian precedent, and in 1616 the Neapolitan jurist Giovanni

Bonifaccio published *L'arte de cenni*—in modern terminology, a treatise on gesture—that provides a retrospective view of sixteenth-century literature about silent language, an exotic echo of much of the substance and figurative expression in Elizabethan discourse. Bonifaccio traces the antique origins of the concept and cites its later expression. Having quoted on his title page the passage in the *Purgatorio* where Dante alludes to "visible speech" *(visibile parlare)*, and having discussed pictorial devices for silent speaking *(parlar in silentio)*, Bonifaccio also quotes Tasso's reference to mute eloquence (*muta eloquenza* [A2ᵛ]). He recalls from Cicero and Quintilian that action, pronunciation, voice, and gesture comprise corporal eloquence (*eloquenza corporale* [Zzz2ᵛ]). Elizabethans could not have known Bonifaccio's work, but they would have known many of his sources and they enacted the taxonomy of the language that he analyzed.

It was a language in which Elizabeth was fluent. In his retrospective *Annals of the First Four Years of the Reign of Queen Elizabeth*, John Hayward (who was himself to suffer imprisonment for his own commitments in written work), describes her typical use of corporal eloquence as public relations:

> Now, if ever any persone had eyther the gift or the stile to winne the hearts of people, it was this Queene; and if ever shee did expresse the same, it was at that present, in coupling mildnesse with majesty as shee did, and in stately stouping to the meanest sort. All her facultyes were in motione, and every motione seemed a well guided actione; her eye was set upon one, her eare listened to another, her judgement ranne uppon a third, to a fourth shee addressed her speech; her spiritt seemed to be every-where, and yet so intyre in her selfe, as it seemed to bee noe where else . . . distributing her smiles, lookes, and graces, soe artificially, that thereupon the people . . . filled the eares of all men with immoderate extolling their Prince. (6–7)

This general description indicates the elusive manner of Elizabeth's effective use of body language. If the silent language of the most powerful figure of her time and place could be multidirectional, that of her subjects was necessarily more circumspect, and that of the dissidents among them subtle and even more constrained. Yet all types found silent language an effective mode of communication.

Treatises, biographies, memoirs, and relevant etymology all afford analytic reflection upon the nature and uses of silent language; belletristic literature offers more casual glimpses, passing glances at its presence. As the epigraphs to this introduction suggest, Shakespeare is a rich source of examples. Claudio speaks directly to the point in *Measure for Measure* when he remarks of Isabella that

> in her youth
> There is a prone and speechless dialect,
> Such as move men.
>
> (1.2.182–84)

Isabella's speechless dialect is the unconscious appeal of youth. More complex because intentionally manipulative is the passage in *Coriolanus* where Volumnia counsels her son Coriolanus to kneel before the people of Rome, "for in such business / Action is eloquence" (3.2.75–76).[2] In *Troilus and Cressida*, according to Ulysses, Cressida's gestures betray her character:

> There's language in her eye, her cheek, her lip,
> Nay, her foot speaks; her wanton spirits look out
> At every joint and motive of her body.
>
> (4.5.55–57)

At first glance, Cressida's gestural language may seem as simple as Isabella's, and so it is, but the rich intersection of meanings in Ulysses' use of "motive" in this passage—kinetic, psychological, and aesthetic—opens paths toward not only the grammar but also the poetics of Elizabethan silent language. The poetry begins, not in ideas, nor in things, but in the body between. The body is intermediary between the abstract idea and the inert thing: if not embodied in poetry, the discursive medium of idea would be too prosaic and the thing itself too earthbound.

It is only to be expected that dramatic works should most frequently allude to the language of gesture, but other kinds of literature also draw upon silent language as a repertory of figures. Sir Philip Sidney's Astrophil woos his Stella not only with his poems but also his "dumbe eloquence" (#61); he infers hope from Stella's "eye's—speech" (#67); his crossed arms signify his status as a lover (song #8), in the gestural cliché that Shakespeare parodically likens to the posture of a rabbit on a spit (*Love's Labor's Lost* 3.1.19). Sidney's Countess of Pembroke's *Arcadia* (now referred to as the *New Arcadia*) represents the role of silent language in constituting the two most important courtly values: his fiction anatomizes the gestures of love ("her cheekes in red letters writ more, then her tongue did speake" [237]) and of chivalry ("the la[n]guage of launces" [416]). Spenser, too, speaks of his lady's "art of eyes I never read in bookes" in his sonnet sequence the *Amoretti* (#21).

Hand gestures form a particularly rich medium of silent language. Spenser's *Epithalamion* (lines 225, 238, 398) emphasizes the role of the hands in the solemnization of marriage and its celebration. Marlowe's lovers Hero and Leander "parled by the touch of hands" (line 185).[3] Romeo and Juliet's parley on hands is an antiphonal sonnet, a prestidigitation that through "mannerly devotion" transfigures the lover's touch as "holy palmers' kiss" (1.5.93–106). The emphasis placed upon manual gestures had a long history in the trust placed upon the touch of hands, as in the handshakes pictured on early Greek vases, the "handfast" signifying marital and other legal contracts in northern European tradition, the metonymic use of the gauntlet as chivalric pledge or the lady's glove as courtly favor—all gestures that appear in Western art and literature as modes of expressing commitment. Macbeth realizes the far-reaching effects of his evil handiwork: not only are his bloody hands permanently stained like the dyer's hands, but he imagines that his may "incarnadine" the green of the sea (2.2.59).

Verses inscribed in the Ditchley manuscript playfully reveal another motive for use of the media of silent discourse, the uses of ambiguity or ambivalence. The verses are dated for November 17, 1584, presumably drafted for the annual celebration of the queen's Accession Day. The poem begins:

> The bold beseacher nedinge to beware
> the penn past feare, the herald of the mynd
> of blynd, and doome, bewraies the case & Care
> by silent Vttraunce, thus to saye assignd.[4]

The tortuous syntax describes a chief attraction of silent language, its capacity for noncommittal expression, safe from the permanency of spoken or written word. The verses comprise a self-reflective commentary upon the pageant as safe port for the launching of unsafe ideas onto stormy seas.

As might be expected, Elizabeth dextrously exploited the full range of nuances of manual gesture. Hayward narrates a famous instance from Elizabeth's coronation entry that dramatizes royal silent speaking in action. At one point on the procession, when a child representing Truth lowered a copy of the bible to the queen, she "kissed both her hands, with both her hands shee received it, then shee kissed it; afterwardes applyed it to her brest: and lastly held it up" (*Annals* 17). In John Bulwer's later (1644) elaborate systemization of the significance of hand gestures, Elizabeth's response would have been accurately classified as what he calls a "visible *Amen.*"[5] Elizabeth also used manual gesture to express her response to approach, extending her hand as favor, withholding it as reproach. The modern expression "on the other hand" comes to mind, one instance among many to follow, of how early modern culture embodied practices that have been transmuted (to revive two more such inert figures) into modern dead metaphor. That she consciously so manipulated the silent language of the hand is evident in her grateful remarks to an orator who welcomed her to Norwich while on progress: " '[Your oration] is the best that ever I heard; you shal have my hande;' and pulled off hir glove, and gave him hir hand to kiss" (Nichols, *Progresses* 1:159).

As the word *manipulate* suggests, the hands are a medium of control, associated with the rituals of social bonding (as in *handsel* and the feudal gesture of homage, *immixtio manuum*) and religion (as in the laying on of hands); and in the transactions of commerce (*manifest*), politics (*manifesto*), and law (as in the manumission of slaves), to touch only lightly upon countless variations. Bulwer's analysis of the gesture "TO OFFER THE BACK OF THE RIGHT HAND TO BE KISSED BY OTHERS" discovers some of the nuances in the movement, "which Pliny calls a religious ceremony used by all nations, is an expression of *state* used by *proud* and *scornful* persons who affect the garb of great ones and are willing to afford a *slight respect* to one they think unworthy of a higher touch" (102). Bulwer would have acclaimed Elizabeth as one of "the great ones," but his description of the reservation implicit in the gesture indicates the ambivalence of the act. Elizabeth was skilled at the legerdemain of withdrawing with one hand what she had given with the other, of not allowing the left hand to know what the right was doing.

If only because of the currency of the term *sign language,* manual gesture may be the first type of voiceless communication to come to mind, but Elizabethans drew upon a huge repertory of other media as well for a variety of purposes. Nonverbal communication was more prudent than words: safer for Sir Thomas Tresham to build his lodge in the shape of a significant triangle than publicly to confess in literal Romanist terms his belief in the Trinity (fig. 1). Nonverbal communication was also more immediate than words: thus Elizabeth chose to spit rather than to speak her disapproval of one Sir Mathew's jerkin, according to Sir John Harington's *Nugae Antiquae* (1:167). Nonverbal communication also offered the politic advantage of ambiguity, as when Elizabeth adapted from the device of Charles V the imperial pillars of Hercules.[6] Above all, silent language could be more effective than words alone, as in two examples I discuss in my text. How many words would have been required to substitute for the economy of Sir Philip Sidney's device on the occasion when, after the birth of a son and heir to his wealthy patron, his uncle Robert Dudley, the earl of Leicester, Sidney appeared in a tournament with a line dashed through his motto "SPERAVI" in order graphically to signify his own dashed hopes for favor from his uncle?[7] And how much more visible and memorable were the canting grasshopper weather vanes that Sir Thomas Gresham (OE *graes* [grass]; *ham* [home]) installed on top of his Royal Exchange (fig. 2) than would have been a plaque or an inscription on a lintel as a way of memorializing his sponsorship of the enterprise? More than four hundred years after Elizabeth's stirring appearance at Tilbury, her dramatic gesture is remembered—even though the possibility that the mustering there of the troops was both mistaken and superogatory is largely forgotten, and even though it may be the case that contemporary accounts of the occasion were largely fabricated. Scholars continue to try to distinguish the historic event from the still-living legend.[8]

The significance of some of this silent language communicates directly even today, but much misleads the unknowing eye and much escapes the uneducated imagination. Apart from acquaintance with Sidneyan biography, Elizabethan tournament, and the story of the Armada, only research into the history of the emblem releases the meaning of Sidney's tournament device and the imperial intention of the Herculean pillars, and only still further research into Elizabethan wordplay reveals the proprietary nature of Gresham's grasshopper. Ad hoc research into these specific questions poses the larger question of the nature of the system of communication that activated and informed emblematic as well as other nonverbal and extraverbal signification. This book is concerned with that system: what it was, how it worked, why it was employed, what values it sustained. To lay open this system for viewing is to conduct an anatomy of its major parts. Like the surgical procedure, this anatomy is not so much an argument as the discovery of the structure underlying the superficially perceptible. As in medical history, the anatomy is an argument only insofar as the necessity and worth of the procedure need rationalization, but the demonstration in itself constitutes its defense. It involves a new look at old elements, seeing with one's own eyes as in an autopsy (Gk. *autopsia, autos,* self + *opsis,* sight) the articulation between the parts and between the parts and the whole body; finally, visualizing with the mind's eye what lies beneath the multilayered surface. The educated imagination may then cautiously simulate the body in motion, the language in action.

Elizabethan silent language drew upon the same semantic resources as did literal language. Inevitably, the subject of much comment about silent language is most frequently Elizabeth, but while the queen may have been the most prominent figure of her age, she was not always the most visible. Most Elizabethans probably never saw her, and even her courtiers complained about her inaccessibility. Although verbal data regarding the queen give the most immediate entry into the culture of her time, other media offer useful, even indispensable, information—verbal, extraverbal, and nonverbal. Primary among these were earlier British cultural practice, selective adaptation of biblical tradition, Tudor historiography, humanist selection and translation of antique culture, as well as the resources of continental culture that were imparted by travelers, ambassadors and other visitors, foreign texts and translations, and the court of Mary Queen of Scots. The memory of foreign monuments as recalled in the imaginations of patrons (and in the minds and hands of the artificers who would simulate those remembered artifacts) was an all-important repository for models for Elizabethan architecture, gardens, and pageantry. Indigenous or denizened codes of gesture and conduct were recorded in the Black Books, heraldic literature, courtesy literature, books of household regulations, and rhetorical treatises. Elizabethan culture is a construct whose matrix was an earlier history and that generated transformations in the lives of all Elizabethans and their descendants, including those who have remained illegible because unwritten. Traces of this wider culture are inscribed in the data of silent language, in the artifacts that wordlessly textualized meaning such as clothing, jewelry, pictures, wall hangings, and pattern books. In sum, the repository of shared traditions, values, and practice constituted what might be called the *mundus significans.*[9] It is worth comment that Elizabethans knew those continental cultures that shaped their own (in every sense of the word *culture*) through the objects that spoke to them of what was different, strange, exotic, and attractive, if not downright seductive, so foreign silent language spoke to them, sometimes in competition with native forms.

This is not to say that the Elizabethans read or used these resources in the same way as the modern scholar who would wish to decode Elizabethan silent language. Much of what the scholar must recover through research in these sources would have been transmitted imperceptibly to one born into that culture. For the occasional highly formalized ceremony that required prescribed gesture and behavior, records do in some cases still exist—the coronation of a monarch, the laying on of the king's Touch, the degradation of a knight, the regulation of a tournament, a banquet in a great house—but presumably most instruction for less important occasions was either superogatory or it was transmitted orally or through observation, so access to this information is more difficult. Still, the historical literature indirectly reveals the meaning of behavior, significance that might otherwise be lost if the subtext is neglected: the queen's anger at a Polish ambassador's insensitivity to the Elizabethan decorum of space; Leicester's fury at the ignorance on the part of Warwick town officials of the unspoken prescriptions of prestation (the protocol of the duty owed to superiors); Sir Thomas Smith's seeming vanity about the absence of a set of plate due his ambassadorial office. The language of legal control precisely dictates some matters—such as the specifications that should govern the painting of a portrait of the queen, or the exact cut, measure, and fabric of costume appropriate to every level of income—but even here Elizabethan precision generates modern ambiguity, in the first case, because of the unfamiliar use of familiar terminology and, in the latter instance, because the excessive repetition of sumptuary proclamations over many years would suggest that these strict rules were unenforced or unenforceable. Still, whether as law or only as draft, the language of these prescriptions articulates Elizabethan social and aesthetic values. Often the period terminology of rationalization needs further explanation, as in the use of the word *natural* to describe highly artificial portraits of the queen, but translation is a necessary part of the recovery and understanding of culture, and if translation can only approximate the historical meaning, that, too, is in the nature of the case.

Apart from the historical literature of memoir, biography, letters, law, chronicle, journal, and historiography, belletristic literature also reveals the workings of Elizabethan silent language. The concept of such communication or the meaning of a specific instance of its use may be explicitly indicated, as in Spenser's representation of the shape of the body-as-architecture in the *Faerie Queene* or Amphialus's weighing his choice of costume in Sidney's *New Arcadia*. Often, literature simply embodies, rather than explains, nonverbal media such as Queen Catherine's vision of the dance of ideal harmony in Shakespeare and Fletcher's *King Henry VIII* or meaningful changes of costume in *Hamlet*. Iconographic, particularly emblematic, allusions also abound in nondramatic literature, notably Shakespeare's sonnets, Sidney's *New Arcadia,* and Spenser's *Faerie Queen*. Sometimes the very shape of a poem is iconic, whether conveyed through typography, as in the pillar-shaped poem honoring Queen Elizabeth, or formed conceptually, as in Sylvester's coronal, which simultaneously mourns the death of Elizabeth and hails the accession of James, the circular mode of the poem itself enacting the mutuality of sorrow and celebration. More often, the architectonics of a literary work wordlessly underlie narrative, and this is particularly true of the use of characters or figures paired, grouped, or developed along a thematic continuum. The specific scheme is left to the reader's inference, the most frequent being the structure of a moral microcosm. Shakespeare, Sidney, and Spenser all three shared the Renaissance attraction to the representation of ideas or values through the use of exemplary characters or situations, and often visual, gestural, or spatial vehicles convey these intentions.[10] As Sidney puts it in his *Defence of Poetry*, the distinction of the poet is the "feigning notable images" of virtue and vice, and his phrase truly exemplifies the literary theory and practice of his age (27). The images of virtue and vice are embodied in word, character, and in nonverbal multimedia addressed to all the senses. The major works of the greatest writers of the Elizabethan period dramatize opposing types of gesture, behavior, and style as exemplary representations for delight and instruction, and they do so with both word and nonverbal media.

More complex than the decorum of the isolated or paired element is the dynamic interplay of the many participants in an entry, progress, or pageant—early "performance art." Many accounts of these presentations survive, some as yet unpublished, and all of them provide a wealth of information about the separate vehicles of silent language already named—costume, emblem, jewelry, gesture, prestation, banquet. Sometimes, the additional treasure of a spontaneous reaction or gesture is recorded: Elizabeth seizing the occasion during her coronation entry to assimilate herself into iconographic identification with Truth the Daughter of Time; Leicester masquerading as Deep Desire, hidden within a holly bush during a pageant improvised for the queen's departure from Kenilworth and from a fictive courtship of several years' duration; Elizabeth protesting to Norwich dignitaries against the need for any gift, then peeking under the cover of the golden cup to find a handsome offering of money within, and bidding farewell to the city with tears standing in her eyes.

Moments like these represent what one must be careful to call, not a truer, but rather a fuller, sometimes a different, picture of Elizabethan values than what the planned program or conventional decorum prescribed, and occasionally these glimpses reveal personal values or feelings that enhance or occasionally undercut the official program or fiction. When taken into account, these details enrich and enliven the more familiar literary history of the time. More importantly, the resulting history is a richer, a more complete resource for one who would appraise the truth of what was. This is not Sidney's "bare *Was*" of history (*Defence* 36), but truth clad in period costume, Hamlet's "abstract and brief chronicles of the time" (2.2.520), played in large-scale production. This approach takes into account the text, the subtext, and the cultural context for what was written, said, or enacted, and for what was left literally unrecorded, unsaid, or invisible. The interaction revives Elizabethan synergy.

In approaching Elizabethan culture, one encounters the big problems that one would in approaching any other: the familiar and the strange. Apart from the initial difficulty that it depends upon only what has survived and gained attention, familiarity breeds other procedural discontents. Modern Anglo-American culture is largely continuous with the Elizabethan past—so much so that many now substitute *early modern* for *Renaissance* to refer to the inclusive period. Hence, many phenomena appear familiar in the earlier semantic system, whether the term is taken literally or is analogously applied to silent communication. Some early modern cultural norms have atrophied or so changed as to be almost unrecognizable, but some, too, have traced a linear development. These last provide dangers similar to linguistic false cognates. For example, the familiar assumption of the masculine norm (only recently controverted in sustained and comprehensive attack) obtained during the period of English history that has come to be named after a female monarch. Should one be diverted by an ahistoric feminism, however, one may fail to observe how

Elizabeth both broke the wedding cake of custom and ate it, too, without intervention of officiating cleric; how she enjoyed the communal spirits of bride-ale without quaffing any bitter cup of matrimony. She exploited conventional style by referring to herself as the Prince of England, but also quite at odds with conventional practice, she resisted efforts to subject her to marriage; she also had it both ways by alluding to herself as the wife of her country, holding up a surrogate wedding ring in a defiant gesture to reify this fictive marriage in order to confirm it.[11] If she was guilty of "feminine" indecisiveness in the matter of the execution of the Queen of Scots, she could also plead that there was no Stuart blood upon her ladylike beautiful white hands after her would-be rival had been dispatched by her male advisors and executioner. If Leicester could argue that the queen's passivity and silence gave him free play to advance his own interests in the Netherlands in ambitious violation of the queen's earlier instructions to the contrary, he nonetheless suffered a very assertive dressing-down when as Elizabeth's "creature of our own" he was reeled back to England for his comeuppance. Whatever the merit of modern disdain for a queen given to hurtful whim and oppressive policy, it is critically necessary also to recognize the historical context for her willful character and behavior.

Manifestations of mixed signals of Elizabeth's manipulation of gendered advantage appear on her portraits. They are graphic example of the need to look carefully beyond ready identification of familiar pictorial elements that often signify values that may be construed by modern viewers as contradictory. On the celebratory, patriotic *Armada* portrait (fig. 3), Elizabeth appears in a sumptuous gown cut in an exotic French fashion and covered with jewels and bows, but she also rests one hand upon the sword of state and the other on the globe of the world. Behind her, depicted in two small insets as triumphal reminder of her combative force, is the defeat of the burning Armada. On the *Ermine* portrait (fig. 4), the ermine, emblem of chastity—the primary feminine virtue—is figured on the queen's left sleeve, but a sword lies on the table that supports this hand, and her right hand is akimbo in the posture that was traditionally a male assertion of power, as on the characteristic portrait of Henry VIII as well as many an Elizabethan courtier, such as Nicholas Hilliard's image of George Clifford, third earl of Cumberland, as the knight of Pendragon Castle (fig. 5). The portrait of Sir Walter Ralegh and his eldest son Walter in the National Portrait Gallery in London represents an amusing variation on the posture, picturing father and boy both posed with left arm akimbo, the son a small shadow of his famous father. Posture, like facial expression, is easily misread, but a contemporary source, the Trevelyon Commonplace Book, clearly labels the stance as "Presumption" in a series of illustrations of characteristic postures.[12] The queenly left hand knew well what the right was doing. Like the Amazonian heroines and those disguised in male costume who appear in the major literary works of the Elizabethan period, the queen combined masculine and feminine characteristics and perquisites. She was, as she herself implied, both king and queen to her country.

Just as a mistaken projection of the modern redefinition of gendered roles onto Elizabethan prototypes can blind one to the queen's ambivalent responses and nuanced inventions, so, too, can the norm of youth be misleading. Like their cultural descendants in the West, the Elizabethans feared sickness, aging, and death, but unlike most of their Western descendants, they heard the hoofbeats of the apocalyptic horsemen weekly if not daily. Sickness came often, aging came early, and death followed soon. The works of Shakespeare, Sidney, and Spenser (as well as several minor poets) all represent heroes who retire in old age from public life and power with varying degrees of nostalgia, reluctance, and regret. The retreat into religious exercises by these fictive hermits would suggest that the life of contemplation was more common among sixteenth-century retirees than among present-day Western pensioners, who are generally more likely to retire to the golf links. Like sixteenth-century poetry and fiction, so, too, do the contemporary nonverbal and extraverbal media such as madrigal, pageant, and portrait register the passing of youth and retirement into old age. The historic retirement of Sir Henry Lee from courtly service is fictively represented in an entertainment performed for the queen at Sir Henry's house at Ditchley—the place that is memorialized by the *Ditchley* portrait (fig. 6) whereon the queen plants her feet on the appropriate section of a map of England. The major sonnet cycles celebrate youth, love, and life, and they express fear and loathing for sickness, age, and death. After a certain age, portraits of the queen represent her with the same unwrinkled and timeless features of much earlier pictures: it is notable that the ageless queen and the "aged" Lee were near-contemporaries.

Yet the Elizabethan norm of youth is not identical with the modern cult of youth, for the youth in question must be differentiated. At a time when the average life expectancy at birth for even the sons of peers was thirty-five years, and old age began with one's forties, youth was the period when the male members of society were cultivating their talents and refining their skills in positions that prepared for the exercise of power.[13] The modern terms *teenage* and *adolescence*, which supposedly indicate a socially protected time for nurturant development, had not been invented because these classifications did not exist in their modern sense. Whereas modern youth is cultivated as a discrete market, Elizabethan young men were valued as perpetuators and curators of family estates. The interests of modern marketers are invested in change of fashion, whereas Elizabethans underwrote continuity and stability of family and property.

These different emphases of value are reflected in relative attitudes to-ward youth. Whatever the degree of wild behavior at large among the young in the Elizabethan period, it lacked the supportive matrix of a youth culture as known to modern adolescents with its presumption of a lack of responsibility created and mutually supported by the experimentation of the young, their commercial beneficiaries, and immature adults.[14] The youth idealized in Elizabethan culture was not the mindless insouciance that is flattered in modern popular culture but the cultivated wit of a young Harington or Sidney. The comparison is invidious, precisely because it is founded on an unequal equation between modern mass culture on the one hand and the Elizabethan elite on the other. As opposed to the homoge-nized youth culture of today made possible by the access of the majority to the requisite time and money, the vast majority in the sixteenth century would have spent their young lives in hard work—unpaid for the girls at home, and poorly rewarded for the boys on the farm, in service, or in a long apprenticeship. For these, record and artifact yield little information be-cause they were invisible, not only to the modern investigator but to their social superiors. Only an occasional glimpse, an inference, a telling absence of record uncovers their culture.

When cultivated Elizabethans regret the arrival of "that time of year thou mayst in me behold, / When yellow leaves, or none, or few, do hang" (Shakespeare, Sonnet 73),[15] they are more often writing in the spirit of the classical *lachrimae rerum* than of modern dispirited popular songs about the passing of summer romance or "golden oldies" recalling to those grown weary of middle age an imaginary perpetual adolescence. On portraits of young men, the usual mood is one of thoughtful gravity, on those of young women, one of constrained chastity. When Elizabethans regret the passing of youth, they do not lament the loss of teenage indulgence in irrespon-sibility but rather the passing of the time of ripening power and increasing responsibility. Certainly sixteenth-century England shared with modern culture the value placed upon sexuality, but even in this respect there is the important difference that the Elizabethan emphasis is upon sex as a pro-creative power as well as a pleasure. Even Elizabeth's undeniable personal vanity about her appearance and her age has a large admixture of concern for her presence as a public person, as an icon of English majesty and power.

If seemingly familiar norms in Elizabethan silent language present diffi-culties of interpretation, so, too, do elements in the Elizabethan nonverbal semantic system that now seem strange. Cognate elements in the culture may go unnoticed or misread because of their seeming familiarity, but strange values may be ignored, misapprehended, or rejected altogether because of modern prejudice, insensitivity, or even for lack of a categorical vocabulary with which to describe them. This is particularly true of aesthetic values. What the Elizabethans prized as gorgeousness may seem surfeit to the modern eye trained on a minimalist aesthetic; effete excess to a homophobic; artificial formality to a studiedly casual couturier. Elizabethan ornament may seem randomly selected incongruity to a modern sensibility accustomed to homogenized revival of other ornamental period styles. Few modern women would care to wear Elizabeth's heavy, uncomfortable gowns or even the burden of her jewels. Similarly, gorgeousness in verse is often antipathetic to twentieth-century critical method and values. On a scale of ethical values, it is difficult now to conceive of magnificence as a constituent of virtue, but so it was construed in Renaissance theory and practice. By the same token, many a modern student finds Elizabethan schematizing of ethical examples in art and fiction to be tediously didactic, at least on first reading. In fact, Elizabethan valuation of the schematic and symmetrical, even when not didactic but merely insistent, can be an impediment to the beginning student who has some sophistication in the arts. Strongly linear emphasis in the visual arts requires sacrifice of the subtleties of chiaroscuro if one is to enjoy a compensatory intricacy of line. The pleasures of blackwork embroidery, linenfold carving, or strapwork pattern on the frontispiece of a book or a building may be surfeit to the taste for understated elegance, or be overly constricted design to the impulse toward freely expressive form. The intensity of Hilliard's pigments rewards a different taste than does the pastel palette of a Watteau or a Gainsborough. A similar astigmatism can also obscure literary delights: in the *New Arcadia*, it is easy to lose the figures of the disguised heroes against the ground of more than a hundred other characters, to dismiss the actions of multiple subplots in the *Faerie Queene* as pointless digression, or to enjoy humor in Shakespeare's tragedies as simple comic relief. Finally, until recently critics have regarded the chimney pots of Elizabethan great houses and the inset vernacular tales in the *New Arcadia* as unassimilated medieval fossils rather than as attractive forms characteristic of the (to use the Elizabethan term) *mere English* style that would be created by the layering of indigenous fossils into an English translation of the continental Renaissance.

In the arts, but also in every aspect of Elizabethan life, another highly important dimension of the semantic system remains to be named explicitly here; that is the hierarchical stratification of society. The primacy of the monarch and of the clergy was the given standard of measure, but relations between the two were sometimes strained. If the monarch received the crown from the hands of one archbishop, another might find himself omitted from the coronation ceremony altogether because of his dissident opinions. Elizabeth may have religiously attended services, but she did not hesitate midservice to rebuke a clergyman whose sermon she found offensive or to secret herself in her closet in order to withdraw from a service that she found unacceptable. On other occasions, Elizabeth found her royal prerogatives challenged, not only in the ways that her father had fancied his own to be violated by ambitious churchmen and courtiers, but in other ways specified by her gender and by the question of succession to the throne. Her most ingenious responses to this challenge lie in her courtly iconography and in her spontaneous seizing of occasion offered by pageant and ceremony.

The rule of hierarchy measured the lives of all, never so urgently as for those nearest in rank to each other, as one observes in countless anecdotes about scuffles regarding precedence on tennis courts and over position at table. Hence the punctilious attention given to decorum of service: who kneels, and when, and to whom; who is seated and on what; who covers or uncovers head or cup; who is seated at the elevation highest by how many inches, and before how many inches of cloth of state. At banquets, what one was served, and how much, and with how much variety, was also calibrated to one's social rank. The grade of bread, the type of dishware, were determined by one's status. One's position was signaled by one's costume: this in turn was further determined by one's income and regulated by exacting legal prescription.

In short, the main elements of the semantic system of Elizabethan silent language were in many cases those of literal language, with resources in religion, in antiquity as translated through humanist tradition, in custom and law, in the continental Renaissance, and in Tudor historiography—syntactic elements translated through word and practice, all of them subject to personal inflection. Assumed as given values were the masculine norm, young adulthood, courtly service, discernment of ethical and aesthetic dimensions in all aspects of life, a comprehensive rule of decorum, and the preservation of religious, political, and social hierarchy. Among aesthetic values, decorous magnificence and gorgeousness, the linear iconic image, symmetry, complexity of figure and ground, and exemplary schematization were honored. Literary and historical studies of these values and their verbal manifestations in the forms so well known abound: analyses of plays, poems, sermons, historical documents of all types. Studies of continental sources and analogues for early modern verbal forms are also abundant. Because this work depends upon them as well as research on the objects of everyday life that spoke to all levels of society, its organization must synthesize both types of investigation.

The chapters to follow articulate how the major vehicles for mute language communicated, complicated, reinforced, or challenged cultural values. The order of inquiry proceeds from the generally simpler expressions to the more complex, from static units of signification to more dynamic interactive expression. Although one may speak of Elizabethan silent language as a system, the model is not a closed or a global one, but a labyrinth. The system of Elizabethan silent language is a system of languages, a system of systems. To borrow a figurative analogy that has proved useful in semiotics, the appropriate diagram for this labyrinthine system is not a maze with enclosed possibilities and dead ends; nor is it a tree with perceptible overall structure and a predictable pattern of generation; rather, it is a net with its unlimited possibilities for connections. Moreover, because it is a structure that changes through time and it is multidirectional, global description is impossible; only local descriptions are possible. One must isolate elements from dynamic configurations, stop time, render into words what is by intent and design nonverbal. Any local description—that is, any possible description of nonverbal language—involves analytic dissection. Because of the paratactic structure of the system, description of any one part necessarily implicates others. For this reason, it is difficult to avoid repetition, on the one hand, or reductive falsification, on the other. Ideally, though, fixing a moment in time and viewing it as a structural component in a dynamic movement reveals the nature of the system. Artificially segmented categories serve heuristic purposes.

This book is divided into four major parts that correspond to four kinds of media for nonverbal communication:

1. Line, plane, surface, and texture
   • Linear expression in graphics, calligraphy, and portraiture, and the use of line and plane on maps and the decorative arts
2. Volume, shape, space, and three-dimensional position
   • Nonverbal expression in such superficial and three-dimensional forms as tapestry, jewelry, costume, coins, sculpture, and architecture
3. Gesture, motion, and duration
   • Nonverbal meaning as conveyed dynamically through gesture, dance, pageant, and procession
4. Figure and ground, convention, indeterminacy, absence, and silence
   • Meaning as conveyed through manipulation of conventional decorum, purposeful indeterminacy, present/absence and absent/presence, and silence

As the outline suggests, if this organization has the advantage of an order of increasing complexity, it also carries the danger of entrapment in static repetition even as the analysis graduates into more dynamic aspects of the system. Having successfully navigated past these shoals, however, the analysis can embark on a fresh approach to Elizabethan culture.

No single book—indeed, no single scholar—can comprehensively describe all of these separate media and categories. A special blessing of this type of inquiry is the large cumulative body of research already gathered by specialists in each separate field. One cannot duplicate the efforts of the giants who have preceded, nor would one wish to do so. Although no single earlier study anticipates my efforts here to uncover the nature of silent language in the material discourse of Elizabethan culture and to exhibit its articulation, many have considered the separate topics that are treated here. It is impossible to credit all of them at this point, but I trust that the notes and bibliography do so. In general, the work of Stephen Greenblatt, Louis Montrose, and Peter Stallybrass has oriented me to the study of the material, social, and political generation of Elizabethan literary culture and its dissemination. Patricia Fumerton and Carole Levin have more specifically analyzed the place—and the placing—of women within a culture with a female figurehead. The references that appear most often below for the history of Elizabethan art are to works by Roy Strong on painting and Mark Girouard on architecture, which occupy pioneering and commanding positions in their fields, but also as invaluable resources for illustrations in this book that necessarily depends upon visual images. Among the studies that are crossing the traditional boundaries between the histories of art and literature, Lucy Gent's and Clark Hulse's research on Elizabethan boundary-crossers and John King's on Tudor iconography are models of the type. Guides through the tulgey wood of the uses of space—whether market, map, stage, or ceremonial—are provided for the wide sweep of early modern culture by Jean-Christophe Agnew, Edward Muir, and Richard C. Trexler, and more pointedly for Elizabethan uses of space by David Bevington, Leah S. Marcus, Lawrence Manley, and Steven Mullaney. Without the orientation to Elizabethan culture and the data regarding its relevant components that are furnished by these specialists, an overview of the silent language of the period would be inconceivable.

The concern of this book lies in the separate media as they relate to each other and as they figure in a larger system for conveying meaning. This study proceeds through a description of salient categories that are exemplified by copious illustration drawn from period accounts together with contextual documentation. Although all parts of the study do incorporate the results of personal investigation of primary sources, each section also depends upon the labors of other scholars and the questions that they have raised. Every effort has been made both to ground the discussion in period sources and to indicate accessible resources, including further illustrations, for the interested reader. The question raised by this book, the nature of the system of Elizabethan nonverbal communication, is one that is, if not unique, a new departure in studies of the period. Because it was a question unasked during the time, it is essential to establish the existence of the phenomenon through frequent citation, always at the risk of recalling the overfamiliar, but in the hope that its placement in an unfamiliar synthesis may uncover new meaning or at least deepen an old one.

As the multidisciplined nature of the categories under investigation would suggest, the topic is pertinent to many fields of Elizabethan studies. The question is open-ended; the methodology, mediatory; the answer, provisional. If it is not possible to represent a detailed map of the world, one must work between the detailed localized insets and the more comprehensive outline. So this study moves between specific instance as revealed in historical data and the significance of the selected example as articulated or implied by contextual data. As is so often the case in studies of the early modern period, belletristic literature and historical resources are mutually illuminating—when they are not mutually frustrating. Consideration of the interrelationships may highlight some details that have gone unnoted or whose significance has been perceived on a diminished scale when measured against the grid of a different territory. If the book reconnoiters some new territory for investigation, if it sketches surveys that generate scholarly interest in drafting yet more precise maps, it will have succeeded.

I

LINE AND PLANE

CHAPTER ONE

DRAWING THE LINE

> Moreover writing is just silent speech, like the nods used
> in the conversation of the dumb.
>
> Erasmus, *De recta Graeci et*
> *Latini sermonis pronunciatione*

> The whole Feate of Architecture in buildyng, consisteth
> in Lineamentes, and in Framyng.
>
> John Dee, preface to *The Elements of Geometrie of*
> *the most auncient Philosopher Evclide of Megara*

HUMANISTS OFTEN CITED Pliny's observation that the Greek master Apelles never "let a day of business to be so fully occupied that he did not practise his art by drawing a line, which has passed from him into a proverb ['No day without a line']": "numquam tam occupatum diem agendi, ut non lineam ducendo exerceret artem, quod ab eo in proverbium venit ['Nulla dies sine linea']."[1] By a significant change in meaning, in northern countries the proverb came to be applied, not to painting, but to writing, so it was inscribed as a commonplace cited often both in private correspondence and as an exemplary classroom motto. A version of the Latin line can be seen, for instance, framed and hanging on the wall in the classroom of a writing master in an illustration printed in a Swiss writing book: "Nulla dies abeat quin linea ducta supersit."[2] Eventually, the original application was separated from painting, possibly because humanists elevated letters to the status of the liberal arts, whereas they consigned painting because of its onerous association with a material medium and manual execution to some other, lower, order of activity, however irrational the hierarchy.

Henry Howard adapts both terms of the proverb, both *day* and *line,* to the urgency of political intrigue in a letter to Essex dated November 17, 1597: "*nullum momentum sine lineâ*" (Birch, *Memoirs* 2:363). The drift of meaning in application of the tag reflects the analogous shift in emphasis from pictorial to literary, and from three-dimensional to linear, from abstract to topical, as the Renaissance moved northward.[3] Linear value was a distinctive quality of northern art, and as the smallest unit of cultural differentiation, arguably the line constitutes what might be regarded as a phoneme in Elizabethan silent language, one of the smallest nonverbal elements that make a difference.

Because the point is smaller than the line, and because the ambiguity caused by the absence or misplacement of a punctuation point fascinated the Elizabethans, the point might seem the more appropriate place to begin. Puttenham recalls the role of amphibologia or rhetorical ambiguity in the history of myth and history, beginning with Greek oracles, and he ascribes the rebellions led by Straw, Cade, and Kett to ambiguous prophecies. He quotes as illustration of the type, "*I sat by my Lady soundly sleeping, / My mistresse lay by me bitterly weeping,*" a confusion that may have been caused for lack of precise placement of commas (*Arte of English Poesie* 160). The clown in *Othello* makes pointed use of ambiguous pointing, and his ambiguity points toward the serious play upon the word *honest* throughout the drama:

> CASSIO: Dost thou hear, mine honest friend?
> CLOWN: No, I hear not your honest friend; I hear you.
>
> (3.1.21–22)

The prologue to the artisans' play within *A Midsummer Night's Dream* (5.1.108ff.) embeds potentially rebellious sentiments in Quince's comedic mispointing, again illustrating the deep import of superficially humorous doubleness.[4] The game of ambiguous pointing depends upon wordplay, however, and Elizabethan manipulation of line has much more to do with nonverbal communication, so extended analysis of line rather than point reveals more about the nature and system of silent language.

Northern linearity is pronounced in Renaissance works of art, but one can actually watch the shift in aesthetic values underway in what Erasmus calls his "monument to the memory of Albrecht Dürer" in the dialogue *De recta Latini Graecique sermonis pronuntiatione* when his speaker Bear considers the nature of painting:

> Bear I admit that Apelles was a prince of painting and that his rival artists could find no fault with him except that he did not know when to stop, a criticism which is a sort of compliment in itself. But Apelles used colour. His colours were admittedly restricted in number and the reverse of flamboyant, but they were colours none the less. Dürer, however, apart from his all-round excellence as a painter could express absolutely anything in monochrome, that is with black lines only—shadows, light, reflections, emerging and reced-

ing forms, and even the different aspects of a single thing as they strike the eye of the spectator. His harmony and proportions are always correct. Above all, he can draw the things that are impossible to draw: fire, beams of light, thunderbolts, flashes and sheets of lightning, and the so-called clouds on the wall, feelings, attitudes, the mind revealed by the carriage of the body, almost the voice itself. All this he can do just with lines in the right place, and those lines all black! And so alive is it to the eye that if you were to add colour you would spoil the effect. It is surely much cleverer to be able to dispense with the meretricious aid of colour that Apelles required and still achieve the same results as he did.[5]

In commenting upon this passage, Panofsky suggests a number of reasons for Dürer's preference for line over color, reasons that obtain also in the work of other northern artists. Prints were much cheaper both to produce and to buy, and hence more popular than paintings: Dürer observed that he would have been much richer had he concentrated on engraving. On the other hand, a major painting was usually executed only on commission, so that the painter worked under the constraints of patronage while the graphic artist was freer to experiment. Whatever the basis for linear value, its aesthetic satisfactions are visible in northern Renaissance artifacts, particularly during the early stages of development of the graphic arts. In the vocabulary of Erasmus and other humanists, the word *pingere* served to denote not only painting, but also those graphic arts more linear in method, another indication of the complications in the migration of pictorial values toward the linear in the north.[6] In fact, Italian precedent for the idea of interchangeability of line and picture lay in Haydocke's translation of Lomazzo, who draws an analogy between handwriting and painting "insomuch as writing is nothing else, but a picture of *white* and *black*."[7]

English humanists also subscribed to this lack of distinction between line as employed in art and line as conceived in letters, with an implicit emphasis on the literal over the pictorial and on the graphic line over the painterly. This is made explicit in a number of statements that were articulated during the long dispute over iconoclasm. The debate has often been recounted as an important episode in the history of the division within the church, but the doctrinal differences between the principals are less immediately significant here than a remarkable similarity in aesthetic premises. One of the earliest pertinent statements appears in the pages that Sir Thomas More added to the second edition (1531) of his *Dialogue Concerning Heresies* in response to the heretical book *The Ymage of Love*. In the course of refuting the argument against the use of images, More observes that not only did Christ imprint the image of his face on the vernicle, but that the heretics themselves honor the name of Christ "whiche name is but

an ymage representynge his person to mannes mynde and ymagynacyon."
A few pages later, More returns to this idea:

> Nowe yf I ge to farre from you to tell it [i.e., a tale] you
> then is the wrytyng not the name it selfe
> but an ymage representyng ye name.[8]

More is concerned with doctrinal dispute, but his premise also carries far-reaching aesthetic implications. He argues that the lines that constitute a letter or a word create an image. This tactical extension of definition of *image* is important in the future development of the Reformation: if the image of the name of Christ is acceptable to a religious community, why should not pictorial images be equally so? It is unimportant how men receive sense images.

This consciousness of line, this concept of line-as-image, figures in other documents of the time. A similar thread of argument reappears in an interchange between Bishop Stephen Gardiner and Protector Lord Somerset during the course of a later dispute about the presence of images in the churches. Removal of images from some chapels at the beginning of the reign of Edward VI prompted Stephen Gardiner, bishop of Winchester, to a lengthy defense of their use. Writing in February 1547 in response to Dr. Nicholas Ridley's sermon opposing the use of images, Gardiner argues that the iconoclasts, if they be consistent, must condemn not only statues, but also books:

> And me seemeth, after the fayth of Christ receyved and knowen, and thoroughlye purged from heresyes, if, by case, ther wer offred a chose ether to retein painting and graving and forbear writing, or, chosing writing, to forbear both thother giftes, it wold be a probleam, seing if graving wer taken away we could have no printing. And therfore they that presse so much the wordes of *Non facies tibi sculptile*, ever, me thincketh, they condeme printed bookes, the originall wherof is of graving to make *matrices literarum*. *Sed hoc est furiosum, et sunt tamen qui putant palmarium.* And therfore now it is Englished, "Thou shalt make no graven images, leste thou worshipe them."
> (Gardiner, *Letters* 258–59)

Like More, Gardiner perceives line itself as constitutive of image.

For his part, Lord Protector Somerset, even though he was Gardiner's most powerful antagonist on the larger question of the admissibility of images into the churches, nonetheless describes images in language that is oddly correlative to Gardiner's: "We cannot but see that images may be counted marvellous bookes, to whom we have kneeled, whom we have kissed, upon whom we have rubbed our beads and handkerchiefs, unto whom we have lighted candles, of whom we have asked pardon and help: which thing hath seldom been seen done to the gospel of God or the very true Bible. Indeed images be great letters: yet big as they be, we have seen many which have read them amiss" (as quoted in John Phillips, *The Reformation of Images* 91). Regardless of his position in the debate about iconoclasm, each perceives three-dimensional images in terms of line, readily conceptualizing the three-dimensional image as a spatialized line. The phenomenon was common in Renaissance culture. In an extreme expression of linearity, for instance, the human body was conceptualized as hieroglyphic line in some French courtly dance, even figuring the names of nobility in a kind of "physical spelling."[9] Moreover, line represented not only shape, but also sound. John Hart set forth the concept of visualization of sound in *The Opening of the Unreasonable Writing of Our Inglish Toung* in 1551. Each letter in his system is "the figure of the lest part of the voice, which we mai also call a maner of Image of the voice." In 1569, by which time he had been created Chester herald, Hart embedded the analogy to painting in the very title of his work on English spelling: *An Orthographie, conteyning the due order and reason, howe to write or paint thimage of mannes voice, most like to the life or nature*, a work illustrated with the ABC pictures of the kind still used to introduce the alphabet to children (*Works* 118).

Other documents also suggest that sixteenth-century Englishmen privileged linear images and, conversely, found it difficult to express concepts of three-dimensional form, sometimes muddling the two, and, as we have seen, reducing three-dimensional forms to their linear components. Lucy Gent has researched many examples of English translators' difficulties with Italianate terminology.[10] Sir Thomas Hoby's translation wrestles with a passage in Baldesar Castiglione's *Book of the Courtier*, for example. Castiglione writes:

> Spesso ancor nella pittura una linea sola non stentata, un sol colpo di penello tirato facilmente, di modo che paia che la mano, senza esser guidata da studio o arte alcuna, vada per se stessa al suo termine secondo la intenzion del pittore, scopre chiaramente la eccellenzia dell'artifice. (*Il libro del Cortegiano* 129)

This Hoby translates as:

> Oftentimes also in painting, one line not studied upon, one draught with the Pensell slightly drawne, so it appeareth the hand without the guiding of any studie or art, tendeth to his marke, according to the Painters purpose, doth evidently discover the excellencie of the workeman. (*Three Renaissance Classics* 289–90)

As Gent concludes, Hoby's England still lacked the aesthetic sense of the design or sketch as a finished work and so translated the subject as a painted work, thus failing to capture the essence of either as an artistic medium. Because the concepts of perspective and of chiaroscuro were similarly lacking, they were translated through clumsy circumlocution. Nor was Hoby the only English translator so to reduce to a simple line or an outline the more complex Italian terminology for distinguishing different types of visual representation. John Dee lost a similar struggle with Alberti's *lineamente*.[11] Haydocke's misunderstanding of Lomazzo's analysis of the "*arte designatrice*" highlights the problem as it continued even until 1598.

It is a commonplace observation that the reformists valued word over image. Elizabeth's aversion to any illustration that she regarded as idolatrous is recorded in a conversation with the dean of Christ's Church, Oxford, in 1561. The dean, thinking to please the queen, had prepared a richly bound volume of the Book of Common Prayer, illustrated with fine cuts representing the Trinity, angels, and saints, but Elizabeth roundly reproved him for his ignorance of her own proclamation against such images.[12] The history of campaigns against religious pictures and roods, representations of the cross, shows some of the more extreme opposition to the use of pictorial images. In Stratford, Shakespeare's father John was made responsible for the obscuring of the Guild Chapel paintings in accordance with the prescriptions of the royal injunctions of 1559 against superstitious and idolatrous images. Dramatically graphic and literal demonstrations of steps taken to obliterate pictures are visible in the chapel at Bramall, in Cheshire, where the Ten Commandments were superimposed upon an earlier painting of the Passion of Christ, and in Saint Margaret's Church in Tivetshall, Norfolk, where Elizabeth's royal arms have been painted over a medieval doom picture.[13]

Moderate religious opposition to imagery considered superstitious or idolatrous was often intensified by zealots into outright condemnation of all pictorial representation, as was demonstrated by iconoclastic devastation in the royal chapel twice after Elizabeth's compromise Royal Order to the ecclesiastical commissioners in 1561.[14] In short, religious and other cultural forces converged to retard the development of easel painting and to reinforce that strong interest in line that is elsewhere evident in Elizabethan culture. The cultural lag in transmission of the Italian Renaissance, the opposition to pictorial image on the part of religious reformists, together with a strong indigenous tradition of manuscript illumination that featured intricacy of linear pattern—all combined to sophisticate linear expression.

Recorded history of art as it was read by the Elizabethans would substantiate and likely validate their esteem for line and outline. Polydore Vergil, for example, traces the history of painting, recapitulating various contradictory accounts of its beginnings. "Albeit, all confesse it began of the drawing of a man with lines. In processe of time it waxed more sumptuous with colours." As thus translated and abridged by Langley in 1546, the story goes on to credit Pliny with the further history of how the potter's art began when a young woman traced the shadow of her lover on the wall and her father filled in the outline with clay (92–93). In 1598, Haydocke's translation of Lomazzo repeated the essential point from Pliny that the first painters worked only in black and white (7). Later, Philemon Holland's translation of Pliny's *Natural History* includes the famous contest of line that reputedly took place between Apelles and Protegenes. In this account, Apelles left as his calling card for the absent Protegenes, whom he had never met, a single fine line drawn upon a blank "mighty large table set in a frame, and fitted ready for a picture." Protegenes, upon his return, did indeed recognize the artist through the skill of his work, and with a "pensill, and with another colour drew within the same line a smaller than it" as his own sign, should Apelles return. Whereupon Apelles, again in the absence of Protegenes, was at first dismayed "to see himselfe thus overcome; but taking his pensil, cut the foresaid colours throughout the length, with a third colour distinct from the rest, and left no room at all for a fourth to be drawn within it. Which when *Protegenes* saw, hee confessed that he had met with his match and his master both."[15] The crux is that each competitor drew an even finer line on top of the other's, fineness of line being the measure of triumph in this prototypical paragone. As in the historical paragone, John Dee supports the case for the importance of line in another art: "*The whole feate of Architecture in buildyng, consisteth in Lineamentes, and in Framyng. . . . Lineamente, shalbe the certaine and constant prescribyng, conceiued in mynde: made in lines and angles: and finished with a learned minde and wyt.*"[16]

Tudor translators rendered the antique stories accessible, and Nicholas Hilliard, the most famous of Elizabethan miniaturists, not only found these examples good but took their implications to heart, expanding upon them in his own theory, and putting them to his own fine practice. In his *Art of Limning*, Hilliard concludes that

> the principal parte of painting or drawing after the life, consiste[t]h in the truth of the lyne, as one sayeth in a place, that he hath seene the picture of her majestie in fower lynes very like, meaning by fower lynes but the playne lynes, as he might as well have sayd in one lyne, but best in plaine lines without shadowing, for the lyne with out shadowe showeth all to a good Jugment, but the shadowe without lyne showeth nothing, as fo[r] exampel, though the shadowe of a man against a whit wall showeth like a man, yet is it not the shadowe, but the lyne of the shadowe, which is so true, that it resembleth

excelently well, as drawe but that lyne about the shadowe with a coall, and when the shadowe is gone it will resembel better then before, and may if it be a faire face, have sweet countenance even in the lyne, for the line only giveth the countenance, but both lyne and colour giveth the lively liknes, and shadows showe the roundnes, and the effect or defect of the light wherin the picture was drawne. (28)

Hilliard's reference to the anonymous painter of four lines modestly alludes to the compliment to himself in Harington's "Historie" notes following the thirty-third book of his translation of Ariosto's *Orlando Furioso*. The passage also indicates Harington's awareness of the commonplaces of art history as well as his own appreciation for graphic line: "I thinke our countryman (I meane M. *Hilliard*) is inferiour to none that lives at this day, as among other things of his doing my selfe have seen him in white and blacke in four lynes only set downe the feature of the Queenes Maiesties countenaunce that it was even thereby to be knowne, and he is so perfect therein (as I have heard others tell) that he can set it downe by the Idea he hath without any patterne, which (for all Appelles priviledge) was more (I beleeve) then he could have done for *Alexander*" (385).

In the best-known passage of his treatise, Hilliard recounts how he limned the portrait of Queen Elizabeth in full sunlight because in conversation he and the queen had agreed on the aesthetic advantages of avoiding shadows. Hilliard argues that miniatures, designed to be viewed in hand, have no need of shadows and benefit most from clear light both in the painting and the viewing. To this practical consideration, he adds an illustrative analogy that suggests resonant metaphysical implications: "beauty and good favor is like cleare truth, which is not shamed with the light, nor neede to bee obscured" (29). Or, as Spenser's Redcrosse Knight puts it in the first canto of the *Faerie Queene*, wherein he explains his lack of fear to enter the Cave of Error, "Vertue gives her selfe light, through darkenesse for to wade" (1.1.12). The concept is graphically represented, too, on Marcus Gheeraerts the Younger's portrait of Queen Elizabeth, *The Ditchley Portrait,* which positions her midway between dark thunder clouds in the background on her left and the bright sky that she faces on her right (fig. 6). The association between truth and light would continue in English culture, to be realized most fully in the third book of *Paradise Lost.*

More immediately, any of Hilliard's works might illustrate his commitment to linear representation as both a decorative component and a significant aesthetic value. The integration of the two is apparent in the well-known *Young Man among Roses* (fig. 7). The edges of the young man's curls, his ruff, and the petals of the blossoms that surround him all follow a tightly curved outline. A looser curve defines the outlines of his inclined head, right sleeve, peascod doublet, cloak (worn Colley Westonward, i.e., fashionably askew), and his languidly crossed legs and feet. A third type of linear pattern repeats in the acutely angular trefoliate forms of the leaves of the bushes and on the lower edges of the young man's bases. Lastly, graceful ovoid forms appear in the slashed patterns on the sleeve, in the outlines of the individual leaves, and at the tips of the feet. The whole painting is executed on an oval vellum, mounted on an oval card. The interplay of related forms is visually pleasing, but more than that, the linear scheme outlines and underscores the note struck by the inscription, which functions as a virtual caption.

Hilliard's lettering is always attractively ornamental, and in this case the inscription also provides a golden key to the work: "*Dat / poenas laudata fides.*" Taken from Lucan (*De bello civili* 8, lines 485ff.), the lines were translated by Ben Jonson thus:

> a praised faith
> Is her own scourge, when it sustains their states
> Whom fortune hath depressed.[17]

Attempts have been made to identify the sitter, all thus far without conclusive evidence, but the sense of the motto would seem to be that the subject's dedication has brought him pain—an observation that at one time or another would have suited any one of Elizabeth's courtiers. The identity of the sitter is, at any rate, less pertinent here than the manner whereby Hilliard has underlined the sense of the theme in his miniature. The young man lounges between a tree and an eglantine bush: he leans upon the trunk of the sturdy tree, the roughness of its bark just barely visible, while the outlines of the thorny eglantine are stark against the blackness of the man's cloak. At this moment, his costume, position, and gesture protect the young man from the threat of surrounding thorns, but movement in any direction will impale him. The sharply outlined thorns prick out the essential point of the image. Symbolic association with the nature of the rose both to reward with its sweetness and to pain with its thorns was a commonplace often repeated in the emblem books. In 1586, under the motto *Post amara dulcia* (After bitter, the sweet), Geffrey Whitney adapted as his own the emblem (no. 30) from Perrière's *Le Théâtre des Bons Engins* (1539; 1548) that represents a man plucking roses (*A Choice of Emblemes* 165). Thomas Combe translated the work in 1614, so the image remained current into the next century. The eglantine, often and widely associated with Elizabeth, is a flower whose name etymologically derives from the idea of sharpness (L. *acus*). In a letter to Christopher Hatton (May 1, 1579), Henry Howard expresses a commonplace conceit: "Eglantine hath ten delights for every other's [i.e., flower's] one, if it had no prickles" (Nicolas, *Memoirs* 116). Hilliard's miniature visually captures these opposing qualities of the rose. The graphic imbrications of pattern, interlining both the courtly elegance of languid ease or surrender and the sharp angularity of thorny apprehension, coexpress the ambivalence of the inscription.

A second miniature may also illustrate Hilliard's interest in line, but to quite different effect. In the case of the larger miniature of *George Clifford, Third Earl of Cumberland, as the Knight of Pendragon Castle* (fig. 5), once again Elizabethan taste in costume serves to underline the artist's own sense of linear pattern, but this time the sitter's mode of address to the viewer is quite opposite from that of the melancholic young man. Cumberland's costume is that of the tilter at a courtly tournament, and he is surrounded by the conventional accoutrements of the role: helmet, gauntlets, lance, cardboard shield with his impresa, and the queen's favor of a glove, worn on his hat. His stance, copied from an engraving of a pikeman by Goltzius, is assertive: his feet solidly balanced apart, his left hand folded into a fist on his hip (once again, Trevelyon's figure, mentioned in the introduction, for "Presumption"), his right hand grasping the lance, which is firmly planted on the ground. The ground whereon he stands is a rise beyond which can be seen in the distance some of the landmarks of London: Westminster Hall, Westminster Abbey, and the Tower.[18] Whereas the landscape barely visible in the miniature of the young man sustains the sense of enclosure and containment within his thorny enclave, the hazy distant view behind and significantly below Cumberland opens onto a boundless horizon. Cumberland, too, is enclosed within a natural space described by a firm line, but the verdure that surrounds him outlines the curve of a protective frame around his self-possessed figure. There is no thorny threat here; rather, the tree serves to support his hanging shield; the rocks and hillocks form stages for display of his helmet, gauntlets, lance, and, indeed, his own elegantly clad figure. He dominates this scene, and the iconography of his tournament costume bears out this theme of personal power. The motif of stars is evident on all of the parts of his armor, including the handle of his lance. On the lining of his hat and tunic appear caducei, olive branches, and armillary spheres. The astronomical motif is also carried out by his impresa shield with its images of the sun, earth, and moon. In sum, Cumberland in his courtly role as queen's champion prevails over not only any challenger who will take up his gauntlet, but also the natural world around him and the civilization visible beyond. Were it made explicit in words, the implicit claim represented by this portrait, as on the picture of the young man among roses, would be rendered overbold, but an advantage of non-verbal medium is what it can leave safely to inference. On both examples, line conveys an implicit political posture.

Extant suits of armor and contemporary portraits, records, and literature all verify the historical reality of fantastic tournament costume like
Cumberland's, but less formal costume was also intricately patterned and
often fantastically symbolic.[19] Another miniature of an elegantly costumed
young man also shows in other ways how Elizabethan enchantment with
line interpenetrated art and life. Isaac Oliver's *Unknown Melancholy Young
Man* (fig. 8) pictures yet another young man in a setting out of doors. This
subject is also wearing a costume with a strongly linear pattern, a striped
doublet with blackwork lace cuffs and collar, the predominant shade of his
clothing being a dense black. He reclines on a grassy knoll, leaning against
a large tree for support. One discarded glove lies beside him, its blackness
giving it a startling emphasis, but unlike Cumberland's rigid gauntlets of
challenge, this glove lies limp and off-handedly disregarded. In the background are a great house, a formally patterned garden with an arcaded
walkway and pergola, and, immediately behind the young man, a low brick
wall that separates him from the social setting of house and garden. As on
the Cumberland miniature, here, too, the subject is foregrounded in a
natural setting that contrasts with the evidence of civilization in the background. Unlike Cumberland's, however, this man's posture, with his arms
and his ankles crossed, bespeaks withdrawal rather than combativeness or
domination. The flowers around him carry none of the natural threat of
the eglantine, but their abundance and wildness do form a contrast to the
highly formal patterns of the house, wall, garden, and walkways in the
background, as do also the irregular small branches sprouting from the
trunk of the large tree that supports his back. The sharp silhouette created
by the foreground scene outlines the contrast between nature and civilization, and it isolates the young man from the courtly scene beyond, framing
him within the wilder setting.

In order to portray a cultivated gentleman seated in an uncultivated
setting that lies just outside a highly cultivated area, Oliver has used line for
his own or his patron's expressive purposes, but he draws upon the conventions of use of line perceptible in a variety of contemporary media. Some
analysis of these adaptations and of the relevant media may reveal how line
is employed as a signifying vehicle, not only in Oliver's painting but also in
Elizabethan culture at large. Many of these elements represent on a miniature scale values that figure large in life, so that the single work is an index
to the world beyond the frame. Analyzing some of these parts within their
social context enlarges the sense of how they enhance meaning. To begin
with one of the smallest components in this and countless other paintings—the embroidery, for instance—is to follow a thread into the whole
fabric of Elizabethan society. For example, the young man's collar and cuffs
on Oliver's miniature are ornamented with the blackwork that was then so

popular, the designs sometimes similar to those on Persian and Italian velvets. Although every other element in his uncomfortable costume be-speaks constraint upon the natural, the blackwork outlines the Elizabethan sense of the natural forms of flower and leaf, so that the young man carries his own coal-black blossoms to this verdant ground. Although this reading may seem overly ingenious, it would not have seemed so to John Taylor, whose poem "The Praise of the Needle" prefaces James Boler's pattern book *The Needle's Excellency* (1631). Embroidery, says Taylor, "doth ART, so like to NATVRE frame, / As if IT were HER Sister, or the SAME" (A3ʳ). The concept of naturalness or liveliness that Taylor praises in this poem con-notes more than mimetic representation of physical appearance; it is the quality of representation of the spiritual essence of the subject.[20] So it is possible for what appears to the modern eye as a highly artificial form, such as the representation of foliage by an abstract outline in black thread, to satisfy the Elizabethan criterion of naturalness.

More important to the Elizabethan aesthetic practice is the quality that Taylor goes on to celebrate, "Moreouer, Poesies rare, with Annagrams, / Signifique [i.e., signify] searching sentences from Names" (A3ʳ). He might well have had in mind the Russell Sowray Cover or *The Shepheard Buss* (fig. 9), whereon yet another man stands encircled by verdure—and this time the pastoral motif is explicit, for the subject is costumed as a shepherd with all of the accoutrements appropriate to his job as it is fictively repre-sented in Elizabethan literature. He stands within an oval, which is in-scribed within a rectangle, in the four corners of which appear four devices taken from Paradin's *Devises* (1557). This rectangle is circumscribed by yet another, larger rectangle, the border frame of which is inscribed with a motto to be completed by rebuses keyed to the adjacent text: "False *Cupid* withe misfortvnes *wheel* hath wonded *hand* and *heart* who *siren* like did *lure* me withe *lute* and charmde *harp* the *cup* of care and sorowes *cross* do clips mi *star* and *sun* mi rose is blsted ad mi bones lo death inters in urn."[21]

Thus the embroidery combines several fashionable courtly modes—pastoral, Petrarchan, and emblematic—in a graphic challenge to viewers to complete the experience of the work from their own knowledge of these conventions. One tantalizing, and probably unanswerable, question re-mains, however: who embroidered this and why? Historical evidence indi-cates that embroidery was considered a pastime suitable for women. *The Booke of Curious and Strange Inuentions . . . Called . . . Needlework* (1596) ex-plicitly separates men's work of sailing, studying, and alchemy as "farre vnfit for tender women kind" and pronounces, instead, "Their milke white hands the needle finer fits," beseeming queens and townswomen as well (3ʳ). Taylor echoes this prescription, advising that women "vse their tongues lesse, and their Needles more" (Aᵛ). Contemporary fiction pictures noblewomen embroidering, as in works by Sidney, Spenser, and Marlowe; historical records and surviving artifacts demonstrate that Mary Queen of Scots and Bess of Hardwick did much needlework. Bess employed male embroiderers, but this exception does not gainsay that *The Shepheard Buss*, representing a conventionally masculine sentiment, would in all likelihood have been executed by a woman. Man proposes and woman complies with her needle in a medium that draws the line between the sexes. More to the point, the embroidered lines, both literal and graphic, explicitly represent courtly address to nature as pastoral theme.

Other portraits record the embroidered forms, natural and geometrical, that Taylor found remarkable for signifying "searching sentences":

> All in Dimension: Ouals, Squares, and Rounds,
> Arts life included within Natures bounds;
> So that Art seemeth meerely naturall,
> In forming shapes so Geometricall.
>
> (A3ᵛ)

As Taylor suggests, the medium of embroidery, by its nature, represents an opportunity to express paradox, in particular the interplay between art and nature that the Elizabethans found so tantalizing, as in the several miniatures and costumes already discussed. A portrait of Frances Clinton Lady Chandos by Hieronimo Custodis shows more specifically how embroidery combined "shapes so Geometricall" as to constitute a number of paradoxes. Lady Chandos wears a gown elaborately embroidered with columns and butterflies (fig. 10), the perpendicular and circular lines of which create a graphic contrast. The natural forms of the butterflies, however, are artificial, stylized almost beyond recognition, whereas the artificial forms of the columns are naturalistically drawn. This chiasmic mode of representation poses a contradiction that subliminally teases the recurrent question of the relationship between art and nature. Moreover, the butterfly is a traditional symbol for evanescence, whereas the column is one for stability and constancy, so the linear opposition underscores an implicit moral antithesis.

The opposition between art and nature was often sophisticated by such complexities, and it found expression in many media. The several miniatures picturing men in natural settings, for example, also represent the contrast between the evanescent beauty of some natural forms such as grass and flowers with the support and stability of other kinds of natural form— the hillock, the columnar trunks of trees. This ambivalent motif signifies pictorially those pastoral retreats represented in contemporary literature wherein courtly figures find both hardship and recreation, as in passages by Sidney, Spenser, and Shakespeare. Moreover, these linear representations convey the ironic contradictions expressed in literature between romantic expectations and the hard realities of a natural setting.

Many Elizabethan artifacts, like needlework, also represent in particular one device historically used in the attempt to understand nature, the armillary sphere, whose appearance has already been noted on Cumberland's portrait and armor. It is a shape that delighted Elizabethans as both curiously linear and intricately symbolic, an artificial device whose function is to locate men in nature. Strong reproduces several examples of iconographic use of the armillary in association with the queen, especially as plea or pledge that she maintain the reformed faith, or that she manifest prudential wisdom, as on *The Rainbow Portrait* (fig. 11), where a celestial sphere appears just above the head of the serpent embroidered on her left sleeve (*Gloriana* 138–41). In a wider sense, the impresa also represents the human effort to comprehend the heavens or to cope with nature. Elizabeth wears an armillary jewel at her left ear on *The Ditchley Portrait* (fig. 6). Used in conjunction with the representation of a landscape bifurcated between stormy and fair skies, the device suggests Elizabeth's need, perhaps her power, to control violent forces. The armillary sphere on Clifford's tilt costume on the Hilliard portrait (fig. 5) refigures an earlier use by Sir Henry Lee, Clifford's predecessor in the role of queen's champion. On a portrait by Antonio Mor (fig. 12), Lee's sleeves are embroidered with the armillary sphere. In combination with the olive branch, as on Cumberland's sleeve and hat, the device would bespeak peaceable maintenance of the faith. In combination with true-lover's knots, as on the portraits of Lee and of Elizabeth (Strong, *Gloriana* 139–41), the device may take on another kind of emphasis.

Knots are omnipresent in Elizabethan culture, and they formed a particular nexus between the frame of embroidery and a wider world beyond. These complex linear designs are also embossed on the badges of many households, on armor, book bindings, embroideries, and wall panels—on any kind of artifact that can bear linear pattern. John Marston satirized the lover whose chamber windows were "strew'd with sonnets, and the glass / Drawn full of love-knots."[22] The 1600 Inventory of the Queen's Wardrobe as printed in Nichols's *Progresses* includes on each of eleven successive pages at least one item ornamented with knots (3:500–12). Noting that the earl of Shrewsbury gave Elizabeth a white satin doublet embroidered all over with interlaced snakes, Nevinson reproduces a repellent example of the type of design.[23] Garments and jewels garnished with knots were a favorite gift to the queen, and while allowing for purely decorative appearances, it is yet certain that the device also often conveys other intentions. To some extent, the Elizabethans themselves explain these conceits. Knots variously figure the complexity of human relationship to self, other, and the physical world.

In two lines of *Orchestra*, Sir John Davies conjoins these commonplace readings. Antinous, the unwelcome wooer of Penelope, plays off against them when he argues to the disdainful lady the reasonableness of dance: "*For of Loves maze it [reason] is the curious plot, / And of mans fellowship the true-love knot*" (*Poems* st. 116).

Courtiers as well as poets manifest an intense self-consciousness about use of the device. In a tortuously knotted letter (May 1, 1579) to his "own dear Cousin," Henry Howard commends a gift to be conveyed by Sir Christopher Hatton to the queen. Howard implies a partial explanation for contemporary fascination with the knot, as he expresses his hope that Elizabeth accept his offering

> if it please her to conceive that some things are as welcome for their figure as other for their weight. . . . [B]ut I am much deceived if, by the turning of one loop or two, her Majesty may not convert it to a truelove's knot. The mean I know, but not the manner, further than that I am assured that no woman of less virtue, grace, and beauty than the best can make this change, because it passeth more by skill than sleight, by wisdom than by hazard: only this I promise, that whatsoever knot her Majesty doth bind shall be my fast in faith; and whatsoever band her fancy shall not like, shall be my loose at liberty. (Nicolas, *Hatton* 117)

Hatton himself had a particular fondness for the knot motif, as shown by its frequent appearance on the costly gifts that he presented to the queen. Thomas Heneage writes to him from Croydon in a letter dated April 2, 1585 to assure Hatton that the queen has received with great affection his gift of bracelets, and "her Highness saith you are a knave for sending her such a thing and of that price, which you know she will not send back again; that is the knot she most loves, and she thinks cannot be undone." A marginal note indicates that this was "The true love knot" (415). For New Year's in 1585/86, Hatton also gave the queen a golden headdress ornamented with "gorden knotts" of costly jewels (Nichols, *Progresses* 2:451), and, unless records have been confused, for New Year's 1588/89, he also gave her a gift of bracelets very similar to that presented through Heneage in 1585/86 (Nichols, *Progresses* 3:1). Heneage, Hatton's courier on the occasion already described, gave another twist to the significance of knots when adapted to his own purposes. Heneage's counter in the collection of medals in the British Museum represents a recursive, open-ended series of loops in a knot design accompanied with the motto "Fast thoe vntyed."[24] Explication of the *fast* of the motto is self-evident, and one can only speculate that *vntyed* conveys the wish of many an Elizabethan courtier tethered by a queen of volatile moods and desires.

That the same word, *knots*, should have been used to refer to patterns of both graphic and garden design suggests a similarity of aesthetic interest and artistic intention across media, as is indeed apparent in contemporary culture. Vasari's praise for Tribolo's plans for the uncompleted gardens at Cosimo di Medici's Castello anticipates Elizabethan fascination with knots and mazes because Vasari articulates the linear emphasis underlying the Renaissance garden. He describes the woods as forming a circle wherein lies a labyrinth formed by a box hedge, "the growth being so equal, and the whole arranged in so beautiful a manner, that they might be taken for a work of the pencil."[25] Granted that *pencil* may imprecisely translate Vasari's *pennello*, still it is the abstract, linear pattern of the labyrinth that attracts Vasari's praise, and it is this quality that particularly appealed to the Elizabethan eye. The transplanted abstract designs in pattern books such as *Excellent and new invented knots and mazes* (1623), attributed to Gervase Markham, or Thomas Trevelyon's manuscript commonplace book of 1608 (Folger Shakespeare Library MSS V.b.232) show at a glance the geometrical intricacy of Elizabethan plots.[26]

Vasari's admiration for the illusionistic interchange between the arts of garden and graphics would also have appealed to the Elizabethan aesthetic. Elizabethans often draw explicit analogy between design in embroidery or gardens and in the other arts. Even as Sir Hugh Platt dismisses the subject of "curious Rules for shaping and fashioning of a Garden or Orchard" because "Every Drawer or Embroiderer, nay (almost) each Dancing-master may pretend to such niceties; in regard they call for very small Invention, and lesse learning," he nonetheless reveals the interconnectedness of the several arts.[27] Marston's third satire invidiously compares the time consumed in setting the folds of a frivolous ruff with the "work in painful perfecting" of the maze at Woodstock (*Works* 3: 276, line 60). More appreciatively, in his *History of the Worthies of England* (1662), Thomas Fuller applies a familiar comparison in order to bridge sections of his exposition: "Pass we from gardening, a kind of tapestry in earth, to tapestry, a kind of gardening in cloth" (364).

Others employ more serious and extensive comparisons between gardening and graphics. For example, the entertainment written by George Peele for the queen's visit in 1591 to Burghley's Theobalds includes a gardener's speech elaborately explaining the allegorical compliment to the queen that, he says, is embedded in the plantings of the enormous garden wherein the flowers figure the Virtues, Graces, and Muses. The explication concludes, "These mingled in a maze, and brought into such shapes as poets and painters use to shadow, made mine eyes dazzle with the shadow, and all my thoughts amazed to behold the bodies."[28] The multiplicity of uses of the interchangeable terms *plot* and *plat* in reference to the structure of fictive narrative, maps, garden plans, and design for architectural construction reflects a commonality of concept of design for which in Elizabethan culture the knot is a visible device. Its linear convolutions resemble the intricacy of the literature, whether one considers literature on the microlevel of the conceit or on the macrolevel of plot. The real garden grounds the imaginary conceit.

Even personal signatures and private letters show homologous graphic and literal complexity. Hilliard's lettering on his miniatures is suitably minuscule, but the downstroke on the capital *A* in the *Aetatis* with which he dates his works is a knotted flourish to which the use of gold adds yet another precious dimension.[29] Signatures of Elizabethan courtiers tend to be large, assertive, and sometimes convoluted into knot-like forms to the point of illegibility, as in, for example, the signatures of Sir William Cavendish, Leicester, Burghley, Essex, Anne Warwick, and Elizabeth.[30] Essex's signature was an offensive weapon, as when Howard, the lord high admiral, saw to his fury that his enemy Essex had signed a joint report to the queen so near the top of the page as to compel the second signature to an inferior place.[31] The queen's signature, although clearly legible, is one of the most knotted and most decorative among the examples just cited, a visible sign of complex, even devious, monarchical authority. One certain indication of William Cecil's power was his access to the royal signature, a control that he restored to the office of secretaryship as one of his early maneuvers during the reign of Elizabeth; he even possessed a stamp of the sign manual, the queen's signature.[32]

To some extent, loops and flourishes in lettering reflect the influence of current popular style (thus demonstrating the adaptability of cultural aesthetic preferences to personal intention), especially as prescribed by exemplary alphabets in manuals such as Jean de Beauchesne's *A booke containing divers sortes of hands* (London, 1571), wherein not only are most descenders of discrete letters knotted or looped, but the last row of letters of the model alphabet are even interlaced with each other in a complex net of knots. De Beauchesne also illustrates many kinds of calligraphy, several of them fancifully conceited, such as "*Lettre couppee*," which is cut through horizontally, and "*Lettre frizee*," which is made up of tightly curled forms (Eii[r]; Gii[r]). In an early example of graphology, he also includes "*Lettre Renuersee Senextre*," a reversed style that is illustrated by a cautionary exemplum regarding the untrustworthiness of sinners (Div[r]).

Handbooks of various sorts compare different crafts to each other on the basis of their similar emphasis upon linear design. Joseph Lawson's "Pennarum Nitor, or The Pens Excellency" (BL Add. MS 36991 [1608]) relates ornate calligraphy to gardening, embroidery, and heraldic design. The complete title of a handbook for glaziers also illustrates comprehensiveness of application, Gedde's *A Booke of sundry Draughtes, Prinicipaly Serving for Glasiers: And Not Impertinent for Plasterers, and Gardiners: Besides Sundry Other Professions* (1615). Most of Gedde's patterns are complex knots. Trevelyon recommends one group of designs as suitable "For Joyners, and Gardeners, as followith 40: Leaues. . . . Heare followith some thinges for ioyners, and Gardeners, as knotes, and Buildyngs, and Morysies, and Termes, with many other thinges to serve their use very well."[33] Trevelyon's signature is a double-paged display of letters embellished with knots (fols. 264ᵛ–65ʳ), and this interest in calligraphy leads Nevinson to speculate that he was a writing master (5). These several handbooks demonstrate effort to suit the nature of text to its linear expression. In a visual pun, de Beauchesne cinches the connection between the pervasive delight in knots and its graphic expression in what he calls "*Lettre entrelacee*," a sample entry of which is entirely interlaced with a cord, tied at the tips (fig. 13).

Many of these uses of the knot or cord embody an old pun, one that ties together many of the paratactic connections between embroidery and the world beyond the frame. It depended upon a homophone that appealed to both the Elizabethans and their Italian forerunners in its use; that is, the association among "con-cor-chord-cord," which offered ground for figuring the concepts of heart, harmony, and the bonds of concord. On Lorenzetti's allegorical fresco of *Justice and the Common Good* in the Salla della Pace in Siena's Palazzo Pubblico, the personification of Concord holds a cord that binds together the representations of Wisdom, Justice, and figures of contemporary magistrates and soldiers. Nearer to home, George Pettie's translation (1581) of Guazzo's *Civile Conversation* illustrated the concept of *discordia concors* through the simile of the cord makers, "who though they winde and twist one contrarie to the other, yet they thereby accomplishe the worke they take in hande."[34] It is this sort of knot that is invoked in *Coriolanus* with reference to Coriolanus's desertion of Rome as having "unknit himself / The noble knot he made" (4.2.31–32).

If cords bound individuals and groups within societies, cords or lines also drew the bounds that defined outsiders. As used in ciphers, rebuses, devices, and other such graphic media, secretive lines bonded confidants and withheld the uninitiated. Minute calligraphic variations marked the codes used in secret court communication, and such codes were often used; Burghley comments, for example, on Elizabeth's cryptographic skills.[35] Heraldry was a recondite language that to some extent signified through line as well as color and position. Certainly it evolved as a system of maintaining social class and status, but its highly codified language was publicly available, and outsiders ignored it at their peril. Rebuses, too, inscribed a line between the sophisticate and the unknowing. They were frequently designed to be self-explanatory only after puzzlement of the viewer, the secretive key to deciphering being an attraction of the medium. Often used to embellish decorative artifacts, rebuses also served to manifest ownership or to affirm patronage. Thus some wall panels originally from Boughton Malherbe Manor and now in the de Young Memorial Museum in San Francisco (Roscoe and Margaret Oakes Income Fund 1981.65) represent the initials of Sir Edward Wotton and of his first wife Dorothy, Wotton's arms, and an elaborate rebus that pictures a number of tuns, the whole design surmounted by a love knot. A stained-glass quarry formerly in Westminster Abbey, now installed in the Burrell Collection (45/223), shows how such playful lines once appeared even in sacred places. The glass pictures a man falling from a tree, to the left of which is the outline of an eye, to the right, the word SLIP, the rebus of Abbot Islip of Westminster. Camden describes the latter and he also supplies many examples of other uses of the tun as device for persons whose names incorporated the syllable *ton* (*Remains* 141).

Rebuses reduce three-dimensional images of the names of things (*res*; ablative pl. *rebus* L.) to two dimensions, the linear abstractions representing pictorial approximations of the sounds of letters, syllables, or words. Like Wotton's or Islip's, rebuses sometimes share a personal joke with the casual observer. Others connote matter with more serious or more deeply personal intentions. Printers' marks, for instance, which identified persons with their craft and business, often employ a rebus that pictorializes the sounds of one's name. Famous examples include again the *tun* or *ton* in which books were transported, and hence an obviously appropriate device for printers whose names ended in those letters, such as Norton, Singleton, and Grafton. A more recondite example pictures the sun, a sheaf of rye, and a hare, representing Richard Harrison (rye for *Ri*).[36] A rebus was accessible on one level of meaning even to the illiterate; to the literate, on a more sophisticated plane; to the historically aware, sometimes at an even more elevated degree of complexity.

Courtiers and other members of the upper social classes distinguished themselves through use of devices, some of which incorporate rebuses, and all of which are designed both to conceal and to reveal. Concealment was sometimes politic, often coy, and always a decorous expression of seeming modesty, but discovery of one's identity by the targeted audience was essential for successful communication. The cryptographic key unlocking many devices like rebuses depended upon phonographic pun. Camden's long discussion of impresas in the *Remains* demonstrates both the usual possibility of identifying the bearer and the occasional confusion caused by ineptitude or ambiguity, as in the case of one who "might seeme to beare a vindicative minde, but I thinke it was for some amorous affection, which bare a flie upon an eye, with SIC ULTUS PEREAM" 183: "Thus revenged, I

shall die" (trans. Dunn 493). He describes a number of fairly straightfor-
ward devices such as the device of one Hartwell, which pictured a hart
racing to a fountain (189). Anagrammatic allusion sometimes signals personal identity, but most of Camden's examples employ more inventive
conceits. Four of these in particular depend upon ingenious use of line in
order to make a difference that matters:

> The Sunne declining to the Weast, with *Occidens, Occîdens, I* being short in
> the first word, and long in the second, shewed that the safetie and life both of
> the bearer and of others did depend on the light and life of the Soveraigne.
> (184)

> A studious lover of good letters framed to himselfe only the figure of *I,* with
> this philosophicall principle, OMNI EX UNO. (184)

> It might seem a craving Imprese, which set nothing but Ciphers downe in a
> roule, with ADDE, VEL UNUM. (188)

> Sir *Philip Sidney,* who was a long time heire apparant to the Earle of Leicester,
> after the said Earle had a sonne borne to him, used at the next Tilte-day
> following SPERAVI, thus dashed through, to shew his hope therein was
> dashed. (190)

Among the various significant motivations of line as communication,
aspiration would seem to be a constant that cuts across social classes. Hope
for improvement in economic and/or social status characterizes at least
three of the four apt descriptions quoted from Camden, and an unspoken
appeal for affirmation of intimacy may also underlie Sir Christopher Hatton's frequent use of pictorial ciphers in his private communications. One
of his devices represents a series of three triangles lined up side by side,
followed by a trailing scrawl, a crude representation of himself as the
queen's "lids," or eyes, an allusion to a pet name that she had assigned him.
His formal autograph is a knot-like inscription. In letters to the queen,
Hatton also uses both the "lids" cipher and another bit of graphic wordplay, signing himself "Your slave and EVER your own," the differences in
script underlining both his dedication to ELizabeth REgina and his hope for
continued maintenance from her (Nicolas, *Memoirs* 28–29). On the most
famous posthumous image of the queen, remarkably similar alternation
between upper- and lowercase expresses a more pious hope. John N. King
points out that the typography of the inscription on the left side of van de
Passe's engraving after a drawing of the queen by Isaac Oliver is so aligned
as to signify through anagram the year of the death of the queen, 1603, or

MDCIII: "*Mortua anno MIserICorDIae*": "Died in the year of Mercy."[37] As for the lower classes, paleographers observe that the signatures and signs used by the less literate often imitate those of their social superiors and that different styles of handwriting arose from not only functional necessity but from aspiration toward social distinction as well. Thus both the occupational signs and cross marks that often served as signatures of the illiterate show effort toward individualization, in what David Cressy aptly calls "the sub-heraldic devices" of the common people.[38]

These individual attempts to express personal aspiration through style of linear expression parallel developments on a larger scale in the history of letters, as a number of historians and critics have observed from the perspectives of their separate disciplines. The kinetic energy of writing is a naturally expressive resource. Jean Claude Schmitt, within the context of a passage wherein he distinguishes the multiple meanings of *geste* that obtained during the Middle Ages when all writing was communicated by handwriting, observes that writing itself is possibly also a *geste*, a gesture, an action.[39] To cite the early Renaissance figure whose expression of the concept anticipates the main line of argument of this chapter and provides an epigraph to it, in his dialogue *De recta Graeci et Latini sermonis pronunciatione* Erasmus draws an important analogy: "Moreover writing is just silent speech, like the nods used in the conversation of the dumb" (397). That handwriting is emotionally expressive has become a modern truism, but an elegy for Queen Elizabeth is, for the early modern period, unusually self-reflexive in its account:

> Mine hand did quake, and with a palsey tremble,
> My letters halfe were straight, and halfe were crooked,
> My teares betwixt each word did blots resemble;
> My sighes did drie my teares, and all ill looked:
> This ague feare, and teares, and sighes compacted,
> Are emblems of an heart farre more distracted.[40]

Moreover, some Elizabethans were sensitive to readers' responses to the difference between handwritten and printed text: John Lyly, in a commentary epistle to Thomas Watson's *Hekatompathia*, confesses reluctance to publish his own love poems lest the printer regularize his expressively crooked handwritten lines.[41]

The linear style of the written letter itself also became an expression of personal affinity for antique style or aspiration toward humanist ideals. Gombrich long ago pointed out the critical role of the humanists' revival of the *littera antiqua* in the creation of the Italian Renaissance.[42] Admired for its aesthetic qualities, antique lettering was also prized as evidence of one's scholarly and cultural awareness; scribes, authors, and, later, printers continued to invest style of script or type with cultural value. During the Renaissance, different kinds of calligraphy or typography set off different kinds of matter, an outgrowth of traditional distinctions that developed in medieval scriptoria, and often these differences graphically indicate hierarchical distinctions as well. Thus the history of the development of the typographical conventions for dramatic texts progresses toward increasingly functional distinctions among parts as well as admitting the use of elegant devices to adorn presentation copies of texts.[43] As newer styles of lettering evolved, hierarchical systems of appropriateness evolved with them, not only in manuscript, but also in type.[44] Whether publication in print did indeed stigmatize the author, courtly writers rationalize their intentions in the *parerega* to many a printed fictive work, thus implying some ambivalence toward publication.[45] On the other hand, typographical format could be used to establish an aura of seriousness of purpose or to set an elevated tone for the printed matter. The format could express a complex of intentions ranging from simple distinguishing of the erudite text from the lowly vernacular to arrogating the humanist aura of classical allusion, and it could even coexpress the fictive intent of the text.[46]

Observance of typographical difference was often motivated by social ambition as well as scholarly or literary aspiration, just as today the engraved invitation carries greater social cachet than the typewritten one, italic type more than roman, by an ironic inversion of an earlier Elizabethan classification of italic as script suitable for teaching to inattentive women (Dawson and Kennedy-Skipton 10). Even the lineation of type could express desire for upward mobility, as in the emphasis granted Drayton's arrival as "Esquire" by its splendid isolation on a line of its own upon his title page.[47] The context for such reading of line as index to one's social status has a convoluted history. If one could save one's life by proving literacy through recitation of a neck-verse, one might also lose it by wearing a pen and inkhorn, like the clerk of Chartham in *Henry VI, part 2* (4.2.105–10). Hamlet, too, comments on the ambiguity as he reflects upon how his fine calligraphy on his forged order has saved his neck:

> I once did hold it, as our statists do,
> A baseness to write fair, and labor'd much
> How to forget that learning, but, sir, now
> It did me yeman's service.
>
> (5.2.33–36)

Fineness of line could save a life, clarity of line could bespeak fineness of culture, intricacy of line could bond social ties. Lines set boundaries between inside and outside, upper and lower, cultivation and wilderness, art and nature. Lines expressed aspiration and they manifested dashed hope. If they depended upon words, they nonetheless coexpressed the literal, often communicating more immediately, or even ironically cutting across the bias of the written message. So line enhanced, underscored, or occasionally contradicted word. In sum, and here the chosen predicates themselves subscribe its significance, line styled personality, it delineated character, it underlined self-definition, it outlined social ambition, it circumscribed power. As a silent medium, line inscribed Elizabethan culture.

In his own lines addressed "To the Ingenvovs Reader" in his translation of Lomazzo, Haydocke highlights the importance of lines. Like the Syracusan Archimedes, whom the enemy Romans invading his fallen city discovered to be busily drawing lines in the sand, the translator-physician Haydocke is

> *heere found drawing of* lines *and* lineaments, portraictures, *and* proportions, *when (in regard of my place and profession) it might better haue beseemed me, to haue bin found in the Colledge of Physitians, learning and counselling such remedies, as might make for the common health: or if I must needesbe doing about lines, to haue co[m]mented vppon this proposition,* Mors vltima linea rerum.

> [But just as Archimedes' discoveries were ornaments of peace and of use in war, so this art will prove] *not onely a grace to health, but also a contentment and recreation vnto Sickenes, and a kind of preservatiue against Death and Mortality: by a perpetuall preserving of their shapes, whose substances Physicke could not prolong, not for a season.* (¶iij^r)

Because, as Haydocke argues, the manner in which lines lay upon a plane is significant, even unto and beyond death, the silent signification of the shape of lines on a page, the forms created by shallow relief are the subject of the next chapter and another stage in the anatomization of extraverbal communication. It is now apparent that lines point to meaning—that they sometimes constitute it. The next chapter demonstrates how the very idea of line as a silent inflexion could turn meaning just as it did in the most complex of rhetorical tropes in verbal form.

CHAPTER TWO

LINE AS INTERSECTION, PLANE, AND IDEA

> One Jesuit [Edmund Campion] made this false
> Anagram on her name,
>
> *Elizabeth.*
> **Jezabel.*
>
> ... [The omitted *T* presaged] the gallows whereon this
> Anagrammatist was afterwards justly executed.
>
> Fuller, *The Holy State*

T O DRAW A GRAPHIC LINE is to set a boundary, to define, to underline, to outline, to delineate, physically to divide space. The metaphorical connotations of these graphic divisions are implicit in the terminology that literally names the act of lining. Other kinds of line serve the same functions, but because these lines exist as inference, as concept, as imaginary construct, their implications are perceived indirectly. Modes of perception are largely conditioned by culture, so communication through the medium of the line-as-inferred idea may be ambiguous to an outsider. Even groups sharing the same written and spoken language may differently interpret the same linear data, and as the codes for understanding them change across cultures and through time, communication is increasingly problematic. It is necessary to try to reconstruct appropriate parts of the originating cultural context in order to understand what was being conveyed through the subtle medium of line.

Beginning with their earliest exposure to letters, Elizabethans were conditioned to see them as multidimensional signs. Children's hornbooks indicated the beginning of the alphabet with a cross, possibly as a signal to make the sign of the cross before starting the lesson, and certainly this sign is also the etymological explanation for use of the word *crossrow* to refer to the graphic arrangement of the letters.[1] The fashion of anagrams, acrostics, and shaped text depended upon this imprinted habit of attending to the patterns created by words inscribed or printed upon a plane, and the ocular habit predisposed the reader to recognize an import more lively than inert typographical pattern, just as a utilitarian initial in the hornbook also signed the cross. Many of these shapes challenge the ingenuity of reader and writer alike, and the most extreme cases are indecipherable without the aid of clues from the deviser. For example, Gabriel Harvey, often given to excess, records an inscription on a ring, engraved in four lines of initials, each of the forty-eight letters standing for a word in the poem that accompanies the ring as a gift to a lady (*Letter-book* 139–40). The obsessively complex acrostic poems by Sir John Salusbury climax in the fourteen stanzas of "Posie IIII" wherein the first letter of the first line of each stanza spells the name of one subject; the first letter of each second line spells another; and the four next lines in the first eight stanzas spell the names of two more persons—so far as a modern editor can decipher.[2] So labyrinthine are Salusbury's works that some of his word game remains a tantalizing mystery, and even Salusbury's Elizabethan readers must have remained lost in the maze.

These acrostics work more as cipher than as literary or pictorial expression, but others attempt to contain and signify the subject of the poem, retrospectively naming the person whom the poem has represented through attributes or achievements. The acrostic frequently appears as the dedicatory poem, as in William Barley's *Booke of Tabliture* of 1596, wherein "Certaine Verses Upon the Alphabet *of Her Ladyships name*" literally spell out the virtues of Bridgett Sussex (Barley, *Lute Music* 7). Thus acrostics often figure in public ceremonies or in the written records of them, as in the official civic welcomings extended or recalled through two acrostics, one dedicated to Will Kemp after he had danced his nine-day journey to Norwich, and another to the queen upon her entry to the same city while on progress.[3] As it praises and names, the acrostic also delineates for those who know their crossrows a mnemonic record of the memorable. Its effect is to herald an arrival or, after departure, virtually to conjure a departed presence, what Elizabethan writers would call an absent presence.

The technique echoes the vocative mode of the litany, adapting it to secular intentions. The religious antecedents for Elizabethan iconographic uses are most apparent in Thomas Bentley's *Monvment of Matrones* (London, 1582), an anthology of selections regarding virtuous women, including several acrostics.[4] Bentley prints a long section of prayers and meditations, "*deciphering in Alphabeticall forme*" the name of Elizabeth, each separate item being introduced by a line from a psalm that begins with one of the letters in the title "Elizabeth *Regina*." Thomas Churchyard rings the changes on Elizabeth as the phoenix, "a bird of gold in Britaine land," to be read in five ways (*Churchyards Challenge* Ff^v). An acrostic announces the title of James Aske's *Elizabetha Trivmphans*, a long poem celebrating Elizabeth's progress to Tilbury in 1588 in order to hearten her troops against the threat from the Armada. The verse associates Elizabeth with myth (Pallas), the Old and New Testaments ("V Vnto *Jehouahs* alters offerings bring, / M Mir, Frankinscence, with euery sweetest flower"), and the Roman triumph, thus combining allusions to the manifold sources of her iconography. Sir John Davies's *Hymnes of Astraea* (1599) is a series of twenty-six acrostics based, like Bentley's and many another acrostic, upon "Elizabeth *Regina.*" Each of Davies's poems praises a virtue or quality, the whole sequence forming an elaborate anatomization of Elizabethan iconography: mythological, lyrical, religious, political. The queen is praised as Astraea, goddess of justice ("Hymne I"), as Petrarchan lady (XI), as angelic creation (XIII), and as saint deserving of the *"Politique Devotion"* of all kings (VIII).

The potency of letters as significant form also underlay many arrangements and rearrangements of letters, arrangements that as arrangements coexpressed extraverbally the literal sense of the words. Puttenham says that he himself "tossed & tranlaced" the phrase *"Elissabet Anglorum Regina"* five hundred times (*Arte of English Poesie* 110–11), an exercise that in its plenitude demonstrated the potency of the monarch. Wordplay with letters could be earnest game indeed: Thomas Fuller attributes to Edmund Campion a demonic variation upon such hagiographics: *"Elizabeth.* / **Jezebel,"* noting that it was "both unequall and ominous that T, a solid letter, should be omitted, the presage of the gallows whereon this Anagrammatist was afterwards justly executed" (*The Holy State* 317). Both the anagram and Fuller's editorial comment demonstrate symbolic inferences from the physicality of letters. The crossrow form of the genre in effect both shapes and modifies the content. If readers expect a predetermined number of lines of extravagant praise, and if the relentlessly formularized nature of that expectation to some degree discounts the excessive claims of the language, the claims have nonetheless been expressed. Attributes that in other contexts would seem incongruous, hubristic, or sacrilegious seem rather to be dictated by the inexorable sequence of initials, and this *"intextus"* thus weaves into the decorous surface of the artifact the warp of idolatry.

Apart from acrostics and anagrams, other modes of graphic alignment coexpress the literal text that they shape or adorn. They may enhance, intensify, or in other ways qualify the words on the page. Shaped text is an ancient mode of signification, as some of the Elizabethans were aware, often citing the same Greek examples in one commentary after another on figured texts, or technopaignia.[5] Roger Ascham's *Scholemaster* (1570) contemptuously dismisses an example by one *"Simmias Rhodius* of a certaine singularitie"* without making clear that the text in question was literally shaped like the mythical egg from which hatched Castor, Pollux, and Helen, but he unquestionably consigns "like folie" to "barbarous nations of ignorance and rude singularitie" (*Elizabethan Essays* 1:32). Gabriel Harvey, for all his own stylistic quirks, also condemns shaped texts by Rhodius and modern imitators as "triflinge and childishe toyes" (*Elizabethan Essays* 1:126). In 1586, William Webbe's *Discourse of English Poetrie* conflates the wording of Ascham and Harvey in his own condemnation of earlier examples of the type *carmina figurata*, with the difference that Webbe goes on to allow, "howsoeuer or wheresoeuer it beganne, certayne it is that in our Englishe tongue it beareth as good grace, or rather better, then in any other; and is a faculty whereby many may and doo deserue great prayse and commendation, though our speeche be capable of a farre more learned manner of versifying" (*Elizabethan Essays* 1:267–68).

Among remaining important Elizabethan commentators on the genre, Abraham Fraunce alludes only to the familiar examples in his *Arcadian Rhetorike* of 1588 (D7^r–7^v), but Puttenham gives the subject extensive coverage together with graphic illustrations in his *Arte of English Poesie* (1589), and he sets the use of figured verse within the wider cultural context of wordless arts. Not because the medium was very popular in Elizabethan England—the commentators tell us it was not—but because shaped text as conceptual structure underlay so much of the most important work of the period, this use of implied line merits some attention as a significant element in the grammar of silent language. Modern readers may tend to underestimate even its limited significance, or dismiss it altogether as a curious folly.

Puttenham gives shaped text the most complete and most sympathetic coverage. He observes the cultural matrix for poetic expression, often alluding to historic precedent and cultural difference in the usage of particular forms. He is also sensitive to analogies between different media, occasionally making comparisons that reveal the coherence of the Elizabethan aesthetic. Some of these are the conventional inert comparisons that recur in poetic discourse, such as the "colors of rhetoric" or "the garment of style," but frequently Puttenham revivifies these dead metaphors within the context of contemporary culture by referring to specific uses of color or costume. He also supplies original analogies that are strikingly appropriate, as in the chapter on "*proportion by situation*"; that is, the variation of "distaunces" between verses for sake of greater delight to ear and eye. To illustrate this technique, Puttenham draws lines of varying lengths that graph the pattern of lines, linking those that observe rhyme and/or equal rhythm. His comments on the attraction of this technique are relevant to his discussion of figured verse that shortly follows: "And I set you downe an occular example: because ye may the better conceiue it. Likewise it so

falleth out most times your occular proportion doeth declare the nature of
the audible: for if it please the eare well, the same represented by delineation to the view pleaseth the eye well and *è conuerso:* and this is by a naturall
simpathie, betweene the eare and the eye, and betweene tunes & colours,
euen as there is the like betweene the other sences and their obiects" (85).

Having here suggested the association between music and poetry, Puttenham also in passing refers to the type of pattern that is created among
concords "by enterweauing one with another by knots, or as it were by
band, which is more or lesse busie and curious," which he illustrates again
through "ocular examples" that show concord in "Plaine compasse" and
"Entertangle" (87). The allusion to knots evokes those many complexities
of linear pattern that were the subject of chapter 1, but that Puttenham
need not specify for his contemporaries. He does, however, use a fresh
analogy in explaining the "band to be giuen euery verse in a staffe, so as
none fall out alone or vncoupled, and this band maketh that the staffe is
sayd fast and not loose: euen as ye see in buildings of stone or bricke the
mason giueth a band, that is a length to two breadths, & vpon necessitie
diuers other sorts of bands to hold in the worke fast and maintaine the
perpendicularitie of the wall" (89). The architectural bands of which Puttenham speaks are most visible today on the great houses that have survived
the assaults of time, destruction, and modernization. Highly decorative,
the repetition of this horizontal motif provides pleasing counterpoint to
the soaring height of Hardwick Hall (fig. 14) and Wollaton (fig. 15). At
Montacute, Rothwell Market House (fig. 16), and Lyveden New Bield (fig.
17), bands also function to support the addition of inscription and the
shields of local families. According to Puttenham, the horizontal bands on
those buildings both bond and support structure and design, as do their
counterparts in Puttenham's proportion by situation in verse, visible con-
junctions of a type shared by different media.

Having discussed the poetics of the abstract patterns created through
length of line and stanza, Puttenham turns to pictorial pattern in verse,
or "figure, so called for that it yelds an ocular representation, your me-
ters being by good symmetrie reduced into certaine Geometricall figures,
whereby the maker is restrained to keepe him within his bounds, and
sheweth not onely more art, but serueth also much better for briefenesse
and subtiltie of deuice" (91). He diagrams fifteen abstract shapes for such
verse, including those frequently to be found in texts that figure devotion
to the queen: the spire or pyramid, the cylinder or column, and the roundel
or sphere (92–97). He prints examples of each, which have been identified
by his editors as probably his own compositions (353ff.). The example of
the spire, taper, or pyramid, "taking both his figure and name of the fire,
whose flame if ye marke it, is alwaies pointed, and naturally by his forme

couets to clymbe" (95). It is a form that thus might signify either exemplary
aspiration or deplorable ambition. An encomium on Sidney that appeared
in the 1605 edition of Josuah Sylvester's translation of Du Bartas's *Divine
Weeks and Works* figures a variation on the conventional shape of a spire or
pyramid, topping it with an arrow tip (the Sidney device of the pheon) and
the Sidney porcupine. The syntax is muddled, but the relevant point is that
the poet reflexively comments upon the inadequacy of words to express the
beauty of form, as in the lines of the first stanza, which typographically
form the top of the shaft:

> ENGLAND's Apelles (rather OUR APOLLO)
> WORLD's-wonder SIDNEY, that rare more-then-man,
> This LOVELY VENUS first to LIMNE beganne,
> With such a PENCILL as no PENNE dares followe.[6]

Puttenham prints two examples representing political, indeed imperialistic, aspiration. Both regard the queen, and the first of these comments
upon its own form. The author also explains that its six-stanza structure is
modeled upon the architects' obelisk, the height of which equals six triangles, forming, he says, a taper, "the longest and sharpest triangle that
is . . . taking both his figure and name of the fire":

> Her Maiestie, for many parts in her
> most noble and vertuous nature to be
> found, resembled to the spire. Ye
> must begin beneath according to the
> nature of the deuice

> Skie.

> ———

> Azurd
> in the
> assurde,

> ———

> And better,
> And richer,
> Much greater,

> ———————

> Crown & empir
> After an hier
> For to aspire

Like flame of fire
In forme of spire

To mount on hie,
Con ti nu al ly
with trauel & teen
Most gratious queen
Ye haue made a vow
Shews vs plainly how
Not fained but true,
To euery mans vew,
Shining cleere in you
Of so bright an hewe,
Euen thus vertewe

Vanish out of our sight
Till his fine top be quite
To Taper in the ayre
Endeuors soft and faire
By his kindly nature
Of tall comely stature
Like as this faire figure
(95–96)

Puttenham also prints his figure for the pillar or column, listing its components as they are used in architecture, once again indicating his perception of a close connection between poetry and other arts, and he supplies his interpretation of the significance of the column, "By this figure is signified stay, support, rest, state and magnificence":

Her Maiestie resembled to the crowned
piller. Ye must read vpward.

Is blisse with immortalitie.
Her trymest top of all ye see,
Garnish   the   crowne
Her   iust   renowne
Chapter   and   head,
Parts   that   maintain
And   womanhead
Her   mayden   raigne

In te gri tie:
In ho nour and
With ve ri tie:
Her roundnes stand
Stre[n]gthen the state.
By their increase
With out de bate
Concord and peace
Of her sup port,
They be the base
With stedfastnesse
Vertue and grace
Stay and comfort
Of Al bi ons rest,
The sounde Pillar
And seene a farre
Is plainely exprest
Tall stately and strayt
By this no ble pour trayt
(97)

The shapes outlined by these poems were frequently associated with Elizabeth, and their usage assumes familiarity with earlier appearances of the form. The spire (or obelisk or pyramid) appears widely in Renaissance iconography, largely because of the humanists' fascination with Egyptian hieroglyphics and also because the obelisk in front of Saint Peter's in Rome had finally been installed there in 1586 through the remarkable efforts of about eight hundred workmen. *Eliza Trivmphans* (1589), an engraving by William Rogers, adapts exotic associations to the celebratory mode of the Armada victory both in the words of the title and the images of the obelisks that flank the image of the queen. The column figures even more often than the obelisk in Renaissance iconography because of its manifold associations through time with pagan myth (the pillars of Hercules), with Christian piety (Samson's pillars; the column to which Christ was bound when whipped; the column that often appears behind Saint Sebastian; the emblem of fortitude), with Italian poetry (as in poems by Petrarch and Michelangelo), and the historic present (as in Charles V's imperialistic adaptation of the association between the pillars of Hercules and the motto *Ne plus ultra*, in his personal device, and in wordplay upon the Colonna family name—this last being updated in the *Hypnerotomachia* through puns and eponymous acrostics keyed to the word *colonna*). So the column was a ready-made attribute for Elizabeth as she appears on the title page of the *Bishops' Bible* (1569), whereon a broken column signifies Fortitude, or, in a more complex adaptation of the image, as she is pictured on the Siena *Sieve Portrait* (fig. 18). On this latter representation, the column on the left of the painting bears medallions that represent episodes from the *Aeneid*, images suggesting affinity between heroic Aeneas and Elizabeth the Virgin Queen. Columns continued to appear as an attribute of Elizabeth until the end of her reign, figuring largely in Sir Henry Lee's entertainment for the queen at Ditchley in 1592, and reappearing on the 1596 engraving by Crispin van de Passe I (fig. 19), which represents the queen standing between two columns topped by devices: the phoenix, symbolizing eternal life, to the right, and the pelican, symbol of self-sacrifice, to the left. Elizabeth personally employed these devices throughout her reign because they allowed latitude for her implicitly to claim physically incompatible qualities: never-ending youth, virginity, and motherhood. Moreover, she was able to capitalize upon the precedent set by Charles V's imperialistic implications in a device that represented the presumption of power without risking the bellicosity of spoken intention.[7]

Most of the forms and devices that are explained by Puttenham are embodied in other technopaignia. In fact, both the phoenix and the column figure in verses that are among the earliest shaped poems in English, published in 1582. In that year, Thomas Blenerhasset's *Revelation of the True Minerva* included a poem shaped like a bird, possibly as an image of the phoenix that is equated with Elizabeth just two pages earlier (xiii–xiv; F^v). Also in 1582, Thomas Watson's '*Ekatompathia* included a particularly ingenious column poem of the "pasquino pillar" variety (i.e., poems that, like the scurrilous poems affixed to the Pasquin statue in Rome, express disaffection, whether of a political nature or, like Watson's, an erotic cast). What may be a visual pun upon columnar associations with Elizabeth appears in Andrew Willet's *Sacrorvm Emblematvm* (1592–98) as an acrotelestic, a poem in which the first and last letters of each line comprise the inscription or an intext.[8] As Willet explains, the text figures the shape of a tree ("*in speciem arboris digesta*"), the first and last letters of each line of the text spelling out "ELIZABETHAM REGINAM DIV NOBIS / SERVET IESVS INCOLV-MEM: AMEN." (A4^v). "*Incolvmem*" denotes the prayer that Jesus support and protect the queen, but it also punningly echoes and evokes iconographic associations with the column. In the year of her death, a collection of elegiac poems was published in Oxford that included two complex variations on an hourglass shape, the one a chronogram, the other a columnar arrangement in which the upper, lamenting half of the shape diminishes to a laconic "*Lugete Anglia*" at the pinched waist of the verse, inverting with *"gaudete Angeli"* to an incremental poem of praise, allusion to the phoenix being a vehicle for the transformation from woe to triumph.[9]

Not all historical examples of technopaignia are prayerful or even solemn: the term itself *(art game or jest)* conveys the playfulness that characterizes many prototypes, beginning with the antique examples invariably cited by Elizabethan commentators, poems shaped like an egg or an axe, and continuing through early Renaissance instances such as illustrate the 1499 edition of the popular *Hypnerotomachia*, like the shapes of vases (g5ᵛ, s2ᵛ, t2ᵛ, x1ᵛ, y2ᵛ) and a basket (q4ʳ). The supposed author of the fiction revealed his identity as Fra Francesco Colonna through an acrostic formed by the first letter of each chapter.[10] The English, too, played with earthy forms, as on the original title page of an early cookbook from the library of Bishop Matthew Parker, shaped in the form of a cup, or chalice:[11]

```
¶                    A                        Proper
    newe          Booke         of         Cokerye,
      declarynge        what        maner         of
        meates      be      beste     in      season,
          for     al     times    in    the    yere,
            and       how       they       ought
              to       be      dressed,      and
                servued     at      the      ta
                ble,      bothe      for
                  fleshe        dayes,
                    and      fyshe
                      dayes.
              With a newe addition, verye nes
                cessarye for all them that
                  delyghteth in Cos
                      kerye.
```

This is no poem, but neither is it so superficial as it might appear if one does not recall the connotations of the decorum of food service for an Elizabethan reader, and in fact the English often put such conventional games to earnest purpose. When Thomas Churchyard constructed an anacyclic poem "to be red fiue waies" in order "to set my Phenix forth" with all her praises, he assured his readers that the point was to "shew what heauenly grace, and noble secret power diuine" dwelt in the "Princely face" of the queen (*Churchyards Challenge* Ffᵛ–Ff2ʳ). Serious implications of the image of the cup appear in the layout of the dedication of the 1596 edition of Spenser's *Faerie Queene*:

TO

THE MOST HIGH,

MIGHTIE

And

MAGNIFICENT

EMPRESSE RENOW-

MED FOR PIETIE, VER-

TVE, AND ALL GRATIOVS

GOVERNMENT ELIZABETH BY

THE GRACE OF GOD QVEENE

OF ENGLAND FRAVNCE AND

IRELAND AND OF VIRGI-

NIA, DEFENDOVR OF THE

FAITH, &C. HER MOST

HUMBLE SERVAVNT

EDMVND SPENSER

DOTH IN ALL HV-

MILITIE DEDI-

CATE, PRE-

SENT

AND CONSECRATE THESE

HIS LABOVRS TO LIVE

WITH THE ETERNI-

TIE OF HER

FAME.

The words of the text solemnize the dedication through explicit use of the language of religious devotion, but the shape of the ceremonial cup renders visible, subliminally tactile, the communion between queen and subject, monarch and poet, secular and divine, heaven and earth.[12]

As an extraverbal medium, technopaignia may, among the examples discussed thus far, like the column, support a text; like the spire or lance, point it; like the cup, uplift or consecrate it. These shapes, constituted by the outline formed through typographical arrangement, are clearly visible, and, in the examples cited, these speak fairly directly to ideas that enhance the verbal text. The typographical shapes render visible a spatial configuration of thought. Other shapes are more subtly contrived, perhaps none so subtly as musical types. John Milsom both describes the working musical model and suggests its underlying schematic mathematical rationale by which "the early Tudor church composer traditionally worked with sets of numbers and ideas of ratio and proportion in his head, schemes relating to the duration of movements and sub-sections that ensured overall balance in the finished product and provided an initial grid on which he could then work out detail."[13] As a modern scholar of the earlier music, Milsom has the advantage of hindsight in perceiving its shape and substance and its relationship to Tudor aesthetics. Like Milsom, sixteenth-century commentators themselves recognized the commonality of musical shape and line in the other arts. Puttenham, for example, draws an analogy between the "*proportion by situation*" of music and poetry (*Arte of English Poesie* 84–85) before proceeding to illustrate its appearance in poetry. In these examples, time coordinates with space in order to create a space and a duration for concept. On a more specialized level of taste, within the context of a scene of coyly salacious rape or seduction, Cutwode's *Caltha "Poetarum": Or The Bumble Bee* (London, 1599) also alludes to musical shape, assuming the titillating vulgar association common in contemporary usage between circles and vaginas: "And this he found,that musick pleaseth best, / Whose moode by prick, in circle is exprest" (st. 177).

Tudor artists used a variety of techniques to work out their schematic shapes. Repetition of musical line, like poetic verse, denotes through a felt roundness of form a harmonious union, in both the technical and metaphorical sense—a primary aesthetic value. The echoing sounds of madrigal and part-song underscore this effect, as in the madrigal printed by William Barley, "Your face / So fair" (*Lute Music* 10). Other forms were expressed through more contrived means. In his *Plain and Easy Introduction to Practical Music*, Thomas Morley says "many Englishmen" have designed canons with "enigmatical words set by them," and he provides a graphic illustration of his own musical figure, a cross without clefs, composed of two staves lined with musical notes. The upright shaft intersects his teasing verse:

> Within this crosse / here may you find,
> Foure parts in two / be sure of this:
> But first seeke out / to know my mind,
> Or els this Cannon / you may misse.

He observes that his composition is "indeed so obscure that no man without the Resolution will find out how it may be sung," and so he supplies a technical explanation and Resolution (285–86). Morley mentions no further thematic significance for the form, however, and it appears that none is intended. One wonders whether any shaped musical forms except the insistently circular would have been perceptible; if so, for the uninstructed they must have generally been more elusive than literary analogues. Yet even some of these also continue to puzzle readers.

Among the shapes that are discussed by Puttenham, the circle, or roun-

del, was one of the most popular and, in its expression, sometimes one of
the most complex. The circle, as an image of the cosmos, was a form that
could speak to humanists and the unlettered alike, dating from earliest
Greek tradition and inscribed in works of art and literature from Homer's
shield of Achilles, through medieval illuminations, to Sir John Davies's
Orchestra. The church propagated the form in many ways, including the
round host, the rosary, the rose windows of the cathedrals—all within the
common experience of the observant public. In London, an elaboration of
the Platonic cosmos was embedded in the medieval mosaic pavement of
Westminster Abbey. The Latin inscription surrounding the roundel of the
pavement labeled the image as *Spericus: Archetipum: Globus: Hic: Monstrat:
Macrocosmum*, but even the illiterate could see in the images of plants,
animals, and sea monsters what the inscription described as "the perfectly
rounded sphere which reveals the eternal pattern of the universe."[14] Thus
the symbolic associations with the circle would have been more accessible
to the commoner during the Elizabethan period than today to many a
scholar of the literature and art of the period.

   In one of its simplest applications, Jennifer Stead recalls the origins of
the term *roundelay,* referring to the round of guests singing the songs or
posies printed on the bottoms of their round trenchers, or "roundels," after
consuming the course of the dessert banquet served on the plain, upper
side of the trenchers, as described by Puttenham.[15] Mark Franko describes
at some length how the circular dance form of the branle figured the
Renaissance concept of harmony while reaching across class boundaries in
its performance.[16] The Fairy Queen Aureola greeted Elizabeth at the entertainment in Elvetham in 1591, bringing with her "a garland, made in the
fourme of an imperiall crowne," and recalling that she would "every night
in rings of painted flowers / Turne round, and carrell out Elisaes name," so
delighting Elizabeth that she called for three repetitions of the dance (*Entertainments* 115–16).

   A more stately circular dance enacts the happy afterlife envisioned for
Queen Katherine in the play *King Henry VIII* that draws upon a broad
continuum of possible interpretations of the meaning of circular form.
Shakespeare's bawdy characters represent something of the prurience of
Caltha in their sexual innuendoes about naughts and "O's"; his noble
characters conjure the outermost circumference of signification in their
references to crowns and globes. Less comprehensive than Shakespeare in
reading the form of the roundel or sphere, and less imaginative in use of
spherical metaphor, Puttenham considers only the most elevated uses of
the circle, but he explains the metaphysical fascination that the shape held
for the Elizabethans, and more specifically, he reveals, too, why poems not
visibly figural are nonetheless discussed in his chapter on "*Proportion in*

figure": "The most excellent of all the figures Geometrical is the round for his many perfections. First because he is euen & smooth, without any angle, or interruption, most voluble and apt to turne, and to continue motion, which is the author of life: he conteyneth in him the commodious description of euery other figure, & for his ample capacitie doth resemble the world or vniuers, & for his indefinitenesse hauing no speciall place of beginning nor end, beareth a similitude with God and eternitie" (98). Puttenham's judgment is corroborated by the broadside poem "Eliza *Trivmphans*" (1597), which concludes,

> The square doth make the surest thing
> Four quarters can diuide the best.
> The circle is the perfectest.
> (British Library Shelflist C.121.g.6 [14])

Puttenham notes that the poet may fashion meter around the circumference like a circle, from the circumference like a beam, or diametrically—which options so complicate perception of the form that, for example, Josephine Waters Bennett must indecisively describe one of Thomas Blenerhasset's figural poems in *A Revelation of the True Minerva* (F2ʳ) as "either a lozenge, or a rondel or sphere" (xiv).

Puttenham prints two examples of his own spherical models that compare Elizabeth to the roundel, neither of which is visibly shaped like a sphere. The title of the first literalizes the most extravagant symbolic implications of the form, "*A generall resemblance of the Roundell to God, the world and the Queene.*" The first two lines of the text of the poem set forth the properties of the sphere: "*All and whole, and euer, and one, / Single, simple, eche where, alone,*" which are analyzed in the body of the poem, with particular attention being paid to the Aristotelian paradox that its center is unmoved in the midst of turbulence and that "*it purports eternitie.*" The last two lines of the poem echo the first two, and the movement of the poem has set up an analogy among God, the sky, and the queen as roundels in their specific spheres, so the poem has come full circle, but in the meanplace it has roundly encompassed some very large claims. Puttenham's second poem also compares Elizabeth to the roundel, and this one sets up the comparison in terms of the three properties of the roundel already described in his commentary and now named in his last line. Thus the poem concludes, "*So is the Queene of Briton ground, / Beame, circle, center of all my round*" (98–100).

As self-reflexive artifacts, Puttenham's poems illuminate the Elizabethan practice of constructing shaped verse whose figure is a notional rather than graphic line, a subtlety that can be missed by inexperienced modern readers and one to which they must be attuned if they are to know the intentions of the poem or song. If this extraliteral dimension of the poem passes unnoticed, the bare text is tedious, especially for the reader unaware of the Elizabethan richness of circular symbol. The echo of similar phrases or lines as in Puttenham's roundels, sometimes in reversed or otherwise changed order, is a familiar device for expressing a perceptibly recursive or spherical design without visibly shaping the text. The plenitude of rhetorical names for types of repetition indicates the antiquity and the popularity of recursive, curvilinear pattern. Puttenham at first lists seven, enough to recall the pervasiveness of repetitive figure: *anaphora* ("or the Figure of Report"), *antistrophe* ("or the Counter turne"), *symploche* ("or the figure of replie"), *anadiplosis* ("or the Redouble"), *epanalepsis* ("or the Eccho sound. otherwise, the slow return"), *epizeuxis* ("the Vnderlay, or Coocko-spel"), and *ploce* ("or the Doubler") (198–202). As Puttenham's anglicized terms make clear, this taxonomy categorizes the kinds of repetition familiar in Elizabethan literature, whether repetition of the first, last, or middle word of a poem, or a phrase, entire line, or verse. Circular form was a comfort to Elizabethans, physical and metaphysical.

Puttenham quotes often from Ralegh to illustrate rhetorical uses of repetition, which could easily be illustrated from the works of any major Elizabethan writer, and some other examples may forcibly recall ingeniously circular figural uses. The correlative sonnet is so structured that the poet is bound to double back over the parts of the division of the theme. Spenser's *Amoretti* XVIII begins with an image that serves as metaphor for the frustrated lover-poet as well as for the mode of the poem: "The rolling wheele, that runneth often round, / The hardest steele in tract of time doth teare." Repetition risks tedium, and the correlative sonnet is particularly vulnerable, granted the restrictions of both genre and specific type. Shakespeare's Sonnet 105 ("Let not my love be called idolatry") reflexively admits the problem ("my verse, to constancy confined, / One thing expressing, leaves out difference"), but seizes the opportunity to express the uniqueness of the single argument that the beloved is fair, kind, and true, which case the poem has analyzed in repetitive detail. The couplet rounds out the argument with a difference: "Fair, kind, and true have often lived alone, / Which three till now never kept seat in one." With its allusion to the Trinity—ironically sacrilegious in light of the denial of idolatry in the opening line of the sonnet—the couplet underscores the circular form and logic of the poem, and it touches upon one of the perfections of the sphere that Puttenham named, its similitude to God.

Shakespeare's Sonnet 113 ("Since I left you, mine eye is in my mind") exemplifies another rhetorical variation upon repetition, the form called *correctio*. After the assertion of the first line, the poet describes the unreceptive response of his mind to visibilia, filled as it is with the image of the absent beloved, so that, he concludes in his last line, "My most true mind thus maketh mine eye untrue." The recursive sound and idea both double back on the first line and move forward with the difference of subtle refinement and distinction.[17] Although the words of the sonnets do not specify the circle, each poem evokes a circular movement of thought that offers the extraverbal satisfaction of patterned resolution to the anxieties verbally expressed.

Natural signs of recurrent change—the daily cycle, the turn of the seasons, and the revolution of the annual calendar—already familiar as visual images on the facades of cathedrals, in books of hours, and as structural popular religious observances provided a ready-made frame for the circular structure of many a sonnet, poetic cycle, or pastoral fiction. Within the *Delia* sonnets, Samuel Daniel includes a run of five (XXXI–XXXV) concatenated poems, joined by repetition of the last line of the preceding sonnet reappearing as the first line of the next, and joined also by allusions to the passing months and seasons, from the April of the first of the group to the winter of the fourth, and the promise of eternal fame in the fifth and last. The poet is courting his mistress in a seasonal variation upon *carpe diem*. He stops the round of the seasons and its inexorable powers of decay in the last of the concatenated group of sonnets with the triumph that the love he expresses in these verses will immortalize his beloved. Less conventionally and more personally, the circular frame of Spenser's sonnet cycle the *Amoretti* is also punctuated with references to time. Sonnet LXXXVI rehearses the weariness of a lover who finds himself wishing "that night the noyous day would end," only then to "wish that day would reascend" as he marks the cycle of time while absent from his mistress.

On a larger scale, the *Amoretti* narrates the inconclusive round of a courtship, the passage of time marked by references to recurrent times and days of the year. The last of the cycle finds the poet alone, awaiting the return of his love: "Dark is my day, whyles her fayre light I mis, / And dead my life that wants such lively blis." Spenser's *Epithalamion* is a long poem of twenty-four stanzas constructed on a numerical model of the hours of the poet's wedding day on the summer solstice.[18] Each of its twenty-three longer stanzas ends with a reprise, with variations, of the couplet that in its final form in the last of the long stanzas reads as anticipation of the end of time and the beginning of eternal bliss for the lovers: "And cease till then our tymely joyes to sing: / The woods no more us answer, nor our eccho ring." The varied repetitions of this couplet move through a series of emotional states, beginning on its first appearance, with the poet alone, to the blissful resolution at its last appearance in the first-person plural, so that the round of hours and of stanzas has progressed from isolation to the perfection of heavenly community. The final stanza, curtailed like the night of the summer solstice, reflects upon the poem as a "goodly ornament" for the bride, "And for short time an endlesse moniment." The words of these poems evoke a world behind the words, the long tradition of visibilia that pictured a circular cosmos. That the words profess to speak only to short time ironically recalls the longer duration of the cosmos beyond the secular, toward which they have constructed a monument. The monument is notionally rounded and literally inscribed. That it is an ornament, even a goodly one, diminishes its value to a reader unacquainted with the significance of ornament in a culture that measured its worth beyond troy or carat.[19]

As the name of the form indicates, the coronet, or corona, of sonnets that often accompanies a poet's longer works is constructed on the lines of a circle, the words and the implied shape together creating the crowning moments of the work. The concatenated identical first and last lines of each sonnet link the chain, which is closed by the repetition of the first line of the first sonnet as the last line of the last one, bringing the group full circle. George Chapman's "Coronet for his Mistresse Philosophie" is an example of the type that pursues a critical argument through the closely-linked form. The corona that accompanies Josuah Sylvester's translation of Du Bartas's *Divine Weeks and Works* exploits the Janus-like device in order to combine an elegy for Elizabeth with a eulogy for James I in the first and last line of the work as a whole: "Our Sunne did sett, and yet noe night ensew'd" (Sylvester 2: app. 887).

Longer, comprehensive architectonic figures are difficult to perceive, and often even more difficult to interpret, especially in an age that has lost both the habit of reading a conceptual figure in a fictive text and the belief in the efficacy of the figure so reconstructed. Fortunately for present purposes, the less complex examples of figural text that were described above serve adequately to demonstrate the nature of this mode of supraverbal communication and to alert readers to its difficulties and rewards. If the single poem or sonnet sequence accommodates the model of a day or an occasional allusion to the passage of a season or a cycle of years, more sustained works offer scope for models on a larger architectonic order. The commentary by the unidentified "E. K." that accompanies one of Spenser's earliest works outlines the design of the twelve eclogues based on the structure of twelve calendar months. The prefatory letter explains that Spenser "compiled these xij. Aeglogues,which for that they be proportioned to the state of the xij. monethes,he termeth the SHEPHEARDS CALENDAR, applying an olde name to a new worke" (¶iij^r). E. K. thus recalls medieval illustration of seasonal occupations in word and image, as most readily seen today, like the cosmographical image, on murals and illuminated manuscripts and also on tapestries, and cathedral facades and capitals. The woodcuts that illustrate Spenser's work topically adapt the tradition to the Elizabethan cultural, social, political, and religious context, as does the poem itself.[20] E. K.'s prefatory *"generall argument of* the whole booke" speaks of the twelve eclogues as "euery where answering to the seasons of the twelue monthes" (¶iiij^r). The arguments and glosses that accompany each of the eclogues more specifically relate the verses to the months and seasons. The "December" argument remarks on the circular movement of the *Calender,* which begins with the poet Colin breaking his pipes in the January eclogue and ends with his abandoning them in December: *"This* AEglogue (euen as the first beganne) is ended with a complaynte of Colin to God Pan. wherein as weary of his former wayes, he proportioneth his life to the foure seasons of the yeare" (M4^v). Remembrance of the traditional correspondences between man and nature is vital to Colin and to the reader's sense of both the despair of the pagan poet and the liveliness of the poem.

Spenser also represents the cyclical change of the hours, days, seasons, and life and death as Mutability's argument for her own godly precedence in the seventh canto of the incomplete seventh book of the unfinished *Faerie Queene.* Earlier, in the tenth canto of the completed sixth book, a complex network of symbolic rings, garlands, crown, and circular dance epitomizes Calidore's vision of perfection. In the center of the circular dance of a hundred naked maidens appear the Three Graces, the naked maidens whose alternating back-to-front orientation toward the viewer symbolizes the reciprocal nature of the grace of civility. The spirit of reciprocal circular exchange so pervades all of the *Faerie Queene* that Patricia Fumerton reads the whole poem as "a circle of gift, an endlessly liminal, transformational round wherein all loss is gain, all giving taking, all dying living." She concludes that this epic is "as much a cultural as a linguistic or aesthetic form."[21] The point is well taken, not for just the *Faerie Queene* but for all of the uses of silent language, embracing as they do so many Elizabethan extraverbal media.

The long poem constructed upon a conceptual figurative model was not unique to Spenser. Sylvester's translation of Du Bartas brought to English readers the text of a massive if incomplete poem in which the author represents the long section called "The Columns" as an explication of the universe, keyed to the mathematical symbols preserved on antique pillars. In a sonnet complimenting the translator, John Davies of Hereford uses an apt phrase that might well describe all Elizabethan use of figurative verse. Of Du Bartas, Davies says his *"Compasse* circumscribes (in spacious Words) / The Universall in particulars" (Sylvester 2: app. 918). Spacious words, too, are George Chapman's in *Ovids Banquet of Sence* (1595), in which critics have analyzed the literal and structural representation of both circle and pyramid as integral to the meaning of the poem.[22]

Another type of graphic illustration speaks immediately even now to the potency of the Elizabethan use of figural line—the chart or map, maps being another linear or planar mode of silent language, one that was under development during the time of Elizabeth. Although the modern eye may be blind to the interests inscribed on the apparently objective ordnance survey or automotive guide of today, it quickly sees the distortions and recognizes the omissions on earlier maps. Heightened awareness of the partiality represented in early modern cartography reveals the nature of mapping as a silent language.

The first example is especially pertinent here because, once again, it is a circular image—more precisely, a series of concentric circles, an image based upon the pre-Copernican model of the universe, adapted to the iconography of Elizabeth. Where the conventional image of man's place in the universe represented a male figure spread-eagled and inscribed within a sphere or a series of concentric circles representing the universe, the image of Elizabeth that appears on the reverse of the title page of John Case's *Sphaera civitatis* (1588) substitutes the image of the queen, and she appears, not circumscribed by the sphere, but outside and above it, apparently embracing it within the folds of her voluminous robes (fig. 20). In a reversal of the conventional image, Elizabeth half circumscribes and crowns the image on which, through pictorial displacement, the universe has metamorphosed as her body. The diagram is adapted as illustration of the structure and the virtues of the Star Chamber, and the virtues are attributed to the planetary spheres, the system of analogy used by Roman imperial theorists to rationalize the Holy Roman Emperor. Because *Sphaera civitatis* was a required text for all undergraduates at Oxford, the image was well circulated there.[23] Even more daringly, the position of Elizabeth at the top of the picture displaces that of the Almighty in the also familiar representation of the concentric spheres that illustrated the holy seventh day in Schedel's *Weltchronik* of 1493.[24] Wordlessly, by iconographic substitution, the woodcut speaks to the expansive power of the queen as words could do only imprudently.

Map lines, both graphic and notional, play a similar role on the *Ditchley Portrait* of Elizabeth by Marcus Gheeraerts the Younger (fig. 6), whereon the sphere, represented in three different ways, is also a significant element. The armillary sphere in the queen's left ear symbolizes the search for knowledge, and the setting for the portrait represents the power of such knowledge. On the left of the painting is a sunny sky, and on the right, a cloudy one; the dividing line between the two is centered over Elizabeth's head. A badly cropped sonnet within a cartouche on the right is now only fragmentary, but enough of the text can be reconstructed in order to see that the poem praises the queen as more glorious and powerful than the pictured forces of nature. Elizabeth stands on the surface of the earthly globe, the circumference of which is outlined in the background behind the hem of her gown, and her feet rest on a map of England, on Oxfordshire, near Ditchley, the site of her famous visit to Sir Henry Lee when she was on progress in 1592, the occasion that this portrait may well memorialize. The position and stance of the queen, together with the foregrounding of the map, constitute the queen's act of possession as the most important relationship within the work.[25] The fragmentary inscriptions also denote signs of dominance: to the right, on the thundery side, "POTEST NEC VLCISITVR [. . .]"; to the left, on the sunny side, "DA [E]XPECTAT"; bottom, right of the map, "REDDENDO[. . .] CE[. . .]." These lines of the inscription literalize the potency of the queen: to be able, to avenge; to foresee; to restore, to return. But it is the lines of the pictorial image that specify, locate, and expand her powers beyond words.[26] Combining device, motto, and explanatory sonnet, the portrait is an enriched emblem that demonstrates the synergy of soul and body, a commonplace in the theory of the emblem.

During the reign of Elizabeth, maps were coming increasingly into their own as tools of power, constructs that could, by the stroke of a line, create the fiction of control, possession, empire.[27] Freed from both rhetorical assertion and discursive rebuttal, maps could pictorially establish categorical claims. Often, attendant illustrations of local costumes, natives and their habitats, fantastic medieval images of monsters, defined difference as Other. Less dramatically, the involvement of the central government with local powers can be charted by the increasing interest in maps as is manifested by reference to maps in records, especially by William Cecil, in the collections of maps, like Cecil's and Robert Beale's, and in patronage of cartography. Beale, clerk to the Privy Council, asserted that counselors and the queen's secretaries should retain copies of Ortelius's maps, maps of England, and notations of local resident powers.[28] Maps were not regularly used in hand then as now in order to find one's way through a maze of streets or highways, and in many respects the maps consulted by the Elizabethans have more in common with the medieval *mappamundi* than they do with modern official ordnance surveys. Like their medieval predecessors, early modern maps served purposes other than what has come to be regarded as scientific accuracy. Typically, the least scientific of early modern maps lacked a uniform method or standard of measure, a scale bar, a compass rose, or a conventional orientation. For instance, Christopher Saxton produced two landmark maps during the reign of Elizabeth and under her patronage—the 1579 atlas and the 1583 wall map. Although these two works together constituted a cartographic view of the country with a skill perhaps unequalled in contemporary Europe outside Austria, they fall short of modern cartographic standards for uniformity and reliability, most especially in the incongruity between regional parts on the atlas and in the incorrect orientation of the Cornish peninsula on the wall map, errors that may reflect the limits of the localized experience of the mapmaker—wordless projections of the interests of his world.[29]

It would be mistaken to suggest that modern scientific cartography, unlike that of the Elizabethans, is without bias. The place whereon the mapmaker stands, the surveyor perches, is staked out now as then by interests, interests of which the observer may be unaware, but that nonetheless determine what is mapped and how it is rendered. Where one looks, how one sees, how one represents what is seen are also determined by history, and it almost goes without saying that when mapmakers are not copying their predecessors, they are attempting to correct them, inevitably conflating the two efforts. The disparity between modern cartographic conventions and a few Elizabethan examples demonstrates the difference a line can make; the difference indicates the use of line as silent language, a concept that today engages cartographers who are trying to integrate the many kinds of information offered by maps.

Many cartographers compare maps and verbal language, with varying degrees of literal application, and their discussion of the nature of the analogy summarily clarifies also the mode of Elizabethan maps as silent language. Robinson and Petchenik argue that, in a general sense, the term *language* can refer to mapping, but they disallow a stricter application because language as "discursive symbolism" differs from the "presentational symbolism" of mapping. Although conceding the linear organization of a sentence as opposed to the two-dimensional form of a map, Blakemore and Harley propose that "the concept of maps as language offers the most appropriate *underlying structure* for the history of cartography." Head supports this view by further arguing that the reading of a map activates the information-processing model of the reading of a linear text. In any case, analogy is not identity, and the objections raised do not gainsay prudent use of the similarity between literal and silent language. Perhaps a more recent definition of map as "any kind of a model of any spatial language" best describes the kinds of maps that served Elizabethan collectors, while also economically paraphrasing the nature of mapping as a silent language.[30]

Most known medieval and early Renaissance maps were designed, not to convey technical geographical information, but rather for other kinds of didactic purposes. Many world maps show their derivation from the ancient concept of history as an encyclopedic record of persons, places, and times—Hugh of Saint Victor's categories of universal knowledge adapted to pious purposes—and many city views embody the abstract quality of a site rather than its physical data in the practice of "moralized" geography.[31] Maps and city views continued to serve exemplary and celebratory purposes through the sixteenth century, long after instruments such as the compass, the astrolabe, and the principles of triangulation were known, devices that might have made possible more geographically correct maps and views if scientific accuracy had been the main motive in mapping. It was not. John Dee outlines the scope of contemporary interest in maps:

> While, some, to beautifie their Halls, Parlers, Chambers, Galeries, Studies, or Libraries with: other some, for thinges past, as battels fought, earthquakes, heauenly fyringes, & such occurentes, in histories mentioned: therby liuely, as it were, to vewe the place, the region adioyning, the distance from vs: and such other circumstances. . . . To conclude, some, for one purpose: and some, for an other, liketh, getteth, and vseth, Mappes, Chartes, & Geographicall Globes. (Preface to *The Elements of Geometrie* [London, 1570] a.iiij^r)

As Dee suggests, aesthetics, nostalgia, sensationalism, and other motives besides geographical accuracy generated interest in maps, and among these, metaphorical expression was historically foremost. Metaphorical motivations for maps may date back to Roman times, and examples certainly exist from the early Middle Ages through the Renaissance. World maps were generally oriented toward the east and Paradise, and a sixth-century floor map of the world might be oriented to place the east at the top to coincide with the eastern end of the church, as in Madaba in Jordan; thirteenth-century English world maps include one at Hereford Cathedral whereon a Last Judgment hovers above the map, and another circular representation in a Latin psalter positions Jerusalem at the center of the world.[32]

Elizabethans, too, metaphorically expressed ambition or possession through cartographic metaphor. One can only question, along with his biographer, Thomas Howard's motivation for displaying in a wainscot frame a map of the world inscribed within the form of an eagle—no doubt his enemies found it ominous—but there is little doubt about the assertive stance of Elizabeth of England standing upon the globe of the earth, her feet planted upon the map of her kingdom on the Ditchley portrait (fig. 6).[33] Several portraits of Elizabeth embody similar adaptations of ancient symbolic uses of geographical images. When globes appear on other portraits of the queen, they represent a symbolic assertion of power. The globe that appears on the right of the *Sieve Portrait* (fig. 18) is so highlighted as to feature its maritime images and so positioned as to lie just below the feet of a triumphal line of courtiers who include, according to Strong, Sir Christopher Hatton, patron of geographers and explorers (*Gloriana* 101–3). On the *Armada Portrait* (fig. 3), nearly a decade later, Elizabeth's right hand rests atop the globe. The globe on neither of these two portraits features a geographically accurate image, the landmass on the latter in particular being fantastically irregular: the intention is symbolic possession. The queen's hand rests on North America and points toward the Spanish Main and South America, possibly indicating expansionist designs.[34] Several of the portraits of Elizabeth, like this one, approximate the syntax of verbal language, expressing the modes declarative, optative, and contrary-to-fact in their representations of a proprietary, imperial, eternally young queen.

Symbolic values are immediately apparent on maps that render cities or landmasses in the metaphorical shapes of living creatures: Rome appears in the shape of a lion on a thirteenth-century plan, and in 1582, Franz Hogenberg's *Leo Belgicus* superimposed a realistic map of the Netherlands on the engraving of a seated lion, a conceit that became popular. Elizabethan mapping adapted this bestiary convention—with the difference that the cartographic image is equated not with a city or a country but a whole continent, and the metaphorical shape with which it is equated is not a heraldic beast but a live human being, the queen of England.[35] If the illustration from *Sphaera civitatis* suggests a metaphorical analogy between the image of the queen and the concentric spheres of the universe, *Queen Elizabeth as Europa*, a Dutch engraving, graphically identifies her body with the map of Europe. Her body displaces the image of a virgin-as-Europe that had appeared in earlier representations. This image fantastically distorts geographical orientation and proportion in order to picture Elizabeth stoutly defending the body of Europe—hers—and the orb that she holds in her right hand—the world—against the assaults of the Spanish fleet and the power of the Roman Catholic Church as represented on board the largest ship in the background by a three-headed figure wearing a biretta, a triple-crowned tiara, and a crown (fig. 21).

More utilitarian purposes motivated progress toward standardized measure, scale, and conventions of cartographic representation. The progress observable on the earlier maps is a nonverbal record of the vested interest of the maker or his patron. Survey maps were consulted over boundary disputes, and some of these are in part impressionistic, disputed acreage being estimated visually in one case, the legal map lacking a scale in another, for example. So late as the end of the century, on the Old Byland map (1598) drafted by the famous Christopher Saxton as evidence in a dispute that involved surreptitious nocturnal removals of boundary stones, essential cartographic features are competently rendered, and Saxton has innovatively color-coded the disputed areas, but his effort to represent relief is inept, with some of the hills even appearing upside-down.[36] The configurations of maps, whether competent or not, often wordlessly graph the chief concerns of the responsible parties.

Elizabethan mapmakers and surveyors complained about the shortcomings of contemporary charts. Edward Worsop, a surveyor, titled his book (1582) *A Discoverie of sundrie errors and faults daily committed by Landemeaters* and complained on the title page about the lack of geometrical instrumentation. Even the most vocal critics themselves, however, often mismeasured, misrepresented, or at best mixed modes and standards of cartography. Ralph Agas pinpointed the main difficulty for incompetent draftsmen: "But the thing indeed which causeth their inevitable errors, & hath persuaded many wise and excellent persons, to doubt whether there be perfection in mapping of landes and tenements for surveigh, yea or not, is the unevenes of the groundes, by their great difference, in hill and dale, from a levell superficies, in that wee are necessarily compelled to put downe our practise upon bookes that are levell and smooth, *Hoc opus est hic labor*" (quoted in Tyacke and Huddy 57). Still, Agas wrestled with perspectival problems in his own map of Oxford (1578–88), whereon, like other contemporary surveyors, he mixed the representational modes of the bird's-eye view and the city plan. His map is oriented from the north because, he says, it offered the best view of the most famous landmarks, but his point of view rationally allowed only one facade of the buildings to be visible in a town wherein the streets mainly intersect at right angles. Thus the map distorts buildings for the sake of presenting more than one face. Moreover, Agas's measurements in all directions together are more than 12 percent in error.[37]

Not all errors reflect special interests, and other complications in this nonverbal mode must be noted. Visual estimation is obviously fraught with the possibility of miscalculation. On the other hand (or foot), pacing is relative to the pace of the pacer (Hurst notes that Agas was crippled [8]). If the surveyor supplies a scale of measurement, it might be calculated in perches (the surveyor's perch, although a common unit of measurement, being one that might actually range from nine to twenty-six feet), daywork (used mainly in Kent and Essex), roods, or acres. Earlier, knotted cords were used to measure until, because of their incalculable response to damp, they were displaced by chains. As late as 1596, John Norden responds in his *Preparative to his Speculum Britanniae* to criticism that he had not used a standard unit and measured every linear distance "so that by intersecting lines the distances may bee gathered according to the same proposition." The demand is impractical, and besides so many stations are obscured by natural phenomena that "to observe them singularlie and precisely, will require the whole time of a man's ripe yeares, to effect the description of

England."[38] An official pass issued to Christopher Saxton so that he might work in Wales indicates how surveyors attempted accurate measurement: the justices are "to see him conducted unto any towre Castle highe place or hill to view that countrey and that he may be accompanied wth ij or iij honest men such as do best know the contrey."[39]

So the lack of adequate scientific knowledge, accurate instrumentation, and the inherent difficulty of transcription of physically observed data to a graphic image were all problems that beset the surveyor and mapmaker. Still, it is apparent that personal values also shaped maps: official administrative interests, Saxton's legal clients, Agas's aesthetics. Apart from the topographical challenge, the surveyor and mapmaker had to contend with conservative resistance to their new-fangled methods, and their possibly political and economic encroaching interests were still felt as threats in the early seventeenth century, to judge from the queries of a local farmer, as sketched in John Norden's *Surveyor's Dialogue*, when he asks, "Is not the field it selfe a goodly Map for the Lord to looke vpon, better then a painted paper? And what is he the better to see it laid out in colours? He can adde nothing to his Land, nor diminish ours: and therefore that labour aboue all may be saued, in mine opinion."[40]

Norden's farmer was digging in his heels on his own turf, and his suspicions were founded on his interpretation of the nonverbal message implicit in the map: the power who paid the surveyor plotted against the farmer or tenant. To attempt to research whether the fears were grounded in reality would be a task on the order of Norden's "whole time of a man's ripe yeares," but certainly many maps are shaped by the interests of the patrons, the mapmakers, or their public. In this respect, Henry Percy, ninth earl of Northumberland, was prototypical: one of the first English landowners to employ scientific surveying, he calculated from the data how to raise his rents.[41] In the late sixteenth century, Irish peasants resisted English invasion by sometimes murdering surveyors in the service of the new English landlords.[42] Tellingly, Sir Ralph Lane writes from Ireland in 1597 to Burghley, commenting on his "liking that actions should (as near as may) be plotted forth by lineal description," and several of the maps of England sketched in Burghley's own hand represent local houses and the residences of recusants.[43]

Evidence of the meticulous supervision of representations of the queen as they appeared in cartographic publications may be inferred from comparison of the two states of her portrait as it appears on the frontispiece of Saxton's Atlas (1579). Seated under a canopy and holding a scepter and crown, she is pictured as the patron of geography, personified by a bearded male holding a pair of compasses and a globe, and astronomy, another bearded figure with an armillary sphere. Differences between the two states of the plate are minor: the hard line of the queen's dress as it lies across her lap has been softened in the second state, and the queen's jewelry is simplified, but the small adjustment bespeaks careful oversight. The engraving may also bear evidence of another kind of invested interest as well. Stephen Orgel argues that the oval impresa mounted in the center of the frieze overhead representing the embrace between Peace and Justice signifies the essential role of the queen's chastity (the nude figure of Peace) in the imperial exercise of power (the figures of geography below and Justice above).[44]

Other kinds of interests also shaped the forms and styles of maps, and some of these can be inferred from the maps themselves. The second stanza of the verse that appears on Agas's Map of Oxford offers another clue. Agas conveys his wish to execute a map of London in honor of the queen:

> The charge not greate, the thinge a woorke of praise
> Her [i.e., London's] present shapp hereafter still to see
> To keepe length bredth and couruinge of the waise
> Number height & forme of buildinges as they be
> Eatch man to knowe his owne by juste degree
> With all thinges else that maie adorne the same
> And leave her praise unto eternall fame.
>
> (Overall 19–20)

The personification of London in this verse and of Oxford in the one following ("Ancient Oxforde, noble Nurse of skill") echoes the medieval tradition of moralized city views, but the Elizabethan reprise introduces a newer note: the map is to show each man his own property, "his owne by juste degree." Not only is the central government interested in maps, but so, too, is the urban gentleman, thus the map charts the social and economic hierarchy. Moreover, the last couplet quoted also dedicates the map to the adornment and praise of the city. *Adornment* meant something more serious to Elizabethans than it does today, but it also meant something quite other than the scientific function of a map.[45] Lastly, proper adornment outwardly manifested inward virtue of the Christian soul, and fame was the public recognition of worldly achievement. The ordered representation of ownership rendered visible the satisfaction in a well-ordered city. The point was not to chart where a city was or how to get there, but rather to picture what it was. What it was was who owned what, and what it was as ideally perceived by an interested observer.

These two focuses of the mapmaker's vision were not entirely compatible, the first requiring the specificity of Norden's "intersecting lines," the second, the abstraction of Agas's selective point of view. Both required the omission of selected details, whether the fen, copse, or hill inaccessible to the perching surveyor, or the backsides of the buildings that Agas showed best facade forward. Maps are by definition abstractions, however, and their mode and motivation reveal perhaps even more about a culture than the territory mapped on the chart. The motto of John Thorpe, surveyor and architect, epigrammatically captures the function and satisfaction of the survey for the estate owner: "*supervidens non videns*," that is to say, conceptually overseeing without physically seeing one's holdings.[46] If the surveyor's map supplied data necessary for economical estate management, it also served pride of ownership.

Maps serving other interests also communicated through lines understood rather than marked. Route maps often feature representations of destinations and personal landmarks along the way as a conceptual line of travel rather than as a clearly marked graphic directional line. The *Memorial Portrait of Sir Henry Unton* (c. 1596) dramatically illustrates this kind of map (fig. 22). The route of Sir Henry's biography begins at the lower right with his birth at Wychwood, Oxfordshire, continues through his education at Oxford, follows his diplomatic career in Italy (Venice, Padua), the Low Countries, and France, where he died, so that the route map dwindles into a funeral processing toward the gigantic representation of the church on the left of the picture. In its ignoring of perspective, its honeycomb of vignettes, and its representation of a route as an imagined line, the anonymous painter continues medieval conventions. The Map of Great Britain by Matthew Paris (d. 1259), for example, approximates the physical appearance of the country, indicating the Roman wall between England and Scotland. It represents the main north-south route between Dover and Newcastle, not by a graphic line, but a series of drawings of buildings, labeled as stops along the way (BL Cotton MS Claudius D.vi. f.12). Robert Adams's map of the Route to Tilbury pricks out with pinholes the route that the queen followed on her journey to hearten the troops stationed there during the threat of the Armada in a line that is virtually invisible (BL Add MS 44839). The map is oriented with the south bank of the Thames ("Parte of Kent") at the top and the north ("Parte of Essex") at the bottom. London is at the right of the map, where modern convention would expect the eastern part of the country to appear, so it is positioned in a less noticeable place than Tilbury, which is pictured on the left. In the Elizabethan shaping of the tradition of moralized geography, this representation is oriented as a triumph for the monarch.

Celebration is also the mode of the decorative maps found in many country houses. A picturesque screen map of Exeter from about 1600 combines points of view in order to represent both bird's-eye and linear perspective on the countryside and its inhabitants.[47] The Sheldon Tapestry Maps, made late in the reign of Queen Elizabeth for the new home at

Weston near Long Compton belonging to Ralph Sheldon, prosperous owner of the Sheldon tapestry business, manifestly celebrate both the patron and his business. Based on the maps of the Saxton Atlas, the tapestries were designed for display. Not only has the designer corrected Saxton's spelling, but he has also added on the Warwickshire map a representation of Sheldon's new house, for which the work was planned. The decorative intention of the work is clear in its sideways orientation, with the north lying to the left, in order to accommodate the dimensions of the room where it was to be hung. Saxton's wall map was hung in the queen's gallery at Whitehall, at Lord Burghley's house at Theobalds, and on the walls of the homes of gentlemen and courtiers. Leicester had some twenty-three maps at Kenilworth in 1588; Archbishop Parker had thirty at Lambeth Palace when he died in 1575; so the decorative use of maps was in itself not innovative, although tapestry maps are uncommon.[48] The tapestries on the walls of Weston, however, spoke to a very different point with their representation of the local landmarks and in particular Weston itself as the achievement of a successful entrepreneur.[49] Sumptuousness as a display of status or ambition introduces quite another element of silent language, and the first of the two chapters devoted to the analysis of matter and material form.

II

SURFACE, SHAPE, AND SUBSTANCE

SURFACE, COLOR, AND TEXTURE AS SUPERFICIAL COMMENT

Come to the Tayler, hee is gone to the Paynters, to
learne howe more cunning may lurke in the fashion,
then can bee expressed in the making. . . . Trafficke and
trauell hathe wouen the nature of all Nations into ours,
and made this land like Arras, full of deuise, which was
Broade-cloth, full of workemanshippe.

John Lyly, prologue to *Midas*

THE POINT, THE LINE—whether a graphic line between two points or the imagined line created by the shape of a text—these were phonemes of silent language, the smallest elements that made a difference. The example of tapestry maps has introduced other, basic elements in the vocabulary; namely, surface, color, and texture. Like their counterparts in verbal language—lexicon, rhetorical colors, and literary texture—these elements deploy the morphemes of the medium for maximum effect. Surface, in the discourse of silent language, often unfolded matter more substantial than the word *surface* (literally, superficial) would suggest. Analysis reveals that close association between textile and text, weaving and writing, that figures in Latin sources.[1]

In his letter (Jan. 23, 1559) describing the coronation of Elizabeth, for example, Schifanoya, an Italian diplomat, time and again selects color and the richness of texture as subjects for comment in his report: the courtiers' jewels and gold collars that sparkled so that "they cleared the air, though it snowed a little," the footmen's crimson velvet jerkins with their massive silver gilt embroidery, the gold brocade with raised pile trimming the queen's litter as well as the mules that drew it, the embroidered relief on the livery, the crimson damask of the Gentlemen Pensioners, the queen's own sumptuous cloth of gold with double-raised stiff pile, the rich tapestry hangings along the queen's path, under her feet on her way to church the purple cloth that was afterward cut away by souvenir hunters (*CSPV* 7:12ff.). Nor was display of richness of texture unique to Elizabeth's coronation ceremonies. Segar makes similar observations regarding the queen's formal procession in 1588 along streets "hung with Blew broad clothes for the seuerall Companies in their Liueries to stand," proceeding from Somerset Place to Saint Paul's, where "a rich Chaire of Estate, and the ground being spred likewise with tapis," the queen knelt to pray at a desk "couered with very Princely furniture" (*Honor Military* [1602] x2^v–x3^r). Obviously, whether to native or foreign observer, magnificence of matter—texture, color, and surface—mattered.

It also mattered to the broad spectrum of culture in Elizabethan England. William Harrison, describing England in 1587 with the sharp eye of the cultural anthropologist or sociologist, compared and contrasted a number of signs that characterized the material culture of his own day with that of an earlier generation:

> The furniture of our houses . . . exceedeth and is grown in manner even to passing delicacy; and herein I do not speak of the nobility and gentry only but likewise of the lowest sort. . . . Certes in noblemen's houses it is not rare to see abundance of arras, rich hangings of tapestry, silver vessel, and so much other plate as may furnish sundry cupboards. . . . Likewise in the houses of knights, gentlemen, merchantmen, and some other wealthy citizens, it is not geason [uncommon] to behold generally their great provision of tapestry, Turkey work, pewter, brass, fine linen, and thereto costly cupboards of plate. . . . But as herein all these sorts do far exceed their elders and predecessors, and in neatness and curiosity the merchant all other, so in time past the costly furniture stayed there, whereas now it is descended yet lower, even unto the inferior artificers and many farmers, who by virtue of their old and not of their new leases, have for the most part learned also to garnish their cupboards with plate, their joint beds with tapestry and silk hangings, and their tables with carpets and fine napery, whereby the wealth of our country "(God be praised therefor and give us grace to employ it well)" doth infinitely appear. (200; interpolation by Edelen, ed.)

Harrison's signs of progress are keyed to an index still in use to assess luxury: material wealth as measured by craft, exotic origin, preciousness, and rarity of material. Less obvious is the subtext that underlies his terminology; that is to say, that the lower classes "have learned" the ways of the richer in "garnishing" their houses with plate and tapestry. As early as 1553, a visiting Parisian priest noted that the English made much use of tapestries and painted cloths that were "well executed" and that there were few houses in which one would not find them (Perlin, "Description" 58–59).

Like Harrison, in his prologue to *Midas*, John Lyly also describes the busyness of England in her fashionable prosperity, and he uses similar artifacts for his examples, among them, tapestry. He metaphorically hints at the depth below the surface: "*Come to the Tayler, hee is gone to the Paynters, to learne howe more cunning may lurke in the fashion, then can bee expressed in the making. . . . Trafficke and trauell hathe wouen the nature of all Nations into ours, and made this land like Arras, full of deuise, which was Broade-cloth, full of workemanshippe*" (3:115). A poster for the first English lottery (1567) pictures a fantastic assemblage of money, plate, and tapestry.[2] The underlying assumptions of the two observers raise questions about the matter silently communicated through material culture. Why were tapestry and hangings so valued? How did a culture that was (on the basis of written evidence at least) so resistant to aestheticism, come to accept and even to admire luxuriousness of material, curiosity of workmanship, and use for "garnish"? What is implied by "learning" these ways? The material artifacts whose substance, shape, and texture made a difference to Elizabethans also make the kind of difference that constitutes silent communication. The evidence of contemporary literature, letters, wills, statutes, and cultural artifacts indicates that textiles (embroidery, tapestry, costume), metals (seals, coins, medals, jewelry, plate), and stone (reliefs, monuments, building materials) were among the most valued of material possessions, and that their substance, surface, and shape mattered. Harrison's pious interjection ("God be praised therefor [i.e., for England's new wealth] and give us grace to employ it well") summarily indicates how pleasure in material luxury was rationalized, but more detailed study of selected examples of each major type of artifact reveals the cultural acceptance of materiality, what kind of difference it made, and the social dynamics of distinctions drawn on the basis of material difference.

One constant in Elizabethan style is manifest in every medium, the use of rich embellishment—whether in the golden flourish of Hilliard's inscriptions, the sugared conceit of the banquet subtlety, the curious fantasy of gold-threaded embroidery upon a lady's sleeve, the interplay of precious stones on a jeweled ornament, or the carved interstices of an architectural relief. Moreover, these garnishments compete for attention with other embellishments or even overlay them: Hilliard's inscriptions encircle sumptuous portraits of subjects dressed in embroidered costume; the banquet subtlety is but one pirouette in a whirl of courses of food; the sleeve on the lady's garment is a side note to a costume whose several parts are equally adorned and among which the intricate jewel is almost lost to sight; the architectural relief surmounts a wall covered with busy tapestries. Pattern-on-pattern obviously delighted as well as dazzled. At first glance, and even more strikingly upon closer examination of the details of these artifacts, it would seem that these gilded lilies, these crystallized violets, bespeak a shallow delight in mere surface, and certainly contemporary expressions of disdain for candied courtesy and sugared conceits show the superficiality of much taste for the decorative. During the Middle Ages, material expression of religious devotion had been richly sensuous, but the visible evidence of Elizabethan pleasure in secular sensuous material would seem to be at odds with the stern rhetoric of contemporary preacher and poet alike in their opposition to indulgence in the things of this world. Recontextualizing some examples of decorative surface reveals under closer analysis their deeper meaning. Moreover, closer study uncovers the role of silent language in effecting acceptance of the cultural transition toward that greater appreciation of material richness in secular life noted by William Harrison in his description quoted above. Rationalization for the shift in cultural values and its acceptance would find place in literature and letters.

Sumptuary prescriptions controlling lengths of fabric appropriate to social rank directly indicate the value invested in display of textile, whether the length of the train of a garment or the amount of fabric in a pair of breeches. The explicit language of the "Breviate" for a nobleman's house of 1605 specifies in exacting detail the cloth of state appropriate for each diner: "a cloathe of estate according to his place, vidz. an earle, to the pummell of his chaire, a marquesse to the seate of his chaire, a duke to within a foote of the grounde," in an exact equation between quantity of fabric and social status.[3]

In addition to the sheer measure of fabric, surface decoration heightened its value. Because textile arts figure in so many ornamental expressions, embroidered objects most immediately demonstrate the interface between line and idea, surface and substance, material and significant matter. In Elizabethan documents, many a lady is represented at work with needle or loom. In 1544, when she was only eleven years of age, Elizabeth wrote out her translation of *The Miroir of Glasse of the Synneful Soule* as a New Year's gift to Queen Catherine Parr and presented it to her in a binding embroidered with the queen's initials and a six-lobed knot pattern. Within the next few years, Elizabeth made as many as four other pious books with similar bindings, possibly embroidered by herself.[4] As queen, she also owned at least two highly decorated bibles, for the second of which, one of the most ornate of the age, Christopher Barker, printer, received in exchange for his New Year's gift, eleven and one-eighth ounces of gilt plate. In 1561, the third year of the reign of Elizabeth, the ancient Broderers' Company was formally incorporated under its first extant charter.[5] One of the two most frequent gifts to the queen—the other being jewelry—was embroidered apparel. Embroidery mattered to Elizabeth.

So did it matter to her rival queen, Mary Queen of Scots. By Mary's own testimonial as well as contemporary account, she was both a prolific and a highly skilled embroiderer. In 1569, Nicholas White reported to Cecil after a visit to Tutbury where Mary was imprisoned under the watchful eye of George Talbot, earl of Shrewsbury, that she worked all day with her needle and that the diversity of the colors made the work seem less tedious. "Upon this occasion she entered into a pretty disputable comparison betwene karving, painting, and working with the needil, affirming painting in her owne opinion for the most commendable qualitie" (Wright 1:310). Mary's "disputable comparison" enlists her in the *paragone*, the comparison among the arts that long occupied Italian artists in the effort to determine the superiority of either painting or sculpture as an intellectually respectable occupation worthy of classification as a fine art. Unique to Mary's discussion is her admission of embroidery as a contender—a possibility not admitted in Italian prototypical disputations—even though she more traditionally does award the palm to painting. Nearly thirty years later, Richard Haydocke would wordlessly represent the same argument on the title page that he designed and engraved for his translation of Lomazzo, *A Tracte Containing the Artes of curious Paintinge Caruinge & Buildinge* (fig. 23). A personification represents each of four arts in the corners: upper left, Juno for painting; upper right, Pallas for weaving; lower right, Daedalus for building; and lower left, Prometheus for sculpture. Only painting is unaccompanied by an Ovidian image of humiliating punishment for hubris, and although Arachne and her webs frame the image of Pallas, the very presence of textile among the arts elevates its status above the lowly position conventionally given to craft. Moreover, because embroidery was a woman's occupation, its elevation to the status of a fine art bespoke respect for woman as artist.

Occasionally idealized as what would be called today "fine art," embroidery also served practical purposes, and among these was hermetic communication. In a letter to Ben Jonson (July 1, 1619), William Drummond minutely lists the "*Impressaes* and Emblemes on a Bed of State wrought and embroidered all with gold and silk" by Mary Queen of Scots. Two of these Drummond describes as seeming "to glaunce" at Queen Elizabeth: two women upon wheels of Fortune, one holding a lance, the other a cornucopia, with the motto "*Fortunae Comites*"; eclipses of the sun and moon with the motto "*Ipsa sibi lumen quod invidet aufert*" (Jonson 1:208–9). However cautiously sidelong, the glances were taken to be the case of a cat looking at a queen, as was possibly also implied by another of Mary's embroidered images, a crowned ginger cat studying a mouse, a detail that Mary embroidered upon the model of the cat that she took from Gesner.[6] Frequently interpreted as dangerously political in implication is another bit of Mary's needlework. She sent a cushion cover to Thomas, duke of Norfolk, who was implicated in a plot for them to marry, a plan that Norfolk most unfortunately failed personally to reveal to Elizabeth at a time when some were scheming to replace her on the English throne by her Scots rival. Mary's embroidery pictured a pruning hook cutting away unfruitful branches, with the motto "*Virescit Vulnere Virtus*": "Virtue flourisheth by wounding." Granted that the emblem pictures Mary's cipher beside the flourishing vine on one side, together with the royal arms of Scotland next to the other, and that this was a gift from the imprisoned queen to her would-be suitor, Elizabeth might well have read this as a cut against the Virgin Queen. In any case, the suspect cushion cover was considered highly damaging evidence in the prosecution of Norfolk for treason.[7] He was financially ruined, ceremonially degraded, and finally executed.

Not all textile works carried such pointed implications, but even in their apparently neutral state as purely decorative objects, they signified more than meets the cursory glance of the modern eye. Invariably, foreign visitors commented upon the amount and richness of the handiwork that they saw in Elizabethan homes. Wolsey's indulgence in tapestry was famous: visitors to his audience passed through eight rooms richly hung with tapestries that were changed weekly, and at Hampton Court, the quality of the pieces increased as one ascended to the presence. In 1522, Wolsey acquired twenty-two complete sets of tapestry, comprising some 132 pieces.[8] Henry VIII had the largest of collections, numbering more than 2,000 pieces; Schifanoya noted some of these hanging at Elizabeth's mass in Westminster Abbey, which he described as the handsomest and most precious ever seen.[9] Tapestries and embroideries were used as bedcovers, table covers, and wall hangings to reduce the cold in great houses like the notoriously drafty Hardwick Hall. Royalty carried tapestries with them to pageants and on progress. Nobility and, later, gentry, collected them, as indicated in the inventories of their goods. As might be expected, Mary Stuart had a large collection of lavishly embroidered, rich textiles, and Norfolk did as well, having assembled the finest private collection in England. Collectors of tapestries embellished them with their arms, as when Bess of Hardwick purchased the Gideon tapestries from the heirs of Sir Christopher Hatton at a price reduced because she would have to remove Hatton's armorial bearings and substitute her own. Having struck her bargain, tight-fisted Bess simply covered Hatton's bearings with hers and added collars and antlers to the Hatton does, thus metamorphosing them into the Cavendish stags.[10] As with the Sheldon tapestry maps, the inclusion of the arms of the owner took possession of the work, affirmed one's right to possession, and asserted pride in the right. In short, decor manifested decorum.

If carefully made of good materials, the monetary value of tapestry is self-evident, but embroideries, too, were made of precious materials, exotic fabrics embellished with costly threads. England exported wools and some linens but imported fine linen from Holland and from Italy silks, velvets, and damasks, much of which was devoted to domestic use. The customs duties on these imports were farmed by Leicester and, later, Cecil, a privilege much desired. Leicester profited twice over: in 1588, the inventory of his goods at Kenilworth reveals that more than half of his thirty-five beds were hung with such imported fabrics as Milanese fustian and green satin from Bruges. Luxurious fabrics confiscated during the dissolution of monasteries also supplied embroiderers. Sir William Cavendish, second husband of Bess of Hardwick, had access to these as commissioner for dissolving of monasteries. An entry in his book of accounts lists some thirty-four copes as well as other miscellaneous rich vestments that he found at Lilleshall Abbey, at least some of which found their way to Hardwick, where they were recycled by Bess for secular use.[11] Mary herself recycled as furniture covers the booty of church vestments seized from the rebel earl of Huntly. Such elegant fabrics, enhanced by ingenious embroidery, made a gift worthy of the queen. Mary Stuart sent Elizabeth an embroidered skirt that required eight ells (ten yards) of crimson satin and a pound of silver thread to construct, and later a petticoat and a pair of sleeves.[12] It has been reasonably conjectured that the brilliant orange cloak that Elizabeth wears on the *Rainbow Portrait* (fig. 11) was a gift from Cecil. The color alludes to Elizabeth's sunlike powers; the eyes and ears embroidered on the garment are symbolic, often read as figuring the attributes of Fame as personified in Virgil (*Aen.* 4.181–83), but also as pointedly alluding to Cecil as the eyes and ears for the queen's intelligence service by those who translate Virgil's *Fama* as "Rumor."[13]

Much extant embroidery from the period is emblematic in design, especially the works attributed to Mary Stuart and to Bess of Hardwick, who worked with Mary during her years of imprisonment. Some, like Bess's octagonal panels at Hardwick, derive from botanical illustrations, in this case, represented within surrounds inscribed with prudential Erasmian *sententiae*. Many, like Norfolk's fatally embroidered cushion, incorporate devices and impresas, conventional vehicles for expression of intentions too dangerous or indecorous for words. Thus Bess embroidered a memorial panel for Cavendish, curiously untimely because she had twice remarried since his decease. The center design pictured tears falling onto quicklime, with the motto "*Extinctam Lachrimae Testantur Vivere Flammam*": "Tears witness that the quenched flame lives."[14] More immediately pertinent to the study of wordless language are several devices of mourning that appear in the border: a cut glove, a snapped chain, a cracked jeweled mirror, a severed love knot, three interlinked and broken rings. In each case, a broken line conveys the sense of loss, yet another variation upon the use of line as signifier.

Textiles conveyed moralistic themes of a more general exemplary nature as well. So important was this function that the two most spectacular rooms at Bess's Hardwick were possibly constructed on their huge dimensions in order to accommodate the hanging of sets of tapestries. The High Great Chamber—at forty-five feet by thirty-one feet, and a story higher than was customary, by far the biggest of period chambers known today— still displays the Ulysses tapestries, and seeing them in situ recreates the sense of how textile spoke to the Elizabethans, whether with the small voice of a device on a gown or the resonant oration of a tapestry surround. Ulysses, of course, was a commonplace type of the male hero, but less often observed is the importance of Penelope, too, as the exemplary woman: quiet, faithful, and busy at her loom—as she appears in one scene on the largest of the set of tapestries.[15] The same subject appears on the only painting listed in the 1601 inventory that is not a portrait and still survives in the house. The Gideon tapestry set, unusually tall at nineteen feet, purchased from the Hatton estate, hangs in the Long Gallery.[16] Elsewhere throughout the house, embroideries represent exemplary figures from religion or myth: the death of Actaeon, the judgment of Paris, Europa and the Bull, the judgment of Solomon, and a set of pieces depicting personifications of virtues. The inventory of 1601 economically describes the full set: "Fyve peeces of hanginges of Cloth of golde velvett and other like stuffe imbrodered with pictures of the vertues, one of Zenobia, magnanimitas and prudentia, an other of Arthemitia, Constantia and pietas, an other of penelope, prudentia, and sapientia, an other of Cleopatra, fortituto, and Justitia, an other of Lucretia, Charitas and liberalitas, everie peece being twelve foote deep."[17] Two pieces from this set hang today in the hall: Lucretia, exemplary heroine who chose death after the dishonor of having been raped by Tarquin, and Penelope, her left hand resting virtuously upon her loom. Behind these works, a pair of other hangings in the passageway represent the Virtues and their Contraries: Faith and Mahomet, Temperance and Sardanapalus.

The subject chosen by a woman in the textiles she purchased or made gave her a voice denied her in the conventional image of the good woman as mute and chaste. In the broadest sense of all, textile work also represented the feminine virtue of the artificer. An attribute of the good girl was her ability to spin, to sew, to embroider; evidence of her virtuous life was the amount of time she spent thus rather than outside the home. So is she represented in countless courtesy books and emblems dating from the earlier Renaissance, and later evidence firmly anchors the concept within the Elizabethan period. In his annotations to William Cavendish's account book, Brodhurst says that during the reign of Mary, when William Herbert, earl of Pembroke, was awarded the riches of the dissolved abbey of Wilton, he consented to restore the abbess and the nuns. The abbess reminded him of his promise when he again banished the nuns during the reign of Elizabeth; his response was, "Go spin, you jade; go spin" (93–94). The spinster stereotype continued throughout the reign of Elizabeth—and, of course, well through most of the twentieth century as a gendered stereotype that had by then lost its etymological association.

Edmond Tilney's *A brief and pleasant discourse of duties in marriage, called the Flower of Friendshippe*, which went through six editions between 1568 and 1587, praised Lucretia for being always at home spinning while other Roman matrons were abroad banqueting (Eiij^v). In 1579, Thomas Salter's *The mirrhor of modestie*, based upon an Italian work by Giovanni Michele Bruto, advised prudent fathers supervising the education of their daughters to substitute exemplary literature and training in the domestic arts, especially sewing, for the unsuitable liberal arts, dangerous music, and the temptations of feasts and entertainments (*A Critical Edition* 79–125). In 1598, *The Necessarie, Fit and Convenient Education of a Yong Gentlewoman*, translated from Italian and French, is still advising against learning for women: "Let the small profit got by learning, be compared with the great hurt that may happen vnto them, and they shall be shewed . . . how much more conuenient the needle, the wheele, the distaffe, and the spindle, with the name and reputation of graue and honest matrons is for them, then the book and pen with an vncertaine report: if in them there be more learning than honestie & vertue" (G2^r). In that same year, Francis Meres's *Palladis Tamia* compiled many pages of sententious commonplaces about women, including many stereotypical anecdotes and examples. Predictably, Penelope is invoked as a model woman: "*Ulysses* though he detested *Calipso* with her sugred voice, yet hee embraced *Penelope* withher [*sic*] rude distaffe" (G6^r), an explicit documentation of the role of textile as voice for the silent woman.

The text for the entertainment presented to the queen when she visited her friends the Russells at Bisham in 1592 shows how embroidery, like literature, figures as a subject to be explicated. The two Russell daughters are identified as Syb. and Isab. in the dialogue with Pan:

> PAN: Not for want of matter, but to knowe the meaning, what is wrought in this sampler?
>
> SYB: The follies of the Gods, who became beastes, for their affections.
>
> PAN: What in this?
>
> ISAB: The honour of Virgins who became Goddesses, for their chastity.
>
> PAN: But what be these?

ISAB: Men's tongues, wrought all with double stitch but not one true.

PAN: What these?

ISAB: Roses, Eglentine, harts-ease, wrought with Queenes stitch, and all right.

(*Entertainments* 45)

The interchange, like the sampler, complimented Elizabeth in her iconographic guise as Virgin Queen, but it also provided opportunity to display two marriageable daughters and what may have been their own handiwork.

Embroidery that appears in literature serves the same purposes as it did in Elizabethan life, sometimes with the added complexity afforded by the synergistic combination of word and image as well as its ecphrastic potential for instruction and exemplary prophecy. Ecphrasis is the literary representation of a work of art; detailed description of the artifact evokes a reaction from the reader, and sometimes from an observer or an objective point of view within the literary narrative. Ecphrasis works through interplay between silent image and verbal response. By nature, the ecphrastic image and its interpretation conflate different places and times, often through the evocation of myth, observed by a viewer for whom the myth is especially pointed. Spenser often embeds ecphrastic passages in his works. For example, his *Muiopotmos* represents both the pleasure of glittering surface and its power to entrap. His mock-epic hero, the butterfly Clarion, is himself a marvel of dazzling surface and texture. Carelessly attracted by the variety and changing beauty of nature, he falls into the web woven by Aragnoll, son of Arachne, who is envenomed by the memory of how Pallas defeated his mother in their weaving competition. In a lengthy ecphrastic passage, Spenser describes the two pieces of embroidery, adding to the Ovidian description of Minerva's representation of Europa and the Bull his own image of a richly textured butterfly:

> The velvet nap which on his wings doth lie,
> The silken downe with which his backe is dight,
> His broad outstretched hornes, his hayrie thies,
> His glorious colours, and his glistering eies.
>
> (Lines 333–36)

It is worth noting, although impossible to pursue, the coincidence that the added butterfly also appears on the embroidered version of the story at Hardwick Hall. The demise of the "fond flie" (line 425) entangled in the web, together with numerous references throughout the poem to his heedless delight in the changeable beauty of nature, point to the hard lesson of the peril of sensuous pleasure.[18] Spenser repeats the lesson through another ecphrastic passage in the first canto of the third book of the *Faerie Queene* when he describes the sumptuous tapestries that line the walls of the Castle Joyeous. There another Ovidian story, the tale of Venus and Adonis and his metamorphosis into a flower, pictorializes the dangers of other kinds of sensuous delight.

It is a lesson often taught in Renaissance literature. A similarly cautionary example of the consequences of unwary pleasure in decorated surface appears in the sixth book of Michael Drayton's *Barrons' Wars*, which is largely devoted to description of the sensuous beauties in Mortimer's tower. The earl enjoys seeing both a bedcover that figures in embroidery his own history and paintings that represent mythological subjects. In these he finds analogies to his own situation, not seeing the irony that his identification with Hyacinth prefigures his own imminent fall. The description of the bedcover sets the tone and reflexively comments, as ecphrasis often does, on its own intention:

> On which, a Tissue counterpoyne was cast,
> ARACHNES Web did not the same surpasse,
> Wherein the storie of his Fortunes past,
> In liuely Pictures, neatly handled was;
> How he escap'd the *Tower*, in *France* how grac'd,
> With Stones embroyd'red of a wond'rous Masse;
> About the border in a fine-wrought Fret,
> Emblem's, Empressa's, Hieroglyphicks, set.
> (St. 43, *Works* 2:114)

There follows a very long passage on the many ominous metamorphoses pictured on the coverlet and on the walls. Like Spenser's Clarion, the earl, disarmed by delight, allows his pleasure to distract him from the approach of his enemies. In many Renaissance works, this kind of literary emblem also figures the seduction of wordly delights as distraction from the more serious mission of life on earth.

In yet another case of ecphrasis inset within a scene of dire extremity, Sidney creates a speaking picture to that effect in the third book of the *New Arcadia*, where the wicked Cecropia visits the virtuous Pamela, whom she holds prisoner. Pamela is patiently embroidering a purse while apparently awaiting her execution (a cruel mock ceremony staged by Cecropia):

by the finenesse of the worke, one might see she had borowed her wittes of the sorow that owed them, & lent them wholy to that exercise. For the flowers she had wrought, caried such life in them, that the cun[n]ingest painter might have learned of her needle: which with so pretty a maner made his careers to & fro through the cloth, as if the needle it selfe would have bene loth to have gone fro[m]ward such a mistres, but that it hoped to return the[n]ceward very quickly againe: the cloth loking with many eies upon her, & lovingly embracing the wounds she gave it: the sheares also were at hand to behead the silke, that was growne to short. (402)

The figurative language of the passage, with its allusions to wounds and beheading, foreshadows Pamela's expectation of execution, but the text spells out the more important point, explaining that the colors for the ground of the design, although a mere detail for the "ornament of the principall woorke," were so carefully chosen "that it was not without marvaile to see, howe a minde which could cast a carelesse semblant upon the greatest conflictes of Fortune, coulde commaunde it selfe to take care for so small matters" (402–3). The purse, in turn, becomes text for dispute between Pamela and Cecropia on the place of aesthetics in the hierarchy of human experience, with Pamela dismissing the purse as a "verie purse" in the face of Cecropia's extravagant praise. For Pamela, the exercise of her embroidering skills is a diversion and a delight, a focus for her imagination even or perhaps especially in light of her seemingly impending execution, but nonetheless her art is no source of lasting value.

In George Chapman's completion of Marlowe's *Hero and Leander*, another ecphrastic passage represents the act of creating an artifact, and it, too, comments upon its own intentions. This passage also suggests a reciprocal function for art that would, ideally, heighten the consciousness of the maker. In the Argument to the fourth sestyad, the narrator summarizes the effect of Hero's scarf: "*Her Skarfs description wrought by fate, / Ostents that threaten her estate*" (85–126). The Argument observes that "Fate" sends into her mind the threatening images of doom that she works into the ends of the scarf "To shew what death was his in loves disguise" (lines 3–4; 110). While she works the embroidery, Hero learns her fate as it is pictured on the scarf; the maker is instructed by the process of constructing her own artifact. It assumes a life of its own, most particularly as she creates the figure of her lover, "And to each thred did such resemblance give, / For joy to be so like him, it did liue" (lines 54–55). She sees an emblem of her own mental state, the division in her own mind, in her embroidered emblem of a "Moone in change" that "did her thoughts running on change implie" (lines 77; 81). As an autonomous work of art, the embroidery delights and illuminates both maker and viewer. On the level of narrative, silent artifact and explanatory word reciprocally create the moment and anticipate its consequences; beyond plot, the interactive modes establish the thematic significance of the poem.

Although then usually deemed a superficial art, the art of textile nonetheless served a number of weighty functions in Elizabethan culture, whether through sheer luxuriousness to contextualize the status of the owner, to serve as currency in payment to servants or as capital for acting companies, to signal wordlessly or extraverbally a dangerous communication, to assert the arrival of the upwardly mobile (the upwardly noble?), to demonstrate the industriousness of the maker, to express emotion, or to manifest a state of mind or ambition. A succinct statement regarding the expressive function of clothing appears in Erasmus's *De civilitate*, often reprinted in England: "Clothing is in a way the body's body, and from this too one may infer the state of a man's character" (*Works* 25:278). In short, besides their central role in the English economy, the textile arts served some of the moral and aesthetic purposes of the fine arts as then conceived, to instruct and to delight. Because the arts of textile, like other material arts, could communicate so effectively and yet so elusively, socially conservative forces were anxious to oversee their use. At the outermost limit of control, as in the case of the execution of Norfolk, penalty for violation of the decorum of superficial artifact could be extreme, but there was a whole spectrum of punishing consequences that could fall short of trial and execution. Some of these modes of control were highly formalized; others were less codified but no less effective.

At the least, the affectation of finery attracted the disdain of social arbiters such as Thomas Wilson, who sneered at those yeomen's sons who would "skipp" into velvet or silk as a jump toward admission into the Inns of Court or Chancery (*State* 19). Much of the opposition to sumptuary finery is more deeply moralistic. *The Steele Glas* by George Gascoigne voices a common complaint:

> Our bumbast hose, our treble double ruffes,
> Our sutes of Silke, our comely garded capes,
> Our knit silke stockes, and spanish lether shoes,
> (Yea velvet serves, ofttimes to trample in)
> Our plumes, our spangs, and al our queint aray,
> Are pricking spurres, provoking filthy pride,
> And snares (unseen) which leade a man to hel.
> (Lines 373–79)

As is to be expected, Elizabeth herself appears as vigilant monitor of costume. Sir John Harington's *Nugae Antiquae* records some telling instances to that effect. A letter dated 1606 to Robert Markham recounts how Elizabeth spied her sulky "servant" Lady Mary Howard wearing an elegant "rich border, powderd wyth golde and pearle, and a velvet suite belonginge thereto, which moved manie to envye; nor did it please the Queene, who thoughte it exceeded her owne." Elizabeth secretly got hold of the outfit and modeled it before her ladies. Eventually, she asked the erstwhile owner whether it were not far too short for the queen's height. Upon receiving the lady's agreement, Elizabeth pronounced that it was too short for herself and "too fine" for the lady "so it fitteth neither well," and thus the indecorous garment was put in storage (1:361). Harington, ever a rich source for observations regarding decorum, comments further on Elizabeth's attention to costume: "The Queene loveth to see me in my laste frize jerkin, and saithe *'tis well enoughe cutt.* I will have another made liken to it. I do remember she spit on Sir Mathew's fringed clothe, and said, *the fooles wit was gone to ragges.*—Heav'n spare me from suche jibinge" (1:167). At other times, if contemporary reports are to be credited, Elizabeth resorted to a more playful type of ridicule of personal decor. On one occasion, Lady Derby wore a miniature around her neck, tucked into her bosom. She was reluctant to show it to the queen, whereupon Elizabeth grew more insistent. Discovering it to be the portrait of Robert Cecil, the queen seized it and tied it to her shoe for a while, walked with it so, and then wore it for some time pinned to her elbow (Nichols, *Progresses* 3:596). She showed similar contempt for the bird of paradise that the Muscovite ambassador sported on his hat: Elizabeth countered his finery by attaching one to her shoe, a gesture that Evelyn recorded approvingly in the seventeenth century because it "shews a kind of contempt of Riches" (*Tyrannus* 27).

In his *Treatise on Playe,* Harington reveals why costume mattered so to the Elizabethans. In this passage, he is rationalizing counterfeit gaming— that is, gambling at cards for stakes artificially inflated for the duration of play—but it is his analogies that are more significant:

> Wee goe brave in apparell that wee may be taken for better men than wee bee; wee use much bumbastings and quiltings to seeme better formed, better showlderd, smaller wasted, and fuller thyght, then wee are; wee barbe and shave ofte, to seeme yownger than wee are; we use perfumes both inward and outward, to seeme sweeter then wee be; corkt shooes to seeme taller then wee bee; wee use cowrtuows salutations to seem kinder then wee bee; lowly obaysances to seeme humbler then we bee; and somtyme grave and godly communication, to seem wyser or devowter then wee bee. And infynit such thinges wee may observe in ourselves, which are some of them commendable in this respect, that, by good and trew endevour to seeme to bee, we may obtayne at last the habyt and grace to become to bee such indeed, according the excellent cownsell, *Labour to bee as you would bee thought.* (*Nugae* 1:209–10)

In other words, we become our habits, so our habits should be becoming. In this important passage, Harington seamlessly explicates what contemporaries would have called the "garment of style," as he shuttles from decorum in cardplaying to decorum in clothing and gesture, shading the discussion from surface to ethics in the style familiar in English discourse from Sir Thomas Elyot to Sir Francis Bacon. English humanists in this way grounded superficial manner in Aristotelian ethic, as in this instance, the philospher's analysis of habit (*Nic. Ethics* 1103ª14–35). To the modern reader, it is also clear that Harington's argument constitutes an implicit defense of fiction, cast in terms of the aesthetic that legitimated imaginative literature even in the eyes of rigorously moralistic critics who would otherwise be inclined to proscribe fiction as feigning, which was as much as to say "lying."

Yet one had to choose carefully the model appropriate to imitate. To copy one's "betters" too exactly or without suitable translation to one's own status was to invite humiliating reprisal for the lie of presumption. Camden repeats the cautionary tale of how in the time of Henry VIII, Sir Philip Calthrop "purged" a shoemaker "of the proud humour which our people have to be of the Gentlemans cut" when the shoemaker insisted that a tailor make him a gown identical to that ordered by Sir Philip. Hearing of the shoemaker's presumption, the knight had the tailor cut both gowns full of slashes so that neither was wearable. The chastened shoemaker vowed never to wear a gentleman's fashion again (*Remains* 197–98). William Turner's *A new booke of spirituall Physik for dyuerse diseases of the nobilitie and gentlemen of Englande* (London, 1555) diagnoses the behavior of "stertuppes, or selfe made gentlemen" (M3ᵛ) as leprosy, a disease for which he prescribes the treatment given to crows by other birds; that is, to pluck them of their finery in accord with his proposed legal provisions. Then nobles, when they spied any "stertup" who could not spend two hundred pounds a year of his own lands, "wearyng silk veluet or any golden cheyne, to cary the crow to the next market towne, and there to plucke the crow, that is to cut his clothes al in peces, and to take hys cheyne from hym, wherof the ryght gentleman shoulde haue the one halfe, and the pouerty of the towne the other" (M5ᵛ–6ʳ). Every type of Elizabethan discourse inveighs against outlandish costume, and ridicule is the weapon of choice. The most familiar graphic example of such ridicule, one that is repeated in the literature regarding costume as early as Harrison's *Description* in 1587 (145), is Andrew Boorde's picture of the typical Englishman as a nude man holding a giant pair of shears in one hand and a bolt of cloth in the other, emblem of his constant search for new-fangled fashion. The image also appeared among a series of murals painted by Lucas de Heere in the London house of Evard Lord Clinton.[19] The origin of the vice of fashion—like that of syphilis—was disowned by every nationality, each of which attributed it to another. By 1604, Robert Dallington was describing the frivolous man of fashion with the shears as a Frenchman (*View of Fraunce* T4ᵛ).

The same attitude of amused superiority characterizes Robert Greene's scathing ridicule of clothing fads in a very popular work that went through seven printings in its first year and many more thereafter. His complete title is key to both the structure of his attack and the reason for taking fashion seriously: *A Quip for an Vpstart Courtier: Or, A quaint dispute between Veluet breeches and Clothbreeches. Wherein is plainely set downe the disorders in all Estates and Trades* (London, 1592). The narrator's description of the two sets of breeches reveals the economic, social, and ethical rationalization for his complaint. He recalls how he saw a pair of headless breeches approaching:

> A very passing costlye payre of Veluet breeches, whose paynes beeing made of the cheefest Neopolitane stuffe, was drawne out with the best Spanish sattin, and maruellous curiouslye ouerwhipte with Golde twist, interseamed with knottes of Pearle, the Neatherstocke was of the purest Granado Silke, no cost was spared to set out these costlye breeches. . . . As these Breeches were exceeding sumptuous to the eye, so were they passing pompous in their gestures, for they strowted vp and downe the Vallye as proudelye as though they had there appointed to act some desperat combat. [Also approaching was] a plaine payre of Clothe breeches, without eyther welt or garde, straight to the thigh, of white kersie, without a stoppe, the neatherstocke of the same, sewed to aboue the knee, and onely seamed with a little couentrie blew, such as in *Diebus illis* our great grandfathers wore, when neighbourhoode and hospitalitie had banished Pride out of *England.* (B3ᵛ–4ʳ)

The objections to velvet breeches are manifold: the fabrics are sumptuous, they are imported, they are wastefully cut to an extravagant profile, and, earlier in the same passage, they are associated with the vagrant and uncouth. Cloth breeches, by contrast, are the plain, homemade costume of the virtuous man of the good old days. Velvet Breeches underscores the point when he challenges a prospective juror, who wears the cognizance of a peacock without a tail, "Why you may gesse the inward mind by the outward apparel and see how he is adicted by the homly robes he is suted in"; he obviously, objectionably in the eyes of frivolous Velvet Breeches, spends his money on alms and hospitality (F2ʳ).

Greene's ironic fictive case was anticipated by more didactic commentators. Thomas Churchyard inveighed against courtiers' costly fashions, which were displacing their forefathers' good country frieze and "kendall greene, in sommer for a show." Greene specifically attacks fabrics with luxurious finish: "Gay golden robes, and garments pownced out, / Silke laide on silke, and stitched ore the same" (P4ʳ–Qʳ). The title of this poem from *Chvrchyards Challenge* spells out the point in advance: "A Discourse of Gentlemen lying in London, that were better keepe house at home in their Countrey," a moral that Harrison's *Description* nostalgically endorses: "Neither was it ever merrier with England than when an Englishman was known abroad by his own cloth and contented himself at home with his fine kersey hosen and a mean slop, his coat, gown, and cloak of brown-blue or puke, with some pretty furniture of velvet or fur, and a doublet of sad tawny or black velvet or other comely silk, without such cuts and garish colors as are worn in these days and never brought in but by the consent of the French, who think themselves the gayest men when they have most diversities of jags and change of colors about them" (148). For Harrison, the insidious exotic setter of harmful trends is French rather than Italian or Spanish, but Harrison, like Greene and Churchyard, sees virtue in homespun.

That most voluble critic of fashion, Philip Stubbes, agrees and targets the unfavorable economic effects of foreign imports, arguing that foreigners wear velvets and silks of necessity, preferring plain English woolens that they import while the English make foreigners rich by importing their finery (*Anatomy* 33). Harrison does allow a "comely" silk and the "pretty furniture" of some velvet or fur, but his final note underlines the mercantile factor involved in so much of the sumptuary literature. He concludes by commending above all English merchants, "for albeit that which they wear be very fine and costly, yet in form and color it representeth a great piece of the ancient gravity appertaining to citizens and burgesses." (148). Shakespeare provides an example of the opposite type, men lacking in gravity. If the merchant's English garb denoted a decorous solemnity, the lover's exotic costume signified frivolity, as in Don Pedro's description of Benedick as a lover: "There is no appearance of fancy in him, unless it be a fancy that he hath to strange disguises—as to be a Dutchman to-day, a Frenchman to-morrow, or in the shape of two countries at once, as a German from the waist downward, all slops, and a Spaniard from the hip upward, no doublet" (*Much Ado about Nothing* 3.2.31–37). In sum, shape and surface differentiated men of substance from the butterflies of fashion.

As late as 1606, Barnabe Barnes was praising Elizabeth for having refused to engage in the "leprosies" of sumptuary competition affecting the "rascall rabble of base ruffians" that led them by an "abhominable and vndecent singularitie" to array themselves at cost and in fashion equal to the wardrobes of barons. The nobility rationalized their exorbitant expenses as necessary to "make a difference of themselues" from their inferiors. Had Elizabeth followed suit in order to distinguish herself from her ladies, the cost would "with ease haue consumed an vnspeakable masse of Treasure." Barnes diagnoses the competitive malady as "vaine ostentation of the mind," a phrase that also unwittingly categorizes sumptuary display as a mode of nonverbal communication. To judge from other contemporary evidence, including Elizabeth's sumptuous portrait costumes, Barnes is more reliable witness regarding the expenses of nobles whose "patrimonies hung in tailors' shops" than he is regarding the restraint on the part of the queen (*Fovre Bookes* D^v). Upstart and noble alike recognized the truth in the old proverb invoked by Harington in his "Advertisement to the reader" prefacing his translation of the *Orlando Furioso*, "the more cost, the more worship" (17).

The foppish male might be taken lightly or brushed aside like the water fly Osric in *Hamlet*, the extravagant underling might suffer the consequences of exceeding his own means, and courtesy literature dismissed the frivolous female as a generic inversion of the responsible and thrifty housewife, but cross-dressers provoked more specific and weighty opposition. Barnabe Riche singles out effeminate gesture or style for particular attack' in *His Farewell to Military Profession* (1581), and two years later Stubbes sententiously invokes Deuteronomy 22 as a curse on cross-dressers, ruling, "Our Apparell was giuen vs as a signe distinctiue to discern betwixt sex and sex, & therfore one to weare the Apparel of another sex is to participate with the same, and to adulterate the veritie of his owne kinde" (*Anatomy* 73). Harrison, too, laments that women's lightness in dress exceeds that of the men, with their "doublets with pendant codpieces on the breast, full of jags and cuts, and sleeves of sundry colors . . . diversely colored netherstocks. . . . I have met with some of these trulls in London so disguised that it hath passed my skill to discern whether they were men or women" (*Description* 147). Harrison, like Stubbes, invokes biblical sanction with a reminder of Sodom and Gomorrah.

Diatribe against females in male garb would intensify in the seventeenth century, and it is noteworthy that then, too, it is the shape of the garment that provoked the writer's wrath, even the shape of what would seem neutral items of apparel, as in the catalog listed in one notorious pamphlet that figured in the controversy, *Hic Mulier: Or, the Man-Woman.* In a passage of invective, the writer lists some of the "garments of Shame" that female cross-dressers have affected, "exchanging the modest attire of the comely Hood, Cawle, Coyfe, handsome Dresse or Kerchiefe, to the cloudy Ruffianly broad-brim'd Hatte, and wanton Feather, the modest vpper parts of a concealing straight gowne, to the loose, lasciuious ciuill embracement of a French doublet, being all vnbutton'd to entice, all of one shape to hide deformitie, and extreme short wasted to giue a most easie way to euery luxurious action: the glory of a faire large hayre to the shame of most ruffianly short lockes" (A4). The shape of fashion draws a boundary between the sexes; ambiguity is intolerable; the line between the two must be firmly held. As Stubbes states, costume is a "signe distinctiue." It signifies a material difference. The most offensive dress violated not only distinction between genders but the decorum of place as well, such as the case of the male in female disguise who intruded into a birth room or those who, in cross-dress, would similarly invade the sacred space of a church.[20]

Ambiguity, however, defies the most rigid of signs and codes, and it would surface in spite of the firmest lines of the code of costume; indeed, the more distinct the boundaries prescribed by those who would conserve antique observances, the less adequate categories became to fix changing social realities. In her own person, Elizabeth generated considerable need for compromise, for exception to rule, and for rationalization, if not in literal discourse, then through the medium of visual imagery. Mary Queen of Scots's reputed affinity for male garb may have counted against her as yet more evidence against her moral character, but as the most prominent figure in England, Elizabeth constituted for her male subjects the embarrassment of a female monarch, the anxiety of one unmarried, who was not only conscious of these disabilities in the eyes of her subjects but also adroit at converting them into strengths.[21] Her courtiers, like herself, became adept at propagating a rhetoric of word and image that exploited her gendered status.

Elizabeth's management of her problematic status is nowhere more artfully demonstrated than in the speech to Parliament in which she confronted the issue head on in 1566, a speech responding to the campaign to have her marry. The speech is too well known to require extensive quotation or analysis, but the gendered visual references are relevant here. The queen begins by chiding those who make her unmarried status a subject of public discussion, "those unbrydelyd parsons whose hedes were nevere snaffled by the rydere dyd rasheyly entere into yt in the comon howse, a publyke place" (*Proceedings in Parliaments* 1:146). Elizabeth has immediately attributed to herself the imagery of mastery closest to the Renaissance male, that of horsemanship. In the next paragraph, in which she recalls her promise to marry and her hope to have children, as expressed earlier to the members, she refers to herself as "theyre Prince," thus employing the advantage of the conventionally masculine reference to the monarch in order to play both ends against the middle. As she draws to a conclusion, once again she evokes the imagery associated with both sexes in her penultimate paragraph: "As for my owne parte I care not for deathe, for all men are mortall; and thowghe I be a woman yet I have as good a corage awnswerable to mye place as evere my fathere hade. I am your anoynted Queene. I wyll never be by vyolence constreyned to doo anye thynge. I thanke God I am in deed indued with suche qualytyes that yf I were turned owte of the realme in my pettycote I were hable to lyve in any place of Chrystendom" (1:148). Thus pulling short the reins and the bit, by a subtle

evocation of the helpless female in her petticoat at the mercy of male kind-
ness, she then creates the illusion that the snaffled men have their heads.

How were her courtiers to reconcile the antique prejudice that women
were to be silent, domestic, and modest, with a monarch who was none of
these? Elizabeth personally managed well through exploiting rhetoric and
iconography that freed her to combine male and female attributes to her
own advantage. So, too, did her subjects, especially through the use of
visual images. Imaginative literature employed Amazonian guise in figures
such as Spenser's Britomart and Sidney's Zelmane in order either to compliment the queen directly or to represent male virtues as attributes acceptable in a female character.[22] Through disguise of male costume, numerous
Shakespearean heroines were freed for display of the physical courage, verbal wit, and assertiveness that society considered properly male strengths,
but that Elizabeth demonstrated continually. Portrait served as an instanta-
neous vehicle for seemingly resolving contradictions between received cate-
gory and Elizabethan reality. Several portraits of Elizabeth immediately
demonstrate conventionally feminine attributes in conjunction with costume showing masculine attributes. On the *Sieve Portrait*, the queen holds
a sieve, which may be the attribute of Tuccia in accordance with the legend
that the Roman virgin proved her chastity by carrying water therein, but
the medallions on the pillar behind her represent both male and female
epic virtues (fig. 18). Her costume on the *Ditchley Portrait* is sumptuously
ornamented in the tradition of the white satin and pearls associated with
the fairy queen, but her position and stance assert power and possession
beyond that permissible for mere woman (fig. 6). If her costume on the
Armada Portrait illustrates the feminine, beribboned and bowed, the sword
and globe represent the extent of her power and the forceful means of
wielding it (fig. 3).

Color was another highly codified and equally ambiguous aspect of the
language of costume. The language of heraldry aimed literally to set forth
the significance of colors, but even within the heraldic context, meanings
shifted and shaded so that without an accompanying explanatory text, it is
usually impossible to ascertain any precise meaning of a color given in
either word or image. The first problem is to know the correspondence
between color and name. The French terminology for green, for instance,
vert was a homophone for *vaire*, a confusion avoided by use of the adjec-
tival *vairé*, but persistent confusion in the spoken form led to substitution of *sinople*, which, unfortunately, also connoted red.[23] Sir John Ferne's
Blazon of Gentrie (London, 1586) sets forth an elaborate chart of heraldic
colors with their associated objects and properties, such as planets, stones,
virtues, and ages of man, but in common usage these relationships were
unstable. Ferne aligns green (*vert*), for example, with the virtues of loyalty

in love, courtesy, and affability; white, with hope and innocence (M.v^r– vi^r). The Tudor colors were taken often to be green and white, said to be derived from the colors of the Welsh leek, but perhaps because of its heraldic association with quicksilver, sea-green also connoted changeability or inconstancy.[24] Changes in fashion and in the technology of dyes rendered semantic shifts inevitable as an ever-growing terminology evolved for naming the new and the fashionable. Harrison's fulminations against fashion convey some sense of the changes taking place during the reign of Elizabeth. Having commended the sobriety of the costumes of English merchants, he castigates some of their younger wives for their taste for curiosity in fashion: "I might here name a sort of hues devised for the nonce wherewith to please fantastical heads, as gooseturd green, pease-porridge tawny, popinjay blue, lusty gallant, the-devil-in-the-head (I should say 'the hedge'), and suchlike" (148).

In their taste for variety, the young wives were imitating their betters—to begin with, the queen. She may have affected green and white as the Tudor colors, and she may have chosen black and white as her own with their signification of constancy and virginity, but her portraits show a range of other hues, and the inventories of her gowns cover an even broader spectrum.[25] The chief attraction of processions and pageants was the splendor and variety of color in the costumes, to judge from numberless accounts of such events, most spectacularly in the reports of Elizabeth's public appearances, as mentioned above. The text for the tilt entertainment presented to Elizabeth in 1581, *The Four Foster Children of Desire*, lavishly describes the costumes of the participants, starting with the earl of Arundel,

> all in Gylt and engraven Armour, with Caparisons and furniture richly and bravely embrodered, having attendaunt on him [twenty-six men] . . . apparrayled in shorte Clokes and venetian hose of Crymson velvet, layd with gold lace, doublets of yellow Satten, hattes of Crymson velvet with gold bands and yellow fethers, and yellow silke stocks. . . . And xxxi yeomen that waited after him apparailed in Cassock coats, and venetian hose of Crimson velvet, layde on with red silke and golde lace, Dublets of yellow taffatie, Hats of crimson Taffatie, with yellowe feathers, and yellowe worsted stockings. (*Entertainments* 69)

The rest of the participants whose costumes are described are equally colorful. On the second day of the same entertainment, the text interprets the significance of the colors adorning the horses that draw the chariot of the challengers. They are "apparelled in White and carnation silke, beeing the colloure of Desire" (82). Even the dress of troops departing for combat is described in similar language of fashion report. When Sir Anthony

Standen wrote to Francis Bacon describing the departure of Essex's fleet for Cadiz in 1596, it was the color and magnificence of the troops that he emphasized: "We have 300 green headed youths covered with feathers, gold and silver lace, at the least ten thousand soldiers, as tall handsome men, as ever I cast eye on, who being conducted by a lyon must work lyon's effects" (Birch 2:15).

Nor were the huge expenses for costuming the occasional exhibition tournament or military expedition unusual among the annual accounts for clothing the nobility. The spectacular occasion was usual in their lives. A large part of their expenses went to clothing. The steward of Robert Sidney, earl of Leicester, one Mr. Cruttenden, reminded Sidney of his excessive spending on clothing. When Sidney was ambassador to France, his purchase of twelve suits and a cloak lined with sables, plus servants' clothing and liveries, totaled more than one-third of his annual income. When ambassador to Scotland, he ordered for his servants cloaks lined with hare-colored velvet and trimmed with hare-color and gold lace, "which iorney was very chargeable to you." Cruttenden repeats that he has often "made boulde to informe" Sidney that he keeps too many servants and dresses them, his many children, and himself too extravagantly. Cruttenden plaintively notes that during his own thirty-four years of service, he has received only two suits of clothes and a black velvet cloak.[26] Cruttenden's indictment so radically contradicts the Sidneyan generosity praised in Ben Jonson's "To Penshurst" that one wonders which of the two pictures is askew, but perhaps Jonson's is based upon an Aristotelian measured liberality and magnificence (*Nic. Ethics* 1122ᵃ). Any neglect, whether real or fancied, would have been particularly galling to Cruttenden because it bespoke an ingratitude worse than the monetary inequity, for as Peter Stallybrass says, "the gift of clothing was the constitutive gesture of social organization."[27]

Moralists often targeted extravagance like Sidney's. In 1607, James Cleland satirized spendthrift dressers: "They haue put their lands, which co[n]-teined a great circuit, vp into a litle trunck, and hold it a point of policie to weare their lands vpon their backes, that they maie see that noe wast be done by their Tennants" (*Hero-Paideia* Dd4ʳ). In his autobiographical poem *Gascoignes woodmanship*, Gascoigne reflects that he had wasted his "purse of prodigalitie" on his "queint aray" so that he "Had pickt his purse of all the Peter pence / Which might have paide for his promotion," only to find "that light expence, / Had quite quencht out the courts devotion" (lines 43–56). When the duke of Norfolk moved between London and Norfolk as he did regularly four times a year, he traveled with a hundred retainers in addition to his large household staff and heralds. Villagers and citizens along the way would line up to watch the procession of velvet coats in passing (Williams, *Howard* 48). Henry Percy learned the cost of flamboyant display during the first year and a half after his succession as earl of Northumberland, when he ran up a debt five times greater than his means. In his *Advice to His Son*, he explains how he recovered: "Well, woods were concluded the next means of relief, so as the axe was put to the tree . . . as within a few years was sold the value of £20,000 well worth £50,000, jewellers and silkmen making their nests in the branches."[28] A fictive character disillusioned with life at court explains the motivation for sumptuary extravagance. Spenser's Colin, having wasted time and money on ambitious display, sourly concludes, "each mans worth is measured by his weed" (*Colin Clouts Come Home Againe* line 711).

Doubtless the motivation for sumptuary display was often personal vanity, notoriously so in the case of Essex, as was recognized early in his career by Marshal Biron when Essex was on expedition to France. Essex appeared in a magnificently plumed hat that provoked from Biron the amused comment, "What, you young gallant . . . are you come hither to brave me with your white feathers? I think I have white feathers too," whereupon he did indeed send for his own finery for a fine-feathered contest (Harrison, *Devereux* 59). Whatever the admixture of vanity about one's person, the main interest vested in costume was the protection of social difference. The character Bellula in the anonymous play *Histriomastix* pointedly expresses the anxiety of inherited wealth when confronted by the well-dressed newly rich: "O, wher's the outward difference of our birth!" (4.1.18). One's servants also embodied one's quality, their livery carrying the stamp of the magnificence of the master of the house. This function could be served even in the absence of the lord, because the colors of the courtier also served to distinguish his powerful friends at court. In 1566, for instance, during the course of a dispute between Norfolk and Leicester (to name another of the biggest spenders of the Elizabethan age), Leicester's supporters at court began wearing blue or purple, and Norfolk's wore yellow, although the rival parties continued outwardly friendly (Williams, *Norfolk* 95).

Costume—in particular, color of costume—could also be manipulated for highly individual statement. Even conformity to convention could be meaningful, as on the occasion of Elizabeth's visit to Oxford University in 1566, when Dr. Laurence Humphrey appeared before the queen in his scarlet gown. One of the most radical of religious reformers in the vestiarian dispute, he had earlier been cited by church authorities for his opposition to priestly garb, so his concession to wear the habit was remarkable (Rosenberg, *Leicester* 129). If it was significant when a sober person appeared in bright garb, it was also significant when a flamboyant character appeared in subdued style. Because Essex was known from an early age for his flamboyant extravagance, when he entered the queen's Accession Day Tilt in

1590 costumed in black as a member of a fictive funeral cortege, the difference in his appearance was memorable. The implicit message in the change was his repentance for the offense of his secret marriage to Francis Walsingham, which the queen had furiously discovered the preceding spring (Strong, *Cult* 152). The most dramatic Elizabethan use of color appeared twice on the scaffold. Coincidentally, it was there that both Essex and Mary Queen of Scots made their last extravagant use of clothing as gesture, and in remarkably similar ways, at their respective executions. Both dressed in black for their last performance. When each partially disrobed for the axe, a red undergarment was exposed—for Essex, a scarlet waistcoat; for Mary, a scarlet petticoat (*CSPD*, 1598–1601:594). Segar's *Honor Military and Civil* (1602) derives red from fire, "the most noble element" and, next to sun, of the greatest brightness, signifying boldness, magnanimity, "ardent loue with charitie" (F^v). Whether signifying the boldness of defiance or the charity of martyrdom—and here is another illustration of the ambiguity of color code—in their choice of bravery, each executed a visual pun.

Literary fictions also reveal the emotional impact of color, Malvolio's yellow cross-garters being the most dramatic instance of gross misjudgment. On the other hand, just how delicately nuanced the choice of costume might be is best shown in Sidney's description of Amphialus's deliberations as he prepares himself to meet the disdainful Pamela, whom he both loves unrequitedly and holds captive unrepentantly:

> calling for his richest apparell, nothing seemed sumptuous inough for his mistresses eyes: and that which was costly, he feared were not daintie: and though the invention were delicat, he misdoubted the making. As carefull he was too of the colour; lest if gay, he might seeme to glorie in his injury, and her wrong; if mourning, it might strike some evill presage unto her of her fortune. At length he tooke a garment more rich then glaring, the ground being black velvet, richly embrodered with great pearle, & precious stones, but they set so among certaine tuffes of cypres, that the cypres was like blacke clowds, through which the starrs might yeeld a darke luster. About his necke he ware a brode & gorgeous coller; whereof the pieces enterchangeably answering; the one was of Diamonds and pearle, set with a white enamell, so as by the cunning of the workman it seemed like a shining ice, and the other piece being of Rubies, and Opalles, had a fierie glistring, which he thought pictured the two passions of Feare and Desire, wherein he was enchayned. (*Arcadia* 367)

Sidney supplied interpretive commentary for his readers because, as Amphialus reflects, the code of costume and device was subject to ambiguity, but the author did not need to specify the Petrarchan contraries that the costume figures forth; nor did he need to comment explicitly on the continuum of the system of signification, from poetry to tournament device, from device to costume, from costume to personal expression, because courtly life assumed these connections and fiction could draw upon them.

Nicholas Hilliard's portrait *George Clifford, third Earl of Cumberland as the Knight of Pendragon Castle* (fig. 5) graphically captures the similarity of costume in history and in fiction. Cumberland is costumed as a mythic character with all of the fantastic accoutrements of legend as it was enacted through tournament, but this bravery is cut from the same cloth as the sumptuary display that is recorded in the inventories, accounts, memoirs, and eyewitness reports of Elizabethan history. Cumberland, whose name must be added to the ledger of extravagant spenders, and whose letters and biography include continual petitions and complaints about his need for money, all too literally took to heart the Spanish proverb that he both quoted and translated in his speech to the queen on her Accession Day, November 17, 1600: " '*Adelante los Abenstados.*': 'Let then [*sic*] hold the purses with ye mouth downeward that hath filled them with mouth upwards'" (Williamson, *Cumberland* 243). Cumberland regarded himself as insufficiently rewarded for his pillaging expeditions on behalf of the queen, and his voice joined the off-stage chorus of those who whispered in the wings their disappointments in Elizabeth's inadequate support for the roles they played. The motto of the Seckford family, "Win't and Wear't," might have expressed the expectations of all of them—Leicester, Essex, Drake, Cumberland.[29] Gerard Legh complains that it was also the unspoken motto of many a bit player as well: "For euery man wil weare, as the best doth, without all order. For now we haue a como[n] saying winne golde and weare it" (Liii^v).

Gloves in particular served as synecdochic evocation of the owner. Ladies' gloves often figure in love poetry, reaching their most extravagant appearance in Henry Constable's "Sonet 2: To his Ladies hand vpon occasion of her gloue which in her absence he kissed": "And I thy gloue kisse as a thinge devine / Thy arrowes quiver and thy reliques shrine." This reverent attitude carries over into the cult of chivalric tournament, too. On his portrait, Cumberland flaunts a glove as fashionable token of what he hoped that he had won by 1590 when he succeeded Sir Henry Lee as queen's champion. On his hat, he wears the queen's glove, sign of her favor, in keeping with the custom that William Smith explains in *Chloris* (no. 29): "Some in their hearts their mistress' colours bears; / Some hath her gloves, some other hath her garters" (*Elizabethan Sonnet-Cycles* 178). Token—more than token, trophy—the glove is synecdochic figure for the hand, the blessing, of the queen, and—perhaps most important—the wearer's triumph over rivals. Recognition of this element in display of a token from the queen would explain Essex's fury upon seeing Sir Charles Blount wearing a chess queen given him by Elizabeth: "Now, I perceive, every fool must wear a favour" (Devereux, *Essex* 1:194). By an ironic inversion of the lady's-glove-as-trophy, Elizabeth displays a tiny jeweled gauntlet on her right side of her ruff on the *Rainbow Portrait* (fig. 11), synecdochic trophy of her triumph over all aspiring contenders in her courtly lists.

Articles of apparel were invested with more than token value. When Henry Machyn describes the passing parades that he so untiringly records, he counts the "coats" that comprise the groups. For instance, he notes in his *Diary* that when Elizabeth, then princess, rode through London at the time of her sister's coronation, she was preceded by "a C. welvett cottes" and followed by another hundred coats of scarlet and "fyne red gardyd with velvett" (57). Thomas Churchyard counted the participants in the procession to welcome Elizabeth when she was on progress through Suffolk and Norwich: in Suffolk, two hundred young gentlemen in white velvet, three hundred men "of the grauer sorte" in black velvet coats and fair chains, and fifteen hundred serving men on horseback in Suffolk. Norwich, not to be outdone, mustered some twenty-five hundred horsemen, six hundred of whom were gentlemen bravely attired. Granted that the population of Norwich was only about seventeen thousand in 1579, this procession represented a sizable proportion of the citizenry, about 12 percent.[30] An entry from the records of the Norwich Corporation may qualify any astonishment at the size and elegance of the turnout, however: "Whereas for the worship of the Cittie agaynst the receyving of the Queen's Majestie, it is thought convenient that 40 bachelours be appointed to attend and waite upon Mr. Mayor, the Justices of the Peace, and Aldermen; and that they should apparell themselves with mandelions cotes, habbits, and slives, all in one suit, and one sashing, in such sort as is appointed. It is agreed, that if any appointed shall refuse to apparell themselves, they shall forfeit 40 *s.* each" (Nichols, *Progresses* 2:130; 133). The number of coats in a procession, the quality of fabric, the coordination of color—these indicated the status of the person so honored.

A lady's glove symbolically represented her person; an official's gown represented his position. Sir Christopher Hatton's jest to that effect has been often quoted. Upon rising to dance at a wedding, he left his gown on a chair, instructing it, "*Lie there, chancellor*" (Birch 1:56). The story nicely illustrates the closeness of association between costume and the wearer's office: synecdoche approaches identity, although the representation may be deceptive, as Shakespeare's Douglas realizes when he resolves to kill all the coats of the king—that is to say, the supporters disguised as the king (*Henry IV, part 1* 5.3.26). Removal of official garment also symbolized deference, as it did most portentously when city officials would customarily remove their gowns on religious feasts before entering Saint Paul's and circling the cathedral before robing again.[31] A similar symbolic bonding also applied to corporate bodies as well as to servants, civic officials, courtiers, and kings. The uniqueness of servants' livery distinguished the house, but the elegance of the garment bespoke both the servitude of the wearer and the liberality or magnificence of the lord, as the etymology of "livery" connotes with its origins in Latin *liber* (free).[32] The wearing of funeral black signified bonding between the deceased and survivors, the wills of those of means having provided the black cloth, appropriately graded by quality and quantity according to the status of the recipient. The great number of coats in a civic procession indicated loyalty and devotion to the monarch; the richness of material manifested the good order and prosperity of the city. If spontaneous demonstration of these qualities by the citizens was unpredictable, it was imposed through sanctions for nonconformity. Decorously magnificent clothing honored the visiting dignitary and it did honor to the wearer. Apparel thus honored donor, wearer, and observer.

In the social effort to protect honor, codes developed, some explicit, some simply understood. If color codes were regulated to some degree by the heralds, other conventions regarding color evolved outside the system and were implicitly understood. Janet Arnold concludes that there were no indigenous theatrical books on color, although Italian ones were known (*Queen Elizabeth's Wardrobe Unlock'd* 90). The multiple degrees of intensity of hue and the many varieties of off-shades and mixed colors so disparaged by William Harrison—not to mention the notorious unreliability of terminology regarding colors—together complicate not only sumptuary control but even posterior analysis of the codes. Opposing colors were instrumental in defining courtly polarities.[33] Black and white, dark and light, somber and vivid represented the opposing values of age and youth, gravity and activity, stability and energy—a useful articulation of the polarization found in Elizabethan criticism of dress. Because this system underlay customary practice, variation upon it or departure from convention called attention to itself as wordless statement.

Courtesy books frequently deplore change in customary dress, and often they offer sociological explanation for such departures, as does *A Health to the Gentlemanly profession of Seruingmen: or, The Seruingmans Comfort*, attributed to Gervase Markham. Within the context of a discussion of upstarts, the text attacks one particular type of sumptuary behavior as indicative of the undermining of social hierarchy:

Now for the ambition and disdayne of the Countreyman, and the Gentlemanly Seruingman.

First for the Yeoman, or Husbandmans sonne, aspyring from the Plough to the Parlor, I holde these, the contempt of his vocation, feare to hazard his life in his Princes Marciall affayres, and the ambitious desire of dignitie, to be the especiall occasions that hath mooued him to change his habite and cullour, from Jerkin to Coate, and from Russet to Blew. (131)

The tone bespeaks disgruntled longing for the good old days when men knew their place and soberly settled into it at an early age, and it echoes the note set earlier (1565) in *A Pleasaunt Dialogn[sic]e or disputation betweene the Cap, and the Head.* The Cap complains about the new-fangled styles of head covering and the faddish ways of wearing and doffing the Cap. It chides the Head: "Thou art not co[n]tented with making me to weare Read, Yellowe, Greene and Blewe laces, but besides that thou encombrest me wyth Byrdes Feathers, thou betrickest me with Brouches, Valentines, Rings, Kayes, Purses, Gloues, yea fyngers of Gloues; thou wrappest me in Chaynes, thou settest me with Buttons and Aglets, thou lardest me with Ribans and Bandes, thou cuttest me, borest me, and slashest me, both aboue and beneath without any compassion or pitie, and so by this dis-fygure me, empayring my dignity, and yet the more to thy shame" (Avi^v–vii^r). The Cap, like the commentator in *The Servingmans Comfort,* reads costume as sign of attitudes toward the social order. In this case, excessive ornamentation indicates the foolish aspirations of the upstart who apes such courtly fashion as the glove worn on Cumberland's broad-brimmed hat, the rightful trophy of a noble triumpher in the tilts. The constraints upon headgear were so restrictive that they governed one's leisure, invading even the privacy of the bedroom, where during sexual consummation the wife's headcovering customarily signaled her chastity. John Stow notes the ostentatious hatband as a fashionable demarcation between gentry and their inferiors, an affectation that could be dangerous on the hat of one for whom the sumptuary prescription was a modest felt cap, made in England.[34]

As it evolved, the broad codification of color allowed scope for some kinds of meaningful variation by those who moved on the upper levels of society, and contemporary observers often note these departures, variations that derived their meaning from their difference. For instance, the conventional association of black with steadfastness and mourning provided a backdrop for a number of reversals. Some of these in turn became them-selves conventional, such as the occasional continental association of white with mourning, as on Clouet's portrait of Mary Stuart, or with the death of women in childbirth. Personal variations were more remarkable, as in two especially notable illustrations of the use of color as statement. In July 1565,

Mary Queen of Scots, already a widow, married Henry, Lord Darnley. A letter to Robert Dudley from Thomas Randolph, ambassador to Scotland, describes the suggestive role of color change in the ceremony:

> She had upon her backe the great mourninge gowne of blacke, with the greate wyde mourninge hoode, not unlyke unto that which she wore the dolefull day of the buriall of her housbande. . . . [In her chamber, later] being required, accordinge to the solemnitie to cast off her care, and lay asyde those sorrowfull garments, and give herself to a pleasanter lyfe. After some prettie refusall, more I believe for manner sake then greef of harte, she suffreth them that stoode by, everie man that coulde approche to take owte a pyn, and so being commytted unto her ladies changed her garments. (Wright, *Queen Elizabeth* 1:202–3)

It is remarkable that it is the men present who remove the pins holding the queen's mourning garb in place, and that Randolph observes the coyness in Mary's "prettie refusall" of their symbolic disrobing of her old mourning self. It is the male who releases the female from the constraints of widowhood, freeing her to resume life as a sexually viable woman. No fiction more effectively dramatizes costume as indicator of one's changing state—not Pyrocles's Amazonian garb in the *New Arcadia*; not the epithalamic arraying of Spenser's brides, nor the stripping of Duessa in his *Faerie Queene*; not even Lear's stripping to his nakedness, nor his pathetic plea for someone to undo this button. Mary's reputed comment to her executioners as they helped her with her final disrobing parodically replays her wedding preparations: "I was not wont to have my clothes plucked off by such grooms."[35]

Lady Essex enacted another inflection of the traditional color code for grief and mourning. It should be recalled that in 1590, Essex had appeared in black as participant in a fictive funeral cortege in the Accession Day tilt by way of penance for his secret marriage. In 1599, he committed another of his continual violations of courtly decorum by precipitately leaving his command in Ireland and, upon his unauthorized return to England in September, forcing himself into the queen's presence, dishevelled and muddy. He was in effect placed under arrest and denied visits from family or friends. Rowland Whyte describes the role of costume in efforts to relieve the prisoner's situation. "November 4: My Lady of Essex is a most sorrowful creature for her husband's captivity; she wears all black of the meanest price, and receives no comfort in any thing. 29th November.—On Sunday, in the afternoon, the Countess of Essex came to Court all in black; all she wore was not valued at 5 *l* [£5]" (Devereux, *Lives and Letters* 2:88). The queen was not to be moved: not until August 1600 was Essex released; it would be only a matter of months (Febraury 1601) before he led the rebellion that led to his execution.

Standards of dress were based largely on custom, but more formal codification also prescribed appropriate costume, and official efforts were sporadically made to enforce these regulations. Heraldic rules were closely monitored by officers jealous of their position and power, and it is curious to see that in the midst of its attack on female cross-dressing, *Hic Mulier* marshals an argument from heraldic proscription as part of the case against the wearing of large ruffs: "From the first you got the false armoury of yellow Starch (for to weare yellow on white, or white vpon yellow, is by the rules of Heraldry basenesse, bastardie, and indignitie) the folly of imitation, the deceitfulnesse of flatterie, and the grosest basenesse of all basenesse, to do whatsoeuer a greater power will command you" (A4^r). Ruffs were a particular annoyance to would-be monitors of sumptuary decorum. A ballad printed in 1566 on the occasion of the birth of a monstrous child with a ruff-like deformation drew this moral:

> This ruffeling world, in ruffes al rolde,
> Dooth God detest and hate;
> As we maye lerne the tale wel tolde
> Of children borne of late.
> (*Collection of Ballads*, ed. [Lilly] 245)

The occasional reference to significant color, the dramatic personal departure from conventional practice, the strained appeal to heraldic practice—these all demonstrate the existence of an implicit code or codes understood as the grid upon which individuals charted their sumptuary progress. Although these data are sporadic in their appearances in contemporary documents and comprise a series of individual cases, they are useful in showing the codes in action. Official efforts at sumptuary regulation, on the other hand, are explicitly stated, minutely codified, broadly applicable, and largely ineffective. Nonetheless, they transparently reveal the motivations for such efforts.

For the lower classes, the rules were simple and clear, consisting mainly of proscriptions motivated by official concern to reserve magnificent display to the upper clases, to differentiate social strata, and to support the English economy, but desire to follow court fashion is omnipresent. Philip Gawdy, lawyer, member of Parliament, and follower of Ralegh, writes to his sister-in-law from London that he has sent her "half an ell of blacke velvett, half a quarter of white satten, and a paire of truncke sleeves," so that she might copy the fabric needed "for the manner of wearing of their hoodes as the courte. . . . Some weare sattin of all collors with their upper border and some weare none. Some one of them weares this daye with all theise fashions, and the nexte daye without. So that I fynd nothing more certayne then their vncertaynty" (Gawdy, *Letters* 49). The better sort did not find imitation by their inferiors complimentary. Time and again, the many proclamations single out "the monstrous abuse of apparel almost in all estates, but principally in the meaner sort" (*Tudor Proclamations* 2:193). Color, fabric, and cut are subject to regulation. Proclamations specify exactly how much yardage may be used "for the reformation of the use of the monstrous and outrageous greatness of hose" (2:189) and they dictate the use of only a single ruff at collar or sleeves.

In the later part of the reign of Elizabeth, the proscriptions about ornamentation are repeated and emphasized. The proclamation of 1580 explicitly relates rank to the degree of ornament permissible "because there are many persons that percase shall be found in outward appearance more sumptuous in their apparel than by common intendment the values of their possessions or goods may warrant." Only earls may wear purple silk, cloth of gold or silver, sable, or gold or silver embroidery. Crimson, carnation, and blue velvet are reserved to barons (2:457–58). Corresponding regulations for women are very similar, with the difference that these rules are even more meticulous about details, such as types of fabric, embroidery, hatbands, and linings. For members of the nobility, the prohibitions are not so well defined as for their inferiors because sumptuary regulations were designed to protect the prerogatives of the nobility, but that is not to say that the rules were any less stringent because unwritten. Custom dictated the garb of civic officials and their wives, sometimes even when they were engaged on daily business in the streets (Tittler, *Architecture* 107). For the miserable apprentice who affected a bit of tinsel, the penalty was a fine. For the aspiring gentleman or noble, if perceived by rivals as a claim to power, his violation of written code or abrogation of convention could at the least motivate dangerous envy and at worst play a role in his downfall, leaving the sumptuous spoils of his extravagance to his covetous enemies. Thomas Platter observes that lords and knights in England customarily leave discarded elegant clothes to their servingmen, who sell them for small sums to actors because they would be "unseemly" if worn (Platter, *Platter's Travels* 167). In this respect, as the implicit model that wordlessly monitored practice, sumptuary regulation was effective. For all of the careful calibrations between personal monetary worth and the correspondingly permissible degree of luxury, the literal proclamations were not effective in their particularity.

The sheer number of proclamations during the reign of Elizabeth indicates their ineffectuality: nine reaffirmed earlier laws; thirteen more were introduced in Parliament, none of which passed.[36] The labyrinthine complexity of specifications and the large number of provisions for exceptions, as in the last proclamation in 1597, were difficult to monitor. An early scholar noted the concentration of effort to regulate within London and the universities, with little effort elsewhere.[37] Still, the upper class monitored the lower, the ins regulating the outs in order to keep them outs, as corroborated by many local sumptuary regulations promulgated by cities and guilds in order to control apprentices, to protect the dignity of civic government, and, the specifications make clear, to enforce the use of domestic materials and manufacture.[38]

Above all, the chief deterrent to enforcement would have to be the sumptuous example set by the upper classes themselves—most powerfully, the queen. Contemporary rumors about the extravagance of her wardrobe may have been exaggerated, but their currency suggests Elizabeth's power as sumptuary model. For example, by John Chamberlain's account (often repeated in modern times, although discredited) upon her death, the queen had two thousand gowns (*Letters* 1:189). Regardless of the exact number of her gowns, any of Elizabeth's portraits represents the lavishness of her wardrobe, and James Melville commented upon her daily change of costume (*Memoirs* 95). Whatever verbal admonitions regarding sumptuary excess may have been promulgated to the contrary, the visible model of the extravagant dress of the nobility set a standard of luxury that the "meaner sort" could only admire; admiring, desire; and, desiring, imitate. Whether one looks to Lady Howard dressing like the queen, the woman adopting male costume, the modest cap bedecked like Cumberland's elegant hat, the frequent comment about the extravagance of the upper class, or the commoner duplicating the gown of the lord, one sees that the lower classes and the powerless enacted their awareness that costume bespoke one's status, achievement, power, and honor. By trying to prevent or to restrain imitation, the nobility, too, affirmed the silent potency of costume, a power so strong that it defeated the word of law.

Surface, color, and texture mattered in the textile arts by manifesting identity, by representing moral exemplars, by expressing aspiration, and by reciprocally doing honor. Beyond these superficial considerations lay other contextual qualifiers. Shape and substance modified matter and inflected silent communication, sometimes with effects more serious.

CHAPTER FOUR

SHAPE AND SUBSTANCE AS
MATTERS OF WEIGHT

I Like no Relation so well, as what mine eye telleth me.
. . . Naturally we carry matter better then wordes, in
which nature tells vs, shee vseth words but for an
interpretour, because our ignorance vnderstandes not
her Language . . . for there is lesse drosse in the letters of
nature, then in words.

Sir William Cornwallis, Essayes

IF SURFACE MANIFESTED or constituted meaning, the more solid matter of shape and substance added another dimension of communication among the separate, generally static elements in the silent language of the Elizabethans. Jewelry, like textiles, was used for adornment with the conventional general value garnered by magnificent display; in the case of jewelry, however, shape or substance or both often further specify meaning. When offered as gifts, jewels carried a meaning more specific, more personal, more precious, and certainly more lasting than most gifts of textiles. Medals and coins shared many of the qualities of jewelry, but having a wider circulation they had different semiotic possibilities. Among small-scale artifacts that were used as silent means of communicating, foodstuffs, perhaps surprisingly, also figured. Jewelry, medals, coins, and foodstuffs—all of them portable media in daily circulation—daily signified meanings that endured beyond their momentary presence as sensible objects. The shape and substance of some larger forms were also semiotic vehicles, signifying more impressively because apprehended only occasionally. In most cases, sculptural and architectural forms figured in larger programs that enacted a more dynamic syntax of silent language. One exceptional sculptural form is the funeral monument, a naturally static artifact that shared something of both the intimate jeweled message, on the one hand, and the public monument, on the other. Lastly, the most visible of privately constructed monuments, the country house, shares the semi-otic intentions of all of the other, smaller forms, enshrining them in a presence so much larger than its parts that it moves into another dimension of significance, one that carries over into the complex uses of place, posi-tion, space, and movement as signifiers. So analytical progression from small-scale shapes such as jewels and coins through sculptural forms such as foodstuffs to larger architectural forms such as monuments and great houses moves toward larger, and more public, ceremonial reception for the mute rhetoric of shape and substance.

Solidity or preciousness of material immediately signifies investment of value in an Elizabethan artifact. This is perhaps not surprising in itself, but the specificity of weight as value in contemporary records of gift exchange sometimes surprises, and the investment of significance in objects of inher-ently negligible worth sometimes dismays. Contextualization of these arti-facts reveals their place in a cultural system of prestation (the traditional offering of gifts as recognition of duty owed) and, if analysis does not ren-der the objects attractive, it does rationalize Elizabethan cultural aesthetics.

Much Elizabethan jewelry strikes the modern eye as too heavy and too heavily overwrought, particularly when one recalls that the large baroque pearl, surrounded by many smaller stones, set in an intricately lacey gold filigree, suspended from a knotted gold chain, and contrived to represent a Moor holding a diamond-studded scimitar, would have been worn as one among many jewels on a gown itself laced with spangled and knotted embroidered design. The point was not to set off the jewel as the single star—singularity and understatement would be valued in the aesthetic of a later age—but to create a dazzling galaxy. The desired effect was that of Elizabeth as she appears on the *Rainbow Portrait* (fig. 11), to name one of her more restrained displays of jewels, whereon one must study enlarged details just to locate and recognize the figure of the crescent on her head-dress or the jeweled armillary sphere on her left sleeve or the jeweled heart dangling from the mouth of the jewel-encrusted serpent there, or perhaps even to notice the little jeweled gauntlet on her ruff, although it is displayed in relatively quiet isolation against the busy ground of the fabric.[1] The overall effect is magnificence—a magnificence that was also the object of rich costume, but jewels carried some special qualities as a medium of communication.

Both men and women wore jewels in profusion. Henry Percy spent more than £1,000 on jewelry in the first eighteen months after succession to his title: a single pearl chain cost nearly £200, and a diamond jewel purchased from Ralegh cost £800.[2] Thomas Fuller concludes his life of Queen Elizabeth with the observation, "She much affected rich and costly apparell; and if ever jewells had just cause to be proud, it was with her wearing them" (*The Holy State* [1642] 319). Fuller's extravagant compliment glances at the reciprocal nature of Renaissance magnificence, both bestowing and receiving glory, a mutuality of value perhaps echoed in modern crowds dazzled by royal appearances or museum exhibitions of crown jewels, which then become conversational capital. Apart from their magnificence, the talismanic properties of precious and semiprecious stone—such as, for example, those supposed powers that forbade the use of any "stone of vertue" in medieval tournaments—attracted Elizabethans.[3] In the works of Sidney, Spenser, and Shakespeare—to name only the major writers from the period—characters allude to the protective or magical properties of gemstones, but it would be misleading to attempt to catalog and explicate these references in search of a coherent system of belief.[4] The allusions belong to fictive characters, often are stated for nonce effect, and in any case, reflect that inconsistent mixture of science and alchemy that characterizes the culture at large. Enough at present to invoke as a general principle the more localized cautionary line from Cutwode's *Caltha*, "stones will tell" (st. 101). Granted the internal contradictions of the system of lapidary reading and the indeterminable amount of credence placed in it, the more fruitful approach is through analysis of specific cases—or, better, types of cases of use of jewels.

The costliness of precious metals would in itself have served to limit their use to the wealthy upper classes, and the guardians of social hierarchy were eager to support that restriction. *The Catalogve of Honor* (London, 1610) looks to antiquity for reinforcement, smugly asserting that in response to abuse by "Chap-men" and "Pedlers," the Roman senate of Julius Caesar's day restricted the use of gold rings to those men with a freeborn patrilineal line and who were valued at forty sesterces. "Heereby it came to passe, that they seemed to be of the Order of *Gentlemen*, which did weare Gold Ringes, for that it was not lawfull for any so to do, but such as had a *Gentlemans* substance" (B3ʳ–3ᵛ). Parliament reaffirmed early Tudor sumptuary regulations, specifying that cloth of gold or silver be reserved to earls, as in the proclamation of 1580 (*Tudor Proclamations* 2:457–58), and local legislation was even more specific in prohibiting the lower classes from the use of precious metals. A member of the Merchant Tailors Company was imprisoned in 1574 for appearing at the company house in a silken cloak, hose lined with taffeta, and a shirt edged with silver. In 1582, the lord mayor and council of London consigned apprentices to plain kersey, whether they would or no, and gold or silver jewels were again specifically forbidden to them.[5]

Apart from the obvious effort to increase the use of goods of domestic origin and manufacture, and apart from the intent to preserve privilege, the regulations aim to restrict circulation (and thus increase the value) of two prized metals. William Heth's handbook for jewelers, *The goulden arte or The Jewell house of gemes* (BL MS Stowe 1071), dating from the last year of the reign of Elizabeth, explains the virtues of gold and silver, and these qualities added value to metals still esteemed for their rarity, malleability, durability, and beauty. Gold, continues Heth, cures many diseases "in so much that nature hath geuen vnto it of peculier property a vertue and pryueledge to comforte the weaknes of the harte and to giue ioyfullnes and mirth to the spirites dysposinge therby the mind to magnaminity and atemptes of great enterprises." Silver, continues Heth, is useful to physicians because "it is modifiable against many euelles" and heals wounds. Both silver and gold, used in the manufacture of tableware, can detect poison (3ᵛ; 9ᵛ; 39ʳ). Heth's combination of physical and magical properties, his blending of practical and spiritual uses, are typical of the lapidary lore of the period as reflected in scholarly and literary works. More to the point, this conflation of physical and spiritual also characterizes actual Elizabethan use of precious substances.

More than any other widely used jeweled artifact, rings were valued for their talismanic and symbolic functions. Men and women both wore rings in profusion, sometimes several on one finger, sometimes between the first and second knuckle, or on the thumb, sometimes tied by ribbons around one's neck, elbow, or waist.[6] Rings figure often in the complications of literary plots and in historical legend, and they are the subject of much speculative comment. That Elizabeth not only kissed Anjou upon the mouth when he arrived in England to court her but that she also gave him a ring was taken by all as a sign of betrothal (Doran, *Monarchy and Matrimony* 187). The tradition of the marriage ring in particular lent itself to fanciful interpretation, none more fanciful than Henry Smith's in his *Preparatiue to Marriage* (London, 1591). In order to illustrate the need for fitness or evenness in marriage, Smith explains the need for banishing the "oddes" between couples: "From hence came the first Vse of the Ring in Weddings, to represe[n]t this euennes: for if it be straighter than the finger it will pinch, & if it be wider than the finger it wil fall of; but if it bee fit, it neither pincheth nor slippeth" (C6ʳ).

Because the marriage ring was such a powerful symbol and because it was so closely associated with Roman Catholic practice, Puritans wished to ban its use, but they might have had greater success had they imitated the cooptative strategy of their sovereign lady (Phillips, *The Reformation of Images* 134–35). Some contemporaries reported that Elizabeth used her coronation ring in a gesture calculated to disarm her Parliament when they would have had her marry against her own wishes. In the course of rejecting their importunity, according to William Camden's account, she chided them, " 'Yea, to satisfie you, I have already joyned my self in Marriage to an

Husband, namely, the Kingdom of England. And behold (said she, which I marvell ye have forgotten,) the Pledge of this my Wedlock and Marriage with my Kingdom.' (And therewith she drew the Ring from her Finger, and shewed it, wherewith at her Coronation she had in a set form of words solemnly given her self in Marriage to her Kingdom)" (*Princess Elizabeth* 29).[7] In his *Watch-woord To Englande* (London, 1584), Anthony Munday's rhetoric indicates the effectiveness of her ploy: "Her Highnesse is the most louing Mother and Nurse of all her good Subiectes, and is lykewise the husband of the common weale, maried to the Realme, and the same by ceremony of Ring as solemnly signified, as any other mariage" (A.iiiʳ). By using the sign of the worth of marriage in order to refuse to marry, Elizabeth was varying her habit of having and her cake and eating it, or having the cake of custom while breaking it—and this time, for good measure, it was a wedding cake.

Ancient Christian association of the wedding ring with the ideal permanence and fidelity of the marriage bond was reinforced by correlative Renaissance belief and device. Sixteenth-century custom assigned ring position according to the station of the wearer: the thumb for doctors, index finger for merchants, middle finger for fools, annular finger for students, and auricular finger for lovers; the fourth finger also had a special association for betrothal and marriage, as the finger that, it was believed, had a direct neural connection to the heart. Thus the York and Salisbury spousal manuals prescribed the placing of the ring upon the bride's fourth finger, left hand, sometimes read as signaling the wife's subjection to the husband (Dugdale, *The Antiquities of Warwickshire* 1:250). The son of Robert Dudley by Lady Douglas, widow to Lord Sheffield, considered the significance of the wedding ring so binding that he entered Dudley's gift of a family heirloom ring to his mother as evidence of his own legitimacy in his abortive suit for Leicester's estate.[8]

The round shape of rings underlay their symbolism as bond and as token of harmony, but one type of ring was more explicit. An unusual shape of wedding ring, the gimmal, formed a specific sign of mutual bonding. Two or more rings were interlinked, one part to be worn by each party until solemnization of the marriage, when the bride then wore both halves (Kunz 219), accurately if inadvertently signing the wife's greater responsibility for sexual fidelity. The biographer of Sir Thomas Gresham illustrates the gimmal ring supposed to have been his subject's wedding ring, aptly inscribed with the scriptural motto, QVOD. DEVS. CONIVNSIT on one half and HOMO. NON. SEPERAT on the other, the motto usually translated as "What God hath joined together, let no man put asunder"—and with symbols of an infant and a skeleton within the cavity inside the bezel.[9] Another gimmal, apparently unnoticed in the literature about the type, had five links, the four inner ones containing a posy by the earl of Hertford that compares the five circles to a "knott of secret might," an allusion that both invokes a common linear device and mystifies it for sake of greater intimacy between parties to a secret marriage. Catherine Grey returned this ring to her husband Hertford, then in prison, together with her wedding ring and another ring with a death's-head as she lay dying.[10] Elizabeth reputedly sent to Mary Stuart half of a gimmal ring that comprised two diamonds in the shape of a heart, a token of faith that failed to save Mary's head, as Aubrey was later to observe (Kunz 184). Perhaps the token signified only Elizabeth's half-hearted esteem, and the possibility illustrates the power of silent language, like verbal, to dissimulate.

Rings signified other sentiments, concepts, and values as well, which gives pause to hasty dismissal of any Elizabethan ornament as mere decoration.[11] Jewelry often carried a memento-mori motif, representing skeletons (as, even, did Gresham's wedding ring), death's-heads, and inscriptions to that effect (as on one of Catherine Grey's rings). Posies on rings frequently enjoined the wearer to behave piously. Other rings have an entirely more secular intent, such as signet rings, which identified the sender, credited the bearer, or certified documents, like Sir Thomas Gresham's famous gifts of grasshopper rings. Gresham, financier and founder of the Royal Exchange in London, used his family badge, or crest—a grasshopper, a canting device for his name (Old English *graes* [grass] and *ham* [home])—on the inside of a number of signet rings that he distributed to friends. Gresham, who did very well by his good deeds as financial adviser to three successive Tudors, may have used the rings to reward those who had done him profitable favors.[12] Neither the recipients nor any Londoner could forget the giver, for he mounted giant ornamental grasshoppers on the roof of the Royal Exchange (fig. 2). Certainly the building earned him much credit, in every sense of the word: he profited about 16 percent on his financial investment (Bindoff, *The Fame of Sir Thomas Gresham* 18).

In the absence of the sender, a ring might also serve as proxy: in his *Life and Death of Cardinal Wolsey*, George Cavendish notes that a gold ring with a rich stone "was always the privy token" for special communication between Henry VIII and Wolsey (105). Leicester forever ingratiated himself with the Inner Temple by persuading Elizabeth to send her ring to the lord keeper in order to halt all proceedings against the Temple in a legal dispute that the Templars had seemed otherwise doomed to lose.[13] Romantic legends abound that associate particular rings with historic dramatic events, and if not all of them can be verified, their long-lived circulation suggests the symbolic power of the ring in the historical imagination. The most famous of these is the account of Elizabeth's rage upon learning of the misdirection of the ring that Essex had tried to return to her when he was under sentence of death. She had given it to him with the assurance of its protective power should he ever need her help. She was so enraged that it was inferred that the earl might have been pardoned had she received in time the desperate message of the ring.[14] Whether it was that ring or not, one Elizabethan observer, John Manningham, records that Elizabeth "caused the ring wherewith shee was wedded to the Crowne, to be cutt from hir finger some 6 weekes before hir death, but wore a ring which the Earl of Essex gave hir unto the day of hir death" (*Diary* 222). It is notable that Manningham, echoing Elizabeth in her speech to Parliament half a century earlier, refers to her coronation ring as her wedding ring, evidence of the effectiveness of her iconographic gesture.

Yet another report attaches special significance to a ring associated with Elizabeth, and that is the "blue ring from a fair lady," Lady Scrope, the sister of Sir Robert Carey. Lady Scrope threw the ring from a window near Elizabeth's death chamber as a signal of the demise of the queen, and Carey then took it by a hard ride to an impatient James Stuart as certain evidence that the heir-presumptive was just a coronation ceremony away from the throne. James had sent the sapphire ring to Carey's sister earlier so that it could serve as immediate certification of the death of Elizabeth well ahead of official notification (Carey, *Memoirs* 59n., 63). Like her son, Mary Stuart also used rings to communicate in dire circumstances. She sent a ring to Thomas Howard, earl of Norfolk, as comfort when he was facing the prospect of imprisonment, and she sent a sapphire ring to her kinsman John Hamilton just before her execution in 1587.[15]

It was perhaps coincidence that the rings employed as silent messengers of the deaths of the two queens were both sapphires, but the attributes of the sapphire as described in lapidary lore were appropriate: sapphire rules and accords those in strife, helps make peace, brings men out of prison, puts away envy, emboldens, and makes the heart steadfast in good (Heth 69ᵛ). Residual belief in the virtues of stones accounts for the practice, often observed on Elizabethan portraits, of wearing a ring on a ribbon under the clothing in order to bring the stone into intimate contact with the body (Oman, *British Rings* 9n.). In the reverent tone of litany, the broadside "Eliza *Trivmphans*" (London, 1597) catalogs the jewels worn by Elizabeth on her Accession Day. Certain evidence of belief in the prophylactic powers of stones appears in a letter sent by Christopher Hatton to Thomas Heneage (September 11, 158[0]) in which he explains his enclosed gift for the queen of a ring "which hath the virtue to expel infectious airs, and is, as is telled to me, to be wearen betwixt the sweet dugs,—the chaste nest of most pure constancy" (Nicolas 155–56). Hatton is exploiting the talismanic associations with stones and at the same time suggesting a metonymic role for the ring.

Hatton's letter, like the rest of his correspondence to or about the queen, characteristically expresses devotion verging on idolatry in language verging on impertinence, or so it seems to the modern eye. Hatton's assumption of intimacy, however, is only an extreme instance—and not the most extreme, which would have to be Essex's—of the fictively erotic courtly discourse that the queen encouraged through her nicknames and her favors. It was a discourse conducted largely through the vehicle of silent language: the courtier's metonymic ring could be placed where his hand dared not venture; the jewel could convey an apology for which words were inadequate. For the queen's part, the acceptance of a gift could convey ambivalent receptivity without the binding constraint of her word, and if she rejected a gift, words were unnecessary.

Gifts, on the other hand, were necessary as part of the exchange of prestation, and their costliness was a requisite part of the unspoken contract. No exchange better illustrates the poisonous element in the Greek origins of the word *gift* than the burden that was entailed for the courtly giver, a burden that Elizabeth was free to deny in return.[16] The manuscript *Certain Observations concerning the Life and Raigne of Elizabeth Queen of England,* written in the year of her death, explains the power of the unspoken obligation of prestation: "She was very rich in Jewells, which had been given her by her subjects; for in times of Progress there was no person that entertained her in his house, but (besides his extraordinary charge in feasting her and her train) he bestowed a Jewel upon her; a custom in former times began by some of her special favourites that (having in great measure tasted of her bounty) did give her only of her own; though, otherwise, that kind of giving was not so pleasing to gentlemen of meaner quality" (Ellis *Letters* 2nd ser. 3:192). Lawrence Stone notes that these gifts were costly, and that they grew increasingly so as the queen aged. At least £100 had to be expended, and many jewels cost much more, like Lord North's £120 in 1577, Sir John Thynne's £140 in 1574, Lord Keeper Puckering's £400 nosegay of diamonds in 1595, or Sir Thomas Egerton's £1000 jewel in 1602.[17]

In his *Journal,* the French ambassador de Maisse names Essex as having instituted an expensive gift as part of the hospitality offered to the queen on progress, which custom then expanded to numerous other occasions as well so that finally if courtiers "cannot give her anything else, she gladly takes a dozen angels" (14). Leicester's will specifies his last gift of jewels to the queen, and the description indicates the lavishness of this bequest. It is a "fair large Table Diamond in the Middest" of three great emeralds, surrounded by many diamonds, and a rope of six hundred pearls to hang the jewel (Collins, *Letters* 1:71). He had intended to present it to the queen when she would visit Wanstead. That he calls this a "token" conveys more effectively than any commentary both a subliminal awareness of prestation as market exchange and the price of remembrance in the silent currency of jewels. In the more common currency of courtship, a gift "token" frequently entailed legally binding promise or contract of marriage.[18] So favors were elicited, fealty was offered, contracts were enacted in the shape of the ring.

These obligatory gifts often figured personal reminders of the giver. When Leicester offered Elizabeth a fan of white feathers set in a gold handle with emeralds, diamonds, and rubies for New Year's Day in 1574 (another obligatory gift-giving occasion), she found each side decorated with a white bear and two hanging pearls, and a rampant lion with another bear, muzzled, at its foot by way of decorous reminder of the giver of the gift and his dedication, for Dudley's device was the bear and ragged staff. The gift is duly recorded as weighing altogether sixteen ounces. When, in 1575 at Kenilworth, he gave her the costliest of entertainments, he presented her with gifts marked with the bear and ragged staff. In addition to many other gifts, including some silver bowls, he also presented her with a set of his silver ragged staves supporting armor from Mars—and, of course, Leicester (Nichols 1:380, 432). Other courtiers also used their New Year's gifts to the queen to commemorate themselves as well as their sovereign. For the 1581 New Year, Philip Sidney gave a tiny, jeweled, gold whip, often regarded as a token of his wordless submission after suffering the queen's displeasure. In that same year, Sir Henry Lee, the queen's champion at tilt, gave her a jewel in the form of a golden lance. Two years later, Sir Christopher Hatton presented a jeweled headdress full of complicated knots, his personal device (2:301; 397).

The jeweled gifts presented on progress often bore a thematic relevance to the motif of the dramatic presentations staged for the amusement of the queen; Leicester's gift of armor from Mars, for instance, figured in a complex mythological scheme that unfolded over several days. On a smaller scale, the Norrises managed to program a series of gifts of jewels so that, when the queen visited Rycote in 1592, the gems reminded the queen of Norris family members absent on service to the queen: a gold dart, an Irish throwing weapon set with diamonds and the motto in Irish, "I flye onely for my soveraigne"; from Flanders, a golden key of Ostend set with diamonds and the motto in Dutch, "I onelie open to you"; a golden sword set with diamonds and rubies and the motto, in French, "Drawen onelie in your defence"; a truncheon set with diamonds and the motto, in Spanish, "I do not commaunde but under you" (*Entertainments* 48–49). During the Anjou courtship, jewels in the shape of a frog, recalling Elizabeth's nickname for her suitor, were popular presents, but literary allegories recalled the predatory nature of the creature by way of indirect protest against the prospective match (Doran 168–70).

Courtiers gave in accord with a principle sententiously expressed by Shakespeare:

> Win her with gifts, if she respect not words:
> Dumb jewels often in their silent kind
> More than quick words do move a woman's mind.
> (*The Two Gentlemen of Verona* 3.1.89–91)

Was the queen moved? Did she remember? Gifts at court did not always motivate reciprocation, as Thomas Churchyard learned to his bitter sorrow. If he proposed, "A dulled horse that will not sturre, / Must be remembred with a spurre," he also regretted that his gifts to courtiers were fruitless, "nothyng did retourne to me, / That I could either feele or se," as he lamented in his valedictory "Churchyardes farewell from the Courte, the seconde yeare of the Queenes Maiesties raigne" (*A light Bondell* C.ij[r]).

Sometimes, sometimes immediately, the queen did remember, as when she reciprocated her New Year's golden gifts with awards of silver plate, but under other circumstances erratically, and in general as cheaply as possible in accord with what Frank Whigham perceptively names the queen's "quantitative linearity."[19] The exchange is meticulously recorded for the New Year of 1579, and it graphically illustrates the quantitative measure of prestation, for the incoming gifts to the queen are registered by monetary worth where appropriate (many were outright gifts of gold), and the outgoing gifts of plate to the givers are listed by weight (Nichols, *Progresses* 2:249–72). Whether, over a lifetime, the exchange was even is incalculable, granted the shifting standard of measure, but the queen's well-known parsimony would suggest that it was not. Leicester, for example, whose will describes Elizabeth as having been "most bountiful" to him, explains he has "lived always above any Living I had" and he apologizes for the smallness of his bequests because "for my hard and broken Estate, being I know not how many Thousand, above Twenty in Debt; and, at this present, not having in the World five hundreth Pounds towards it" (Collins, *Letters* 1:70–71; 74). Actually, Leicester underestimated his indebtedness by nearly 100 percent. In 1590, a probate inventory of his goods was conducted during proceedings to seize Leicester House in payment of the debt that he owed to the queen at his death, a sum of £35,087.[20] Leicester was extravagant, but so, too, were the imperatives of prestation, and even at £35,087, his outstanding debt to the Crown was not the largest: Sir Christopher Hatton, whose favors from the queen were exceptionally large, died owing the Crown about £42,000, but Leicester's case illustrates the dynamics of the round of the system and the price of being caught in its loop.[21] The outward glitter of inward magnificence was all gold, and it cost the courtier a pretty pound. For some courtiers who found themselves shortchanged by the queen, on the one hand, on the other enjoyed gifts of plate weighing in from hopeful or grateful petitioners. Burghley's collection of plate was worth almost £15,000, but even so, it was worth only one-tenth of the value of Wolsey's hoard at Hampton Court.[22]

Apart from plate, the most common gift of the queen's role in tangible prestation was the gold chain, which was popular in England under Henry VII and may have derived from Italian fashion (Evans, *A History of Jewellry* 98). John Ferne lists the "engines of Knighthood by the sword" as the gold ring, gilded spurs, and the gold chain (*Blazon of Gentrie* H.vii^v^). The queen's New Year's gift to Sir Christopher Hatton in 1588/89 shows her occasionally extravagant favor: he received four hundred ounces in plate. Later in the same year, her gifts of a number of gold chains were sometimes very weighty pieces (Nichols 3:15; 23). One wonders how the honored recipient, thus necklaced, bore his honor, yet bear up he did, as is evident on many an Elizabethan portrait and in many an Elizabethan document. Foreign visitors observed that the chains of the mayor, lord chancellor, and the lord treasurer hung down as far as their girdles or saddles, both back and front.[23]

The careful weighing of chains is one indication of their potential usefulness as capital; the ultimate disposition of some of them may be indicated again in the 1588/89 list that records Elizabeth's order that two collars of esses (i.e., linked *Ss*) be delivered to the jeweler to be made into buttons for her use, and in 1600, short of funds, the Crown both seized some of Sir Francis Knollys's plate and money that had been left in the charge of the Exchequer and planned to sell off its own out-of-style holdings in plate.[24]

Not only were chains valuable as capital and as recyclable precious metal, they were also visible signs of favor, public position, and social status. The collar of esses was a special dignity: the lord mayor's was a gift to the aldermen during the reign of Henry VIII, at which time it was ruled that no one under the rank of knight might wear any gold collar of esses, and efforts to restrict the use even of enameled chains through sumptuary regulation continued in the reign of Elizabeth.[25] Chains were part of the official insignia of honorary orders like the Garter and St. Michael's—Segar specifies that the Garter collar is to be made of garters and knots, enameled with white and red roses, weighing thirty troy ounces and garnished with precious stones (*Honor Military* F3^r^). Chains were also an honorific gift to visiting dignitaries. Sir Nicholas Throgmorton, for instance, urged Dudley to move the queen to send a chain of four or five hundred crowns to the envoy of the duke of Savoy, to whom she had neglected to make a gift upon his recent visit (Wright, *Elizabeth* 1:59). A French ambassador noted that because the Dutch ambassador had flattered her beauty, Elizabeth awarded him a chain twice as valuable as those given others (Aubrey, *Memoires* 256).

Many a contemporary observer calculates the display of magnificent chains worn by nobles and gentlemen on public occasions. Thus the recorder of Elizabeth's entertainment at Elvetham in 1591 describes how the earl of Hertford rode out to meet the queen with a train of more than two hundred men, most of them wearing gold chains around their necks, and Churchyard tallies three hundred in a similar procession that met her at Suffolk.[26] Like the velvet coat, the chain represented the man: Chamberlain says that the lord mayor prepared to meet the queen for her Accession Day in 1602 "with his troupes of 500 velvet coates and chaines of gold" (1:171–72). When the queen died the following year, the ceremonial delivery of the official proclamation on parchment, slipped under the city gate, was accompanied by the collar of esses of the lord treasurer (Handover, *The Second Cecil* 297).

The implicit obligation that accompanied the gift of a chain engendered the antique topos of golden fetters that inspired many Renaissance moralists, such as Alciati and Thomas More (Simonds, *Myth* 172–73). The high visibility and symbolic significance of chains made them a prominent target for social criticism. The deference accorded to chains provoked a sarcastic passage in the work already mentioned in chapter 3, *A Pleasaunt Dialogn[sic]e or disputation betweene the Cap, and the Head* (London, 1565), wherein Cap questions Head's bow to a man passing by who is wearing "a fayre chayne." Because the passer-by is unknown to Head, Cap triumphantly concludes Head is bowing to the chain (B.iiij^r–iiij^v). Cap's may have been a capital hit against Head, but his target is precisely the point of material honors, so a campaign against display is a cause lost from its inception. Yet even rightful wearers of the chain parodied its cachet. One of the articles of the Order of the Knighthood that was jokingly presented at the Prince of Purpoole Christmastide entertainment at the Inns of Court in 1594 prohibited any knight of the order to pawn his collar for a hundred pounds, with the corollary provision that anyone who should retain the collar for the same price would then be a knight "by reason of a secret Vertue in the Collar" because "the Knighthood followeth the Collar, and not the Collar the Knighthood" (*Gesta Grayorum* 42).

Like gold chains, gifts of silver, too, might be recycled through the chain of prestation. Silver, like gold, might be bartered, and it served always as exhibit of one's status. So prized was a collection of plate that Roger Ascham addressed a letter to Cicero, who had singled out the absence in Britain of silver artifacts along with learning and letters as evidence of its barbarity, so Ascham exulted that now there was more "comely plate in one city of England than is in four of the proudest cities in all Italy, and take Rome for one of them" (Ascham, *The Schoolmaster* 150). Some nobles had large collections; Henry Percy, ninth earl of Northumberland, reputedly had 931 pieces of silver plate and 532 of gilt from his wife's family (Batho, "Finances" 437). Elevation to public office, admission to a corporate body—this type of public occasion required of the party so honored a gift of silver, sometimes of a specific weight and design.[27] In his *Blazon of Gentrie*, Sir John Ferne rationalizes the laws restricting the use of precious serving utensils as a way of reserving honor to gentles (Fviii[r]), but to little apparent effect, for wills of the middle class often make bequests of silver. In 1553, nearly one-tenth of the estate of an Oxford plumber was invested in plate, and a Litchfield baker who died in 1570 left two dozen silver spoons, a salt, a goblet, and a silver mounted goblet (*The Elizabethan Midlands* 12). The salt was, to all appearances, the most prestigious item. Harrison observes that formerly, if there were four pieces of pewter in "a good farmer's house," one would be a salt (*Description* 201). One foreign visitor commented that it was a bad farmer indeed who had no silver cups, spoons, and salts (Klarwill, *Queen Elizabeth* 342). William Harrison uses the increase in silverware as one of his main indices to the growing wealth of England, and his reference to the cupboards of plate in farmers' houses recalls the original purpose and appearance of a cupboard: boards were mounted to display cups and other silver service (*Description* 128). The cupboards of the wealthy required many "stages" or shelves—as many as ten on royal cupboards, the number diminishing along with reduction in rank: seven and a half for a duke, five for a marquise, three for an earl.[28]

Although table service of treen, tin, or pewter might have served the needs of the lower class, gold, silver, or, surprisingly, glass signified the mead of the upper strata. Once again, Harrison supplies a sociological explanation: "It is a world to see in these our days, wherein gold and silver most aboundeth, how that our gentility, as loathing those metals (because of the plenty), do now generally choose rather the Venice glasses, both for our wine and beer, than any of those metals or stone wherein beforetime we have been accustomed to drink; but such is the nature of man generally that it most coveteth things difficult to be attained" (200). Some may have engraved their silver with *sententiae* in order to provoke thought or discussion about wise matters so that "some parte of tyme shall be saued, whiche els by superfluouse eatyng and drinkyng wolde be idely consumed," as Sir Thomas Elyot had recommended (*Gouernour* 1:25–26), but extant pieces of plate show intent less moralistic, particularly the extravagant salts made of silver. They are more in keeping with the spirit of Russell's injunction in *The Book of Nurture* to "emperialle" the noble cupboard with silver and "gild fulle gay."[29] Certainly it was this sense of the decorousness of fine plate as befitting to power that provoked Sir Thomas Smith's annoyance at the absence of the queen's plate that should have been accorded his state as ambassador in France, although his four-year prosecution of the case was excessive. It was also a matter of pride that, two years later, the French king presented him with a cupboard of silver plate, weighing, he wrote Elizabeth, 1,154 ounces.[30]

The salt was a large receptacle, usually made of highly ornamented silver if belonging to a noble household, where it stood on the high table. As the marker that delineated "above the salt" and "below the salt," it certainly savored of status, as well as seasoning. Cellini's famous piece is a most ornate example; Leicester's, a fantastic Elizabethan variation that signified Dudley's military ambitions as well as serving its functions as saltdish and table marker. The description of Leicester's salt in the Dudley papers at Longleat imparts a sense of its massiveness and ornateness, sounding like a Hollywood parody of itself: "A salt, ship fashion, of the mother-of-pearl, garnished with silver and divers works of warlike ensigns and ornaments, with sixteen pieces of ordnance, whereof two on wheels, two anchors on the fore part, and on the stern the image of Dame Fortune, standing on a globe, with a flag in her hand" (quoted in Wilson, *Sweet Robin* 80). Colonna's *Hypnerotomachia*, a work widely circulated in England, fantasizes the uttermost excess of precious table service, including a bejeweled wheeled cupboard "in fashion like vnto a shippe, and the rest like to a triumphant Chariot," in a description that runs on for more than fourteen pages in the English translation of 1592 (P2ʳ–R2ʳ).

Leicester's salt and Colonna's surreal fantasy may be extreme examples of the type, but Tudor table service made of silver often displays very elaborate decorative motifs. The Gibbon Salt, which belongs to the Goldsmiths' Company, gestures toward antiquity by representing Neptune within a pillar of rock crystal so that he seems to be under water; the silversmith surrounds him with columns in the middle of each side in an Elizabethan adaptation of the classical orders.[31] The Vintners' Company Salt, made in 1569, is decorated with flowers and other natural forms, but also with panels representing the cardinal virtues, a moralistic inspiration that Thomas Elyot might have approved. The Vyvyan Salt would also have pleased him: it is faced with panels of foil and glass that represent three of the Nine Worthies and prudential devices cautioning against overindulgence.

Cups, too, when intended for ceremonial use, were made of highly decorated, massy silver. On stately occasions, the ceremonial cup would be awarded to the presiding servant of the queen; traditionally at the coronation banquet, it was given to the lord mayor of London after he served her (*A Collection of Ordinances* 123). Many Tudor examples of such cups, like their Italian prototypes, are fashioned in extravagant forms and embellished with animal, marine, and floral decorations. One purpose of ceremony is to isolate a segment of experience and to call attention to it by extending time and enhancing process. Much of the regalia and accoutrements proper to ceremony serves this function through physical properties that retard rapid or thoughtless gesture and compel redefinition of the use of the artifact. This can be achieved through, for example, massive structure, cumbersome weight, or delicacy of design. The heavy, often top-heavy form, balanced upon a stem that is knobbed so that it can be grasped at all, so large as to require cautious decanting or fastidious sipping, forces the focus of attention upon the ceremonial purpose of drinking rather than its pleasurable or practical aspect. The Glynne Cup is the epitome of the ceremonial type, so ingeniously shaped as to be difficult to use, but of particular relevance to the study of shape as silent language during the Elizabethan period, for the cup is elaborately formed as the pelican in her piety. She is plucking her breast to feed her young with her own blood, as in bestiary lore and in the Christian iconography appropriated by Elizabeth in order to emblematize her devotion to her subjects.[32] The cup is a monument to the union of useful and ceremonial, carnal and spiritual, secular and Christian, of display and devotion. It is the special virtue of magnificence to make a show of harmonizing polarities.

Liturgical vessels carried a particularly weighty significance. Eamon Duffy remarks that a "staggering list of objects" were traditionally required of the laity for medieval daily religious observances, and the objects, from the chalices to the walls of the graveyard, visibly bore their history. The name of the donor engraved on the cup ensured that, when the priest elevated the eucharistic wine, the remembrance, too, would be raised; the donated tabernacle, the inscribed book, vestment, or tomb—all these inscribed the memory of the giver. Little wonder, then, that the Reformation sought to banish, erase, or convert these religious objects from the memory of later generations. Elizabeth, conscious of the symbolical power of form, decreed that all chalices were to be beaker-shaped, a form that made it difficult to celebrate the old rite of the Mass. The font, or stoup for holy water, became a trough for swine, priestly vestments were unstitched and recycled, pyxes became counterbalances on scales—a measure for a more secular culture.[33]

Plate also served more mundane purposes. Those who paid debts and taxes often had to use their plate as currency, from the Hostess in the second part of *Henry IV* (2.1.140–42) to Peregrine Lord Willoughby and the earl of Shrewsbury, because of what today might be called problems with cash flow on a national scale.[34] Royal plate was mainly used for display, as foreign observers often noted. In 1578, Bernardino de Mendoza reported Elizabeth's displeasure at the paucity of royal plate on view during a feast given for Alençon's ambassador and the consequent bitter dispute between Sussex and North regarding the matter.[35] Lupold von Wedel describes how, in November 1584, he and other visitors to an exhibition of silver and gold plate in the Tower were allowed to touch some huge vessels, including one set with two hundred large diamonds on the cover alone, as well as countless more, and a highly ornamented salt "valued at one ton of gold" (Klarwill, *Queen Elizabeth* 330). The visitors' awe registers the effect desired. Philippa Glanville quotes Henrician documents indicating that the nonuse of silver on display enhanced the distinction of the host—a demonstration of conspicuous nonconsumption (286). That even the sovereign might have rented the glitter on show indicates a deep division between superficial impression and substantial fact. Then, too, the monarch might find practical use off-stage for precious metal. Much of the royal plate and metal was consigned to the mint during the reign of Elizabeth, one lot being sent for recycling as service utensils for Alençon's envoys in 1581, possibly as tardy recompense for the niggardliness of service three years earlier. Highly prized collars of esses and knots of gold with enameled roses were made into buttons. Even the first Great Seal (at some point after being superseded by Hilliard's design for the second in the series) was transmogrified into two silver jugs, and by 1600 many religious objects were recycled as well (*Jewels and Plate* 24; 67; 586–87). Transformation of shape followed change in values, the new form often debasing an older one intended as permanent manifestation of honor.

If the precious metals of highly honorific symbols could be impressed into lowly service, so, too, could the lowly metals of the coin of the realm be new-minted to mimic their betters. Secret and highly profitable debasing of the currency had taken place repeatedly during the reigns of earlier Tudors, and English currency was falling into disrepute on the international market. In 1560/61, Elizabeth recalled debased coins, largely at the instigation of banker Sir Thomas Gresham (who, as mentioned above, would later build the Royal Exchange). By stabilizing the currency, the recall immediately benefited at least Gresham, the Crown, financiers, and merchants, but throughout the reign of Elizabeth a shortage of coin moved merchants to paper exchange at the upper end of the market, and to the use of lead tokens at the lower end among those who profited less from revaluation.[36] If professional traders could distinguish between a debased coin and one of higher standard, others could not, so when the government revalued coins according to actual silver content, they had to be stamped in order for the distinction to be made clear to those who depended upon direct correspondence between shape and substance with word or image. William Heth is explicit on the need for literal stamp upon precious substance in order to render it current in popular usage. He describes the making of the gold or silver ingot, perfected only "by the stroke of the stampe which imprinteth vpon it the figure by the prince commanded by which is it easely knowen and wtout it cannot be properly called money till by the printe it be brought to the trewe forme."[37] Substance, shape, and sign—the trinity mutually validate.

Elizabethans were well aware of the symbolic uses of coin. The entertainment of 1594 for Elizabeth by the Inns of Court lists the ways for a prince to render magnificence visible, and high on the list is the advice that "your Coin be stamped with your own Image; so in every part of your State there may be somewhat new; which, by Continuance, may make the Founder and Author remembred."[38] Coins by definition are a medium designed for circulation, and hence also naturally suited for broadcasting iconographic changes or refinements. With the issuance of new coins, Elizabeth seized the opportunity to improve her portrait and to circulate the devices with which she is associated in the decorative arts, as well as on paintings and engravings. The words *Rosa Sine Spina* appear on her hammered silvered coins from 1561 throughout her reign; devices of the ermine and the eglantine appear throughout the 1570s; and the 1582/84 issue of the rose noble updates the traditional image of the monarch in a medieval ship by placing Elizabeth aboard a sixteenth-century galleon embossed with a Tudor rose. Earliest circulation of these coins would have called attention to themselves with these changes, but eventually they would have passed unnoticed. In the long run, Elizabeth's reformation of the currency was regarded favorably. Maurice Kyffin's *Blessednes of Brytaine* (London, 1588) singles out for praise her institution of "*perfect Gold, and pured Siluer cleane / Which passe for comon Coynes, her Realms throughout*," and asks, "*When was this Realme so rich of glittring* Gold, / Of plated Siluer, pearle, *and* precious stones?" (A4ʳ–4ᵛ).

Precious metals were also used in the chains and badges that were worn by servants. These heraldic labels differentiated the house that one served as well as one's own status among the hierarchy of servants: knights wore their badges around their necks or on livery chains, lesser servants wearing them on their caps, sleeves, or backs. This display demonstrated the extent and the power of the forces that supported a lord in return for maintenance and protection under the system of bastard feudalism.[39] Badges, if made of lead, also branded one's official status as a convict or an official beggar, the base metal substantiating the debased status of the wearer (Beier, *Masterless Men* 154). Medals and seals are less subject than coins to inattentive habituation in handling; they are occasional; they are less conventional; they are less widely circulated. During the controversy over iconoclasm, the dispute between Bishop Gardiner and Lord Protector Somerset regarding the Saint George on the Great Seal had illustrated the power of the imagery of sign and seal to focus debate. On the one hand, Gardiner's allusion to the "St. George" on the seal echoed common usage, but on the other, as Somerset was quick to point out, this was a misperception of what was in fact the image of the king on horseback, as the inscription on the seal clearly labeled it. Somerset argued that Gardiner's confusion was evidence of the dangerous nature of images and cause for the need for vigilance over them on the part of the authorities in order to distinguish false from true (Foxe, *Monuments* 6:26–30). Spenser would later exploit all sides of the argument in his use both of the identification between the monarch and Saint George as well as of the ambivalent nature of images in the first book of his *Faerie Queene*, in many respects itself a fictive embodiment of the iconoclastic dispute.

The Great Seal was the most important of all seals because it certified all important state documents. It was kept by the lord chancellor, and its importance in defining and dignifying his office explains Cardinal Wolsey's historic reluctance to surrender it when he was toppling from power, as is dramatized in *Henry VIII* by Shakespeare and Fletcher (3.2.228–349). Elizabeth's first Great Seal (1559) comforted her subjects by repeating the familiar general pattern of her predecessor Mary's and by continuing the image of the crowned monarch, but it was also stamped with Elizabethan difference: the obverse improved the spacing of the earlier composition, and, more significantly, the reverse introduced both the motif of the Tudor rose and the Protestant motto PVLCHRUM PRO PATRIA PATI.[40] Her second Great Seal (1584–86) made more important departures from all preceding great seals, because here the traditional images of the monarch, both enthroned on the obverse and on horseback on the reverse, are enhanced by the imprint of the divine. Heavenly hands support the queen's mantle on the obverse, and other-worldly clouds and rays halo her head on the reverse, giving official circulation to the mythology of the fairy queen.[41] After the death of Chancellor Thomas Bromley in 1587, Elizabeth gave the seal to "young" Sir Christopher Hatton, then in his late thirties, causing what an early historian of the seals calls "the universal amazement." She also allowed Nicholas Bacon to keep the seal of dignity after his resignation from the chancellorship, an honor that Bacon sought to perpetuate by having a cup made of the seal with an inscription that it was intended as an "Heyrloome to his house of Stewkey" (Bloom, *English Seals* 43; 85).

Coins and medals that supported and extended Elizabethan iconography also carried topical relevance. Elizabeth is represented as Venus on two medals that had special political implications. On a medal representing Philip de Marnix (1580), the reverse pictures Venus in a swan-car, crowning a soldier on horseback, read as the duke of Anjou in a symbolic expression of the belief that Elizabeth would marry Anjou and come to the aid of the United Provinces against the Spanish (fig. 24; also, Hawkins, *Medallic Illustrations* I: no. 84). On a counter struck in Hainault, Elizabeth as Venus is represented restraining Philip II as Mars, an image expressing the Roman Catholic hope that Elizabeth's mediation would forestall attack by Philip (fig. 25; also, Hawkins I: no. 104). Also related to the campaign in the United Provinces is a counter that represents on the obverse Elizabeth distributing the divine favor of nectared roses to two deputies from the United Provinces (MACTE . ANIMI . ROSA . NECTARE . IMBVTA: Take courage, the rose is imbued with nectar); on the reverse, two Spaniards eat hay from a manger, with the motto, SPRETA . AMBROSIA . VESCITOR [sic]: Despising ambrosia he feeds upon hay (fig. 26; also, Hawkins I: no. 86).

The Spanish invasion and the English response triggered a silent campaign of coins, medals, and counters. One medal, pictorial reminder of the part played by religious opposition, represents Elizabeth trampling on a hydra, or the Beast of the Apocalypse, and Leicester interceding for five provinces, here personified as five naked boys bearing appropriate shields. The reverse pictures the pope and other ecclesiastics falling from heaven (fig. 27; also, Hawkins I: no. 99). Many medals register the controversy with which Leicester's role was surrounded. By picturing two proverbial emblematic devices on a silver counter, the Belgians represented their fear that they had surrendered too much power to an untrustworthy Leicester: on the obverse, a Belgian, frightened by Spanish smoke, falls into Leicester's fire; on the reverse, a Belgian ape smothers its offspring, liberty, through being oversolicitous (Hawkins I: no. 95). Suspected in England, too, of excessive ambition, Leicester was recalled by a furious queen and was obliged to confront her displeased council. He, in turn, pressed a medal into service in his own behalf (I: no. 100). Camden describes it and, at the end, pithily sums up the role of metal in the battle:

> At his Departure he privately distributed amongst some whom he had drawn to his Faction certain Medals or Tokens made in Gold, on the one side whereof was his own Picture; and on the other side a Flock of Sheep, some Sheep straying, and a Dog ready to goe away looking back behind him. Near the Dog was, *Invitus desero*, that is, Unwillingly I forsake, and near the Sheep, *non gregem, sed ingratos*, that is, not the Flock, but the Unthankfull. And no doubt but he had it in his Head to usurp the Government. But these People have by their Policy and Wisedom not onely retained their ancient Freedom, against both the Power of the Spaniards, who have the Knack also to fight with Gold and other Arts [but also the wiles of the French, the English, and the Prince of Orange]. (*Elizabeth* 304)

Medals were used not only as a vehicle "to fight with Gold," however. The most famous of the medals associated with Elizabeth are celebratory in nature, and many of these appropriate religious images to the queen. The medal commemorating her recovery from smallpox in 1572 adapts the emblematic device of a hand shaking a serpent into the fire, as Saint Paul did after shipwreck, a biblical allusion (Rom. 8.31) strengthened by the accompanying motto, SI DEVS . NOBISCBVM . QVIS . CONTRA . NOS: If God be with us, who can be against us? (fig. 28; also, Hawkins 1: no. 48). The Phoenix Badge interests for a number of reasons as an adaptation of another device familiar from mythology and often used in allusion to Christ. Hawkins, noting Elizabeth's relatively plain costume, comments that she issued a sumptuary proclamation in 1574, the date on the reverse. He also infers from the legends some fear for the life of the queen. The motto on the obverse carries added resonance for the study of Elizabethan aesthetics: +HEI MIHI QVOD TANTO VIRTUS PERVFSA DECORE. NON HABET ETERNOS INVIOLATE DIES.: Alas! that virtue endued with so much beauty, should not uninjured enjoy perpetual life (fig. 29; also, Hawkins 1: no. 70). The line is from Walter Haddon's *Poemata* (P.2ʳ), and the word *decore* inscribes through its association with *decor-decorum-decoration*—that union of ethics and aesthetics that ideally substantiates Elizabethan decorative arts.[42]

Medals were made more useful as objects of display when mass-produced in less expensive materials and fitted for suspension as pendants. As Strong points out, this widened their distribution to include those unlikely to have access to the more costly prototypes and so proved a useful vehicle for propagation of the mythology of the Virgin Queen (123). The *Dangers Averted* (fig. 30; 1589) pendant may have referred to the execution of Mary Stuart, the defeat of the Spanish Armada, or other past political threats. The image of the queen on the obverse is encircled by the motto, DITIOR . IN . TOTO . NON . ALTER . CIRCVLVS . ORBE: No other circle in the world more rich. The motto may play upon both the orb that the queen holds and the circle formed by the motto surrounding her. The reverse pictures the device of a bay tree on an island, two distant ships, and a motto based upon herbal lore regarding the bay tree as impervious to lightning, NON . IPSA . PERICVLA . TANGVNT: Not even dangers affect it.[43] A medal more specifically referring to the defeat of the Armada was struck in Holland in 1589. The obverse shows Elizabeth seated in a triumphal car, as on her historic procession to Saint Paul's after the defeat of the Armada. She holds a palm branch and an opened prayer book inscribed in Dutch with the beginning of the Our Father (fig. 31; Hawkins 1: no. 128). Like so much of Elizabeth's iconography, the medal combines seemingly incompatible elements, incorporating the imagery of both Christian thanksgiving and pagan triumph, thus impressing in miniature the fusion of Christian and Renaissance cultures. The defeat of the Armada was the most triumphant and the most memorable event during the reign of Elizabeth. Four hundred years later, the event was still vivid enough to generate numerous memorial services, publications, and exhibitions that included the extant medals struck at the time of the first celebration of the English victory, evidence not only of the power of the event, but also of the power of the associated imagery to shape perception and memory of the event.[44]

Because shape and substance were significant together, and because metallic artifacts were both durable and widely circulated, coins and medals weighed heavily in silent discourse, but other media, less durable, less visible, or less widely circulated, could nonetheless be shaped as language. The most ephemeral of substances so pressed into service was foodstuff. The material substance lacked inherent value, and its perishability further limited its viability, but its malleability rendered it an expressive medium, and presentation within the context of ceremonious magnificence enhanced its part in the silent rhetoric of occasion. Graded for quality, bread and salt respectively supported and savored social distinction, and, granted the portentous symbols associated with bread, it also served as a vehicle for ethical imperatives. The author of *A Restitvtion of Decayed Intelligence*, Richard Verstegan, for instance, sets out his etymology for names of various social degrees. The word *hlaf* or *laf*, he says, originally referred not just to the shape of bread but to its very substance:

> Now was it vsuall in long foregoing ages, that such as were endued with great welth and meanes aboue others, were chiefly renowmed . . . for their howskeeping, and good hospitallitie, that is, for beeing able and vsing to feed and sustaine many men, and therefore were they particularly honored with the name and tytle of **hlaford** which is asmuch to say, as *An afoorder of laf*, that is, *A bread-giuer*. . . .
>
> And yf wee duely obserue it, wee shal fynd that our nobillitie of *England,* which generally do beare the name of **Lord** haue alwayes, and as it were of a successiue custome (rightly according vnto that honorable name) maintained and fed more people, to wit, of their seruants, retayners, dependants, tenants, as also the poor, then the nobillitie of any countrie in the continent, which surely is a thing very honorable, and lawdable; and moste wel befitting noblemen, and right noble mynds. (Rr2ᵛ–3ʳ)

From *leafdian* (i.e., bread-server), Verstegan derives the name *lady*: "Whereby it appeereth that as the **Laford** did allow food and sustenance, so the **Leafdian** did see it serued and disposed to the guests," which custom of ladies carving and serving continues to the present (Rr3ᵛ). Thus does Verstegan connect food with noblesse oblige. Thus, too, does Verstegan rationalize the social division of labor according to gender: man provides and woman serves. Mythographers might detect here a variation upon the most ancient Western myth that explains the division of labor according to gender as having resulted from woman's act of serving food: "She took of the fruit thereof, and did eat, and gave also unto her husband with her; and he did eat" (Gen. 3.6). Both instances convey that terrible power of myth to figure reality, in particular here the engendering of role and caste. Bread was the staff of life, and the process of its dispensation outlined the staffing of all walks of life according to degree. The title page of Gervase Markham's *English Hus-wife* assumes as an ethical imperative the association between food and gender for the middle-class woman: *The English Hus-wife, Contayning, The inward and outward vertues which ought to be in a compleat woman. As, her skill in Physicke, Cookery, Banqueting-stuffe, Distillation, Perfumes, Wooll, Hemp, Flax, Dayries, Brewing, Baking, and all other things belonging to an Houshould. A Worke very profitable and necessarie, gathered for the generall good of this kingdome.* If the obligation of the noble lady, the leafdian, is to serve the lord's bread, the obligation of the housewife is to bake it. A letter from Lord Herbert to his father-in-wardship Sir George More in 1602 explicates the significance of the shape of a loaf from Shrewsbury that he sends as a gift; moreover, he nicely articulates the relationship between form and substance in terms that, from the Elizabethan point of view, illuminate many symbolic associations between shape and substance: "Measure not my love by substance of it, wch is brittle; but by the forme of it, wch is circular, and *circulus* you knowe is *capacissima figura*, to w'ch that mind ought to bee like, that can most worthily love you. Yet I would not have you to understand forme so as though it were hereby *formall*; but, as *forma dat esse*, so my love and observance to be *essentiall*" (*Loseley Manuscripts* 354–55).

Herbert's reverent attitude toward bread may be a secular echo of religious sacrament, but if the shape of bread could signify prestige, love, and unity, it could also symbolize religious division, and one of Elizabeth's earliest proclamations aimed to settle this as well as other religious controversies. The proclamation of 1559, *Announcing Injunctions for Religion*, orders that communion bread is to be made of the same "common fine bread, for the more reverence" as it was during the time of Edward VI, and that it "be made and formed plain without any figure thereupon, of the same fineness and fashion round, though somewhat bigger in compass and thickness as the usual bread and wafer, heretofore named singing cakes, which served for the use of the private Mass." Compromise is hinted through reference to Roman Catholic ritual; difference is established through slight change in shape and in plainness of surface. This injunction further differentiates Elizabethan observance from all other, as is indicated by a modern editorial note that in this long proclamation of fifty-three injunctions, this was one of two that were outstanding because they countered the rubrics prescribed in the Book of Common Prayer (*Tudor Proclamations* 1:131).

Other foodstuffs lent themselves to more fantastic forms and more profane intentions. Both the table service and the food itself might be shaped ingeniously, and sometimes to very specific purpose. Two banquets presented to Leicester when he was in the Netherlands on diplomatic mission illustrate this type of intention: food was shaped or served in such a way as to figure the Netherlandish appeal for Queen Elizabeth's support against the provinces. In Delft on Christmas Eve 1585, the feast highlighted a crystal castle on a pearl rock, surrounded by silver streams, fowl, fish, and beasts, "some hurt, some slaine, and some gasping for breath, on the top of which was a fair virgin lady leaning and giving her hands over the castell to succour them."[45] Animal forms shaped another wordless appeal to Elizabeth, from Utrecht in the following spring, when, to one side of the absent queen's trencher, heraldic beasts bore arms; on the other side lay fowls such as peacocks and swans "in their naturall feathers spread as in their greatest pride, which sight was both rare and magnificent" (Stow, *Annales* 717). The lion, king of beasts, lay couchant at her trencher in silent compliment to the supreme power of the Virgin Queen. Because hunger wonderfully concentrates attention on food, the program could not have passed unnoticed.

Under less urgent circumstances, food also served as more generalized compliment to the queen. Many accounts supply the staggeringly large figures for quantity and cost for food during visits from Elizabeth when on progress, but the description from the entertainment at Elvetham in 1591 is unusually specific about the food at one banquet. In Renaissance times, the term *banquet* generally referred to a light dessert; the one at Elvetham, however, comprised a thousand dishes, and the description lists the great variety of shapes executed in "sugar-worke." These included the queen's arms and those of all the nobility and a whole hierarchy of natural creation, including every species in the food chain from worms to humans, thus figuring the queen's command over all these lesser creatures (*Entertainments* 115; 165 n.95). The centerpiece of the banquet table usually featured the marchpanes, or sugarwork showpieces, such as, in 1562, the models of Saint Paul's Cathedral, a tower containing men and artillery, and a chessboard, each presented to Elizabeth by one of her servants.[46] Hugh Platt gives recipes for such confections whereby one can "*cast Rabbets, Pigeons, or any other little bird or beast, either from the life or carued molds,*" and one can heighten the artifice by dredging the figures with bread crumbs "so they wil seeme as if they were rosted and breaded. . . . By this meanes a banquet may be presented in the forme of a supper, beeing a verie rare and strange deuise" (*Delightes for Ladies* B3ᵛ–4ʳ). Ingenious subtleties that mimic in sugar other forms of foodstuffs, or that imitate at an Elizabethan banquet the more substantial courses of a dinner, and sometimes even disguise themselves as the very tableware—the whole conceit is an elaborate form of conspicuous consumption. The artifice is so highly contrived that it calls attention to itself instantaneously as a form of consumption, causing reflection upon the distinction between art and reality. It is the ultimate self-regarding, self-consuming artifact.[47] As the most necessary of material things as well as the most ephemeral, in a palindromic exchange between consumer and consumed, food consumed much time, energy, and effort to rationalize the significance of consumption.

Most other Elizabethan sculptural forms were more outer-directed, oriented toward posterity. The sculptural relief in the great house played a relatively private role in the overall scheme of decor, and was placed so as to be seen within the context of the larger whole in a manner to be considered later, together with other aspects of movement as a mode of silent communication. Tomb sculpture, on the other hand, the most prevalent sculptural form during an age with relatively few other types of sculpture in Britain, was designed to be appreciated by quite another viewing public and in quite another rhetorical mode of address.[48]

Tombs were designed to edify both the departed and the survivors, and so these monuments constituted yet another medium for magnificent display. They were paradoxically self-regarding of a self already consumed, and they counseled viewers with regard to their own end. A ghoulishly witty epitaph from the tomb of John Daye, printer, composed by his widow, who had been remarried to a man named Stone, puns upon the self-regarding aspect of contemporary tombs. It recounts the highlights of Daye's life as a printer, including marriage to two wives, the second of whom (the widow), "mourning longe for being left alone, / Set vpp this toombe, herself turned to a STONE" (Ravenshaw, *Antiente Epitaphes* 32). This epitaph is typically Elizabethan in its direct address to the reader with regard to both the achievements of the deceased and the anticipation of the death of the survivor. In such anticipation, many tombs were ordered long in advance of need by the prospective inhabitant, and detailed discussion often preceded actual construction of the monument. Lady Russell, for instance, writes to Sir William Dethick, garter king of arms, regarding her concern for the decorum of her funeral, concluding, "Good Mʳ Garter doe it exactly, for I finde forewarninges that bidde me provide a pickaxe." The elaborateness of her tomb testifies to the respect with which her remains were interred.[49]

Elizabethans were anxious that their tombs represent them decorously to posterity and that their monuments speak for them to those who followed.

Many monuments stylistically evoke the past, or rather, a selective past, whether a Gothic atavism representing a Roman Catholic, or a High Renaissance evocation of antiquity representing the aesthetics of a humanist. The Doric pilasters on the tomb of the brothers Hoby (Mann plate xxb) bear out the Italianate taste of Thomas, translator of Castiglione's *Book of the Courtier*. The particularized costume and casual ease of the reclining posture of the Hobys—an innovation that would be often imitated, as on Sir Henry Unton's monument (fig. 22)—bespeak values that are literally worlds apart from contempt for the flesh. Other-worldly orientation does appear on some tombs, often in the bifocal form of two representations of the deceased—on the upper level of the tomb as in life, and on the lower level as a skeleton. The Cecil monument concretizes the transition from medieval to Renaissance forms, combining the essentially northern medieval transi images of Cecil (in life and in skeletal death) with the Renaissance costume of the cardinal virtues that support him.[50]

Nigel Llewellyn's work on Elizabethan tombs has led him to conclude that a hierarchy of materials, size, and style conveys the sense of the degree of the deceased, and that tombs not only register status but create it.[51] The data confirm this observation; funeral monuments, themselves immobile, were sometimes used as substantial leverage for social advancement post mortem. Wills for members of the lower classes rarely mention any sort of monument: in three volumes of wills from Essex, Emmison reproduces only three that make provision for a stone monument. Camden's *Remains* explicitly endorses a decorum for funeral monuments: "[M]onuments answerable to mens worth, states, and places, have alwaies bene allowed, yet stately sepulchers for base fellowes have always lyen open to bitter jests" (319). John Weever lifted this passage verbatim in his *Ancient Fvnerall Monvments*, further prescribing that "[s]epulchres should bee made according to the qualitie and degree of the person deceased, that by the Tombe euery one might bee discerned of what ranke hee was liuing" (B5ᵛ). Of the media available, gilt bronze was reserved for tombs of royalty, if only because of its costliness, while other materials, arranged in descending order of status, included alabaster, marble, wood, and plaster. The contract for the tomb of Richard Kingsmill, drawn up by his son-in-law Sir Thomas Lucy, well illustrates this matter of material and status. Lucy specified three effigies to be executed: the figure of Lucy, the self-important patron, was to be made of good alabaster, the most prestigious of stones, whereas those of Kingsmill and his lady, the supposed chief subject of the monument, were to be carved of an inferior material.[52]

Size and style also assert the supposed importance of the resident of a tomb. All of the tombs discussed above are large, but the massive tomb of Sir Christopher Hatton, who died in 1591, was scandalously so, and a popular rhyme snickered, "Philip [Sidney] and Francis [Walsingham] have no tomb / For great Christopher takes up all the room" (Esdaile, *English Church Monuments* 47–48). Style is an index of status because the monument expresses the aesthetic refinement of the patron's taste in sculpture. Francis Willoughby, builder of Wollaton, concerned that the monument that he erected in 1591 to his father Henry should reflect Willoughby aspiration to gentility, contracted for stone carving of high quality from London, site of the better and more fashionable craft. Ornate and gilded, the monument aspires to the condition of magnificence, as did Sir Francis.[53] Style of costume worn by the image of the deceased also documents contemporary dress, in itself a sensitive barometer of status calibrated by efforts at sumptuary regulation. The sumptuous dress worn by the effigy of Elizabeth Willoughby, wife of Fulke Greville, with its elaborate display of red kirtle, petticoats, false sleeves, and a mantle of red trimmed in gold reflects her position as an extremely wealthy heiress. Moreover, the effigies of the daughters among her fourteen children are dressed like their mother. Ann Digby wears a similarly complicated dress and for jewelry wears three gilded chains around her neck, one bracelet on her left wrist and four on her right, and rings on all her fingers, two on some. Humphrey Peyto's will specified "a tomb of alabaster with two pictures made of alabaster for myself and my wyfe and pictures of all my children: my oone armes and the armes of the famyles." His wife's jewelry displays her worldly status: rings on the first, third, and fourth fingers of each hand, and no fewer than twelve chains around her neck.[54]

Sometimes costume signifies other than a taste for fashion and display. John Gage, for example, insisted that his two wives be represented in somewhat antiquated costume. He chided the engraver Gerard Johnson for designing a monumental brass that "sett owte my two wyves wth longe heare wyered," their gowns girdled, and their feet exposed. Gage ordered restoration of more old-fashioned costume.[55] His specifications may simply reflect conservative taste or religious constraints, but other monuments represent an antiquarian effort wordlessly to align one's self and family with tradition. Although their tomb dates to the latter half of the sixteenth century, Sir John Horshey and his son lie in Gothic armor on a chest, represented in a style imitating fifteenth-century alabaster. In a similarly anachronistic style, Sir Gawan Carew appears in mailed armor, his legs crossed in imitation of early fourteenth-century monuments. Sir Gabriel Poyntz built and reconstructed monuments of himself, his son, and six direct ancestors in order to create a petrified family tree rooted in the reign of Edward III. John Lord Lumley's revisionist project was the most ambitious antiquarian reconstruction: fourteen monuments imitative of earlier styles, arranged in chronological order, head-to-toe, in a revival of dead styles.[56]

Nor were the Elizabethans concerned only for their ancestry. Their descendants, too, were represented on the parents' monuments in dismaying numbers. Images of ten children appear on the Peyto monument; on the Greville monument, fourteen; and on the Parret brass, an astonishing nineteen. It is perhaps less astonishing that the inscription on the last indicates that Elizabeth Parret died in childbed.[57] So common was this cause of death that a monumental iconography evolved to signify it: typically, the representation of a woman lying in bed, a swaddled child lying nearby.[58] Both the appearance of children on monuments and the conventional representation of women dying in childbirth speak to the importance of family-as-posterity in Elizabethan society. Lawrence Humfrey cites approvingly the ancient Roman custom of displaying "formed shapes of ware" representing the images of men by their tombs, "So ateuery mans buriall, was prese[n]t all his race" as moral familial example (*Nobles* eii[r]).

The preeminent example of funeral monument as bond between past and posterity is the tomb of Elizabeth, completed under the command of James I. Maximilian Colt, the sculptor, repeats the forms that were used in the original ceremony. As Llewellyn puts it, "bier, effigy, *baldacchino*: truly, the monument is a permanent memorial of the funeral."[59] Monuments on this scale move into the dimensions of architecture, and they incorporate architectural forms and motifs. The recessed center opening, the arched roof, the banded pediment, the sculptural niches, and decorative obelisks on the Unton tomb on the left side of the *Memorial Portrait of Sir Henry Unton* (fig. 22) convey a sense of how the Elizabethan tomb presents itself as a great house manqué.

Three types of great houses are especially pertinent insofar as the shape of these buildings forms a significant motive, the expression of a concept or aspiration. Great houses historically express the magnificence of the great man who built them. Aristotle even regards the house as "a sort of public ornament" (*Nic. Ethics* 1123[a].5), but Elizabethans inflected their architectural language with a more specific rhetoric of which three examples illustrate three main types. Kenilworth Castle is notable as a monument to its medieval past and to Leicester's Elizabethan magnificence. The ruins of Kenilworth tell the story. Robert Dudley became owner of the site in 1563 and spent ten years renovating in preparation for his lavish entertainment of the queen, generally preserving the ancient buildings as he found them. He modernized only where required for greater comfort and elegance, building his aspirations for the future upon antique foundations. The stones of the demolished Kenilworth Abbey that had stood on the site until his father garnered them as spoils from the Dissolution provided much of the building material for his renovation.

Dudley's building also looked forward and out, as reflected in the amount of glass that he installed. He widened the old narrow, round-topped windows of the twelfth-century Norman keep, installing rectangular windows instead, and he used many tall, mullioned windows in his own buildings constructed on the site for the entertainment of visitors. The increased use of glass throughout Elizabethan England characterized Renaissance style: it signified greater sense of physical security against assault; it was more outward-looking; and it made a display case of the house itself, an effect that the Elizabethans themselves noted as a shift in style. Harrison comments upon the increased use of glass everywhere (198–99), and Robert Langham's *Letter* particularizes the dazzling effect at Kenilworth, "every room so spacioous, so well belighted, and so hy roofed within. So seemly too sight by du proportion withoout: a day time on every side so glyttering by glass: a nights, by continuall brightnes of candell fyre and torchlight transparent throogh the lyghtsom wyndoz, az it wear the Egiptian *Pharos* reluceut untoo all the Alexandrian coast: or els . . . thus radiaunt, az thoogh *Phoebus* for hiz eaz woold reast him in the Castl, and not every night so too travell dooun untoo the *Antipodes*" (69). Langham's allusions to the edification of antique myth and the illumination of magnificence would have pleased Dudley.

In other respects as well, Dudley's reconstruction looked behind to Arthurian associations and beyond to classical antiquity, as well as outward to its contemporary setting. The large, artificial lake had been created for defense at the beginning of the thirteenth century, but by fortifying and shoring up the causeway, Leicester converted it to a setting for medieval entertainment for Elizabeth. As Catherine Bates observes, the ambiguity regarding which Mortimer it was whose arms Dudley carved into Mortimer's Tower left open the possibility of his affinity with both the Arthurian Roger Mortimer and his grandson the earl of March, who also loved a queen—an ambivalent signification that enhanced Dudley's position as conservator of tradition and as suitor to the queen, as once again Dudley looked both fore and aft with a bifocal vision uniting past, present, and, he hoped, future prospects (*The Rhetoric of Courtship* 55–57). By converting an earlier defensive structure into what came to be called the Gallery Tower, he provided an outlook for spectators for tilts conducted below. Leicester's gatehouse is a paradigm of his inflection of styles. The four turrets and battlements overlooking the garden were designed for display, as were the classical design of the portal and the elaborate decoration of the fireplace within, both structures transported from elsewhere, probably Leicester's Building in the Inner Court.[60] By a paradox implicit in the Renaissance, Leicester's atavistic classical ornamentation was avant-garde design. It had its desired effect, as Dugdale witnesses in his praise of Leicester's work at Kenilworth, because he "spared for no cost in enlarging, adorning, and beautifying thereof; witness that magnificent Gatehouse towards the

North, where, formerly having been the backside, he made the Front" (*The Antiquities of Warwickshire* 1:249). Dugdale's selection of structure is telling: the gatehouse, the way into Kenilworth and passageway to fictive reconstruction of the past. His emphasis upon Leicester's reorientation and ornamentation of the entrance appreciates the rhetorical intention of the change, and Dugdale's choice of the term *magnificent* to express his praise signifies that the rhetoric has made the desired impression.

Similarly ambitious in shape and in effect is Hardwick Hall, the triumph of Bess of Hardwick, countess of Shrewsbury (fig. 14). Bess has enjoyed or endured a reputation for being ambitious herself, either for herself or for her granddaughter Arabella Stuart as a claimant to the throne. Four times married, mother of eight children, hard-headed and tight-fisted businesswoman and supremely competent manager, Bess has also suffered the denigration accorded any woman who traverses cultural definition of appropriate feminine behavior. In any case, if she had political ambition it was thwarted by her own imprudent actions and by Arabella's recalcitrant behavior, so that Bess's scheme came to nothing. Hardwick Hall, on the contrary, remains as a monument to the aspirations of an extraordinary woman.

The house could have entertained royalty, although there is no record that such a visit took place. It is a structure that impresses first of all with its great height. It is built on a hilltop, not only so that the owner can oversee the surrounding domain, but also so that the house can be seen. The facade emphasizes its height through the use of tall windows. That these were designed according to a plan for exterior effect is obvious because some of the tallest windows are false, and other tall, single, windows open on the interior onto two stories of low-ceilinged rooms. The Hardwick building records indicate that the decision to heighten the windows in this fashion was made during the actual course of construction and that the decision must have been made by the countess herself.[61] "Hardwick Hall, more glass than wall," goes an old saying, and as at Kenilworth, the glitter of glass illuminates magnificence, and once again, the spectator cannot forget whose house this was. The Dutch-inspired grace notes at the top of each turret herald her initials, and, more traditionally, her coat of arms, supported by the Hardwick and Cavendish stags and surmounted by the countess's coronet, dominates the frontispiece. Hardwick Hall speaks the silent language of prodigy houses with the special accent of the countess of Shrewsbury. Before one enters the hall, the principal function of the Elizabethan prodigy house has been signaled: to assert dominance, proprietorship, achievement, and aspiration. Entrance to the hall will wait upon a later chapter given to movement and process, however, because movement within Hardwick ascends beyond shape to another dimension of meaning.

The last type of building to be considered because of significant shape is the kind that obsessed Sir Thomas Tresham. More modest in scale than Kenilworth or Hardwick, less self-aggrandizing than either, more reverent in intention than both, Tresham's structures are monuments to his religious conviction. A Roman Catholic, Tresham spent much time in prison for his beliefs, and he devised some of his ingenious plans for his structures while incarcerated. He owned possibly the most comprehensive Elizabethan library of architectural books, including at least one copy of virtually all the most important antique treatises and continental works (Gent, *Picture and Poetry* 72; 80–86). His papers, like his buildings, document his concern for classical proportion and detail as well as his obsession with a personal system of religiously significant number.

The most secular of Tresham's surviving buildings is his Rothwell Market House (fig. 16), a highly visible, functional monument to his civic dedication and a gift to the town where he was lord of the manor. In two places he underscores his motivation. A Latin inscription running around the building on the lower frieze reads, in translation: "This was the work of Thomas Tresham, Knight. He erected it as a tribute to his sweet fatherland and county of Northampton, but chiefly to this town his near neighbour. Nothing but the common weal did he seek; nothing but the perpetual honour of his friends. He who puts an ill construction on this act is scarcely worthy of so great a benefit. A D One Thousand, Five Hundred & Sev.[in fact, 1578]" (Gotch, *A Complete Account* 18). Having thus disarmed would-be critics, Tresham then bonded the upper frieze with the shields, bearing coats of arms, of ninety landed county families: an effective, extraverbal representation of communal fealty (HMC, *Report on Manuscripts in Various Collections* 3:xxxv).

Lyveden New Bield (fig. 17), which Tresham called his "garden Lodge," was designed to carry twelve dozen shields (HMC, *Manuscripts* 3:1; liii) as another expression of his sense of community. This structure also testifies to his interest in classical architecture and his deep commitment to his religion. The architect was Robert Stickells, himself interested in antique precedents, and a letter from Stickells to Tresham reports that he has "mayd the ordnance" according to Tresham's request, "by the Simetry or measwer agreinge withe the Doricke Architrave frees and corniche." In quoting this letter, John Summerson concludes that it may refer to Lyveden, which fits this description, and he further suggests that some drawings among the Tresham papers show a roof tower framed in according to plans devised by Serlio, which would have crowned the building had it been completed.[62] Built on the model of a Greek cross, Lyveden is even more certainly testament to Tresham's religious convictions than to his interest in Renaissance architecture. The fragmentary inscriptions on the frieze of the upper entablature refer to the passion of Christ and to Mary, the spacing of the letters so arranged that the names Jesus and Mary appear on the main wall in corresponding positions on the right and the left of each wing. The exact numbers of letters and running feet of inscription were calculated in multiples of five, seven, and nine—numbers that Tresham associated with salvation, the Godhead, and the trefoil associated with his own name and coat of arms in a canting device (three in chief and three in base, equaling nine leaves in each).[63] Thus this structure edifies his three essential values—communal, aesthetic, and religious—in a structure that also spells out his own familial identity.

Tresham's Rushton Triangular Lodge is an even more insistent expression of these interests (fig. 1). Here he carries his canting device and his numerological symbolism to eccentric extreme. The structure itself is triangular, and the trefoil appears inside and on every exterior wall. Each face of the building is dedicated to a different Person of the Trinity. For example, the north side figures the second Person, the Son of God, as the inscription on the entablature makes plain: QUIS SEPARABIT NOS A CHARITATE CHRISTI: *Who shall separate us from the love of christ?* The emblems of the pelican in her piety and of the hen and her chickens signify the charity of Christ, and the number of chicks in the original conception is also significant: nine, the number of Tresham's own children.[64] No one has deciphered all of the complex mystical terminology, but Tresham is working, sometimes exponentially, with biblical numbers and numbers associated with personal and religious significance.

This last example is itself an exponentially complex illustration of the use of architecture to shape meaning. Tresham's buildings are extreme examples of a type of Elizabethan interest in architecture that found expression in several buildings. Longford Castle, like Tresham's lodge, also expresses the concept of the Trinity through triangular form.[65] The circle was adapted by Lady Anne Clifford for her almshouse at Beamsley in Yorkshire and by Henry Oxinden in Kent. Oxinden explained his motivation in doggerel, "I imitated the great Architector, Loe / Both Earth & Heaven, hee hath framed soe." John Strode coexpressed the religious motive for his E-shaped plan for Chantmarle House in Latin: "Constructa est in forma de Littera E, sc. Emmanuel; id est, Deus nobiscum in Eternum."[66]

In all sizes of three-dimensional objects—from the smallest, whether coin or finger ring, to the largest, the great prodigy house—the shape and substance of Elizabethan artifacts worked as units of nonverbal or extraverbal communication, grounding communication with the gravity of the things of this world. Material, whether bread or gold, substantiated meaning, and form bodied it forth. The next chapter considers how bodies in space—their position, displacement, motion—generated other syntactic transformations in silent language. When moving from consideration of shape and substance as signifiers into the more dynamic dimensions of silent language, it is well to recall with de Maisse, the French ambassador, that high officialdom was seated—physically seated—in Parliament on material reminders of the lowly origin of English prosperity. He describes in his *Journal* the order and relational positions of all participants, noting in particular, "All the seats are covered with red cloth, and in the middle are four great mattresses, full of wool and covered in red, on which they sit; these are very high and well stuffed; they say that it signifies the prosperity in England which comes from wool."[67]

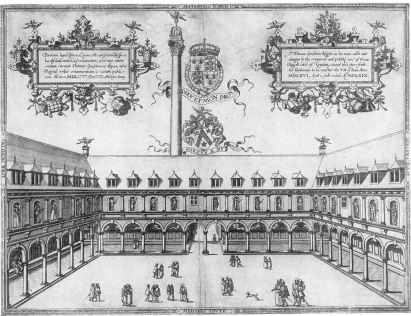

(top) FIGURE I. Triangular Lodge, Rushton. North side. 1594–97. Photo by Marvin Zuckerman.

FIGURE 2. Franciscus Hogenberg (?). The Royal Exchange. 1566–68. © The British Museum.

FIGURE 3. Attributed to George Gower. *The Armada Portrait*. 1588(?). By kind permission of the Marquess of Tavistock and the Trustees of the Bedford Estates.

FIGURE 4. Attributed to William Segar. *The Ermine Portrait*. 1585. Courtesy of the Marquess of Salisbury. Photo: Courtauld Institute of Art.

FIGURE 7. Nicholas Hilliard. *Young Man among Roses.* c. 1587. Victoria and Albert Museum. Victoria and Albert Picture Library.

(top left) FIGURE 5. Nicholas Hilliard. *George Clifford, Third Earl of Cumberland, as Knight of Pendragon Castle.* c. 1590. National Maritime Museum, Greenwich, London.

(bottom left) FIGURE 6. Marcus Gheeraerts the Younger. *The Ditchley Portrait.* c. 1592. By courtesy of the National Portrait Gallery, London.

FIGURE 8. Isaac Oliver. *Unknown Melancholy Young Man*. c. 1590–95. The Royal Collection. Reproduced by gracious permission of Her Majesty the Queen.

(top right) FIGURE 9. *The Shepheard Buss*. c. 1596. Victoria and Albert Picture Library.

(bottom right) FIGURE 10. Hieronimo Custodis. *Frances Clinton, Lady Chandos*. 1589. By kind permission of the Marquess of Tavistock and the Trustees of the Bedford Estates.

NON SINE SOLE
IRIS.

(above) FIGURE 11. Attributed to Marcus Gheeraerts the Younger. *The Rainbow Portrait*. c. 1600. Courtesy of the Marquess of Salisbury. Photo: Courtauld Institute of Art.

(top right) FIGURE 12. Antonio Mor. *Sir Henry Lee*. 1568. By courtesy of the National Portrait Gallery, London.

(bottom right) FIGURE 13. Jean de Beauchesne. *A booke containing divers sortes of hands, as well the English as French secretarie with the Italian, Roman, Chancelry, & court hands. Also the true & iust proportio[n] of the capitall Roma[n]e*. London, 1571. Photo Courtesy of The Newberry Library, Chicago.

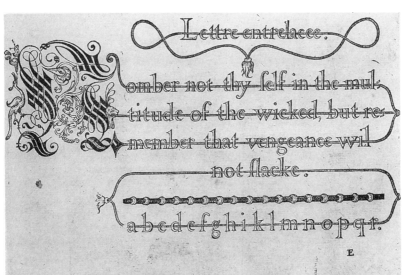

(above) FIGURE 14. Hardwick Hall. © The National Trust Photographic Library. Photo by Geoff Morgan.

FIGURE 15. Wollaton Hall. RCHME, © Crown Copyright.

(top) FIGURE 16. Rothwell Market House. Photo by Marvin Zuckerman.

FIGURE 17. Lyveden New Bield. Photo by Marvin Zuckerman.

FIGURE 18. Quentin Massys the Younger. *The Sieve Portrait.* c. 1580–83. Pinacoteca di Siena. Alinari/Art Resource.

(top right) FIGURE 19. Crispin van de Passe I. *Queen Elizabeth.* 1596. © The British Museum.

(bottom right) FIGURE 20. John Case. *Sphaera civitatis.* Oxford, 1588. Title page. Photo Courtesy of The Newberry Library.

ELIZABETA D. G. ANGLIÆ. FRANCIÆ. HIBERNIÆ. ET VERGINIÆ
REGINA CHRISTIANAE FIDEI VNICVM PROPVGNACVLVM.

SPHÆRA CIVITATIS

(above) FIGURE 21. *Queen Elizabeth as Europa.* Sutherland Collection. Ashmolean Museum, Oxford.

FIGURE 22. Artist unknown. *Memorial Portrait of Sir Henry Unton.* c. 1596. By courtesy of the National Portrait Gallery, London.

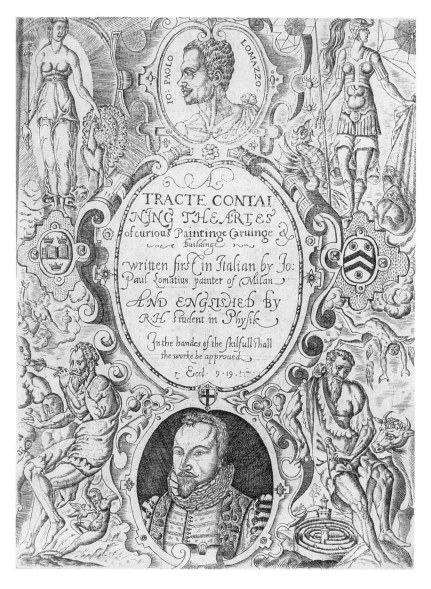

FIGURE 23. R[ichard] H[aydocke], trans. *A Tracte Containing the Artes of curious Paintinge Caruinge & Buildinge. . ..* By Paolo Giovanni Lomazzo. Oxford, 1598. By permission of the Folger Shakespeare Library.

FIGURE 24. Philip de Marnix. Elizabeth as Venus. 1580. © The British Museum.

FIGURE 25. Elizabeth mediates peace. 1587. © The British Museum.

FIGURE 26. Assistance to the United Provinces. 1585. © The British Museum.

FIGURE 27. Protestants supported in Belgium. 1587. © The British Museum.

FIGURE 28. Recovery from smallpox. 1572. © The British Museum.

FIGURE 29. The Phoenix Badge. 1574. © The British Museum.

FIGURE 30. *Dangers Averted.* 1589. © The British Museum.

FIGURE 31. Defeat of the Spanish Armada. 1589. © The British Museum.

FIGURE 32. The Gates of Honour. Photo by Marvin Zuckerman.

III

POSITION, GESTURE, MOTION, AND DURATION

CHAPTER FIVE

PLACE, BOUNDARY, AND POSITION

> Some have fallen from being Princes of this land, to be
> prisoners in this place [the Tower]; I am raysed from
> beeing prisoner in this place, to bee Prince of this land.
> Hayward, Annals

> For a while you may see these great lords in vast pomp
> and magnificence, and the next instant you behold them
> under the hands of the executioner.
> Stephen Perlin, "A Description of England"

FOUR DAYS AFTER HE WAS SENTENCED to be executed, on January 20, 1572, Thomas Howard, duke of Norfolk, wrote a farewell letter from prison to his children, cautioning them, "place hath no certainty." Painfully conscious of his loss of position, aware that he would soon cross the threshold to eternity, imprisoned in the narrow confines of the doomed, Norfolk's letter frequently employs spatial metaphor: "my fall," "beware of high degrees," "throwes [one] downe," "every thing . . . falls" (Wright 1:402–5).

Norfolk was speaking metaphorically of social position, but to understand the dynamic resources of silent language, it is important to recover some of the physical dimensions of the Elizabethan sense of place and position, liminal and interstitial boundaries, that generated such metaphor. The same spatial metaphors are still applied with similar intent to social position, but—as with so many inert figures of speech—the tenors have changed over time. Behind Elizabethan verbal communication lay the syntax of the silent language of the period. It is worthwhile to concretize again some of the physicality of spatial metaphor, not because the metaphor is misunderstood—it is not—but because the tenor tells much about the historic workings of silent language—workings that may otherwise be ignored.

Customary observation of place and position and of movement between them generally passes unremarked except as a sign of the solemnity of an occasion or the dutiful conformity of the subject. Preservation of a traditional substructure might ease a major shift in values because the following of old routes for public processions conveyed a sense of continuity, even as the significance of the event became more secularized.[1] It is the remarkable change of spatial relationships, the moment of risk of loss of place, the implication of movement across a threshold, up or down a passage, that attracts contemporary notation or comment and provides evidence of the difference made by traverse of place.

Elizabethan concern about place and position largely continued earlier, even antique, values and practices. In *Honor Military and Civil*, William Segar schematizes the honors due the worthy, such as proximity to the most honorable personage at dinner, the position nearest the wall when moving through the streets, or an appropriately "delicate" diet (S4ʳ). Even in death, position indicated favor: it would have been an ominous insult to be buried face downward or with one's head pointing in unconventional position, thus violating the prescribed posture from which to greet the angel of the resurrection (Cressy, *Birth, Marriage and Death* 466). For the instruction of young noblemen in his *Hero-Paideia*, James Cleland frequently prescribes the order of honorific seating, position, and movement by invoking examples from classical literature. Diarists and historians were pleased to compare the order of processions and triumphs to Roman tradition. Medieval drama ingeniously interchanged biblical places with local names in order to bring home timeless truth. Decorum of place was systemized by guardians of rhetoric, art, literature, and heraldry. This much of the background is both too broad to document and so generally accepted as not to require it, but within Tudor history, two events in particular had dramatized the political significance of place. Both were associated with Calais and both exemplify the link between medieval and Elizabethan concepts of place.

The events surrounding the Field of Cloth of Gold are legendary for the cost and effort expended in their preparation. A similarly punctilious extravagance also characterized the display of courtesy and exchange of favor among the principals during the attendant series of processions and meetings. Thus if the French organist accompanied the English singers for the first introit at Cardinal Wolsey's mass, the English organist accompanied the French singers for the second. The same sense of reciprocal courtesy also dictated the chiasmic use of place. When Henry VIII met the Emperor Charles on their way to Calais for the second round of events, the venue had to be at a point midway between Calais and Gravelines, then under the emperor's jurisdiction. Even-handedness literally manifested itself thereafter on their trip to Gravelines, with Henry maneuvering Charles into position on his right hand for so long as they were on English territory, and with Charles exchanging the courtesy and the position together with its implicit assertion of power when they passed the bridge of boats marking the boundary stream between the two territories.

Medieval history offers striking precedent for sensitivity both to a river as boundary between opposing parties and to position on the right as sign of rank—an honorific distinction that Segar assumes in his calculus of the greatest injuries in combat or triumph as those that touch any part of the right side of the body (*Book of Honor* K3^{r-v}). William Bercher's *Nobility of Women* rationalizes early modern continuation of medieval honoring of the right side:

The place of creation/ shewethe playnelye the dyfference of o^r parfection/ for every man knowethe that a woman is formed in the lefte side/ and man in the right side of the bodye/ and every man seethe that the right side gevethe the ffyrst mocon to man/ and he that movethe by reason settethe his right foote before/ and in doenge of anye thinge the right side is promptest/ wch is well declared by the names of bothe/ in o^r tonge we call the lefte side the Imparfect and the side of wante./ the wh^{ch} the mocons of the heavens declare/ wch is from the east to the west/ as from the right to the lefte/. And the order of the Earthe is for honors sake to put a man to the right hande and the Scripture sayethe/ that at the last daye/ when every man shalbe iudged accordenglye/ the good shall go on the right side/ and the evill on the left/ (108–9).

In his *Interpretacion of Dreames* (1576), Thomas Hill professed the distinction to obtain even in dream as index to the superiority of male over female, basis also for Nicholas Knyght's claim in 1600 to superior spiritual power over Elizabeth because she carried the sword in her left hand and he in his right.[2]

As for the strength of amity or agreement following the pageantry of 1520, the second event associated with Calais demonstrates its tenuousness for many years thereafter. The early biographer of Sir Thomas Smith reports the efforts of Smith, Elizabeth's ambassador extraordinary, and Sir Henry Norris, ambassador in ordinary, to demand the return of Calais to the English in 1567, according to the Treaty of Cambrai eight years earlier. Strype's account stresses the significance of physical location in the fruitless ceremony: "Not as though they thought the governor would deliver it, but to avoid all cavillations which the French might invent, (for by law it was to be demanded at the very place,) and being not delivered, the sum of 500,000 £. was forfeited to the Queen . . . which he did with this formality: + he demanded Calais first at the gates of the town next the sea, in a loud voice in French, by the sound of a trumpet . . . and next coming to the French King, he demanded Calais again" (*Life of Sir Thomas Smith* 95).

Smith may have stood his ground; the French were not to give place. The unsuccess of the claim is irrelevant to the immediate point, which is the manner of its delivery, with its emphasis upon ceremonial possession of actual physical location. The literal insistence upon physical grounding of a claim continued the similar medieval surrender of title through transfer of a handful of earth, as in the ceremony of *levatio cartae*, whereby the parchment, pen, and ink to be used in writing a charter were placed upon the land to be transferred, thereby assimilating chthonic forces.[3] Kissing of the earth signified earthly contact, possession, and, paradoxically, submission—a recognition of place. Within the religious context of ceremonies such as clerical investiture and creeping to the cross, the submission is complete, a gesture of humiliation. It is worth noting that Elizabeth discontinued the royal ceremony of creeping to the cross, even as, although she proscribed other religious processions in 1559, she preserved the ancient observance of rogation days, whereby the clergy and parishioners of substance walked their parish boundaries in a procession designed to demonstrate the proprietary rights of the village and to educate observers, especially the young, regarding future claims.[4]

Strype, writing with the hindsight of a century later than Smith's ceremonial claim to Calais, suggests that the English recognized the disjunction between symbolic gesture and political reality even as they physically enacted the literal terms of the law. Nonetheless, the prescription of the gesture was of a piece with the whole cloth of a culture that preserved faith in the virtue of physical place. The ritual of coronation prescribed measured consideration of spatial relationships as what Ilse Hayden calls "a highly condensed microcosm of the world" that symbolically within the ceremony located all social classes. The queen was crowned within the Coronation Theatre: Saint Edward's chair, the seat for actual coronation, is located between the altar on the east and the throne on the west, symbolizing the harmony of religious and secular powers; the royal gallery and peers are on the south side, peeresses and bishops on the north (Hayden, *Symbol and Privilege* 148). The layout represented the powerful classes of the society that endorsed the coronation.

No traditional structure can inscribe social structure as it evolves through time, however, and stresses along the fault line inevitably surface with the passage of time. Occasional realistic or even cynical awareness of the emptiness of a given observation signals the tension at least subliminally present in any society, especially one undergoing the changes afoot in sixteenth-century England. Elizabethan attitudes toward place and the uses of position still reveal a substantial investment in physical location as a manifestation of power. In *Worlds Apart: The Market and the Theater in Anglo-American Thought, 1550–1750*, a brilliant study of the relocation of the market from place to process to principle to power, Jean-Christophe Agnew has traced the gradual dematerialization of market exchange during the early modern period. As he describes it, that part of the change of concept of the market that falls within the Elizabethan period would also fit the overarching developments in the value and use of place in silent exchange of other kinds of meaning as well as monetary. Agnew observes, for example, that the market cross at Cheapside was the site for many legal transactions, including executions (28, 56). We might note that the Little Conduit at Cheap was also one of the eleven sites where Elizabeth paused during her coronation procession, asking at that particular location the significance of a pageant being presented before her. "And it was tolde her Grace, that there was placed Tyme. *Tyme*? quoth she, *and Tyme hath brought me hether*" (Nichols, *Progresses* 1:48). Through this bit of astute repartee, she insinuated herself in the place of Truth, the Daughter of Time, adding another legitimizing function to this traditional venue. As a well-known device had it, *loco et tempore*; the motto accompanied a picture of a bomb, signaling the power of one who exploits the right time and place.[5]

Elizabeth was enacting a sense of drama that was well placed and timely, but no more so than would characterize other performers when their location in the liberties, appropriately so named, would allow latitude for play. Steven Mullaney has imaginatively mapped the association between place and play as "a rhetoric of space" (*The Place of the Stage* 17). This was the latest spatial trope in the evolution of British drama as the locus of performance gravitated from church to marketplace to theater, removals that signify changing roles for drama. Other historical data confirm the critical importance of the physical location of the boundaries of the City of London. The first is that the protection of the city offered sanctuary to the villein or bondman who lived there for a year and a day, "For so great is the prerogatiue of that place, that it giueth protection to the villen or bondman against his lord while the saide bondman shall be resiant there."[6] One infers that the fugitive migrant worker might change status if he changed his place, provided that he escaped detection. Another glimpse into the historical situation raises unsettling ambiguities, however. The archives of the city unfold a long dispute about the actual location of one of the boundaries during the course of controversy regarding the liberties and privileges of the Tower of London, a quarrel that began long before the reign of Elizabeth, as early as 1465, during the reign of Edward IV. In 1582, the dispute was renewed because the porter of the Tower was exacting payment in kind from victuallers passing by the Tower into the city, imprisoning those who refused to surrender payment, and thus, according to the lord mayor, discouraging trade and hurting the London market. The subsequent deliberations uncovered other differences regarding the privileges, such as habeas corpus, proper to the city as opposed to the Tower. The Privy Council ruled on these issues, but the issue regarding the boundary remained unresolved. The boundary stone that marked the place where the sheriffs of London received prisoners from the Tower for execution had been removed by order of the lieutenant of the Tower. The ensuing fracas involved the settling of tenants in the disputed territory, a march-in, or "perambulation," as the lieutenant called it, and long litigation. The determination of the boundary in question was not made until 1687, after which time still further litigation ensued.

Civic awareness of the significance of boundaries was also imaginatively inscribed in what Lawrence Manley calls "the discursive nature of the form" of civic pageants, particularly those arriving by water, which through word and image symbolized the liminal relations between such sets of oppositions as inside/outside, chaos/order, nature/civilization.[7] The removal of the boundary stone mentioned above was not a unique occurrence: the nighttime spiriting away of stone markers also troubled the controversy over Old Byland (Beresford 59–60). Not even religious observances were free from disputes about boundaries: Rogationtide processions to beat the boundaries of a parish were sometimes occasion for violent encounters between rival groups, each certain that the other was driving demons over the line between them (Duffy, *Stripping of the Altars* 136).

The seizure and destruction of monasteries during the reign of Henry VIII had caused another type of liminal dispute, a massive dislocation, and a sense of loss intensified by the associative powers of place. David Starkey calculates the profits from the Dissolution as amounting to £1,300,000 by the end of Henry's reign. Disturbing as the eviction of human beings was, Margaret Aston suggests that the effect of the devastation of monastic places may have been even more upsetting. The dislocated residents became assimilated into society, but the ruins of their former establishments remained as silent monuments to the violence of the destruction. Henri Lefebvre differentiates the complexity of a spatial work from the complexity of a text: "In space, what came earlier continues to underpin what follows. The preconditions of social space have their own particular way of enduring and remaining actual within that space" (*Production of Space* 229). In light of a succession of attitudes toward the religious use of space, the multiple metamorphoses of Westminster Abbey under a succession of Tudor monarchs with a variety of religious convictions created a monument to layered change (Foster, *Patterns of Thought* 70–71). On every hand, what Henry's commissioners were unable to demolish or remove, the combined depredations of wind, weather, and scavengers attacked, leaving gutted shells and bare, ruined choirs that would haunt observers for several generations thereafter.[8] Many of those who profited from the Dissolution by purchase or award of property were slow to build on the church sites, whether because of uncertain religious settlement or residual reverence for places formerly consecrated to religious purposes, but the Dissolution did release an enormous amount of land and materials that were recycled for secular purposes, particularly once the accession of Elizabeth gave an air of permanence to the Henrician changes in religion. Destruction of the old church building was the most certain way of erasing memory of its former dedication, and this was the usual course taken by new owners, who then converted the monastic dwellings to their own use as home and setting for magnificent display.[9] The transformation in appearance of place materialized both the displacement of old values and the elevated position of the new tenant.

William Petre's Ingatestone is a case in point, as is that of one who was elevated even higher—Leicester's reconstruction of Kenilworth Castle, detailed in chapter 4. The son of a tanner, Petre served as Thomas Cromwell's deputy in ecclesiastical affairs, and in this capacity he conducted visitations of monasteries in London and elsewhere. Like many Tudor officials, Petre supplemented his small salary with other perquisites associated with his work. Thus he received annuities from nineteen monasteries, with a forty-year lease on manor property from the nunnery of Our Lady and Saint Ethelberga of Barking, gifts presumably offered in hope of alleviating the impending dissolution of their institutions. After paying the Crown just under £850, Petre pulled down the old house, modified its medieval name, and superimposed an embattled house of fashionable brick with a symmetrical entrance imposed upon an essentially asymmetrical medieval arrangement of the interior—a combination that was to be often used during the Elizabethan period. The hall could seat as many as a hundred diners, but Petre himself most often used his private dining room next door, a custom that he shared with many another Tudor owner, and one that spatially represented the changing alignment of social classes, the newly arrived superiors seeking the luxury of privacy and visible separation from their inferiors. With some sixty rooms, large hall, courtyard plan, use of wainscot, glass, and many fireplaces, Ingatestone was a relatively modest example of the Tudor country house of an aspiring courtier. One telling detail is the fact that Petre received from the Crown in 1551 a "licence to embattle," together with a pardon for having already done so, even if the embattlement was more decorative than defensive in nature: the place reflected both the social transition from Petre's status as son of a tanner to Tudor courtier as well as the stylistic transition in architecture from medieval to early Tudor to Elizabethan Renaissance.[10] The social and aesthetic transformations were interrelated, bonded in stone and brick.

On a far grander scale, Somerset House on the Strand in London was in many ways the prototypical great house, and it, too, concretized religious, political, and aesthetic transitions. Pevsner has minutely analyzed the respects in which this is true, from the combination of early Tudor elements with Renaissance innovations to the influence of this style on Elizabethan structures.[11] Construction of Somerset House began with stones from the demolished cloister at old Saint Paul's, and behind the symmetrical Renaissance facade was an eccentric Tudor structure. If the design introduced the continental Renaissance balustrade, superimposed orders of columns, pilaster and frieze, fenestration, and triumphal arch, it also preserved the Tudor chimney and the even earlier English asymmetrical entrance to the hall. Edward Seymour enjoyed only five years of glory as duke of Somerset before his execution in 1552, but his house remained as monument to the passage from medieval models to the crossing of the threshold to Renaissance style.

The architectural influence of Somerset House is marked at Burghley House, the Northamptonshire seat of the protector's secretary, William Cecil, who not only survived the political changes that led to Somerset's execution but lived on to thrive as Elizabeth's chief minister. Burghley House, too, registers the upward mobility of its owner, and about this Cecil was explicit, accounting for his great building as "of competency, for the mansion of his Barony"; that is to say, he was transforming the comfortable manor suitable for the knight he was into the magnificent mansion appropriate to the baron he had become.[12] This ambition is most evident in the enormous size of the building, the prominent display of the family coat of arms, and in the fashionable translation of classical elements learned from architectural treatises, continental models, and Somerset House. It was this scale of magnificence, especially when affected by the gentry, that prompted contemporary moralistic comment. An ambiguous entry in Sir Roger Wilbraham's *Journal* records amusement at one builder's obsession: "Per W. Gerrard: one said by [i.e., about?] Puckering L. keper: he was acquainted with him verie familiarlie, & had neither great lerning nor welth till that advauncment, but now he perceved the operation of a L. keper's place was to purchase a manor every moneth" (9). In his *Steele Glas*, George Gascoigne refines the role of architecture as concrete evidence of the moral state of the ambitious builder: "The sumpteous house declares the princes state, / But vaine excesse bewrayes a princes faults" (288). Barnabe Barnes early in the Stuart period cautioned counselor-builders not to exceed their means to support and furnish out their magnificence, "for the worthiness of a good house holder is mentall, and not corporall" (*Fovre Bookes* I^v–Iij^r).

While building Burghley House, Cecil corresponded about it with Thomas Gresham, the royal agent at Antwerp, who also built under the influence of the example of Somerset House when he put up the bourse in

London with its arched colonnades (fig. 2). Like many another Tudor construction, Gresham's Exchange is a record of displacement as well as ambition. Some sixty houses on the construction site were auctioned off to those who would remove them; more than eighty houses were demolished, causing many serious injuries. According to Stow, "all whiche chargis [for demolition and clearing] was borne by yᵉ citizens of London, and then possessyon gyven by sertayn aldarmen to Syr Thomas Gressham, who layed yᵉ fyrst stone (beynge bryke) of yᵉ fowndacion," one of the hundred thousand bricks of which it was constructed having been donated by the city along with the land on which it stood.[13] The statues of the kings of England in the niches above the arches in the courtyard signified national pride (Buxton, *Elizabethan Taste* 62). Gresham's canting grasshoppers mounted on the roof signaled his leap to the height of his financial achievement. The second part of Thomas Heywood's *If You Know Not Me, You Know Nobody*, a eulogistic dramatization of the building of the Exchange, represents Gresham as explaining that the shops will be "like a parish for good Cittizens," where they and their wives will be so well attired that courtiers "shall come in traines to pace old *Greshams* Burse" and they will "sweare they ly'd when they did scoffe" (lines 1231–39). He reminds the queen of her promise "to giue the name / To *my* new Burse," whereupon to the sound of trumpets, Elizabeth names it the "*Royall* Exchange" and raises Gresham to knighthood (lines 2098–2107 [emphasis added]). Heywood's simile is telling: the burse is displacing the parish; the courtier will pay court to commerce; the noble will patronize the bourgeois. Later, Fuller comments that the populace familiarly refers to the "Change" rather than the "Royal Bourse" because it is the site of so many changes in fortunes. Michael Berlin aptly observes that the Elizabethan citizenry was typically dedicated to private affluence and public squalor—a reluctance to pay for the reconstruction of Saint Paul's as an outstanding example—with the notable exception of mercantile institutions such as the Exchange.[14]

The comparison between parish and bourse draws upon a contemporary phenomenon of displacement to be witnessed at Saint Paul's, as may be inferred from Thomas Norton's complaint in 1569 about the papists who "be common rumorspreders, of whom the publike fame is that there be or haue bene certaine notable and noted walkers in Paules and such places of resort, so common that the very vsuall places of their being there, are ordinarily knowen by the names of Papists corner, and liers bench, sauing that I heare say now of late many of them flocke more into the middle isle, which is supposed to be done partly for better harkening, and partly for more commodious publishing" (*Warning* G.1ᵛ). In Saint Paul's, the threshold of the place of worship had become the publishers' location, and, according to other reports, even more mercenary transactions took place there. One pier within was known as "the serving-man's pillar" because men waited there for prospective employment (Phillips, *The Reformation of Images* 158). In 1608, in *The Dead Terme* Thomas Dekker personifies the steeple of Saint Paul's as lamenting that the middle aisle has become a Mediterranean Sea whereon merchants and pirates rove: "Thus am I like a common Mart where all Commodities (both the good and the bad) are to be bought and solde" (*Non-Dramatic Works* 4:51–52). Heywood projects the consequences: the Exchange figuratively replaces the church as parish, as community. In that direction, far ahead, lies the modern mall.

London might attract the most wealthy and powerful, but town and countryside allowed the lesser nobility and gentry greater scope for the exercise of localized power in relative seclusion from immediate supervision by the central government. The architecture and furnishings of town halls were visible traces of their growing power as limen between past and present, marketplace disorder and civic hierarchy.[15] Even when more modest in scale than the extravagances of the most powerful, country houses were nonetheless often ambitious in intent, adapting continental Renaissance architectural elements to personal and regional conditions.[16] Figuring an example of the ambitious, not to say nastily so, was the largest Elizabethan mansion in Berkshire, Shaw House, constructed by Thomas Dolman and completed in 1581. Dolman's own inscriptions register what might be called his superliminal motivation for extravagance. Over the porch, he inscribed the Greek motto "Let no jealous enter," and over the window above, the feral Latin inscription "The toothless envies the eater's teeth, and the mole despises the eye of the goat." A clothier, Dolman retired from his business when he built this monument, provoking from the townfolk in Newbury a rhyme that registers their subliminal recognition of the economics of Dolman's unedifying values: "Lord have mercy upon us, miserable sinners. / Thomas Dolman has built a new house and turned away all his spinners."[17]

The first step in constructing a monument to one's own magnificence was the choosing of a location. The countryside was highly desirable, whether because of the location of family holdings, the desire to retreat from the pressures of court or city, or the translation of classical value of *otium* to English circumstances. As for the actual siting of the house, if one built on the remains of an ecclesiastical structure or an inherited family seat, this decision about location was already made, but when ambitious Elizabethans started from scratch, the first footings were often sunk into the top of a hill. The association between physically elevated position and display of power is archetypal, as manifested in the tower of Babylon or top place on the wheel of fortune, and as traditionally observed in the positioning of royal apartments and the manifest hierarchical order of guest quarters.[18] Elevated position properly belonged to royalty: *The Queenes Maiesties En-*

tertainement at Woodstock (1585) describes how the queen dined in "a place by art so reared from the ground" some forty feet (B4ʳ). Such aspiration was dangerous in lesser folk. *Leycesters Common-wealth* indicts Leicester for failure to observe the decorum of assignment of the highest rooms at court (64). In Spenser's *Colin Clouts Come Home Againe,* one of Colin's chief indictments of ambitious courtiers is that they "purchace highest rowmes in bowre and hall" while truth and honesty wander unattended (line 726). Stow's *Survey* cites a cautionary number of merchant builders who were cast down for their haughty ambition to overgo their neighbors and so failed to enjoy their lofty structures (Manley, "Of Sites and Rites" 49).

Wollaton is the preeminent example of the ambitious Elizabethan prospect still extant: a tall house on a hilltop, its elevation enhanced by the addition of a prospect room on the roof—a room from which one can view the surrounding county, and that renders the house highly visible (fig. 15).[19] Although the first entry in the OED (2nd ed.) for the noun *prospect* in the sense of "look-out" is 1586, the phenomenon existed earlier, and in fact Andrew Boorde nearly fifty years before had recommended a good "prospect" as pleasant for both resident and viewer (*Introduction* 234). At many great houses, banqueting rooms on the roof serve similar purposes, as originated at Longleat and appearing also at nearby Hardwick Hall (fig. 14) and at Montacute in Somerset. In the *New Arcadia,* Pyrocles/Zelmane praises the siting of Basilius's lodge because "it gives the eye lordship over a good large circuit" (91). John Norden indicated the contemporary appreciation of vista when, in 1610, he praised Castle Ashby as "a very fayre House mounted on the browe of a Hill havinge a very goodly perspecte farr over the Countrye" (*Speculi Britanniae* 46). Sir Henry Wotton elaborately echoes Sidney's phrase when he in turn names the motivation and the pleasure of prospect as

> the *Royaltie* of *Sight.* For as there is a *Lordship* (as it were) of the *Feete,* wherein the Master doth much ioy when he walketh about the *Line* of his owne *Possessions:* So there is a *Lordship* likewise of the *Eye* which being a raunging, and Imperious, and (I might say) an *vsurping Sence,* can indure no narrow *circumscription;* but must be fedde, both with extent and varietie (*The Elements of Architecture* 4).

Through the concrete antonomasia of architecture whereby the house edifies the qualities of the owner, the prospect room supported the old desire to be king of the hill, monarch of all one surveys. Moreover, in some houses, like Wollaton, it also furnished a private surveillance point from which to oversee the interior prospects of one's kingdom in the hall below.

For those closest to Elizabeth and for those who wished to be among them, the size of the house was determined by the hope, expectation, or fear that the queen when on progress might visit herself upon them. Sir Christopher Hatton's lofty rhetoric, as so often is the case, sets the highest pitch of the discourse, and again as so often, it sounds to be designed for the ears of the queen. Hearing its echo across the centuries may explain his sometime reputation, according to Fuller, as a "mere vegetable of the court" (*Fuller's Worthies* 291). In a letter to Sir Thomas Heneage dated September 11, 158[o], Hatton announces that he is about to visit his Kirby, which he has never yet surveyed, "leaving my other shrine, I mean Holdenby, still unseen until that holy saint may sit in it, to whom it is dedicated" (Nicolas, *Hatton* 155). Hatton rarely visited either property—at most, Kirby every other year—but he entertained extravagantly (Chettle, *Kirby Hall* 6).

Contemporary correspondence of a more certainly private nature discloses the anxiety and even understandable alarm with which other prospective hosts received the word or, worse, the rumor that Elizabeth and her enormous entourage might be moving in their direction, minimally requiring the removal of their entire families to other quarters and the securing of troublesome, expensive provisions, gifts, and entertainments.[20] An oft-repeated conversation between Sir Nicholas Bacon and the queen illustrates the magnitude of the problem of providing adequate accommodation for the royal party. Elizabeth, visiting Sir Nicholas at Gorhambury while on progress, observed, "You have made your house too little for your Lordship," to which Bacon, lord keeper of the Great Seal, reputedly answered, "No, Madam, but your Highness has made me too big for the house" (Nichols, *Progresses* 2:56n.). After this visit, Bacon added wings to his house, including a gallery and two apartments, one of which was designated for the queen and sealed off after Elizabeth's visit "that no other step might pass the same threshold" (1:602n.). Fuller prints a less-often quoted account of Thomas Gresham's supposed overnight division of the courtyard at Osterley House into two parts upon the queen's complaint that the original space was overly large. The report goes that the quick alteration illustrated "it was no wonder he could so soon change a building, who could build a 'change,'" or that a house like Gresham's "is easier divided than united" (*Fuller's Worthies* 243).

Emphasis upon the impressively ornamental becomes increasingly important during the Elizabethan period, an emphasis that is visible in changes to the presentation of the facades of important houses. The first record of a London courtyard with a streetside presentation of an ornamental railing and gate is at Salisbury House, which was rebuilt for Sir Robert Cecil in 1599 (Schofield, *Medieval London Houses* 43). The approach and the threshold to the Elizabethan house were highly symbolic, so much so that Dudley, we recall, reoriented the approach to Kenilworth in order that what had formerly been the backside of the site would put up a good front, one ornamented with turrets and battlements, an elegant paraphrastic variation upon medieval function, a renovation that was later duly singled out for commendation by Dugdale (*Antiquities* 1:249). At both Holdenby and Kirby, Sir Christopher Hatton constructed impressive gateways, rerouting the roads at Kirby for more impressive approach to the house. He also demolished outlying buildings and constructed a grand outer courtyard there with a loggia, all the better to set off the approach to the second, inner courtyard and the classicized frontispiece of the house beyond. Surrounding fields were enclosed and the land became part of the estate, leaving the former villagers without livelihood; an early owner, either Hatton or his successor, apparently displaced some tenants by demolishing nearby houses for the sake of the setting for Kirby Hall. At his Holdenby, too, the twenty houses around the village green were reduced to fourteen on the plan of 1580, and the eight that remained on the 1587 plan were rebuilt to the west of their former position, the southern half of the parish having become a park, the fields having disappeared, and Holdenby having acquired a walled and gated courtyard in front of the main entrance.[21] Other Tudor houses, such as Montacute, Burghley, Castle Ashby, and Sir Thomas Smith's Hill Hall, presented similarly imposing courtyards, so many that the type could provide architectural tenor for John Caius's delightful kinetic metaphor, the Gates of Honour, at Gonville and Caius College, Cambridge. There the scholar entered the college through a series of three gates, the first a low, simple Gate of Humility, medieval in style, which one had to stoop to enter; the second, unassumingly Renaissance, the Gate of Virtue; the last, by which the student left the college to receive his degree, the Gate of Honour, an imposing if incongruous domed structure representing a triumphal arch surmounted by a temple front, with obelisks at each corner (fig. 32).[22]

Generally, having processed across the ceremonially spacious approach and having traversed the dramatic courtyard before a great Elizabethan house, visitors passed over the threshold of a doorway centered in an imposingly symmetrical frontispiece. Once inside, they were confronted by a screen separating the entrance from the hall beyond. Like the approach to the house, the courtyard, and the threshold, the screen, too, served as a "portal trope."[23] The screen in some cases functioned practically to shield the hall from direct exposure to drafts from the entryway, but it also served to separate stranger from guest, outside from inside, outdoors from indoors, natural setting from artificial interior. It was here that the household officers could judge the suitability of the visitors for admission to the hall and distinguish their relative social rank, which in turn determined the appropriate seating arrangements for meal service. The orders to be observed at Wollaton by the servants of Sir Francis Willoughby emphasize the primary role of the usher both in seeing that dogs are kept outside the hall and in separating the social sheep from the goats within it.[24] William Turner, incensed by what he metaphorically diagnosed in his *Spirituall Physick* (London, 1555) as the infection of ambition among the lower classes, recommended that the great houses maintain a quarantine of three dining arrangements, one for the uncleanly folk, one for honest plowmen, artificers, and those under the rank of gentleman, and a third for one's own friends (K3ᵛ–5ʳ).

The screen, like the arch, constituted a most significant limen within the ceremony of entry into a defined communal space, and subsequent participation in the activities to be shared therein. A schematic example of this function is the screen at the Temple Inns of Court, which marked clear division among grades of diners: one table outside the screen was designated for yeomen (benchers' clerks); the four inside tables were hierarchically arranged to seat at separate tables the clerks' commoners, masters' commoners, fully qualified barristers, and masters of bench.[25]

Orders for more private spaces are equally rigid, often conveying a military model. Richard Braithwait describes in detail the customary offices of the servants in *Some Rules and Orders for the Government of the House of an Earle.* The marshal in a great hall is "to carry in his hand a white rodd, and to appoint the Yeomen Vshers to place all strangers according to their degrees, as he shall direct them" (20). The language of "A Breviate touching the Order and Governmente of a Nobleman's House" (1605) extends the military connotations: if the lord keeps a hall, then the steward and the comptroller "are to marshall that place, bearinge theire white staves in theire hanndes." The military metaphor becomes even more explicit when it specifies the "office" of the yeoman of the ewery, an echo of famous descriptions of the arming of knights in literature:

> Hee is alsoe to arme the carver, fouldinge his arminge towell full three fyngers broad or more, and that to putt about his necke, bringinge both sides of the towell even downe to his girdell, and puttinge them under his girdell faste, a littell waye, the endes are to hannge from thence right downe. His lordes and ladies napkines to bee laide faire, on his lefte shoulder, his owne napkine on his lefte arme, and so the carver beeinge armede, the gentleman usher is to present him to the table from the ewerie. Hee is to arme the sewer with a towell, of the like foulde, to the carver, and is to putt it baudericke wise, about his necke, with a knotte thereof, so lowe as his knee, and both the endes of the towell to hannge lower at the leaste by a foote then the knotte, and so hee beeinge armede, to goe to the surveyinge place or dresser, for the lordes meate.[26]

In Gervaise Markham's *English Housewife* (1615), even the housewife is impressed into service to "marshal" the foodstuffs: "if [the housewife] want skill to marshal the dishes, and set every one in his due place, giving precedency according to fashion and custom; it is like to a fencer leading a band of men in rout, who knows the use of the weapon, but not how to put men in order." He then lists the order in which the dishes are to be "delivered" to the table at the command of the housewife. Markham addresses himself to her because, he says, "we allow no officer but our housewife . . . she shall first marshal her sallats, delivering the grand sallat first, which is evermore compound; then green sallats, then boiled sallats, then some smaller compound sallats" (121). Granted his prescriptions for a military type of service, one wonders whether Markham is punning upon *sallat*, a decorative helmet.

The punctiliousness of procedure, the terminology of military arms and decorations, the submission of lesser officers to the scrutiny of the superior—all of this conveys the image of military order in the preservation and defense of civilization itself. Good form is described with the obsessive detail of a drill sargeant: no "halfcaps & salutations which you make for fashion sake" will do, as James Cleland commands (*Hero-Paideia* y^v–y2^r). Militaristic, too, are the censures of lapses: thus one servant recalls being forced to execute a hundred "leggs" in perfect form for having made one unsatisfactorily in haste before his lady while carrying a covered dish, compelled to restart the count if any were imperfect (*Berkeley Manuscripts* 2:386).

Clark Hulse suggests that the screen, as decorative object and as backdrop to the feasting and dramatic entertainments that took place in the hall, linked the verbal and visual arts, and he notes that the screen was reproduced as background on the early stages and festival arches for entries and pageants (*The Rule of Art* 13). More likely, screens recalled earlier continental triumphal arches, but whichever way the influence flowed, the screen was undoubtedly an architectural showpiece. It made the most of the occasion for display of elegant treatment of post and lintel or arched entranceway, and it was support for generous use of wood and alabaster carving, whether quotation from classical motifs, strapwork, or mere English relief. The screen at Burton Agnes is a most elaborate example of the last, representing on a series of superimposed levels a complicated program of imagery: the twelve tribes of Israel, the nine Sibyls, personifications of virtuous types, the four evangelists, the twelve apostles, Elizabethan ladies, and crusader knights flanked by angels. All of this rests in top-heavy position above a carved wooden set of two arches flanked by paired sets of Ionic columns. The iconography may be too complex for ready deciphering, and the style may be wildly eclectic, but the moral intent is imposing, not to say overbearing.[27]

Passage through the hall and the remainder of public spaces in an Elizabethan house was designed to initiate visitors to familial values, whether dynastic, moral, aesthetic, or most likely some combination of these. At Burton Agnes, the house in which so much Elizabethan carving remains on display, the initiation to high moral purpose that began with the screen is furthered by the alabaster chimney piece in the hall, representing the wise virgins (who are, like good Elizabethan girls, busy at their washing and spinning) and the foolish (who are, like frivolous Elizabethan ladies, singing, drinking, and dancing). Through the farther end of the hall, in the drawing room beyond, another carved chimney piece intensifies the moral instruction with a cautionary representation of a Dance of Death, and another in the queen's state bedroom represents personifications of Patience, Truth, Constance, and Victory, together with three contraries, Tribulation, Fraud, and Danger, plus Reason, this work not having been completed until 1610. Finally, yet another carved chimney piece now in the dining room, but originally in the gallery above, would have capped the visitors' upward progress with representations of seven virtues and three vices.

The figure of upward progress is advisedly chosen, as warranted by both the design and early descriptions of Elizabethan houses. Burghley's letter to Hatton, written after a visit to Holdenby on August 10, 1579, recreates the experience of approaching, entering, and visiting one of the largest of Elizabethan houses. First, Burghley describes how, in Hatton's absence, he was met on his way by some of Hatton's servants,

> all showing themselves, as by your direction, glad of my coming. But approaching to the house, being led by a large, long, straight fair way, I found a great magnificence in the front or front pieces of the house, and so every part answerable to other, to allure liking. I found no one thing of greater grace than your stately ascent from your hall to your great chamber; and your chambers answerable with largeness and lightsomeness, that truly a Momus could find no fault. I visited all your rooms high and low, and only the contentation of mine eyes made me forget the infirmity of my legs. And where you were wont to say it was a young Theobalds, truly Theobalds I like as my own; but I confess it is not so good as a model to a work, less than a pattern, and no otherwise worthy in any comparison than a foil. God send us both long to enjoy Her, for whom we both mean to exceed our purses in these. (Nicolas, *Hatton* 126)

Burghley's reverent allusion to the queen anticipates Hatton's effulgent reference of the following year to Holdenby as his "shrine" for "that holy saint" (155). A generation later, Norden's terminology preserves the sacral aura (which may have been quite literal) when he describes the hall in Holdenby as featuring "three Peramides very high standinge insteade of a

Shryne, the midst whearof ascendeth unto the Roofe of the Hawll, the other two equall with the syde Walls of the same Hawll, and on them are depainted the Armes of all the Gentlemen of the same Shire, and of all the Noblemen of this Lande."[28] Whereas the keynote at Burton Agnes was insistently moral exemplification, at Holdenby surviving evidence would indicate that the mode was magnificent praise of the upper reaches of the social order. Visually and kinetically, as Burghley and Norden testify, Holdenby exalted the mighty.

Holdenby was constructed for the express purpose of entertaining the queen and her large retinue, although she never did visit there, and Hatton only seldom—a conspicuous example of lack of practical consumption of extravagant investment on a royal scale—although Barnabe Riche in *His Farewell to Military Profession*, while extravagantly praising the house "for the bravery of the buildings, for the stateliness of the chambers," commends Hatton for keeping daily hospitality in his absence for a neighborhood six or seven miles in compass (131–32).

Other tall houses embody other kinds of aspiration. Wollaton and Hardwick Hall are well-preserved examples. Wollaton dominates a commanding view of the surrounding countryside of Nottinghamshire, the creation of Sir Francis Willoughby, an early Midlands magnate who invested in woad, cloth production, iron, and coal, and expended more than £8,000 of his profits in the building of this monument to his position (fig. 15). Both the house itself and historical records about Willoughby create the image of the builder as a prototypical Victorian industrialist, a Dickensian profile of the type. The house features many consciously medievalizing details that emphasize the height of the structure: towers, turrets, and chimneys, the fantastic ornamentation on top, the tracery windows of the hall and prospect room. The most certain evidence of the intentionality of the medievalizing, however, must be the hammer beam ceiling of the hall. It is, says Girouard, a "fake" because it serves no useful function and is in fact slung from, rather than supporting, the roof.[29] As Pevsner comments, these stylistic paraphrases may represent the builder's wish to impress with atavistic reminders of his family connections to the Dudleys, Seymours, and Lady Jane Grey, who was a first cousin.

Willoughby was anxious to impress with his taste as well as his lineage, so the ornamental detail at Wollaton was contrived as evidence of his humanistic learning.[30] On the exterior, niches on the towers support busts of exemplary ancients such as Virgil, Aristotle, Plato, and Cato, together with Minerva as inspiration for all such sages, the whole complex serving in turn as wise inspiration for the approaching visitor. Precedent for this type of exterior display of classical roundels existed in the Italianate work at Hampton Court, Whitehall, and a few of the houses of Henry VIII's more ambitious courtiers, so the imperial mode of the style attracted Willoughby, too (Wight, *Brick Building* 192–97). Moreover, John Shute's *First & Chief Groundes of Architecture* (1563) articulated another humanistic motivation for such display of heroic exemplars, and in fact for all magnificent building, when he reminded Elizabethans of the many antique philosophers who had praised the art and its patrons, such as Plato, Aristotle, Pliny, and Caesar (Aijᵛ). Inside Wollaton, the carved screen continued the mixed quotation, paraphrase, and innovation of the decorative detail of the exterior, with the combination of antique pillars, metopes, and strapwork. Chimney pieces also expressed a similar eclecticism.

As at Holdenby, the loftiness of aspiration would be felt at Wollaton through the physical movement of approach, passage, and ascent. The prospect room expressed the height of this kind of architectural conceit; one could enter its blazing light only after ascent and passage up a dark winding staircase, an experience analogous to passage through Caius's Gate of Honour. The spatial organization of the house, moreover, outlined the implicitly masculine normative basis for such heights of aspiration and achievement. Rooms on the ground floor were largely devoted to masculine prerogatives of overseeing the household, business, management, and the activities of the hall, and to the master's quarters—the power base of the house. Upper floors, approached ceremoniously and hence less accessible, were dedicated to activities shared by men and women; the public rooms for entertainment were large, formal, and stately. The plan expresses women's isolation and segregation into positions more decorative than powerful.[31]

Hardwick Hall, on the other hand, expresses the aspiration of an exceptional woman, the formidable Elizabeth Shrewsbury, who refused to be cabined in any quarters less than magnificent or to be confined to woman's place out of sight or mind. Whereas the eye of the visitor approaching the entrance to Wollaton is drawn upward to view the busts of exemplary men from antiquity displayed in niches in the towers, at Hardwick it is the initials of Elizabeth Shrewsbury that dominate the ornamental finials on the towers of her house (fig. 14). If Bess spent her time on the upper floors of her tall house, it was because those were the most important spaces at Hardwick. The traditional hall of earlier Tudor houses was losing its place as focus of both the daily and ceremonial activities of the lord and lady. In this respect, Wollaton was transitional, preserving the large, traditional screens passage (that is, a passageway behind screens at a hall's entrance), while Hardwick retained only certain vestigial aspects of the appearance and function of the hall, thus looking forward to later developments in the layout and function of the great country house. Girouard refers to the "cross-hall" at Hardwick, a term that usefully encapsulates the change in position and purpose of the hall. At Hardwick, the hall runs through the house, its length situated perpendicular to the long axis across the house, and it is two stories high, thus allowing for its assimilation into a symmetrical plan for the house as a whole. The screen, more open than most, is a simple, pure classical-columned structure that allows full view into the length of the hall, so that the carved chimneypiece is clearly visible with its prominent Hardwick coat of arms, surmounted by the countess's coronet, supported by the Cavendish stags.[32] Thus the visitor is immediately made aware of the significance of dynastic connections at Hardwick, associations impossible to forget while touring the house.

Impossible to forget, too, is Bess's strategy of playing both ends against the middle as she maneuvered traditionally female iconography across the field of conventionally male power, a strategy at which her sovereign was most adept. If every floor of Hardwick Hall, indeed almost every room, recalls an exemplary female such as Minerva, Penelope, or Lucretia, it is also true that reminders of family connections are omnipresent as a discreet hint of power, or the desire for it, expressed through the ploy used at many a master's country house, as at Wollaton. The most memorable aspect of Hardwick, whether viewed from outside or experienced through a long climb up the two staircases inside, is its great height, a feature that supports the stately function of the spaces within. These rooms were not located functionally—otherwise the dining spaces would have been placed much nearer the kitchen rather than up that long stairway, for instance—but rather in ascending order of state, a hierarchy that is reflected in the graduated heights of the windows. As Girouard puts it, "on each floor the rooms grew more ceremonial," and every room that Bess often used was furnished with her own high chair and stool, upholstered with fine metallic thread, as befitted her station (*Hardwick* 33–35).

In the High Great Chamber, where Bess and her guests formally dined on public occasions, they would have been edified by the Ulysses tapestries, the frieze of Diana with its implicit allusion to the Virgin Queen, and thirteen paintings, including all of the Tudor monarchs. The royal coat of arms surmounted the carved chimneypiece, and it was featured also on the rare mirror in that room. Within this context of royal compliment stood a table, very probably the "Eglantine" table, which is inlaid with the family arms, eglantine, images of leisure activities such as games and musical instruments, and two Cavendish stags in the center supporting the motto "The redolent smele of Aeglentyne / We stagges exault to the deveyne" (*Hardwick* 71). In light of the poetic association of eglantine with the queen, it was Bess's fortunate coincidence that the flower also figured in the Cavendish arms, allowing an ambiguity both complimentary and daring.

The allusions to royalty and to Bess's family connections echoed and heightened an association already posed in the drawing room on the floor below, although less elegantly and less insistently there than in the more ceremonial setting of the High Great Chamber. Moreover, a procession through the Long Gallery next door, the other important stately room of the top floor, would both widen and enhance the noble context for presentation of family credentials. Typically, galleries in the great houses exhibited portraits of English monarchs and sometimes other European rulers, too, and the social function of the gallery to exhibit the magnificence of the owner was well-recognized, as when Sir William Petre's surveyor described Ingatestone as having a "fair and stately gallery or walk meet for any man of honour to come into" (Emmison, *Petre* 32). At Hardwick, the conventional arrangement of hanging portraits provided setting for additional display of more personal images. The 1601 inventory of Hardwick Hall lists eighty-two pictures, one-fourth of which were portraits of Elizabeth Shrewsbury and her family. These family portraits were hung in the company of the kings and queens of England and other European monarchs.[33] The guest who passed through the gallery was impressed by the company the family kept. Ultimately, whatever Bess's designs upon movement upward beyond the domain of her great house, they came to nothing and in fact came perilously close to ruination, but the house itself is a magnificent achievement.

A foreigner's description of Theobalds, visited in 1602 by the duke of Stettin, reveals another kind of scheme for using the gallery to create a context for grand design. The duke's secretary, instructed to record every day's activities, took minute account of what he saw at Theobalds:

> Especially noteworthy were the three galleries. In the first were representations of the principal emperors and knights of the Golden Fleece, with the most splendid cities in the world and their garments and fashions. In the next, the coats-of-arms of all the noble families of England, 20 in number, also all the viscounts and barons, about 42, the labores Herculis, and the game called billiards, on a long cloth-covered table. In the third, all England, represented by 52 trees, each tree representing one province. On the branches and leaves were pictured the coats-of-arms of all the dukes, earls, knights, and noblemen residing in the county; and between the trees, the towns and boroughs, together with the principal mountains and rivers.[34]

Together, the galleries virtually represented the whole of England, or at least that part of it that concerned the Cecils, and set the power of England within the context of power as it was pictured in western Europe. A tour of the three galleries represented a review of this alignment, the physical passage from gallery to gallery enacting kinetically and on a microlevel the geographical area covered by a sweep of the eye. In a gesture thoroughly in keeping with the humanist ethic, the presence of a representation of the Labours of Hercules among the artifacts lent to the whole program of the place the weight of the most popular exemplar of male virtue. On a grand scale, the galleries at Theobalds signified the development of the great house as setting for secular magnificence. In this respect, as Theobalds appeared in 1602, the sensuous attractions of its galleries could easily have fed the dire suspicions of one early observer of the pleasures of the great Tudor house. John Knox's bitter indictment of Somerset proleptically recognized the displacement of the medieval hall and its communal functions in favor of the gallery and upstairs ceremonial rooms with their attendant social display. Knox complained of Somerset, "he wald ga visit his masonis, and wald no dainyie himself to ga frome his gallerie to his hall for hiering of a sermone."[35]

Elizabethan structures organized the flow of traffic so that physical movement enacted the disclosure of meaning in a gradual sequence. The process of communication depended upon a system of spatial organization usually taken for granted, so that departures from it would, subliminally at least, signify meaningful difference. The very serving of food moved on an upward course that paralleled the upward ascent of the human hierarchy. The rigid order of seating, the graded quality of utensils, the number of courses, the marshaled order of presentation, the proportional quality and quantity of the foods offered, the reverential manner of the serving, all indicated the social status of the host and of the guest. The very foodstuffs bespoke an epideictic ceremony for which the physical setting was the stage. Physical elevation signified elevated social status, the ascent beginning with the climb to the upstairs location of the dining chamber, rising to the high table raised upon a dais, the upward movement materially represented by the upward sweep of the stages of the cupboard and the height of the footed salt, crowned by the rooftop location of the banqueting rooms. The ascent was kinetically enacted by a series of processions: the guests processed to table, the food processed to the guests, some selected guests processed to the dessert course. At last, an inverted procession carried leftovers down to the kitchens to be carted out to the gates for charitable distribution to those on the lowest rungs of the social ladder.

Unusual emphasis upon conventional position bespoke intensification of traditional values, such as the primacy accorded to the right hand or side. Thus the elaboration of emphasis upon position and place at Calais that was detailed at the beginning of this chapter heightened awareness of the honor at stake in the negotiations. Increased emphasis upon formal composition of space intensified the solemnity imparted through ceremonial spatial pattern, as at the great houses expecting royal visitation. Variation suggested adjustments in values, as when the decor of a great house increased the space devoted to customary exhibition of artifacts bearing reminders of dynastic connections, or when traffic patterns changed in Saint Paul's, or when internal spaces of a house became more separate in function, a consideration heartily recommended by Francis Bacon in "Of Building."[36] These interior adjustments were reflected in the plan and facade of the Elizabethan house, and, indeed, in 1563 John Shute coined the word that named the value, *symmetry,* in the first English treatise on architecture.[37]

Most of the uses of place, position, and spatial organization discussed thus far were conventional, or so discreetly different as not radically to shock conventional expectation. Within the parameters of political and social decorum, it was permissible to introduce emphasis, elaboration, and even personal variation. Apart from the massive displacement following the devastation of the monasteries, individualistic violation of customary spatial use was relatively uncommon. Reversal or inversion of place, position, or spatial organization was rare; assertive and potentially dangerous, it suggested incontinent ambition or even outright challenge.

Apart from architecture, other media sometimes provided the setting for more immediate and more daring assertion. The frame of pageant outlined a protected space within which negotiations about power might be presented; within drama, the fictive frame of pageantry offered safe space for the expression of potentially dangerous challenges to monarchy.[38] Occasional examples of eccentric use of position or space in order to differentiate personal, political, or religious values can nonetheless be found in a wide range of behavior and artifacts, many of them on a microlevel easier to observe than on the scale of a great house. There was historical precedent for such displacement and departure; cases associated with earlier monarchs show with schematic clarity the workings of alteration of place on a conventional grid.

Foxe's *Acts and Monuments* is ever alert to the semiotics of position and place, particularly as manifested in royal entries. The description of the entry of Philip and Mary into London includes several telling details. The stations of the pageantry included a painting of Henry VIII as one of the Nine Worthies, a representation that in itself elevated the status of Henry by altering the historic configuration of nine heroic figures. Traditionally, the Nine Worthies included three Hebrew leaders (David, Joshua, and Judas Maccabeus), three pagan (Hector, Alexander, and Julius Caesar), and three Christian (Arthur, Charlemagne, and Godfrey de Bouillon). Early in his reign, Henry had been celebrated in verse as the tenth Worthy, but now he had boldly displaced one of the original nine. An occasional substitution of one ancient historic figure would occur, but displacement in favor of a near-contemporary was extraordinary. Even more extraordinary at a later date would be the addition of Christ, Saint Peter, and Queen Elizabeth to the scheme engraved on a set of silver spoons in order to increase the number of Worthies to an even dozen, and with the inclusion of a female.[39]

Foxe is even more concerned, though, with another displacement in the same celebratory picture, the book in Henry's hand, labeled *Verbum Dei*, the word of God, a detail that so disturbed the bishop of Winchester lord chancellor that he called the painter knavish, treasonous, and villainous, and ordered him to remove it because it would better be attributed to Queen Mary, the true reformer of religion. The painter departed; "but, fearing lest he should leave some part either of the book, or of 'Verbum Dei,' in king Henry's hand, he wiped away a piece of his fingers withal!" Foxe then describes how, in a complimentary innovation upon the configuration of the Worthies, verses celebrated Philip as one of "the five worthies of the world: Philip of Macedonia, Philip the emperor, Philip the bold, Philip the good, Philip prince of Spain and king of England." Foxe turns next to an account of how the rood was erected in Saint Paul's to welcome Philip to the church, the cross and the rood lofts being the object of a major displacement during religious controversy (*Acts and Monuments* 6:558).

Uneasy watchfulness for any manipulation of position and space by suspect parties was often warranted by other behavior or subsequent events. Like Philip, Henry, earl of Darnley and consort of Mary Queen of Scots, was a source of anxiety and resentment among the subjects of his queen, and, like Philip's, the ambiguity of his political status provoked careful scrutiny of the implications of his actions and the underlying iconography of his public presentation. A silver coin issued in commemoration of the marriage of Mary and Darnley that placed his name before hers was quickly withdrawn, and the device on the obverse of another coin that represented a tortoise climbing a palm tree did nothing to alleviate suspicion that he sought upward nobility.[40]

In England, outsiders and ambitious insiders recognized the uses of displacement as a wordless bid for an improvement in their own position, too. Flamboyant courtiers provide egregious, occasionally inventive, examples of aggrandizement of space and position. On official documents, Robert Devereux, earl of Essex, habitually signed his name too high on the page to allow any other to top his, a stroke that prompted Lord Howard literally to undercut him by slicing out Essex's signature (Handover, *The Second Cecil* 136). A device written by Essex for the entertainment of Elizabeth imparts the same sense of extravagant appropriation when it represents the queen as recipient of a courtier's gifts of gold, incense, and myrrh—biblically, the gifts brought by the Magi to the Christ child. Verses in the device laud her as ruler of an incomparable land: "*Never did Atlas such a burthen bear* / *As she, in holding up the world opprest*" (Devereux, *Devereux* 2:502, 504). The outlandish praise of her place would have delighted Elizabeth, but Essex's inability to know his own did not, and for his boundless indiscretions, he would ultimately pay with his life. In fact, in one of his last manifestations of rebellious indecorum, he appropriated the streets of London for the performance of a play—possibly Shakespeare's—about Richard II, much to the annoyance of Elizabeth, who recognized its potential relevance to herself.[41]

Robert Dudley, Essex's chief rival for place in the queen's favor, betrayed an ambition comparable to his, but Dudley, unlike Essex knew his place, even if he did sometimes dangerously give sign of discontent with it. When, at Kenilworth during the entertainment of the queen by a pageant featuring the Lady of the Lake, the Lady referred to the lake as having been hers since the days of King Arthur, the queen quickly interposed ad lib that she thought it had been hers, "Well, we will herein common more with yoo hereafter" (Nichols, *Progresses* 1:431). Elizabeth mildly put Leicester in his place with this spontaneous response to his hint of pride of place, but Leicester's lavish entertainments gave Oxford grounds or pretext for charging that Leicester was actually fortifying Kenilworth under color of dazzling the queen with fireworks (*CSPD 1581–90* 39). That the queen knighted Dudley at Kenilworth signified that he had successfully curried her favor, but a more outrageous offense while he was on diplomatic mission to the Low Countries in 1586 provoked a furious dressing-down from the queen. Leicester had exceeded his place by accepting the governorship of the United Provinces, and before he returned to England he symbolically made deferential amends to his absent queen by insisting upon a stool in the presence of her unoccupied place of state at the ceremonial banquet in Utrecht, "for he would haue no chaire" (Stow, *Annales* 716). Eventually, the queen was mollified and showed his restoration to a place of honor when, on her triumphal appearance at Tilbury in 1588, she was flanked by Essex and Leicester. On the other hand, Wotton dates the beginning of the fall of Essex to this appearance, when the queen "much graced him openly in view of the Souldiers and people, even above my Lord of *Leicester*: the truth is, from thenceforth he fed too fast" (*Reliquiae Wottonianae* 178).

A third prominent courtier, George Clifford, earl of Cumberland, privateer and the queen's champion at tilt after Sir Henry Lee retired in 1590, used, like Essex and Leicester, the fictive device of royal entertainment in order to express his aspiration for a better place in the queen's favor, and again like them he grounded his appeal in figures having to do with location. In a speech delivered on Coronation Day 1593, he begins by referring to himself as the "Knight of Pendragon Castle," and excuses a two-year absence from Coronation Day ceremonies because in the "meane space" he has been on the queen's business, consorting on dangerous enterprises with seafarers for profit and reward. Upon his return, he "found the Old Castle which was founded in Westmorland and once removed to Westminster, now strangely erected in Windelysore," a reference to Cumberland's ancestral Pendragon Castle in Westmorland, associated with Arthurian myth, on the one hand, and on the other with the locations of Elizabeth's ceremonies at Windsor and Westminster.[42] On this occasion, Clifford's speech relocates his castle and, of course, himself with it, first in a prophetic couplet: "When Windesore and Pendragon Castle doe Kiss / The Loyon shall bring the Red Dragon to Bliss." A second prophecy concludes the speech, and the last lines more topically locate Clifford through reference to the knight of Pendragon's seafaring:

> When Nature shall spend all perfections in one
> When all for that one of themselves shall thinke worse
> When duety shall move very castles of stone
> When Albion prospers by outlandish curse
> And when the Red Dragon led shipmen on dry land
> Then blest be the Earth for a maide in an Iland.
> (Williamson, *Cumberland* 122–23)

By this geographical translation, Pendragon contrives to construct the seat of power from the building blocks of his ancestral stones and to base the triumph of the queen upon his own. As usual, flattery was welcome but ineffective in redressing the financial imbalance of prestation, and Cumberland, like other lavish spenders, was chronically in financial straits. He may have exhibited the queen's glove upon his fine tilting bonnet (fig. 5), but her favor was purely poetic and would pay none of his astronomical expenses. None of her most extravagant courtiers considered himself adequately rewarded, so in the long run the competitors were engaged in a profitless chase, but it was Essex at any rate who triumphed as queen's favorite until he contrived his own downfall.

If these historic celebrations and events incorporated fictions about place, fiction in turn embodied historic events and values associated with the significance of place. The silent language of space was current in the order of art and life. Shakespeare's King Henry IV dies happy in the recognition that the prophecy that he "should not die but in Jerusalem" (*Henry IV, part 2* 4.5.237) is to be fulfilled when he expires in the Jerusalem Chamber of Westminster Abbey, a dramatic geographical translation that shares some of the ironic play between word and place that characterizes Cumberland's speech. The Jerusalem trope is an instance of a type that has a long and varied history, revealing a continuing fascination with seemingly providential punning in dislocation and relocation.[43] Later in his career, in *Macbeth*, a drama much concerned with "measure, time, and place," as the last speech of the play reminds us, Shakespeare varies the trope of reorientation toward geographical location in another, more secularized, expression. Birnam Wood physically comes to Dunsinane, and the wild forest moves within the pale of a castle soon to have a new order of civilization.

In the *New Arcadia*, Sidney adapts the concept of passage through space as an unfolding of meaning. Often his text simulates the temporal succession of moments of revelation. The first instance occurs in the first chapter of the first book when Strephon, Claius, and Musidorus watch the approach of the shipwrecked Pyrocles. The text represents the increasing clarity of their vision through a series of recursive self-corrections: "a ship, or rather the carkas of the shippe, or rather some few bones of the carkas" (9). The opening passage thus sets the keynote as the change in physical perspective on the remains of the shipwreck simultaneously changes the reader's point of view on the fiction.[44] Following soon upon this passage, others describe places that figure symbolically in the construction of character and the moralized architectonics of plot: Basilius's star-shaped lodge with its satellite comet where Pamela dwells; Cecropia's castle . . . every change in location resonates with changes in perspective and a new dimension of symbolic significance. These topical changes render in greater detail the larger contrasts between pastoral, courtly, military, and other scenes.

Among the major writers of the period, Spenser provides the most useful illustration of Elizabethan concern with position and place because his work both embodies it upon the most comprehensive scale and comments upon it continually. The sustained allegory of the human body as locus of a hierarchy of values in book 2 of the *Faerie Queene* is a virtual paradigm for the latter half of this chapter. Just as the Elizabethan house channels the movements of visitors spatially and figuratively through an initiation into the culture of a family, so Spenser's knights are physically directed through an anatomy of the human body as a figurative architectural structure that articulates a hierarchy of values in the quest for the virtue of temperance. Only after conquering the enemies of the bodily structure do the hero knights Arthur and Guyon gain admission to the Castle of Temperance, whereupon they are first entertained by the Lady Alma in the hall, "shewing her selfe both wise and liberall" (2.9.20), these being the qualities of virtuous hospitality. She then leads them to the castle wall, the skin of earthly slime. The shape of the castle, like the forms of such historic shaped buildings as the circular almshouse at Beamsley or the triangular Longford Castle, or Tresham's Lodge at Rushton, is significant:

> The frame thereof seemd partly circulare,
> And part triangulare: O worke divine!
> Those two the first and last proportions are;
> The one imperfect, mortall, foeminine,
> Th' other immortall, perfect, masculine:
> And twixt them both a quadrate was the base,
> Proportioned equally by seven and nine;
> Nine was the circle sett in heavens place:
> All which compacted made a goodly diapase.
>
> (2.9.22)

Unlike the triangular forms that figure the Roman Catholic iconography of the Trinity at Rushton and possibly Longford, the triangular component of Spenser's structure represents rather the imperfect female form; the circle, in the traditional Renaissance reading considered the image of perfection, is here attributed to male form, the numerical proportions being mystically significant.

After a stately meal in the hall, the knights physically enact a detailed anatomy, ascending from the kitchen and Port Esquiline whereby all the "noyous" waste from the feast is "avoided quite, and throwne out privily" (2.9.32). Alma leads them to an assemblage of the affections, who are grouped in a "goodly parlour,"

> That was with royall arras richly dight,
> In which was nothing pourtrahed nor wrought,
> Not wrought nor pourtrahed, but easie to be thought.
>
> (2.9.33)

Here the knights are entertained by a party of courting couples, who nevertheless defer to the tempering presence of Alma; in particular, Arthur and Guyon are instructed by ladies chosen from the company, Prays-desire and Shamefastness.

The knights continue to articulate the anatomy throughout their ascent until they reach the topmost turret, the top-of-the-body prospect room, "lifted high above this earthly masse, / Which it survewd" (2.9.45). The workmanship of this part, the head, excels all other worldly work, "And likest is unto that heavenly towre, / That God hath built for his owne blessed bowre" (2.9.47). Here dwell the three sages who counsel Alma on how to govern—personifications of imagination, judgment, and memory. Imagination, or Phantastes, who has the power to see future possibilities, resides in the first room of the turret. The walls are painted with "infinite shapes," images that busily trouble and confound, representations of the dangers of uncontrolled fantasy. In the second room, the personification of judgment meditates upon the walls that are "painted faire with memorable gestes" of wise men and exemplary "picturals" of all arts, science, and philosophy. The innermost room, an allegorical version of the muniment room of the great family house, is hung with ancient documents, and here the personification of memory records human history. Arthur discovers *Briton Moniments* among the records, and Guyon, the *Antiquitee of Faery Lond.* Through the reflexive stroke of having his heroes discover their appropriate texts, Spenser brings the reader out from the innermost recesses of consciousness to the fictive frame and exemplary intention of the poem. The synergetic relationship between the two modes of knowing, history and myth, generates the mode of the *Faerie Queene* itself, just as the intercalation of history and myth, public record and private hope, was represented in the public spaces of the Elizabethan house in order to generate subliminal awareness of the achievements and aspirations of the owners.

Spenser's treatment of the body as architectonic is systematically discovered, as an anatomy must be, and highly analytical, as a moral allegory needs to be. His treatment of liminality in the sixth book of the *Faerie Queene* is appropriately more fluid in method. This book continually represents characters breaking bounds, intruding as they cross thresholds, some intentionally rude, others inadvertently indecorous. Book 6 begins and ends with wandering interruptions. The proem begins by commenting on how the "exceeding spacious and wyde" ways of Fairyland have tempted the poet to interrupt his work, "nigh ravisht with rare thoughts delight, / My tedious travell doe forget thereby." The twelfth canto ends with a double interruption: the Blatant Beast, boundless in its aggression, has broken its chains and is running loose; Spenser interrupts his conclusion to enter his poem and comment upon the fate of his own verses. In between these major intrusions, many others have taken place: a discourteous knight has interrupted Aladine and Priscilla, Calidore has interrupted Serena and Calepine, Arthur and the Savage Man have invaded Turpine's castle, and so on. The most significant intrusion in the book occurs when Calidore, courtly knight-disguised-as-shepherd, happens upon the dance of the Graces, a vision conjured by the poet-shepherd Colin. Enchanted with the sight, and "resolving, what it was, to know" (6.10.17), Calidore ventures to approach the dancers, but the vision immediately disappears. He abjectly apologizes to Colin for this "luckelesse breach," the invasion of one "who rashly sought that which I mote not see" (6.10.29). Calidore's thoughtless physical intrusion metaphorically enacts a spiritual indiscretion. In this, the book of the virtue of courtesy, the essential courtesy is to respect the threshold, to know one's bounds.

It was also the essential courtesy in Elizabethan society, essential even to survival, as some courtiers learned to their cost. Violation carried heavy sanctions; on the other hand, invitations of welcome beyond customary limits conveyed special favor. It is well to recall, too, that the sense of inviolable boundary underlay bodily decorum, as observed by all social classes. Riots were incited by one self-described gentleman's pirouette upon the stomach of an apprentice sleeping near a playhouse. The putative gentleman "did turne upon the toe upon the belly of the same prentice," as assertion of his superior status.[45] Literary representations of the nuances of liminal decorum employ spatial structure as setting and as metaphor. Thus in Shakespeare's *Lucrece*, Tarquin penetrates a series of increasingly private spaces belonging to Lucrece: the threshold of her home, her bedchamber, and her body. A similar kind of narrowing gyre of intimate spaces, although under very different, welcoming circumstances, was replicated in James Melville's initiation into the queen's private quarters where, at her invitation, he viewed her miniature portrait of Robert Dudley.[46]

The queen monitored the decorum of place and the primacy of her own position with her own sensitive antennae and those of her busy anthill of intelligencers and informers. Most pointedly, an act of Privy Council dated August 30, 1600, forbade as unseemly the practice of circulating popular engravings of anyone other than the queen (*Acts of Privy Council* 618–20). Thomas Norton, the first remembrancer of London, wrote out a set of guidelines for the mayor of the city, reminding him of his duty to preserve London as the queen's own space: "You muste, next God, have a care to serve her Majestie and content her. Remember that London ys the Queenes [Chambre (Collier's emendation)], that owr Queene hath committed London to you, and to London yt selfe; when I name London, I name no small thinge" ("Instructions to the Lord Mayor" 3:9). Not only within London but throughout the kingdom, all physical thresholds were construed as welcoming the queen through the implicit system of prestation, and if welcome were lacking, the host soon knew it, whether through immediate confrontation, early departure, or later disfavor.

The iconography associated with the queen posed territorial claims that exceeded the boundaries of London and of England and expanded her authority far beyond. These claims would have been indecorous or even outrageous if expressed literally, and it is relevant now to recall that the portraits of Elizabeth often represented superhuman attributes and excessive power, as discussed at some length in chapter 2 above, qualities that were often pictorially represented through disposition, gesture, and posture. On a woodcut initial illustrating Foxe's *Acts and Monuments*, she sits on a chair of state above a fallen pope.[47] On the *Ditchley Portrait*, her stance upon that part of England where the home of Sir Henry Lee her host was located, and on the globe itself, visible in the background, suggests proprietary domination of the earth and its parts (fig. 6). Other images reinforce the suggestion: the *Armada Portrait*, whereon her hand rests upon the globe (fig. 3); the title page illustration to John Case's *Sphaera civitatis*, whereon she embraces the representation of the pre-Copernian universe (fig.20); the *Rainbow Portrait*, whereon she holds the rainbow in her hand like a hoop (fig. 11). On two portraits, she stands upon a threshold. On an engraving by Crispin van de Passe I (fig. 19), Elizabeth stands between two pillars, an imperialistic device appropriated from the Emperor Charles V, on which the columns recall the pillars of Hercules that signified the ne plus ultra of human ambition, but that, according to Thomas Floyd, after Columbus, with the promise of yet more daring places to conquer, was translated to plus ultra.[48] The queen is poised on the edge of a quay; behind her lies the sea, to which there is no access visible except between the pillars where Elizabeth occupies all the space. On *Elizabeth I and the Three Goddesses* by the monogrammist "HE," Elizabeth stands at the top of the three steps leading to the entrance to an interior that features her canopy of state, the orb and scepter in her hands.[49] From this superior position, she puts to dismay the goddesses who have lost to her in the judgment of the divine contest, Juno, Venus, and Minerva. Elizabeth stands on the threshold between human and divine, history and myth, uniting the two and even shaping and controlling them. More topically, her interpolation into the ancient myth also displaces her female predecessors in use of the story in the iconography of earlier queenly progress. Not only do these images represent ad hoc assertions of the power of a monarch; as a body of representations, they constitute a remarkable exception to Renaissance conventional portraits of women.[50]

This chapter has investigated some of the ways by which Elizabeth manipulated the uses of place, position, and liminality. Her example has concluded this section because she was finally the most powerful figure of her age, but that power was demonstrated in relief against a background that is more fully understood in light of the practice of her courtiers. This is generally true of Elizabethan silent language, even in the case of public ceremonial observances, the main subject of the next chapter, which will consider the uses of forms incorporating the dimension of duration into ceremonial expression, such as pageant, progress, and procession.

CHAPTER SIX

MOTION, MEASURE, AND MEANING

> For God hath dealt with daies as with men . . . some of
> them hath he blessed and exalted, as kinges and princes:
> & some of them he hath sanctified, and appropriated to
> himselfe, as Prophets and Priestes: but some hee both
> cursed and brought lowe, and put them in meane estate.
> John Howson, *A Sermon Preached . . . in defence . . .*
> *of her Maiesties Coronation Day of November, 1602*

T HE SUBJECT OF THE LAST CHAPTER—place, position, and liminality—often spilled over its own bounds and onto the subjects of this one and the next to follow, which are concerned with two of the main ways by which Elizabethans limited, controlled, and styled nonverbal communication. This chapter will be concerned with the shaping of motion and the control of time; the next will be more particularly dedicated to the uses of decorum and protocol, but both will necessarily consider expression through ritual, ceremony, and public performance.[1] To some extent, this chapter will note some of the Elizabethan developments of earlier concepts of time: time personified and time as duration, conjunction, or sequence of events. Difference from precedent marks Elizabethan inflection of the syntactical control of time and motion as elements in silent language. Because Elizabeth dominated her time, contemporary records and modern research often reveal her as both subject and object of these inflections, so this chapter pivots around her manipulation of time. After considering her first appearance as monarch in her coronation procession, her prototypical public appearance, this chapter will be concerned mainly with occasional or unscheduled appearances without a tightly prescribed protocol. More formal observances having literal or strongly traditional prescribed procedures will logically find their place in the next chapter.

It has long been a truism among historians, including specialists in the history of art and technology, that a primary distinction between the Renaissance and earlier history was a new interest in the nature of time and especially in its more accurate scientific measurement.[2] A corollary development was observation of relational position, motion, and consequent change, as manifested, for example, in Leonardo's notebooks and Vesalian anatomy. Interest in temporal progression also motivated the long duration of the Petrarchan triumph as a motif in art, literature, and public performance. Representation of the sequential triumphs of Love, Chastity, Death, Fame, Time, and Eternity captured at once both the momentum of physical change and spiritual dominance over it as each successive personification triumphed over the one preceding. The human desire for the reassurance of continuity in the midst of change also lay behind later perceptions of temporal pattern, and other efforts to discover coincidence, recurrence, direction in the flux of time. The less secure one's belief in the ultimate triumph of eternity over the vicissitudes of time, the stronger the need for temporal satisfaction. As cultures became more secularized, more of the temporal prerogatives formerly belonging to religious authority were transplanted into secular control, and attributes formerly signifying spiritual power over time were grafted onto secular figures. The transition and resultant mutations are manifest in the silent language of Elizabethan culture.

After the death of the queen, Thomas Dekker noted a temporal coincidence in her life that epitomizes the Elizabethan search for meaning in the passage of time. In *The Wonderful Year*, Dekker approvingly comments regarding the birth and death of the queen: "She came in with the fall of the leaf and went away in the spring—her life, which was dedicated to virginity, both beginning and closing up a miraculous maiden circle, for she was born upon a Lady Eve and died upon a Lady Eve" (*Dekker*, ed. Pendry 37). The supposed circularity of the pattern gratified the Renaissance sense of perfect form. Ironically, the aleatory symmetry of the dates of the birth and death of the queen bracketed the Elizabethan management of public observation of important days in her life to correspond with, or, more precisely, to displace, significant dates in the Roman Catholic calendar. From the very beginning of her reign, devotion to the Virgin Queen began to displace former devotion to the Virgin Mary; to the immense displeasure of the Italian visitor Schifanoya, the English litanies used in the queen's chapel omitted all reference to the Virgin, along with other Romanist observance (*CSPV* 7:11). Her birthday on September 7 overshadowed the birth of the Virgin Mary on September 8, cause for congratulation by many of her subjects, especially because the coincidence provided opportunity for Elizabeth to assimilate the very language of praise for the Virgin.

Richard Niccols reports in his elegiac poem *Englands Eliza* (London, 1610) that crowds hailed her with "*Auies*" when she rode "*in Princely State.*" In a few lines, this poem blends the religious and pagan allusions that so frequently color the iconography associated with the queen; the crowd's religious salutation greets Elizabeth when "*She goddess-like in chariot high hath sate*" (Eee7^r).

When Elizabethan observance omitted some former holy days, reformists like William Harrison were pleased at the consequent reduction in number of feast days, regarded as temptations to idleness and drunkenness (*Description* 36). But just as Reformation physical structures embodied memories of the institutions that they displaced, so too did newer rituals and calendars. Some resistance rallied around the feast of Saint Hugh, which was overshadowed by the celebration of Elizabeth's Accession Day on November 17, for which Archbishop Grindal in 1576 issued a special prayer. As David Cressy points out, a later version of this prayer aligns Elizabeth among the kings of the Old Testament.[3] Sermons broadcast apologies for the highlighting of Elizabeth's days. Thomas Holland preached an "*Apologie or Defense of the Church and Common-wealth of England for their annuall celebration of Q. Elizabeths Coronation day the 17. of Novemb.*" in which he argued on the one hand that Saint Hugh's day was no longer orthodox, and on the other that the celebration of Accession Day in its place was spontaneous, "meere voluntarily continued" by a thankful people.[4] He also defended the celebration of the queen's birthday on September 7 with the coincidental downgrading of the birth of the Virgin on the next day on the grounds that the Church of England did not designate Elizabeth's a holy day (L2^r). Dated 1599, Holland's sermon also retrospectively broadens and further sanctifies the allusion to Elizabeth as a phoenix, the device that most directly represents Elizabeth's power over time, by comparing her welcome appearance in England to the return of the dove to the ark with a laurel leaf in its mouth (K2^r). In another sermon preached at Saint Mary's (Oxford, 1602) defending the celebration of November 17, John Howson brought to bear the weight of divine institution and historical precedent among the Jews, the Christian emperors, and Elizabeth's predecessor Queen Mary for revering days that were not in the earlier calendar of feasts. These apologies contrived to associate the queen's days with religious sanction, a sanction intoned by the ringing of church bells to celebrate the queen's day. Even Lodowick Lloyd, whose *Triplicitie of Triumphes* (London, 1591) argues a lengthy case for the magnificence of Elizabethan triumphs as superior to those of pagan history, at the same time exhorts his compatriots to celebrate her day as one appointed by God for their rejoicing: "[A]s farre as heauen surmounteth the earth, or as the glorie of God excelleth the pompe of man," so far did she exceed in virtues that all

English may say, "*Haec est dies quam fecit Dominus exultemus & laetemur in ea*" ("This is the day which the Lord has made; we exult and rejoice in it") (H4^v–I^r). Was it literal truth or irony, then, that prompted Henry Howard's closing comment in a letter written on November 17, 1597, to Essex, regarding court intrigue? His comment ran: "In haste the feast of St. Elizabeth, whom, if I were pope, I would no longer set forth in red letters in the calendar of saints . . . but the best is, the power is now wholly in herself to canonise herself, because she will not stand to the pope's courtesy" (Birch 2 :364). In either case, Howard is spelling out the unvoiced significance of the calendrical rubric.

In effect, Elizabeth had no need to canonize herself. She was already enshrined in the rhetoric, the public performances, the great houses of her courtiers, and, if contemporary report is credible, the hearts of her subjects. She created the public perception of herself as a saintly—even divine—figure, largely through a combination of the nonverbal devices of costume, portrait, personal presence, and patronage, and the most important variable in the use of these vehicles was her manipulation of time. Her costumes do not age, and it is only the occasional foreign observer who confides in personal correspondence any sense of incongruity between the queen's advancing age and her timeless style of the maiden. Almost all observers comment, rather, on her gorgeousness and her accomplishments. The whitened, youthful mask of beauty that was virtually legislated as the template for graphic representations of the queen propagated the image of her as divinely ageless, but the ageless divinity also knew the politic uses of time. The fortunes, lives, and honor of her courtiers depended upon the exquisite timing of her granting or withholding of her presence or her patronage. One certain result of the unpredictability of her management of time was the creation of an aura of superhuman power.

When inductively observing data regarding Elizabethan silent language—in particular, the uses of time—one may be surprised to see how many of the queen's devices, techniques, and stratagems inflect those that characterized the spread of the Roman empire to the Greek provinces. The point is not exhaustively to mix and match the two cultures, but to recognize a prototype for Elizabethan practice in order better to understand the use of public performance, entry, and progress. For instance, Elizabethan practice incorporated local communal culture into public appearances of the queen, an echo of the Roman effort to embrace all levels of the local communal culture in provincial celebrations.[5] Adaptation of traditional local festivals to Roman occasions brought the emperor into contact with local culture, and adjustment in the traditional local calendar was a primary way of assimilating the culture into the Roman ethos. Strikingly, too, the image of the Emperor Augustus does not age, all representations conforming to only a few standardized types, and often imperial images draw upon traditional images of the gods. In an even more specific anticipation of Elizabeth's practice, Roman emperors made progresses through the provinces in what Elizabethans imagined as prototypes for many of their analogous devices and patterns.

Elizabeth's first procession as ruler was her passage through the streets of London from the Tower to Westminster for coronation, accompanied by a thousand attendants in appropriate costume, following the traditional route from the river, across the city, toward Westminster, physically tracing the lifeline of the city in a passage that outlined the new monarch's taking possession of the city, the throne, and the country. A pamphlet published within ten days of the event describes the coronation procession in great detail, *The Passage of our most drad Soveraigne Lady Quene Elyzabeth through the Citie of London to Westminster, the daye before her Coronation, Anno 1558–9.* Her progress occasioned several stops along the way, where the queen both effectively demonstrated her power over her subjects and ostensibly subjected herself to their power over her as they instructed her through tableau and speech in the virtues and obligations proper to their queen. The pamphleteer describes eleven such pauses along the way, and twice the pamphlet summarizes the importance of the sequential nature of the events. Elizabeth witnessed tableaux that represented her descent from the union of the houses of Lancaster and York, her possession of virtues, the hope for her exercise of the beatitudes in office, and lastly, another pageant figure offered her the aid of a bible in English as textual mainstay in her effort to live as Truth the daughter of Time. In another variation on the effects of time, an allegorical landscape represented a flourishing commonwealth and a decaying one as the setting for this last pageant, about which the writer of the pamphlet observes, "The mater of this Pageant dependeth of them that went before." Because she was so instructed by Time and Truth on the state of the commonweal, the writer concludes, Elizabeth "therefore cannot but be mercifull and careful for the good government therof" (Nichols, *Progresses* 1:51–52). Both the pageantry and the pamphleteer's comment upon it establish the reciprocal nature of the meaning conveyed through mainly visual media, but Elizabeth scarcely needed the instruction. When confronted on her procession with the personification of Time as the father of Truth, she had already appropriated the role of Truth with a ready quip. Pausing to ask the identification of the character, and upon being informed that it was Time, her response was, "*Tyme?* quothe she, *and Tyme hath brought me hether*" (1:48).

After narrating how Elizabeth passed still more tableaux, the reporter once again and even more pointedly summarizes the incremental nature of the whole series: "Thys ground of this last Pageant [of Deborah as exemplary governor] was, that forsomuch as the next Pageant before had set before her Graces eyes the florishing and desolate states of a Commonweale, she might by this be put in remembrance to consult for the worthy Government of her People ... and that it behoved both men and women so ruling to use advise of good counsell" (1:54–55). So it is that the commentator binds the connective thread of the procession, ever looping backward to reinforce an earlier lesson, ever casting ahead for application to the future rule of the queen, mindful always of the lesson to be learned by passage from station to station, a virtual Way of the Crown. An essential aspect of the event was Elizabeth's physical movement through the stations, as the meaning of the program unfolded through time, looking back to her predecessors, praising her character, looking ahead to the future of her rule. The pauses at the stations punctuated the movement with time for recollection, what Thomas Wright called in music "paused grauity."[6] The citizens' instructive pageants suggested a contractual element in their relationship with their new sovereign, but their terms were more in the nature of hope than sanction.[7]

For her part, Elizabeth's frequent pauses on her progress served as markers for her taking possession of the city, much in the manner of the Roman emperors, whose analogous entries were punctuated by similar pauses. Indeed, in form and function, the whole procession carried strong resemblance to the *adventus* of antiquity—form and function following fiction— the purpose of which was the establishment of consent and the formulation of corporate identity. Elizabeth did not simply follow the prescribed program: interested in the planning of the event, she seized the opportunity to make the day her own.[8] Her recorded responses confirm her use of the occasion to define her own role as gracious sovereign and Truth, daughter of Time. The contemporary pamphlet account clocks the steps of her progress, noting her enthusiastic reception by the crowd, and the writer notably insinuates a masculine quality into Elizabeth's profession of gratitude, no doubt by way of refuting objections to feminine rule:

And on thother [i.e., the queen's part] side, her Grace, by holding up her handes, and merie countenaunce to such as stode farre of, and most tender and gentle language to those that stode nigh to her Grace, did declare herselfe no lesse thankefullye to receive her Peoples good wyll, than they lovingly offered it unto her. . . . The People again were wonderfully rauished with the louing answers and gestures of theyr Princesse. . . . [Other spectacles included] the People's exceding comfort in beholding so worthy a Soveraigne, and hearing so Prince like a voice, which could not but have set the enemie on fyre. (1:38–39)

The language of this description reveals one of the functions of royal public appearance mutually beneficial to the spirits of ruler and subject: the "exceding comfort" of the people, which is reassuring to both parties. Much later, Sir Christopher Hatton, too, refers to the "comfort" to be derived from beholding the queen's passage from Hampton Court to Saint James's, in a letter dated November 27, 1583, to the lord mayor of London, apprising him of the expediency of publishing notice of her plans so that the citizens may observe her movements on the anticipated date.[9] So responsive was Elizabeth to the crowds watching her coronation ceremonies that Schifanoya complained to the castellan of Mantua that when Elizabeth emerged from Westminster Hall, "she returned very cheerfully, with a most smiling countenance for every one, giving them all a thousand greetings, so that in my opinion she exceeded the bounds of gravity and decorum" (*CSPV* 7:17). Nonetheless, her dazzling approaches to the public often drew approving comment from foreign visitors such as Baron Waldstein, who witnessed her procession to chapel at Greenwich, when, "glittering with the glory of majesty and adorned with precious gems, [she] entered into the view of the whole assembly and stretched her arms out wide as if to embrace everyone present" (*Diary* 73). Seventeenth-century historians, too, would repeat the observation that people crowded in great numbers to see her, "And she (having observed that her Sister, by the sullenness of her Behaviour, had much disobliged the People), frequently looked on them with a chearful and pleasing Countenance, and returned the Respects they paid her, with great sweetness" (Bohun, *Character of Queen Elizabeth* C4ᵛ). This retrospective comment implies the Machiavellian element in Elizabeth's cultivation of public goodwill, an element made even more explicit by John Hayward's judgment that she knew "right well that in pompous ceremonies a secret of government doth much consist, for that the people are naturally both taken and held with exteriour shewes."[10]

This is not to begin to construct a case that Elizabeth's performances were simply cynical diversions to placate a restive people. Like the coronation procession, less solemn Elizabethan appearances were also grounded in ritual, traditional ceremony, or at least in precedent. Like all ritual and ceremony, Elizabethan observances enacted their significance and created meaning; over time, they generated their own patterns and expectations so that they assumed the character of more formal ceremony. They may have been political strategems, but the queen's public appearances also comprised elements more complex than mere circus, such as the gathering of intelligence first-hand regarding the state of her kingdom, the bonding of reciprocal pledges and promises, and even the construction of her persona. The last of these important functions is the one that most depended upon the resources of silent language for effectiveness, and it is the one most concerned with the uses of time.

When Elizabeth insinuated herself into the role of fictive Truth, she enacted an oxymoron, the apparent contradiction between fiction and truth, thus establishing the mode of performative fiction that throughout her reign would characterize her persona with its paradoxical attributes of holy virgin and wife, jealous lover and unattainable lady, Christian saint and pagan goddess. Her observance of Maundy Thursday (L. *mandatum*, command; *manus*, hand) exemplifies her use of a traditional religious ritual, the washing of the feet of the poor in imitation of Christ's washing the feet of his disciples, to constitute a public perception of her character, and it, too, enacted a contradiction. A manuscript now preserved in the College of Arms describing in detail how the ceremony was observed by Henry VIII gives little indication of the monarch's personal impress upon the service. Rather, it prescribes the order of procession, robing, praying, gifting, and washing the feet of the poor. The manuscript specifically details how the king is to go from the hall "in to the wardrop of his robes there to put on the gowne which he shall geve to suyche one of . . . the pore men as shall lycke his grace" (Coll. Arms MS 8 temp. Hen. 8 fol. 26ʳ).

Elizabeth made the occasion indelibly her own by literally updating it and adding gender-specific touches. On Maundy Thursday, Elizabeth would don a long white apron (a feminine adaptation) and wash the feet of poor women and give them gifts of clothing, food, and money. Elizabeth's accents upon this traditional observance enhanced its obvious political capital, putting it on a new footing. Her poor were not only reminded through the reading of the gospel that the ceremony began with Christ: they were also reminded that it continued through the grace of Elizabeth. When Edward III was fifty years of age, he distributed food, clothing, and fifty coins to fifty poor men, and Henry VIII continued the reminder of the monarch's age by apportioning the number of Maundy coins given to correspond with his own age. Elizabeth observed the practice with occasional variations.[11] William Lambarde explains that thirty-nine ladies attended the queen for Maundy in 1573, "for so many were the poor folks, according to the number of the years complete of her Majesty's age," and thirty-nine small white purses contained a gift of thirty-nine pence "after the number of the years of her Majesty's age" (Nichols, *Progresses* 1:326). Elizabeth's observance conformed to traditional practice, but she also gave the women yards of broadcloth to make gowns, and a second set of purses containing twenty shillings "for the redemption of her Majesty's gown, which (as men say) by ancient order she ought to give some one of them at her pleasure; but she, to avoid the trouble of suit, which accustomably was made for that preferment, had changed that reward into money" (327). On

her Maundy Thursdays, Elizabeth improvised departures to suit her conve-
nience, her public image, and perhaps her vanity. In 1573, she may have
adjusted the chronology of the gift of money to reflect a younger, fictive age
for herself, and she again manipulated time by altering her age in 1579 and
in 1589.[12] In light of the comments about Elizabeth's personal touch, it is
germane to note that the women's feet had been prewashed by the yeomen
of the laundry in one of those behind-the-scenes gestures that staged a desired fiction (Nichols, *Progresses* 1:326). Elizabeth as performer of Maundy
humility was protected by the apron and the prewash; as for her charity, it
was reciprocally bonded with and rewarded by subjects' loyalty.

Well might Elizabeth focus the program upon her own role in the event
as a public symbol of her beneficence. In 1572, Elizabeth's parliament
enacted a poor law that was, in the words of one modern historian, "certainly the most harsh of Elizabeth's reign." The act prescribed whipping,
ear-boring, and even death for vagabonds—a term that included unli-
censed wandering players and university scholars.[13] Moreover, the number
of vagrants sent to London's Bridewell hospital for judgment and punishment increased eightfold between 1560 and 1601.[14] Nonetheless, at the end
of the seventeenth century, Bohun praises how "she by her Laws reduced
the Inhabitants of the Countrey-Villages from Laziness and Beggary, to
Labour and Husbandry," so the rationalization for severe Elizabethan policy endured without prejudice, and with it coexisted the image of the
bountiful queen (E6ʳ).

Elizabeth's progresses through the southeast of her kingdom offered
wide latitude for the creation and display of her public persona, an image
reinforced by other entertainments offered by her courtiers. Twenty-two
progresses during forty-four summers, beginning with the summer of 1559
and the last occurring only in the summer of 1602, created a temporal
structure that bracketed her entire reign and provided a syntax for every
conceivable conjugation of time as a dimension in the silent language
shared by queen and subjects.[15] The rhetorical momentum of the multimedia, gathering iconographic images as it moved forward, energized each
subsequent entertainment. The season of the royal visits, the timing of the
schedule, personifications of time, metaphorical representations of time,
intertextual temporal allusion, both diachronic and synchronic—the possibilities were limited only by time itself.

Indeed, the most audacious conceit used on many of these occasions
represented the stopping of time. The "Letter" attributed to Robert Langham that describes at length Elizabeth's visit to Kenilworth in 1575 spells
out Dudley's use of the device. It is both an early and a literal example of
many more elaborate to follow during the regime. The letter writer explains that on Caesar's Tower there were two magnificent clock faces, one

turned toward town, the other toward the country. Both the bell and the clock were stopped upon the arrival of the queen:

> But mark noow: whither wear it by chauns, by constellacion of starz, or by fatall appointment (if fatez and starz doo deal with diallz,) Thus waz it in deed: The handz of both the tablz stood fyrm and fast allweyz poynting too just too a clok, still at too a clok. Which thing beholding by hap at fyrst; but after, seriously marking in deed, enprinted intoo me a deep sign and argument certein. That thiz thing amoong the rest waz for full signifiauns of his Lordships honorabl, frank, freendly and nobl hart toward al estatez. Which, whither cum they to stay and take cheer, or straight to returne: too see or too be seen: cum they for duty too her Majesty or loove too hiz Lordship, or for both: Cum they early or late: For his Lordships part, they cum allweyz all at too a clok, een jump at too a clok. . . . [T]hiz poynting of the clok, (too my self) I took in amitee as an Oracle certein. (74)

The passage comments usefully upon Elizabeth's mythic power, but it more remarkably shows how the attributes of the queen radiated toward her favorites. Honor extended to the queen reflected honor to the giver; favor radiating from the queen attracted favor from others. Langham's note records how the stopped clock stood as Leicester's wordless but highly visible and profitably ambivalent memorial for courtly power over time. That it was a wordless signal safely left to obliging interpreters like Langham any possibly hubristic inference regarding just whose power it was to stop time.

Whether attributed to Elizabeth, to Leicester, or both, this secularized conceit of the end of time is radically different from earlier imagery as it figured in triumphal representation throughout the Renaissance. Neither Langham, the device that he describes, nor Elizabeth's processions in general are directly connected with Petrarch's *Trionfi*, but the tradition was the main source for the iconography, the themes, and the vehicle for the association between time and triumph. The difference in imagery embedded in Elizabethan allusion to triumph over time is a significant departure from Petrarchan tradition, even as it was known at second or third hand in England in the forms relevant to Elizabethan practice. As conceived in the Petrarchan succession of triumphs, it is Eternity that triumphs over Time.

About 1503, in a youthful exercise, Thomas More had devised a set of painted cloth hangings and accompanying verses depicting a series of triumphs that expanded Petrarch's group, concluding with a triumph of the poet over all, including Eternity. The poet advises the reader to put all trust in God, who will give eternal life: "Qui dabit eternam nobis pro munere vitam, / In permansuro ponite vota deo" (*The English Works* 1:335). Other

English redactions and adaptations were also moralistic in character. As translated by Henry Parker, Lord Morley, in the early sixteenth century, Petrarch's Fame "is no nother to be named but a second death" ("Tryumphe of Tyme" line 201), Time is the passage to decay, and the final triumph in the series belongs to Divinity.[16] The Petrarchan tone of grave piety is preserved, and secular triumph is represented as a cautionary example of the vanity of earthly goals. The descriptions of triumphs in Stephen Hawes's *Pastime of Pleasure* elaborate concrete images of the personifications, with particular specification of the destructive attributes of Time, which can be redeemed only through virtue. As Eternity cautions at the end of the poem: "Tyme past with vertue must entre the gate / Of Ioye and blysse with myn hye estate" in order to translate into life everlasting (lines 5785–86).

In ways analogous to the literary triumph, pictorial arts that would have been accessible during the Elizabethan period also represent time and its movements. The tapestries picturing the Petrarchan triumphs that were bought by Cardinal Wolsey and are at Hampton Court illustrate both the magnificence and the evanescence of worldly triumph. Among these, the triumph of Time over Fame is uniquely expressive in representing the movement of time. With only one exception, on all of the extant tapestries the triumphal cars travel in the same direction, left to right, the defeated personifications on their own wagons following the forward-moving triumphators who have overcome them. On the Triumph of Time alone, one of the triumphal cars, the wagon belonging to Fame, faces the viewer's left in a graphic reversal of fortune. The figure of Fame sits dejectedly on her defeated wagon, facing backward, toward her former triumph over Death. On the right half of the tapestry, Time towers over her captive figure, seated in the front of his wagon, her glance still directed backward as the Triumph of Time takes off into the empyrean where the ultimate triumph will belong to Eternity.[17]

By way of contrast, the *Memorial Portrait of Sir Henry Unton* (about 1596; fig. 22) betrays a more worldly concept of time, even as it pictures the life of the subject in a medievalized set of static vignettes representing highlights in the life of the ambassador. Because it is structured as a cross-section of many interior scenes interspersed with processional passages between them, the painting manages to approximate the inflections of time in works that make more sophisticated use of perspective and anatomy in simulating the movement of time, change, and motion. Unton's portrait is a graphic representation of passage, passage through time and space, passage through states of life, and passage through metaphysical states.

Much of the composition of the work is bifurcated between, on the right half, views of the life of Unton as soldier and diplomat and, on the left, his death and interment. Unton's birth and death scenes anchor the lower right and left corners of the picture, the symmetry being emphasized by the homologous insets that represent Unton lying across the lap of a woman, first on the right as a newborn, and last on the left as a corpse. In the middle space, a stream or a river symbolizes the progress of life. The masque that appears in the lower right of the picture is of particular interest because of the manner in which it shows the ascent of the masque figures, including some naked cupids, on one side of the staircase, and the apparently simultaneous emergence of hooded figures marching in Unton's funeral procession from the underside. The most emphatic representation of the transition from life to death, and death to eternal life, appears in the chiasmic figures of the skeleton on Unton's left, offering an hourglass, and the trumpeting angel on his right, offering an eternal crown. Upon closer inspection and second thought, however, one sees that the angel bears the spotted wings emblematic of the antique image of Fame and that the image of Unton is much larger than the scale of all of the rest of the picture, including the image of the church in the background on his right. He sits writing at his desk, and on it rests the image of the queen, which he wears suspended from his neck on a golden chain. The image has been carefully turned on its side in an unnatural position for the benefit of display to the viewer. This central image of Unton is the picture's most memorable, dominating everything else there portrayed and physically located in a position to oversee Unton's own funeral procession, which passes through the space beneath his desk like a trail of insects. Once again, Elizabeth and one of her courtiers have triumphed over time and perpetuated earthly glory, and once again, the identity of the triumphator is slightly ambiguous: Unton? Elizabeth? Or Unton, by grace of Elizabeth?

By nature, portraits create the illusion of triumph over time by recalling the image of one absent or dead, but the Unton portrait goes further by representing processional movement and by evoking traditional associations with the perpetuity of the final triumphator. More than static portraits, live processions and entertainments could implicate other temporal dimensions for added meaning. Entertainments for the queen provided a literal stage and a metaphorical guise for nonverbal communication of private intentions that would have been indecorous or even outrageous if articulated in words. This possibility was always present in any entertainment, but if the presentation was one of several in a series, duration over time offered the chance to develop a conceit, to intensify an appeal, to refine a concept, to repeat a proposal or to revoke it altogether. Also, the frequency of entertainments presented within a fairly small group of able hosts extended the opportunity for borrowing back and forth of the images developed in a system of circulation that interacted with the whole complex of Elizabethan iconography. Thus several entertainments shared related motifs or figures, one outstanding recurrent example being the hermit type developed by Sir Henry Lee.[18] A brief rehearsal of its appearance reveals how the cycling of a character type developed an idea, and in this case, some striking uses of time; and even a curtailed sketch indicates how entertainment and other cultural forms interacted.

Hemetes the Hermit appears at Woodstock in 1575 as the narrator of a romantic tale, highly complimentary to the queen, concerning a knight called Loricus. A hermit reappears in the undated Ditchley manuscript wherein his rhetoric recalls the Woodstock entertainment and he delivers a little speech on mutability of the seasons, the elements, and the meaning of eternity—a theme that would reappear in much English literature, and one that Spenser would more fully develop in the "Two Cantos of Mutability" of the *Faerie Queene*. The hermit indicates that a curate has advised his parishioners "of a holiday which passed all the Pope's holidays, and that should be on the seventeenth day of November," another bit of explicit evidence of the intention to displace Roman Catholic observance with Elizabethan feast days.[19] Also in the Ditchley manuscript, a poem dated November 17, 1584, refers to how the blind and dumb presenter must communicate "by silent Vttraunce" (Chambers 271)—a phrase apposite to describe the whole broad concept of silent language. Immediately following, the manuscript then includes an address to the queen that refers to an oracular old hermit (Yates 101). In the Accession Day tilt of 1590, another reference to hermit-like retirement appears in Lee's own farewell to his role as queen's champion at tilt in the poem "My Golden Locks Time Hath to Silver Turned." A variant of this poem as set to music by John Dowland epitomizes the unlikely fusion of disparate images that marks Elizabethan iconography. The poem describes how the knight is lured from his "cell," whence he has retired from court, by a glorious light emanating from where his goddess dwelt: "Aye me, he cryes, Goddess my limbs grow faint, / Though I times prisoner be, be you my Saint."[20] Knight and hermit, goddess and saint, the imagery conflates religion and court, pagan and chivalric myth.

Lee's entertainment of the queen at his home in Ditchley in 1592 brings full circle after nearly two decades of development a concatenation of imagery, theme, and devices, many of which thread through the whole fabric of Elizabethan culture. Self-reflexive comment on their appearance in the Ditchley entertainment exposes the deliberate nature of their immediate use and of this type of entertainment, and these relevant passages also implicate the larger context of Elizabethan culture. The first day's entertainment begins with poetry recited by speakers imprisoned in the trunks and branches of the trees in a grove—a device to be found in Ariosto, Spenser, and many another Renaissance pastoral—whereby literal "tongues in trees" (*As You Like It* 2.1.16) moralize landscape. A brief echo verse follows, a device that itself echoes verses used in earlier progresses, such as the Kenilworth visit in 1575, and, more memorably, in the closing pages of the second book of Sidney's *Countesse of Pembrokes Arcadia*. The queen is led to a hall "hung with allegorical pictures" that she is to decipher: "Drawe nere & take a vew of euerie table / in them no doubte some secreats are concealed" (Chambers 281). This device, too, often appears in Elizabethan literature, as in countless occasional ecphrastic passages, such as the parade of portraits during the course of Phalantus and Artesia's triumph in the first book of the *Arcadia*, or in the sustained explication of the "secreats" of a single pictorial representation in the mode of the speaking picture—for example, Lucrece's long consideration of the picture of the fall of Troy in Shakespeare's *Rape of Lucrece*.

The Ditchley entertainment also glances at the ambition and aspiration that motivated pageantry and the iconography incorporated in it. An old knight delivers a long poem that comments on the function of courtly pageantry: "For he that mightie states hath feasted, knowes / Besides theire meate, they must be fedd with shewes" (282), and an oration on the next day explains that, when tilting, the old knight was "manifesting inward Joyes by open Justes, the yearlie tribute of his dearest Loue." Together, these comments specify the political and psychological roles of pageantry, but the orator's further explanation for the hermit's retirement also hints at the more personally ambitious motivation for competitive pageantry: the knight had desired only the reputation for having loved, "till the two enimies of Prosperitie, Enuie and Age . . . cutt him cleane off from following the Cowrte, not from goyng forwarde in his course" (291). As for the allusion to the enemy Age, repeated references in these entertainments to the old age of the hermit-knight located compliments to the timeless Fairy Queen within the time and space of the quotidian world of the court, serving to heighten the fantastic aura that insulated the queen from mortal change. If successful, the fantasy would have banished from the memory of all present the uncomfortable coincidence in the year 1533 of the birth of both the aged hermit and the ageless queen.

As for the queen in whose honor these pageants were performed, aspiration, and possibly even the second enemy Envy, or ambition, are symbolically associated with her figure, too. The most prominent iconographic device in the entertainment, the crown and pillar, alludes to her power, both earthly and divine. The pillar evokes association with the pillars of Hercules, the device of Charles V that had been appropriated to Elizabeth as the monarch who would indeed enact the exhortation implied by the accompanying motto *(plus ultra)* and go beyond human limits. At Ditchley, the chaplain's oration on the second day spells out the current iconographic adaptation: the "owlde Knight, now a newe religious Hermite" has retired with his chaplain to a cell that he calls the Crowne Oratory: "and therefore aduansed his deuise on the entrance after the Romaine fashion in a Piller of perpetuall remembraunce" (290; 292). The "dying Loricus" makes his last will and testament to the crowned pillar in the last poem of the entertainment. Yet once more, Elizabethan iconography has synchronized the crown, the Romans, and Christianity through the timely stroke of a visual device.

Allusion is also often made to the Fairy Queen, and indeed in another entertainment that appears earlier in the Ditchley manuscript, the introduction of a "Knight clownishly clad" (270) parallels the allusion to the "clownish younge man" who will plead a boon from Spenser's Fairy Queen, according to the poet's prefatory letter (137). During the 1592 entertainment, Elizabeth is represented as having the superhuman powers of this mythic queen, including divine healing powers, so that she has cured the old knight of his ailments, as his page reports in the last speech of the entertainment:

> the sole vertue of your sacred presence, which hath made the weather fayre, & the ground fruitfull at this progresse, wrought so strange an effect and so speedie an alteration, that whereas before he seemed altogether speecheles, now Motion (the Recorder of the Bodies Commonwealth) tells a lyuelie tale of health, & his Tongue (the Cocheman of the Harte) begun to speake the sweete language of affection. So tourning him selfe about to the ayre & the lyght, O wretched man . . . fixing his eyes on the Crowne, he sayd Welcom be that blessed Companie, but thrise blessed be her coming aboue the rest, who came to geue me this blessed rest! (Chambers 295)

The page recalls that an irresolute debate followed between the chaplain and Loricus whether God or the queen had performed this "miracle," with Loricus yet crediting her "diuine power."

The page then reads the legacy of Loricus to the queen, his "Whole Mannor of Loue," a conceited allegorical itemization of his acts and feelings, represented as a lordly house and the surrounding landscape, for example,

> Arrable Lande of large promisses,
> Riuers of ebbing & flowing fauors,
> Gardens hedged about with priuate, for succorie, & bordered with tyme: of greene nothing but
>> harteseASe, drawen in the perfect forme of a true louers knott.

(296)

In their symbolical subjection of nature to monarch, these fictive testaments would have been fitting texts to accompany *The Ditchley Portrait*, largest of the portraits of Elizabeth, painted by Marcus Gheeraerts the Younger about 1592, which was formerly hung at Ditchley (fig. 6). Elizabethans commonly used gardens to represent personal values, whether through plantings of significant herbs and flowers, the figurative shaping of the beds, or the placement of statues of heraldic beasts or emblematic plaques. Indeed, Lee's Loricus bequeaths to Elizabeth his "Queene Apples, Pome Royalls, & Soueraigne Peares," in the course of the delicious wordplay of the last testament of his manner of love. The *Gesta Grayorum* (1594) is a contemporary example of the type, rendered very specific, describing the ideal garden with its water, beasts, birds, and fish as creating "*in a small Compass, a Model of Universal Nature made private*" (47). *The Ditchley Portrait* pictures the privatization of the universe of Elizabeth with its representation of the queen standing upon a map of England, her feet resting on Oxfordshire, near Ditchley, and with the outline of the curve of the surface of the earth visible in the background. It shows her dominance over the elements—sun, earth, thunder, ocean—as she stands between a simultaneously sunny sky on the left and a thundery one on the right. The fragmentary inscriptions and sonnet also bespeak her power and suggest the similarity of this image to Spenser's Fairy Queen. Strong cites this painting as the first to associate the sovereign with cosmic control of nature (*Gloriana* 137–38).

Because Lee originated the Accession Day tilts, because the records of his entertainments cover so many years and permit a glimpse of the development of a continuous theme, and because his later entertainments present a self-consciously retrospective view of the temporal dimension in pageantry, the model of the Ditchley entertainment of 1592 illuminates brief mention of other, more self-contained and localized uses of time in other occasional pageants. Possibly in the sixteenth century, and certainly in the twentieth, the most widely known of Elizabeth's occasional public observances were those connected with the defeat of the Armada in 1588. The queen traveled to Tilbury in order to conduct a review of her troops. Tilbury was mustered ten days after the Armada had been defeated at Gravelines on July 29, and in any case it was on the wrong bank of the Thames if it were to block the likeliest route an invasion would take.[21] In effect, however, the occasion had more to do with myth than fact, as both contemporary description and modern memorial confirm.

The occasion incorporated a great deal of visual display; indeed, visual display was the event. When the queen arrived with her escort of thousands at Tilbury, she was flanked by her two handsome if unreliable favorites: Leicester, returned to favor, and Essex, not yet having lost it. James Aske's long poem *Elizabetha Triumphans* (1588) recalls that the queen arrived with a "court-like stately troupe," like to Mars's own (Nichols, *Progresses* 2:565). To view the visual splendor was ecstasy:

> He happy was that could but see hir coatch,
> The sides whereof beset with emmerods,
> And diamonds with sparkling rubies red,
> In checker-wise by strange invention,
> With curious knots embrodered with golde,
> Cast such a glimse as if the Heavenly place
> Of Phoebus were by those his foming steedes
> On foure round wheeles drawne all along that way.
> Thrise happy they who sawe her stately selfe,
> Who, Juno-like, drawne with her proudest birds,
> Whose tayles do hold her heard-man's hundred eyes,
> Passed along through quarters of the Campe.
>
> (2:567)

The quoted passage typifies the insinuation of mythological allusion into the language of historical description in order to glorify the queen. Comparisons designed to enhance the power of the queen as well as her splendor embellish the narrative. Here the allusion to Juno evokes only magnificence perhaps, but several allusions to Bellona and Amazonian queens, and an explicit comparison to Voada and Vodice all attribute mythic military power to Elizabeth. Thirty years after her accession, Aske's rhetoric thus implies the need to maintain defense against the antifeminists in her kingdom. The poem begins on a note of apology with praise of the "Virgin Queene, / A Maiden Queene, and yet of courage stout" (2:548). Elsewhere, on the one hand, Elizabeth appears as mythic warrior queen with mysterious attributes ("strange invention," "curious knots"), and on the other, as prince and general. Her gestures in particular convey the image of masculine authority: she goes "marching King-like on" (2:566); she was "Most bravely mounted on a stately steede / With trunchion in her hand (not used thereto)" (2:570). Elizabeth's speech also implies the need to demonstrate manly courage. She begins by noting that she has come to Tilbury in spite of cautions to the contrary because she need not fear her subjects as tyrants must. "I know I have but the body of a weak and feeble woman; but I have the heart of a king, and of a king of England too; . . . rather than any dishonour should grow by me, I myself will take up arms; I myself will be your general, judge, and rewarder of every one of your virtues in the field" (2:536).

The readers of Aske's poem would have been relatively few, but countless thousands would have seen the queen in procession and in visual evocations of her as king and general, as Amazon and virgin queen, as living embodiment of the charisma of antique paganism as well as Christian election. In Richard Niccols's *Englands Eliza* (London, 1610), the iconography of Aske's poem is paralleled, with Elizabeth appearing as Tomyris queen of Thrace, astride a white horse and wielding a "martiall staffe" (Hhh4^r). A representation of the queen at Tilbury, on horseback and holding her staff, appears on a playing card as the queen of hearts and on an early seventeenth-century painting still at the parish church of Saint Faith, Gaywood, crudely expressing popular perceptions. No matter that there is no trustworthy eyewitness report to verify Elizabeth's costume, her gestures, or even her speech. The drama of her appearance was what mattered to her subjects, and it is what has lived on for four hundred some years after the performance.[22]

If the equestrian image of the queen fixed an impression of her manly or Amazonian courage and power on earth, another assimilated her to the divine. The queen's procession to Saint Paul's for thanksgiving after the victory inspired many visual representations, procession being a ready-made conveyance for both antique and Christian significance. Niccols's description fuses the two as he recalls how the queen rode under a gold canopy while people along her passage shouted their "Auies" (Iii4^v). The list of attendant dignitaries is long and specific, down to the "Queene's cloake and hat, borne by a Knight, or an Esquier," and a letter from the lord mayor to the livery companies ordered their attendance in livery and best apparel, with threat of having to answer at their peril for failure to comply (Nichols 2:537–38, 541). Elizabeth is represented in her triumphal chariot on a medal struck in Holland in 1589 commemorating the defeat of the Armada (fig. 31). On this image, she holds, not her truncheon, but a palm frond and a book, on which is inscribed the beginning of the Our Father in Dutch (Hawkins, *Medallic Illustrations* no. 128). Niccols voices the translation from pagan to Christian association visible on the medal: Elizabeth prayed "to th' *Olympian* Kings great Deitie" in her thanksgiving (Iii4^v).

Like her review at Tilbury, timed safely after serious threat had passed, the procession that followed was also scheduled conveniently. Although the Tilbury review took place in early August, it was not until November that the thanksgiving procession took place, in closer coincidence with the queen's Accession Day on November 17, and the lord mayor's letter of instruction to the livery company indicates that the first plan had been for it to take place on the day following, but it was deferred until November 24. November 19, meanwhile, was kept as a holy day throughout the realm, with sermons, bonfires, and livery appearances, so that the citizenry was well prepared in anticipation of the queen's appearance on the following Sunday in a chariot-throne under a canopy surmounted by the crown imperial (Nichols 2:538). If Elizabeth was the first monarch to observe dates from English history with special celebrations (Cressy, "Protestant" 34), she made this occasion extraordinarily memorable by extending its duration over many days.

The long duration of memory of the defeat of the Armada continues today. At least two of the pictorial images associated with the defeat of the Armada continue to be widely circulated in reproduction: William Rogers's engraving *Eliza Triumphans* (1589) and George Gower's painting, the *Armada Portrait* (fig. 3). That one extant impression of the engraving is much worn indicates that it was a popular print in its own day, according to Arthur M. Hind, who reproduces it as the frontispiece to *Engraving in England in the Sixteenth and Seventeenth Centuries*.[23] Roy Strong describes it as the first separate popular print of the queen and an early identification of the queen herself as the personification of Peace (*Gloriana* 113–14).

Elizabeth's subjects responded to her use of time with acute sensitivity, themselves creating fictions that manipulate time, occasionally for highly personal intentions, sometimes under inventively poetic guise, and rarely, dangerously, as expressions of ambitious political or economic motives. As a creator, manager, and participant, Robert Devereux, earl of Essex, combined these qualities in his uses of time in pageantry. If he was not the most ambitious of Elizabeth's courtiers, he was certainly the most indiscreet. Wotton attributes Essex's start upon the road to ruin to his inordinate haste following Elizabeth's public show of favor to him at Tilbury: "from thenceforth he fed too fast" (*Reliquiae Wottonianae* [London, 1685] 178). His pageantry displayed his bad timing: Alan Young comments that Essex made the queen's Accession Day Essex's Day as much as Elizabeth's (*Tudor* 37).

In the Accession Day tournament at Whitehall in November 1590, Essex appeared as part of a fictive funeral procession, all in black in a chariot drawn by black horses, the mourning color signifying his sorrow for either the death of Sidney in 1586, as George Peele's *Polyhymnia* (*Minor Works* 1:231–43) would have it (lines 110–12), or the queen's fury at her recent discovery that he had secretly married Sidney's widow (Strong, *Cult* 152). In either case, as George Peele's *Polyhymnia* describes the tournament, among the thirteen couples of tilters colorfully costumed, Essex and his company appeared "in funerall blacke," his chariot "full of deepe device, / Where gloomy Time sat whipping on the teame" (lines 100–101; 110). On Accession Day 1595, in an allegorical entertainment dramatizing a competition among occupations and loyalties, Essex, like Lee and Nashe earlier, employed the figure of a hermit, soldier, and secretary, in a thinly veiled invidious comparison between himself and Burghley and Cecil during the contest for appointment as secretary.[24] Essex represented himself as "tormented with the importunity" of the other three characters on this, the queen's own day (quoted by Young 173). Having denigrated the other's sense of timing, Essex proceeded to monopolize the rest of the afternoon and the evening as well with his self-centered pageantry, but if his own use of time was indecorous, he was alert to his queen's sensitivity to its passage. Tournament speeches composed by Essex or Bacon, and likely intended for the same day's performance, allude to a Blind Cupid who regains his sight, and as Seeing Cupid, presents the queen (then sixty-two) with the gift of perpetual youth (175).

Essex's earlier uses of time may have been clumsy, indecorous, offensive, but his last dramatic strokes were his most untimely. On the eve of his abortive rebellion, Essex's followers paid the Lord Chamberlain's Men to stage a drama about the deposition and death of Richard II (the play likely was Shakespeare's).[25] Elizabeth identified herself with Richard in a conversation with William Lambarde, as had some of her courtiers earlier, so suspicions of treasonable intent by the Essex party—although not on the part of Shakespeare's play, printed four years earlier—were reasonable. Strengthening the case against Essex was Sir John Hayward's dedication of his book on Henry IV to Essex as "*futuri temporis expectatione*," an expectation that some read as Essex's design upon the throne in future time. In the final analysis, the staging of this play weighed in the case against Essex. If it was Shakespeare's play that the Essex faction patronized, Richard's line shortly before his murder: "I wasted time, and now doth time waste me" (5.5.49) resounded for Essex with proleptic irony.

Time more often figured in the epideictic theme of royal entertainment than in outright rebellious schemes. Thomas Nashe's *Summer's Last Will and Testament*, performed at Archbishop Whitgrift's palace in Croydon in the summer of 1592, dramatizes the contest among the personified seasons with some of the most poetic of lines about the passing of time. The prologue describes the entrance of Summer, drooping, and pleads: "Go not yet away, bright soul of the sad year; / The earth is hell when thou leav'st to appear." Summer responds, "Summer I was, I am not as I was," but that "Eliza, England's beauteous Queen, / On whom all seasons prosperously attend" has ordered his death to be postponed until the end of her summer progress.[26] Shortly, Summer meets Solstitium, "*like an aged hermit*," who carries balanced hourglasses, one white, one black, emblems of the day and night, favor and downfall. Even in the midst of this melancholic farewell to seasonal beauty, Summer offers a subtle reminder of the flow of political power as he supplies the motto for Solstitium's device: "A mighty ebb follows a mighty tide" (158–59). As the work ends with the anticipation of his death, Summer wills his last fair days to the queen (then fifty-nine), commands Autumn and Winter to observe a charmed circle around her, and addresses Elizabeth: "Ah, gracious Queen, though Summer pine away, / Yet let thy flourishing stand at a stay" (203).

"Stand at a stay" time did quite literally at Beddington in August when Elizabeth visited late in her reign. Sir Hugh Platt concludes his *Floraes Paradise* with the "pretty conceit" of how Sir Francis Carew found himself caught up in the fictive calendar of the queen. For at least a month "after all Cherries had taken their farewell of England," Sir Francis retarded the ripening of his cherry orchard so that it should coincide with her appearance. This he managed by covering the trees with canvas and watering them artificially, keeping them from the rays of the sun, which would hasten their ripening, until he was assured of her schedule (M7^r–8^r).

From July 31 to August 2, 1602, Elizabeth visited Lord Keeper Thomas Egerton at Harefield, and there she was entertained by allegorical personifications whose self-reflexive discourse annotates such laborious compliment: "PLACE *in a partie-colored roobe, like the brick house.* TIME *with yeollow haire, and in a green roabe, with a hower glasse, stopped, not runninge.*" The ensuing dialogue between the two incorporates the usual compliments regarding the inadequacy of Place to accommodate the queen, "for noe *place* is great ynough to receive her," and the indecorous haste of Time, whose wings have been clipped by the queen (then sixty-nine) and his hourglass stopped—as it would be in ironical fact with the death of Elizabeth within the next year. If the separate devices were by then overfamiliar, the representation of time and place as coordinates locating the queen's presence uniquely mapped her progress toward divinity, as Place comments: "And doth not she make *Place* happy as well as *Time*? What if it she make thee a countynewall holy-day, she makes me a perpetuall sanctuary. Doth not the presence of a Prince make a Cottage a Court, and the presence of the Gods make euery place Heauen?"[27] Elizabethan transformation of place was a material coordinate of anxiety to stop time. Best if this domination could be effected within a sacral aura and with the loving assent of subjects. Place ends the entertainment by presenting Elizabeth with a jeweled heart.

A contemporary letter records that Egerton made Elizabeth a rich gift of jewels and an embroidered cloak, one jewel being worth £1,000, and the heart that dangles from the mouth of the serpent on her sleeve on *The Rainbow Portrait* (fig. 11) may well memorialize this occasion. Not all of Elizabeth's hosts could afford to be so extravagant, as is indicated by one motif that recurs over time in her civic welcomes. A number of places that were economically depressed at the time of the queen's visit seized the opportunity to apprise her of their hardship and delicately to imply their need of support. At least three such cities resorted to the same technique, an evocation of historical typology, for masking their timely appeal as an apology for the smallness of the gift offered to the queen. In 1566, when she visited Coventry on her way to the earl of Leicester at Kenilworth, the city presented her with a purse filled with £100, only a fraction of the value of Leicester's or Egerton's gifts, but larger than some offered later by other cities. The city recorder delivered a speech in which he recalled the "first advancement and flourishing state of this City" under former monarchs, detailing the generosity of the earlier Tudors, and alluding to the "lamentable ruin and decay" of the city at present, determined to "pass it over in silence, with great good hope conceived of a speedy repair thereof"—thus both maintaining his silence and loudly breaking it, too, under cover of rhetorical *occupatio*. The grace note to his "silent utterance" is his closing allusion to the updated example of the poor ploughman's gift of his handsful of water to the Persian king Artaxerxes.[28]

The recorder's welcoming speech at Warwick seven years later followed the pattern of the Coventry model, applying ancient history to present time, with minor differences: more classical allusions, and now the gift of water is offered to Alexander, by a poor soldier. On this occasion, the "faire wrought purse" held only £20, all in sovereigns—perhaps as a punning compliment to the monarch (Nichols, *Progresses* 1:315). In 1575, the city of Worcester also greeted Elizabeth with the contrast between former prosperity and present decay. Again Elizabeth was reminded of the generosity of her ancestors, and again the speaker resorted to *occupatio* in order gracefully to mask appeal. This time, however, the recorder's description of the economic hardship is graphic: where formerly 380 looms supported eight thousand men, now only 160 remain for the declining population of five thousand. The orator concludes by invoking the responses of both Artaxerxes and Alexander to their poor gifts as lesser types of Elizabeth's graciousness. If records are complete, this time, too, the gift is small: a gilt cup filled with gold, the whole worth about £51 (1:546–48).

The city of Norwich, by contrast, was careful to distinguish itself from less flourishing towns when the queen visited in 1578. Her entertainment was carefully programmed and updated by the civic authorities to represent the city as industrious and well-governed, and this time there was no appeal to exemplary Alexandrian trope. Preparatory renovation involved clearing, painting, and rebuilding where required; removing the pillory and cage; widening passageways. Forty bachelors were ordered under pain of fine to appear in prescribed costume to attend the city officials. The queen received a covered gilt cup bearing £100, and civic officials had agreed that no member of her train should be unbidden to both dinner and supper on any of the six days of their visit. A series of pageants and masques adverted to themes familiar from the queen's earliest public appearances, beginning with her coronation procession: Judith, Deborah, and various Old Testament texts set the tone for the first day. The difference was that whereas the coronation pageantry had represented the "Causes of a florishing Commonweale" as fear of God, virtue rewarded, and chastening of vice—the virtues of a good ruler and a submissive subject—twenty years later at Norwich, the emphasis has shifted toward the more specific qualities of a disciplined work force—the cherishing of labor, the expulsion of idleness (1:51; 2:143). These were illustrated by paintings of workers at seven looms weaving different kinds of cloth, and on the stage below by two groups of small girls spinning worsted yarn and making hose. A child representing the commonwealth of the city spells out the moral: "The idle hande hath here no place to feede." He concludes his verses with good mercantilist self-congratulation, "We bought before the things that now we sell," and the possible non sequitur that prosperity has come with the queen's help and divine aid (2:144–45). On the eve of her departure, a masque also recalled earlier progresses as once again pagan gods and goddesses presented emblematic gifts. This time, however, the heavenly train is introduced by Mercury, "the god of merchantes and merchandize, and therefore a favourer of the citizens, being thought meetest and chosen fittest to signify the same" (2:159).

The queen's response to the pageantry was enthusiastic: she pronounced the schoolmaster's oration the best she ever heard, knighted the mayor, and, shaking her riding rod, promised never to forget Norwich, "wyth the water standing in her eies" (2:166). Elizabeth appears to have been genuinely moved, and it is interesting to speculate why. Allowing always for the fragmentary nature of the evidence and the partiality of the recorders, it is nonetheless highly probable that she was impressed with the industry of the workers—in particular the female child laborers—the regimented cleanliness and order of the city, and the updating of the myths from old pageants to the economic specifics of a city staging a show of exemplary financial independence and prosperity. The queen enjoyed both a tight-fisted economy, on the one hand, and a reputation for open-handed generosity, on the other. She also rejoiced in the financial independence of her subjects, on the one hand, and their submissive decorum, on the other. Norwich extended her the luxury of having it all. In this respect, too, Norwich was exemplary, for a near-contemporary, Sir Robert Naunton (1563–1636), infers similar generalizations from her lifetime of public appearances:

> It is manifest, she left more debts unpaid, taken up upon the credit of her privy seals, than her progenitors did or could have taken up that were in a hundred years before her, which was an enforced piece of state: to lay the burden on that horse which was best able to bear it at the dead lift. And for

such aids it is likewise apparent that she received more, and that with the love of her people, than any two of her predecessors that took most, which was a fortune strained out of her subjects through the plausibility of her comportment and (as I would say without offense) the prodigal distribution of her grace to all sorts of subjects. For I believe no prince living that was so tender of honor and so exactly stood for the preservation of sovereignty, that was so great a courter of her people, yea, of the commons, and that stooped and descended lower in presenting her person to the public view as she passed in her progresses and perambulations and in the ejaculations of her prayers upon the people. (*Fragmenta Regalia* 44)

As much as to see, the purpose of Elizabethan progress was to be seen. Loricus's page in Sir Henry Lee's entertainment at Ditchley may have commented only as an aside that Motion is "the Recorder of the Bodies Commonwealth" (Chambers, *Lee* 295), but Elizabeth was fully aware that hers was the commonwealth's body, and she knew the political capital to be gained from visibly manifesting through motion the health of her body and hence that of the commonwealth. Countless letters and memoirs record her constant movement, walking, hunting, dancing—above all, dancing, and especially dancing to impress visitors and ambassadors. These reports register the intent of the activity. In 1565, Maximilian's ambassador wrote that he had seen Elizabeth performing some Italian dances in her apartments (Klarwill, *Elizabeth* 228), and the Scots ambassador Sir James Melville reported that he had been detained in England by Elizabeth for two extra days so that he "might see her dance, as I was afterward informed" (*Memoirs* 97). In 1599, John Chamberlain reported to Dudley Carleton that the queen had danced with the earl of Essex in order to honor the Danish ambassador (1:62), and in 1602, the duke of Stettin observed her "walking as freely as if she had been only eighteen years old" (von Bülow, *Diary* 51). The memory of her dancing at the age of seventy for Orsini, duke of Bracciano, lived on in history, for "then did the Queen dance a galliard very comely, and like herself, to show the vigour of her old age."[29]

What dance recorded on the microlevel, the procession and progress revealed on a larger scale of motion: the health and vigor of the queen's two bodies—the body of the aging monarch and the body of the enduring commonwealth. If the concept of the monarch's two bodies was a legal fiction, it was also a fantasy given historic expression in the queen's public performances. If the king never dies, then by the same logic the queen does not age; she lives in a perpetual present. So it was that the Virgin Queen danced her way into Elizabeth's old age, and the Fairy Queen traversed Elizabeth Tudor's kingdom on her progress toward eternity. Contemporary report of some of the last words of the dying queen record her significant complaint about the "chaine of yron" around her feet. When urged by the lord admiral to show her usual courage, Elizabeth answered, "I am tied, and the case is altered with me."[30] The progress of the one body of the commonwealth had halted; the motion of the other was stopped. The two bodies were disjunct. Time had stopped for Elizabeth Tudor, who, on her progress to the throne, had once stopped for Tyme.[31]

IV

FIGURE AND GROUND: CONVENTION AND INDETERMINACY, ABSENCE, AND SILENCE

CEREMONIAL DEPARTURES AND INDECOROUS PRESENTATIONS

The self is in part a ceremonial thing, a sacred object
which must be treated with proper ritual care and in
turn must be presented in a proper light to others.
                    Erving Goffman, *Interaction Ritual*

"Much company, much knavery," as true as that old
adage, "much courtesy, much subtlety."
                    Nashe, *The Unfortunate Traveller*

PROGRESSES AND TOURNAMENTS naturally allowed some latitude of movement and flexibility of program: scheduled at the queen's discretion, they offered contingent temporal and spatial elements as significant media of communication, like the examples cited in the last chapter. Narrower constraints bound the fixed ceremony, historic ritual, and some other events ruled by traditional proprieties: christenings, coronations, formal processions, chivalric rites, executions, and funerals, the subjects of this chapter. Before the Reformation, for example, the timing and the routes for civic ceremonies were determined by the division of the year into a ritualistic half and a secular half, the former affirming religious and social cohesion and running from Christmas to the feast of Saint John the Baptist on June 24, at midsummer; the other half of the year was devoted to economic activity and civic ceremony. Over time, the mayoral ceremonies of the second half became increasingly market-oriented in every sense. If economic constraints reduced the frequency and lavishness of civic feasts, and if the changing geography of the observances nonetheless charted the dominance of mercantile interests, these alterations reflected evolving market pressures rather than the willful imposition of a powerful individual (Berlin, "Civic Ceremony" 21). No less constricting than those regulating historic formal public ceremonies were the prescriptions of law, written order, or custom that implicitly governed even apparently informal events such as exchange of gifts; these remained largely outside control of the participants. Egregious violation of the decorum governing this type of occasion and the sanctions that shaped it constituted an idiomatic mode of abstention, dissent, or resistance.

English preservation of historic practice gratified writers of courtesy books and other arbiters; anxious concern to protect social hierarchy generated rigidity of prescription. Miri Rubin observes that "ritual, and especially processional ritual, possesses an inherent destabilizing element," and the necessary imposition of a linear form upon fluid social relations "distorts experiences" (*Corpus Christi* 265). The tension between the flux of social interaction and ritual prescription sometimes erupted into resistance, and each perceptible transgression sharpened anxiety to maintain social distinction through the visible signs of difference. Supervision of ritual and social formula was always difficult, sometimes impossible. The ineffective efforts of Italian officials legally to regulate the behavior of prostitutes stood as a cautionary precedent. So effective as an indicator of class was social form that prostitutes continually mimicked the modes of costume and gesture appropriate to the upper classes in order to assume their social advantages even though such presumption was subject to legal punishment.[1] The history of Tudor sumptuary regulation traces a similar cycle of rule, sporadic enforcement, and defeat.

Vigilant effort to preserve decorum dates from antiquity, and it motivated feudal punctiliousness of ceremony and permeated Mediterranean cultural protectiveness toward concepts of honor and social status. Fossil remains of this multicultural history of propriety are embedded in traditional Elizabethan ceremonial decorum. By nature, conventional occasions bore the cumulative weight associated with all historic civilized ritual, so any departure or variation became a channel for individual expression. Even apparently spontaneous occasions like gift giving and seemingly casual leisure activities were circumscribed by the unspoken ceremonial protocol of rank, so manipulative individuals played against those implicit prescriptions as well. On the other hand, transgressions risked disfavor or worse penalty. The unspoken protocol of rank abrogated the rules of game, whether at cards with the queen or at the tennis courts with nobility. The exchange of gifts was fraught with the possibility of offense unless both parties observed a nuanced decorum of gift exchange. Both the exemplary rule that would control social interaction and any deviation or spontaneous inflection of expected behavior constituted a mode of silent or extraverbal communication. So significant were departures that, at their most extreme, they might even be read as signals of treasonous intent, as in the seemingly trivial observance of the custom of removing one's hat in the presence of superiors. Failure to uncover was interpreted in this light in various cases of would-be assassins and rebels, such as the Marian martyrs, Gowrie's conspirators, and the earl of Essex—all of whom failed to doff their hats deferentially at critical moments.[2] Because the scheduling of coronations generally lay outside personal control, the orchestration of one coronation during the Tudor period exhibits the prototypical resources of manipulative improvisation on traditional coronation ceremony: the crowning of Anne Boleyn. Among all of the wives of Henry VIII, she was the only one besides her immediate predecessor to be honored with a coronation.[3] The purpose of her magnificent procession and coronation in the sixth month of her pregnancy with Elizabeth was obvious to contemporaries, as the causally conjunctive syntax of the report in Holinshed's *Chronicles* reveals: "After that the king perceiued his new wife to be with child, he caused all officers necessarie to be appointed to hir, and so on Easter euen she went to hir closet openlie as queene" (3:778). But if the pageantry was successful at manifesting Anne's queenship as a fait accompli, it was less so at ingratiating the new queen with many of Henry's resentful subjects.

Henry's management of the order of participants in subsequent public appearances of his children also bespoke changes in the royal hierarchy, the import of which was obvious to the principals, if not to the modern reader. Had Catherine of Aragon, his erstwhile queen, followed Henry's commands, the infant Elizabeth would have been carried to her christening in the same expensive shawl that had wrapped her half-sister Mary seventeen years earlier, but Catherine refused to surrender the garment for use in the ceremony. Later, when traveling during the childhood of Elizabeth, Mary was demoted to a litter behind that of Elizabeth, who was in pride of position, and later at the christening of the infant Prince Edward both Mary and Elizabeth were degraded in turn to a lower status in the ceremonial train. Mary had to be positioned by force on her litter behind Elizabeth.[4] After Mary's coronation, she displaced Elizabeth from her accustomed precedence to a degraded position behind the countess of Lennox and the duchess of Suffolk (Neale, *Queen Elizabeth I* 34). As so often is the case, drama articulates the cultural perception of departure from royal ceremonial decorum: in the play by Shakespeare and Fletcher *King Henry VIII*, Norfolk says of the Field of the Cloth of Gold (to name another significant and even earlier Henrician pageant), "Order gave each thing view; the office did / Distinctly his full function" (1.1.44–45). In these several cases, the view revealed the new order to which the old must give way. The view inscribed the new hierarchy, proscribing the old.

With Mary on the throne, Elizabeth suffered further indignities of lese majesty. An incident that figures twice in the works of Thomas Heywood records a blatant indication of Elizabeth's degradation. In *Englands Eliz-*

abeth, Heywood describes how Sir Henry Bedingfield, her "gaoler" (a term that Sir Henry resented), mistreated Elizabeth when, at Mary's command, she was transferred from the Tower to Woodstock (H6ʳ ff). Mary had ordered that Elizabeth be respected, but she was nonetheless deprived of the cloth of state behind her chair that would properly have been accorded to a princess. The display and the precise length of a cloth of state were signs of honor traditionally prescribed by rank (Segar, *Honor* V5ᵛ). According to Heywood, Bedingfield abused his authority and, in a further show of his contempt, sat himself in the chair that, together with two cushions and a rich carpet, had been prepared for Elizabeth, and from that exalted position he loudly called for his servant to pull off his boots (H8ᵛ). The episode is also dramatized in the first part of *If You Know Not Me You Know Nobody* (lines 901ff.). The intention of insult is obvious, although not, perhaps, the enormity of it, nor the reason why a chair should so readily become the dramatic prop for its expression; during the Tudor period, however, the decorum of seating was carefully calibrated according to degree, ranging from benches for the lowest of diners in the great halls, through stools for the "more worthy" company, and chairs for those classified as "the better sort," to the cushioned chair of state for the most elevated. Thus, in the second part of *If You Know Not Me You Know Nobody,* for example, when Hobson wishes to show respect to his visitors the merchant family Greshams, he calls, "Stools for these Gentlemen, your worships welcome" (line 270; emphasis added). Although chairs became plentiful only after the Restoration, it was the significance of the object rather than its rarity that served to underline Bedingfield's insult. The chair signaled the place of the master—in some cases, such as that of Bess of Hardwick, the mistress of the household; or it could, as a courtesy, mark the elevated status of a dinner guest.[5]

When Elizabeth came into her own as queen, as a mode of personal expression she, too, varied the behavior expected on conventional occasions. These departures began before her coronation. As dramatic signal of the new order that she would institute, she enacted her disapproval of the Roman Mass as it had been celebrated during Mary's reign by walking out of the chapel royal when Bishop Ogelthorpe, contrary to her instructions, elevated the host on Christmas Day. When she entered London before her coronation, at Highgate, where bishops kneeled in allegiance before her, she extended her hand to be kissed by each of them except Edmund Bonner, bishop of London, "which she omitted for sondry seuerities, in the time of his authoritie," according to John Stow (*Annales* [1615] Ggg4ᵛ). The bishops retaliated for her intransigence by refusing to crown her, although Ogelthorpe, bishop of Carlisle, eventually did so on the principle of choosing the lesser evil, lest the queen, rejected and enraged, become more adamantly heretical (Ridley, *Elizabeth I* 78). Elizabeth's alterations in traditional ritual continued through her coronation ceremony, an occasion heavily bound by the prescription of precedent. Ogelthorpe would have found it particularly rankling that his conciliatory performance of the crowning was followed by a mass at which, in accordance with Elizabeth's orders, the host may not have been elevated. Moreover, the traditional order of homaging was changed at Elizabeth's coronation so that after the bishop (presumably Ogelthorpe), the temporal peers followed, and at last then the other bishops, the ranking of the last two groups being a dramatic reversal of the order followed by Mary. In yet another conspicuous departure from precedent, Elizabeth allowed only the presiding bishop the ten yards of scarlet that were earlier, at Mary's coronation, allotted all the bishops. This wordless short shrift may have been only circumstantial testimony to Elizabeth's religious independence, but it does create compelling suspicion of her motives.[6]

Following Bedingfield's insult—if there is anything to the above account of it—and certainly in light of Elizabeth's former indeterminate status during the reigns of both Henry and Mary—the new queen must have taken satisfaction in the formal setting for the dinner that celebrated her coronation. A contemporary English account of the event begins with the observation that, after the service, "she dined in Westminster-hall, which was richlie hoong, and everie thing ordered in such roiall maner as to such a regall and most solemne feast apperteined" (Nichols, *Progresses* 1:60). A lengthy series of manuscript drawings of the coronation setting and procession also includes a sketch, perhaps unfinished, showing the queen, robed and crowned, seated alone under a canopy at a long, empty high table, before a cloth of state. Below her are four long, covered but empty tables.[7] Never was the term *splendid isolation* more graphically illustrated.

Elizabethan chroniclers took particular care in recounting the order of processions, the richness of costume and panoply, the details of ceremony at a length that is difficult to understand unless one is aware of the value placed upon order and protocol as inherent values, or, more precisely, as outward manifestation of the inward virtue of the social being or the good government of the well-regulated state. The meticulous sketches of the setting for Elizabeth's coronation, for example, indicate precisely where the cushions are placed upon which she will kneel when being anointed, when offering, and when praying (Egerton MS 3320 fol. 20^v–21^r). Verbal descriptions of such pompous ceremonies are also explicit, and it is in light of the value implicit in such reports that the impact of egregious deviation can best be understood. Accounts of openings of Parliament convey interest in relative position of the participants, in precision of execution, in the unfolding of the process itself in its temporal dimension. In their wealth of detail and sequential particularity, the accounts recreate the event and simultaneously its magnificence, index to the meaning of the event. A herald's account of the opening of 1572 is minutely circumstantial, so it is necessary to quote a very long paragraph in its entirety in order to reproduce the manner of the telling because it is constitutive of the significance of the ceremony:

> The Quene's majeste did take her coche at the garden dore of St James and was conveyed thoroughe the parke by her nobles, prelates and gentlemen and ladies *etc.* to White Hall where her Majeste stayed the space of one hower and there put on her robes and a diadeame of gowld with riche stones and jewelles on her hed. This done, she came from her pryve chamber in White Hall with her nobilite thorough the chambers to the hall and so to the common brydge called the Water Gate where her Highenes toke her barge and was rowed to the Kinge's Bridge at Westminster, wheras her coche was reddy with all her nobles and bushops in theyre robes on horsback, all men in order placed. And her Majeste beinge sett in her coche the gentlemen pensioners with theyre axes, the sargentes and [officers of arms (editor's brackets, indicating crossing out in the manuscript)] set were [sic] on horsback and the esquiries with others on foote on eache side of her Highnes' coche in good order. Next to her Majeste rod th'Erle of Kent with the cape of mayntenance and th'Erle of Rutland bearinge the sword next before. Then th'Erle of Oxeford, Lord Great Chamberlen of England, and with him th'Erle of Worcester, being for that tyme appoynted to be Erle Marshall, caryed the rodd next before. Then the Lord Admyrall beinge appoynted to be Lord Steward for that parliament. Then Mr Garter Kinge of Arms with ij gentlemen hushiers, he ryding in the myddest betwene them. Then the ij Archebushoppes, of Canterbury and York. And so every noble man and the bushoppes and barons ij and 2 *etc.* in theyre degrees and places in order, with the herauldes on eache syde. And so cam her Majeste thorough the pallays into the Kinge's Street and from thence to the north dore of the cathederall churche of St Peter in Westminster where there was made redy a place with carpettes, stole and cushions for her Majeste wher her Majeste allighted. And beinge placed therin the Deane of Westminster with divers other of the chanons, prestes and queresters beinge redy at the said dore to receyve her Majeste, the Deane kneled downe and sed a chapter with certyn prayers; which don he delivered unto her Highnes the rod of sylver and gylt with a dove in the tope of it which her Majeste toke and caryed in her hand. And then ther cam six knightes with a canapie under the which her Majeste was conveyed from the same litell north dore with the hole quyer of chanons and queresters singinge unto the west dore of the quyer, and so to the upper end of the same where was prepared a travers into the which her Highnes was conveyed, where she

continewed duringe the sermon that was made by the Bishop of Lincolne. The sermon being done her Majeste was conveyed under the canapie agayne and so with her nobles, prelates, barons and ladyes *etc.*, every man in order as before, brought her to the est dore of the churche and so to the west dore of the parliament howse where at the stayer foote the cannapie was taken away and delivered to the footemen which were reddy there to receyve the same as a fee dewe unto them. Then her Majeste was conveyed up to the parliament howse wher ther is a place made redy to withdrawe her selfe; stayed there a litell space untill the lords and bushopes had taken theyre places. And then her / Majeste cam forthe, the hatt of mayntenance, sword, the Lord Marshall and Lord Chamberlen, and Garter King of Heraldes and gentlemen hushers goinge before to make place, she was brought to the royall seatte prepparred on degrees with carpettes, cheyre, stole, cushions, under a riche clothe of estate. The Lady Leneux caryd the trayne all this tyme. Thus her Majeste beinge sett in her chayre of estate th'Erle of Kent with the hatt standinge on the right hand and the Lord Chamberlen with him, th'Erle of Ruttland and th'Erle of Worcester with the sword and rodd on the left hand, *viz* all placed, the lower howse cam into the same place. The Lord Keeper stode up on the right hand of her Majeste['s] clothe of estate, havinge a place there made for him, began an oration declaringe the cause of her Majeste's sommoninge of this highe court of Parliament: which done the knightes and burgesses beinge appoynted to repayre to the lower howse to chose theyre Speker. Then her Majeste cam downe from her seat to her withdrawinge chamber where she put of her robes and in the meane tyme the lords shiffted them. Which don, her Majeste cam forthe and the lordes and gentlemen went on before with the sword and rod caryed and the heraldes on the sydes of the noble men. And so cam downe the pryve stayres on the est syd of the parliament howse to the Queen's Brydge where she tooke her barge, the sword and Marshalle's rodd delivered to the gentlemen ushers. Other lordes departed and her Majeste was rowed to Whitehall stayres whereas she before had taken barge and so went thoroughe the howse to the parke where her coche was reddy, and with dyvers noblemen and ladyes retorned to St James agayne. And this was the end of the fyrst daye of her Majeste's goinge to the parliament howse *viz* viij[th] of Maye 1572 *anno* xiiij[th] of the Quen's Majeste's reigne. (*Proceedings*, ed. Hartley 1:267–68)

Because several qualities of this report are characteristic of Elizabethan description of ceremonious events, it has been worth quoting the passage in full as a narrative demonstration that simulates in its telling how duration constituted a dimension of honor and magnificence. The length of the passage is in itself typical, generated as it is by observation of material detail—especially, rich and costly detail (the jeweled gold diadem, the silver rod with "a dove in the tope of it"), gesture (who carries what), position (particularly right/left orientation), and movement. Moreover, the frequent repetition of the precise inventory of all persons and objects in the exact order in which they appear at each stage of the procession creates a predictability of stately rhythm. The heraldic intention is to describe ceremonial order: David Dean describes the demonstration of monarchical power in judicial, religious, social, and political realms as the processional embodiment of "the stable and ordered universe of Elizabethan England." He notes the conspicuous absence of the members of the House of Commons as evidence that the procession represented the medieval image of Parliament, and on the other hand, the conspicuous presence of the cap of maintenance, formerly a symbol of papal support, as a more recent cover for royal supremacy.[8] Presence and absence both testify to the transitional nature of the procession.

The text emphasizes order in other ways, too. The word *order* itself appears four times in the quoted paragraph, and with its meticulous circumstantiality and paratactic style (the word *then* appears eight times, together with many synonymous expressions as well), the passage reads with the narrative rhythm of a medieval romance or chronicle. This is not to suggest disorder; rather, the order is the very circumstantiality of the event, which the herald is fictively reconstituting in the manner of the telling.[9] The affect created through the repetition of series—of names, of persons, of offices, of actions, of removals—generates the reassurance of fairy or folk tale, the magical aura of litany.

Elizabethans would also have appreciated the value added by the slowly unfolding nature of the process—the enhancement of magnificence through duration of its display. As detailed in chapter 5, magnificence of procession extended even to the order of food service. For example, as the site for table service gradually was removed upstairs in the great houses like Hardwick, the procession of dishes mimicked the ceremonial ascent of the guests. The metaphorical prescriptions of household books encode cultural values that go far beyond the meal of the day.

If the hierarchy of salads and the procession of dishes required marshaled order, how much more the order of funerals? The length of the procession signified the status and magnificence of the deceased, as Lady Russell reminds Sir William Dethick, the garter king of arms, in the letter prompted by the forewarnings that bade her "provide a pickaxe." She proleptically orders the decorum of her own funeral march, enjoining Dethick to "set down aduisedly and exactly in euery particuler by it selfe the number of mourners due for my callinge beinge a Viscountesse of Birth, with their charge of blackes and the number of Waittinge Women for my selfe and the women mourners" (Coll. of Arms MS 151, 2:325). The procession for Edward, the earl of Derby, in 1572 included 500 yeomen in the last discrete section alone, and the corpse of Edward, the earl of Rutland, was escorted in 1587 by some 560 people (Stone, *The Crisis of the Aristocracy* 573–74). So many accompanied the hearse of George, the sixth earl of Shrewsbury, in 1590 that the heralds who arranged the procession with a crowd reputed to number twenty thousand, were hard pressed to order them all properly within the distance between the earl's castle and the church (Hunter, *Hallamshire* 98). Funeral expenses could be enormous: for Walter Devereux, earl of Essex, more than £1,100; for the earl of Leicester, £4,000.[10] Even though the costs of Essex's funeral included the expense of moving the corpse over mountains, the largest outlay was, as was usual, for the black cloth that outfitted mourners and all of the ceremonial decor.[11] The number of mourners in a procession indicates the cost of the ceremony. It may not be possible to calculate the exact number of participants in Elizabeth's enormous funeral procession, whether as pictured on William Camden's incomplete Funeral Roll (BL Add. MS 5408) or as Henry Chettle outlines it in his contemporary (1603) description entitled *Englandes Mourning Garment* (F2^r–3^v). Chettle does specify that 240 poor women led the group, and in the next five columns of text he lists all of the many officers who marched thereafter, ending with the whole guard who brought up the rear, "their halberds downward" in the manner that Lodowick Lloyd ascribes to ancient Roman custom (Lloyd, *Order* I2^r).

Lloyd, like many of his contemporaries, was eager to establish the antiquity and hence the exemplary decorum of current practice, so he looked to ancient Rome for the prototype for Elizabethan funerals. For instance, he lists a number of observances for the fallen Roman warrior: during the funeral procession, points of swords were turned downward, pikes trailed down behind the officers, ensigns were folded inward, horses were sheared and clipped. Elizabethan performance of many of these observances can be seen on Thomas Lant's roll of drawings of the funeral of Sir Philip Sidney that illustrates the magnificence of Elizabethan funeral ceremony and dramatizes the significance of scale. The inscriptions on Lant's roll describe "*The horse for the field . . . led by a footman, a Page rydinge, trayling a broken lance,*" and "*The Barbed horse . . . ledd by a footman, a page rydinge carying a Batlax the head downwarde*" (Hind 1:134). The long inscription that precedes the pictures explains that the halberds, pikes, and ensigns were all trailing, and that the drums and fifes played very softly. By inverting the normal physical position of the properties of combat, symbolic gesture silently expressed martial impotence, and by reenacting reputedly antique ceremony, the procession also embodied continuity between the two cultures, honored classical value being thus assimilated to early modern context.

In his description of Elizabethan funeral practice, Lodowick Lloyd demonstrates the power and intent of such nonverbal communication by applying the phrase *dumb Musick* to the effect of antique funeral processions. Lant's memorial drawings simulate something of the rhythm of procession in a silent but tangible, even kinetic, recreation of Sidney's lavish funeral. The roll measures about forty feet in length and is so designed that it could be displayed as the representation of a continuous procession in motion, whether mounted as a frieze or unrolled between two dowels. The length of Lant's roll is commensurate with the length of the procession that, according to Lant, numbered some twelve hundred marchers (132), and the slow progress of its unrolling mimics the retarded pace of the original march. Lant indicates on his roll the significance of number among the marchers, including as it did "*so many poore men as he was years ould viz 32*" (133), the customary symbolic participation of the poor representing society as the socially powerful wished to be represented—that is, a community embracing the whole spectrum of social classes. Although Sidney was only a knight, the participation of seven official mourners accorded him an honor conventionally reserved to barons, and the presence of Dutch officials recalled the political cause in defence of which Sidney had died, the English support of Dutch resistance to the Spanish king and his Roman Catholic religion. Moreover, the lord mayor of London, aldermen, and other influential citizens represented their special respect for the dead hero.[12] These differences silently marked the uniqueness of this funeral in its departures from the observances ordinarily accorded a mere knight.

So magnificent was Sidney's funeral that to the present it has often been mistaken for a state funeral, and so agreeable to the keepers of decorum that it apparently passed without specific objection to any departures from convention—if only because its grand display marched to the political and religious tunes of a state that was not in fact paying the piper. On a wider scene and over a long period of time, infractions of funereal convention drew bitter comment. Twenty years before Sidney's funeral, Gerard Legh was already complaining about "things that are out of order. Wherof morning at burials is not one of the least, at this day" because artificers, no gentlemen they, were giving to their burials "Viii. black gowns with hodes, & al they shalbe morners. And an Earle by law and order of Armes, may haue no moe" (*Accedens* Liiii[r]). Henry Barrow bitterly complained that money could buy the proper orientation of an ignoble corpse with the attendant ceremony "as if Duke Hector, or Ajax, or Sr. Launcelot were buried" (*Writings* 459). Segar echoes the cry in 1602, calling for the queen or the lord marshal to prescribe the number of mourners appropriate for each degree, the chief mourner being of the same degree as the defunct, no man being permitted to have mourners of a degree greater because "for some times we haue seene the buriall of an Esquire more costly then was fit for a Knight, and a Knights funeral such as might become a Lord" (*Honor Military, and Ciuill* Y^r). Vincent repeats a "remembrance" of a controversy between Garter and Clarencieux that arose when the latter had "intruded" into Garter's perquisites by burying the mayor of London as a knight because Sir John had been served at table in the manner appropriate to a baron (1:182–83).

Most discourse about funeral decorum concerns the proper ordering for burial of male members of the nobility. Glimpses of attitudes toward the burial of females appear in the interstices of written comment, and these reveal sidelights on ceremonial difference. According to Weever, even the mode of bearing the coffin in a properly ordered service signaled an important gender-based distinction: male corpses were properly borne at shoulder height, female at arm's length "to signifie, that being inferiour to man, in her life time, she should not be equalled with him at her death" (Weever, *Ancient Fvneral Monvments* B6^r). The funeral of Ophelia illustrates other differences that distinguished women's funerals on the basis of gender, marital status, and patriarchal power. Suicides were ordinarily denied conventional Christian burial, but Ophelia, a possible suicide, is allowed the customary "virgin crants, / Her maiden strewments" proper to symbolize female chastity, as well as the "bringing home / Of bell and burial" that signified the funeral of a Christian. These "maimed rites" are permitted Ophelia only because "great command o'ersways the order" prescribed for the common suicide, which dictated still greater obscurity (*Hamlet* 5.1.219–34).

A description of a closing of Parliament early in the reign of Elizabeth shows some of the other important contingents involved in ceremonial order of procession. The report is attentive to the seating arrangements within the house. Not only did the woolsack signify the source of much wealth in England, as noted by the French ambassador de Maisse in his journal (30), but relational positions thereon were also scrupulously observed. The parliamentary report, dated January 2, 1567, locates by name and office precisely who sat on each of the compass points of the woolsack, beginning with the most important: "And one the upper woolsacke sate the Lord Keeper till the Queene came, and then wente to his place at the raile on the right hand the cloth of estate," a maneuver that demonstrated both his power and its limits.[13] He sat at the upper point (the place of honor) until a higher authority arrived, at which point he arose and stood (signs of deference) at the right (the more honorable) side of the queen. The choreography is minutely programmed to orchestrate the relationships among powers. Against the grid of such conventional protocol and expectation, individual variation would egregiously display ignorance, singularity, or rebelliousness.

Having already signaled her religious difference during the events attending her coronation, Elizabeth continued to assert this and other differences of style in ceremonies thereafter. As is frequently the case, a foreigner is especially alert to deviations from expected order. Schifanoya's letter to Octaviano Vivaldino, dated January 30, 1559, reports at least three such variations in Elizabeth's procession to Parliament, which he describes as no more nor less magnificent than her entry to London. He notes two unusual aspects of the queen's costume. She wore a royal crimson robe lined with ermine, but not the hood generally worn by previous sovereigns, and a necklace with a "most marvellous pendant," thus individualizing her dress in the idiomatic manner that would characterize her style for the remainder of her days, even on the most formal occasions. The spectacular jewel was prelude to the gorgeous displays that would adorn her public performances and that are represented on her portraits.

A sententious comment in Thomas Bentley's *Monvment of Matrones* illuminates the cause for remark upon the queen's omission of the traditional hood. Bentley prescribes the *"ceremonie euerie woman ought by Gods word to vse in the time of praier, publike or priuate,"* and although this occasion was not religious in nature, Bentley's rationalization for mandating a head cover may nonetheless be relevant to Elizabeth's neglect of the hood: woman's head is the head of her topmost authority; to cover her head is a sign of her subjection to man because she is of man, given to man, so she should not have power over her head, that is to say, be headstrong (B8^r). Schifanoya's notation of the absence of the hood—even if formerly worn only dangling down the back as a vestigial sign of deference—suggests both the effectiveness of Elizabeth's omission and its possible intentionality. Also portentous was her command to the monks with torches who had come to lead her: "Away with those torches, for we see very well," dismissal of a piece consistent with her earlier rejection of Bishops Ogelthorpe and Bonner during her coronation celebrations (*CSPV:* 7:22).

Detailed descriptions, illustrations, and sketches block out the floor plans and the order of processing or seating for other kinds of important occasions: christenings, ceremonies of the knights of the Garter, guild affairs, dinners in the great houses, entries, civic events, executions, and funerals. The illustrated usual order in itself affords a glimpse of an important Elizabethan value, but the modern eye soon glazes over as yet another book of household orders unfolds or the whole series of descriptions of funeral processions unrolls in Machyn's *Diary.* Upon closer examination, however, the figure in the carpet takes shape, and, interestingly, so too do the stains, which are often even more telling. The carpet may figure the norms and ideals of the culture; stains outline the impress where an individual foot was put down. The difference distinguishes idiolect from cultural dialect, and so, quite apart from the impracticality and tedium of rehearsing the conventional ordering of all of these events, highlighting the occasional change or infraction more clearly focuses ceremony and protocol as a vehicle for silent language. Often a violation of conventional proxemics underlies the cause for notice, concern, or outrage. The language of proxemics—the culturally appropriate use of space—is ancient, implicit, and omnipresent, although the sense of appropriateness varies across cultures and may thus generate misunderstanding or conflict. Proxemics implicitly both prescribes spatial decorum and explains attendant personal discomfort or resentment at violation of underlying cultural assumptions. For example, the legendary explanation for King Arthur's invention of the Round Table as a means to eliminate sense of pride of place demonstrates the antiquity of anxious concern for relational position, a rationalization that Segar pointedly repeats in 1602 (*Honor Military* E4^v).

Contemporary observations illustrate Elizabethan sensitivity to an understood decorum of space. In a letter to Essex (July 26, 1597), Robert Cecil describes one of the most frequently discussed violations that took place in the royal presence. Cecil writes at Elizabeth's insistence so that Essex should hear of her triumph over the bumptious Polish ambassador: "He was brought in attired in a longe robe of black velvett, well jewelled and buttoned, and came to kisse her Majestie's hands where she stood under the state, from whence he straight returned ten yards of, and then begun his oration aloude in Latin, with such a gallant countenance, as in my lyfe I never behelde." He berated the queen at length for tolerating mistreatment of his countrymen, whereupon the queen, abrogating the customary delivery of a response by the Lord Chancellor, herself in extemporaneous Latin gave the offending ambassador a dressing down because "although I perceave you have read many books, to fortifie your arguments in this case, yet I am apt to believe that you have not lighted upon the chapter that prescribeth the forme to be used between kings and princes; but were it not for the place you hold, to have so publickly an imputation throwne upon our justice, which as yet never failed, we would aunswer this audacitie of yours in another style." She then appointed council "to see upon what ground this clamor of yours hath his foundation, who shewed yourself rather an heralde than an ambassador" (Wright, *Queen Elizabeth* 2:478–80). The emphasis in both Cecil's letter and the queen's own words upon the abuse of spatial decorum ("ten yards of," "prescribeth the forme," "so publickly," "this clamor of yours," "rather an heralde than an ambassador") highlights the implicit decorum that should have moderated the ambassador's style. The attack was grave, but Elizabeth seems to have been more offended by the formal indiscretion of the presentation than the substance of the accusation, to which she accorded the courtesy of a quiet review by her advisers.

Concern to enforce heraldic regulations against upstarts is often manifested during the time of Elizabeth. In his *Accedens of Armory* (London,
1568), Gerard Legh makes bitter jest of what he perceives as the decay of
heraldry, recounting (or perhaps inventing) a number of examples. He
blames partly the laxity of the nobility, such as those "gentle vngentils" who
would "rather sweare armes then beare armes. Who of negligence, stop
mustard pottes with their fathers pedegrees, or otherwise abuse them." A
large class of villains comprises those "stubble curres" who bear no legiti-
mate claim to arms, such as the one who, when challenged by the herald to
present his coat of arms, produced a jacket that he tried to sell to the herald.
Upon being instructed in coats of arms, "Armes quod he, I would haue
good leggs, for myne armes are indifferent" (Aiii^r–iiii^r). Other works, such
as Puttenham's *Arte of English Poesie* (105–6) or Sidney's elaborate parody in
the characters Dametas and Clinias in the *New Arcadia*, similarly mock the
clumsy efforts of ignorant upstarts to affect noble devices.

The queen was personally jealous to protect the privilege of class, as is
evident in the heralds' explanations for their actions; historical and belletristic documents indicate the eagerness of the privileged to institutionalize
their advantage through control of ceremonial observances and restriction
of the visible language of costume and device. A manuscript entry dated
"20 July 1591" prescribes the sanctions for a group of possible offenders and
it is explicit in describing the queen's minatory interest in the affair. The
order commands men to appear, bringing with them their arms, crests, and
evidence of pedigree for justification, the common concern for official
visitations. "The Queens most exelent Matie: being desyrouse that the
nobillitie and gentery of this Realme should be preferred in every degree of
honore as in worshyppe," Rougecross will "reprove comptroll and make
knowne Infamous by proclamation" all false claimants. Like Rougecross,
Clarenceux struggled with resistant offenders to enforce heraldic rules. A
communication dated "19. N. 1591" orders a miscreant to appear before
Shrewsbury under pain of fine and "further peryll & trouble that may
ensue" if he fails, as he has in the past, to comply with the heralds' attempts
to register those worthy of gentle status (BL Harl.69 fol. 54^r–54^v). William
Segar generalizes the rationale for concern: "*For as good order is an ornament
of great excellencie: so confusion causeth discord, and is the roote of many most
dangerous questions: which moued the Philosophers to say, that the losse of
worldly wealth is lesse grieuous to men of generous minde, then the priuation of
place and honorable estimation*" (*Honor Militarie* S2^r–2^v).

The queen also sharply rebuked her own officers for deviation from
accustomed order of ceremony. An undated communication addressed to
William Burghley, Charles L. Howard of Effingham (the lord high admiral), and Henry, Lord Hunsdon (chamberlain "of our house"), occasioned

by "many accidents of arms & Chivalry" following the death of George, earl of Shrewsbury (November 18, 1590), rationalizes Elizabeth's concern for heraldic order and summarizes serious violations. The errors, she says, arise "for want of due regard had unto the Actions of our Officers of Arms, Kings Heraulds & Pursuivants," and this negligence is "to the dishonour of our Nobility & Chivalry and to the disgrace of sundry familys of Ancient Blood bearing ye arms of their ancestors in applying & appointing the ancient arms Badges & Crests of some of our Nobility & Chivalry & of the Gentlemen of ancient Blood, to men that were & be strangers in Blood to them & not inheritable thereto." Nor, apparently, was it a case of simple negligence. The indictment continues with matters more serious. For gain, officers have appointed arms, crests, badges "for some other persons of Base birth or of mean vocation & Quality of living that were meet for persons of birth & lineage to receive honour either for service in Politick government or in Martial Actions wch Errours and disorders we of our Royall & princely dignity from whence all Inferiour honour & dignitys ought to be derived and protected," do authorize several officers with temporary powers to serve as earl marshal and to revoke any such unlawfully given arms.[14]

Of course, any deviation from the customary order of ceremony by the queen herself was cause for gossip, comment, and legend. Sometimes historical records reveal her direct involvement in the reordering of a ceremony, registering both her intervention and the interest of contemporaries in its significance. The investiture of knights, for example, occasioned comment upon ceremonial departures. It was a solemn occasion, one weighted with history and tradition, and one that Elizabeth was vigilant to preserve as a restricted and special mark of grace. She threatened, for instance, to "disgrade" some of the thirty-nine knights whom Essex had raised extravagantly during the campaign in Ireland. Only Cecil's argument dissuaded her from an extraordinary proclamation to that effect because it would "wrestle with the great seale of England, and bringe the authoritie therof in question," as John Chamberlain explained to Dudley Carleton in a letter dated July 1, 1600 (*Letters* 1:104–5). The queen was in such bad temper that Sir John Harington confided to Sir Hugh Portman, "In good soothe I feard her Majestie more than the rebel Tyrone, and wishd I had never received my Lord of Essex's honor of knighthood" (*Nugae Antiquae* 1:317). So in the end, Elizabeth backed away from her impulse to undo the new order created by Essex, but only because of her commitment to the sign of a larger order.

On the other hand, Elizabeth was also capable of benign, even playful actions during ceremonies when she officiated, secure in her primacy of position, improvising gestures that dramatized her command of subject and occasion. When she raised Dudley to the peerage at Westminster, for example, "with great solemnity, the Queen herself helping to put on his ceremonial," the Scottish ambassador James Melville observed that she could not resist tickling Leicester on the neck in a gesture that immortalized her favor (*Memoirs* 91–92). On another occasion, Elizabeth showed an extraordinary interest in young Herbert of Cherbury as he, along with the customary spectators, watched her ceremonial Sunday procession through the presence chamber to the chapel. Pausing, with an oath, she inquired of his identity, expressed regret at his early marriage, and with another oath extended her hand for him to kiss, clapping him softly on the cheek twice with another oath (Neale 217). Thomas Fuller recounts another of Elizabeth's gestures that lived on in legend as revelation of the humanity of the queen in her relations with courtiers. Because Burghley was troubled with gout, Elizabeth would insist that he remain seated in her presence, protesting "*My Lord, we make much of you, not for your bad legs, but for your good head*" (*The Holy State* 268). Francis Bacon relates how on still another occasion the queen seemingly pretended to have forgotten to knight a group of gentlemen who were waiting, kneeling in an order hierarchically ranked by Lord Burghley. Affecting to recall herself after having forgetfully passed by the line of gentlemen, the queen then knighted them from the lowest to the highest order, explaining later, "*I have but fulfilled the Scripture; The first shall be last, and the last first,*" wit thus serving to preserve in legend as well as chronicle another ceremonial aberration (*Works* 7:157–58). Only a monarch or a fool could insouciantly break the rules.

On less formal occasions, or rather occasions presumably less formal, infringements upon royal prerogatives or a nuanced social hierarchy—whether real or fancied in the imagination of a hypersensitive monarch—quickly drew the queen's angry response. If one was in disfavor because of a supposed violation, the usual avenue to a return to grace was through the offering of a gift, but the offering in itself occasioned yet more anxiety about all of its attendant circumstances: what to give, how and when to offer it. The offering of a gift was an occasion weighted with meaning and with pitfalls for the ignorant or the unwary. Hence the necessity for formal prescription regarding the offering of a gift to royalty. The repertory of suitable gifts was established in historical religious and diplomatic precedent for Tudor practice, and the types often appeared in the records of analogous Italian occasions: cups, chains, plate, and lengths of cloth. In *The "Libro Cerimoniale" of the Florentine Republic* Francesco Filarete, the first herald of the Signoria, systematized the protocol observed in public ceremonies during the 1450s, many echoes of which resonate in Elizabethan practice. Filarete prescribed the correspondence between the value of the gift offered and the social rank of the recipient. This calculation was rendered particularly delicate by the need for cities to be careful not to outgo the magnificence of the visitor in what Filarete's modern editor calls "rhetorical overkill," embarrassing the visiting party through an overwhelming excess (64).[15] In England, the calculus of prestation was further refined: according to one foreign visitor, a newly elected lord mayor of London "may demand a gift of some thousand pounds from the city, not more than £10,000 however, and the smaller the demand made, the greater the honour" (Platter 157–58).

The giver had carefully to assess the gift as a reflection of the honor of both giver and receiver. The articles ordained by Henry VII for regulation of his household (1494) stipulate that when a queen comes over London Bridge for her coronation, the city must receive her "in most royall wise with a great guifte, for their owne worshippe," thus suggesting the reciprocal honor of the gift (*Collection of Ordinances* [1790] 123). Even the messenger bearing a royal gift might share in the honor of giver and recipient, as Sir Nicholas Throgmorton reminds Dudley in the letter (1560) in which he urges that Dudley move the queen to make amends for the egregious lack of a gift for the envoy of the duke of Savoy on an earlier mission. A delegate should bring the duke "a chayne of four or five hundred crownes from her Majestie, yt should well repaire all that is past, and your Lordshippe shuld wynne to yourselfe moche honour."[16]

The decorum of prestation was most highly institutionalized in the offering of New Year's gifts, an ancient observance that George Whetstone represents in his *Heptameron of Civill Discourses*, commenting upon the contrast between English and Italian custom: "This order the *Italians* use, the best giveth newe yeares giftes to his inferior freendes, and in England cleane contrarie. The Tennaunt giveth his Lord: the meane Gentlemen, to Knightes: Knightes to Barrons: Barrons to Earles: Earles, Marquises: and Dukes, to their soveraigne Prince," which order, says Whetstone, is nearer the original Roman practice than its later Italian inversion (199). As was often the case, honor displaces equitable material retribution. The English variation was controlled by a prescription dating even earlier than the time of Henry VII. An old manuscript conveys the sense of the occasion as a closely observed exhibition of one's social rank and status in royal favor. The clothing to be worn by the king is minutely specified, dictating that if the king's ermine "pane be V ermine depe, a duke shall be but iiij; an erle iij." His majesty is to sit at the foot sheet of his bed to receive gifts, and in return to give his servants their rewards, their value to be calibrated according to a schedule described. The queen's costume is similarly prescribed in detail, and she, like the king, is to sit at her foot sheet; her rewards, "I trow they shall not be all things so good as the King's"—the reduction in value of the "rewards" being thus scaled down to the lower status of the queen.[17] As explained in chapter 4 above, the extant inventories describe in specific detail gifts of jewelry and clothing made to Queen Elizabeth, calculating their costliness of materials and craftwork; the records also document the weight of the gifts of plate that were made by the queen in return. Ideally, prestation institutionalized the courtiers' sense of their place in the hierarchy of noblesse oblige, their expression of dutiful gratitude to the queen, and her reciprocal material recognition of their service.

In practice, there was often some admixture of self-interest invested in gift-giving, especially in the presentation of gifts that fell outside the formal structure of prestation. Leicester, according to the French ambassador de Maisse, introduced the custom for the host to give the queen gifts upon her departure from his home when she was on progress, even though he would already have spent a great deal on her lodging and entertainment. The custom became so popular on all of the queen's special occasions that all courtiers offered gifts, and "when they cannot give her anything else, she gladly takes a dozen angels" (*Journal* 14). These gifts were regarded as capital investments in goodwill, but other occasional gifts were more immediately market-oriented.

In a letter to an unidentified correspondent, Sir John Harington describes his hesitations and doubts regarding the planned offering of a gift to Elizabeth at the time when a lawsuit was pending to recover some of his forfeited ancestral land holdings. "I will adventure to give her Majestie five hundred pounds, in money, and some pretty jewell or garment, as you shall advyse; onlie praying her Majestie to further my suite with some of her lernede counsel, which I pray you to find some proper tyme to move in. This some hold as a dangerous adventure, but five and twentie manors do well warrant my tryng it."[18] The editor notes that in 1572 Harington did indeed give the queen a gold heart encrusted with diamonds, rubies, pearls, and emeralds: "thr q^{trs} di. and farthing golde weight," according to the bookkeeper of New Year's gifts. Others also personally imprinted their gifts: Sidney's gift of a tiny jeweled whip, presented at a time when he was in disfavor, and those other New Year's gifts that through allusion recall the giver—Walter ("Water" to the queen) Ralegh's jeweled bucket, Hatton's jeweled knots. On neither hand were the New Year's gifts disinterested. Rowland Whyte describes to Robert Sidney the links in the chain forged in 1595 between one courtier and the queen by favor and gift:

> Her Majestie is in very good Health, and comes much Abroad: Vpon *Thursday* she dined at *Kow* [*sic*], my Lord Keapers Howse (who lately obtained of her Majestie his Sute for 100 £ a Yeare Land in Fee Farm.) Her Intertainment for that Meale was great and exceeding costly. At her first Lighting, she had a fine Fanne, with a Handle garnisht with Diamonds. When she was in the midle Way, between the Garden Gate and the Howse, there came Running

towards her, one with a Nosegay in his Hand, deliuered yt vnto her, with a short well pened Speach; it had in yt a very rich Iewell, with many Pendants of vnfirld Diamonds, valewed at 400 £. at least. After Dinner, in her Privy Chamber, he gaue her a faire Paire of Virginals. In her Bed Chamber, presented her with a fine Gown and a Juppin, which Things were pleasing to her Highnes; and, to grace his Lordship the more, she, of her self, tooke from him a Salt, a Spoone, and a Forcke, of faire Agatte. (Collins, *Letters* 1:376)

Whyte's letter captures in short compass the element of tit-for-tat evident to contemporary rival suitors, and it also demonstrates how they valued the queen's spontaneous response. She had, after all, already received costly gifts in overplus at Kew, but her spontaneous seizure of plate items as souvenirs was read as a gesture to "grace his Lordship the more." Such queenly grace might be costly, and it could also be greatly inconvenient. Sir William St. Loe wrote to his wife Bess of Hardwick about his own experience with the imposition of queenly favor: "The quene yesterdaye her owne seylff rydeng upon the waye craved my horse; unto home I gave hym, resevyng openlye for the same manye goodlye wordes." St. Loe shows no resentment or irritation, but his next and last sentence of the letter expresses his wish that he were home (Hunter, *Hallamshire* 108).

The offering of the special gift as token of apology or plea for favor was not conventionally coded by tradition or written inventory, and its indeterminate nature heightened the anxiety of an occasion already fraught with the caprice, indifference, coldness, resistance, or anger of a volatile queen. Historical literature suggests that Elizabeth calculated her displays of disfavor as a strategic weapon, and her unpredictability kept courtiers off balance. On their part, the courtiers, too, manipulated their attentions and especially their gifts so as to lead the queen to take notice of her neglect. Although often not a reliable source, *Leycesters Common-wealth* makes the plausible suggestion that Leicester contrived temporary fallings-out with the queen as a way of enhancing his favor in her eyes in the long view: "For if her highnesse fall not out with him as often as hee desireth to gaine this way, then hee picketh some quarrell or other, to show himselfe discontented with her, so that one way or other, this gainefull reconciliation must bee made, and that often for his commodity. The like art hee exerciseth in inviting her Majesty to his banquettes and to his houses, where if she come, shee must grant him in sutes, ten times so much as the charge of all amount unto: so that *Robin* playeth the Broker in all his affaires, and maketh the uttermost penny of her Majestie every way" (91). On the other hand, Leicester did sometimes genuinely provoke the queen's anger, and when he did, a gift was the specific palliative. For instance, while he was in the Low Countries as her representative, supposedly acting under explicitly limited powers, rumors of his ambitious behavior infuriated the queen, as mentioned in chapters 4 and 5. Thomas Dudley reported Elizabeth's suspicions to Leicester on February 11, 1585, cautioning him to moderate any apparent extravagance and to mollify the queen by writing her and to "bestowe some two or three hundred crownes in some rare thing for a token to hir majestie" (*Correspondence of Robert Dudley* 113–14).

Leicester's tokens, offered over many years of courtship, may have contributed to his indebtedness at the time of his death, but for others less favored by the queen, even a single peace offering could be financially ruinous on both sides of the grave. The case of Robert Carey illustrates the potential size of the burden. He was advised by his father to placate the queen for her angry disapproval of his recent marriage by appearing at court to participate in the Accession Day triumph in 1593. He complied by participating in the ceremony as the Forsaken Knight, and his caparison together with the gift cost him "above four hundred pounds"—this expense for a man whose income was only £100 a year from the exchequer "during pleasure," and who was £1,000 in debt, as the editor of his *Memoirs* notes (28).

Like the offering of a gift, its acceptance, too, was weighted with momentous possibility. During her entry into London for her coronation celebration, the first public offering of a gift to Elizabeth from her subjects created a particularly tense situation. Confronted with the gift of a bible, symbol of her conformity to Protestant expectations and thus a potential source of offense to Catholic Spain, her ally against France, Elizabeth tried to deflect the political implications of her personal acceptance by deputizing a courtier to receive the gift in her behalf. Defeated in this ploy by the insistence of the city worthy that rather she personally receive the book when lowered to her on a silken thread, Elizabeth still controlled the reins by deferring this commitment until she should first have received the city's gift of money, a sequence that in the telling makes clear her tactic and her triumph in wordlessly enacting her use of giving ceremony as a mode of control.[19] On another occasion, Elizabeth was more thoroughly successful in controlling the circumstances of receiving a gift and negotiating its implicit attendant contract of obligation. At the Gesta Grayorum revels of 1593/94, she deferred her reciprocal presentation with a promise of a gift to be delivered at some future, undetermined time in response to the honor accorded her (Apple, " 'And Attend that in Person' " 123–36).

The occasion for presentation to the queen of a gift as reconciliation or petition had to be as minutely planned as its cost. Unless the offering was embedded in a conventional ceremony with a prescribed format for gift giving, it was critical that the encounter be contrived to appear as at once decorous, opportune, and spontaneous. Granted time for reflection and the binary categories operative in response to a request for formal interview, the queen would likely deny access to a disgraced petitioner. To grant access was already to concede. On the other hand, a seemingly spontaneous meeting allowed the queen the latitude of choosing to hear a suitor without the commitment implicit in admittance to a formally scheduled hearing. Thus Rowland Whyte wrote to Robert Sidney that after Elizabeth had repeatedly evaded a promised meeting with Lady Leicester, the queen was surprised on Shrove Monday in 1597 by her appearance at the comptroller's "with a faire Jewell of 300 £" (Collins, *Letters* 2:92–93). The proferred gift had to be costly, commensurate with Elizabeth's perception of the gravity of the petitioner's offense or that of a third-party beneficiary like Essex, who would presumably benefit from the gift offered by Lady Leicester.

Acceptance of a present naturally affirms a social bond; rejection of a gift bespeaks an alteration of the relationship between the parties, as Drake unhappily recognized when "some prime Courtiers refused the gold he offer'd them, as gotten by piracy," according to Fuller (*Holy State* 137). If Barnabe Barnes specifically allowed that the treasure distributed by Clifford, Drake, and Essex was, on the other hand, not piracy, but the spoils of professed enemies that would legitimately benefit the state of England (*Fovre Bookes of Offices* Biiij^r–iiij^v), Drake's men were more likely mindful of the indebtedness incurred by the recipient. Antonio de Guevara's *Menosprecio* had long ago cautioned (in the 1548 translation by Sir Francis Briant): "The giftes makes a man muche subiecte that receiueth the[m] for assone as any man doeth take of another an horse or a goune, or often sitte with him at his table, he bindes himselfe therby to beare him fauour, to defende his quarel, to kepe him company, to take his parte, and to loue that that he loueth" (Briant, *A Dispraise* h.v^r). If a horse or a gown could so bind parties, how much more a child? The English practice of sending their children to learn manners through service in others' great houses was a custom that institutionalized the bonds of reciprocal giving. It was remarked by one foreign visitor in 1500 as evidence of the English lack of affection, but the children in effect were hostages to peace between great families.[20] William Cornwallis offers a more cynical manipulation of gift, earned-wage-as-present: the statesman should not reward immediately for services rendered but at some future time, "when it shall looke altogether like your bountie" (*Essayes* part 2, Mm^r).

For ordinary mortals to accept a gift constituted a concession, but for Elizabeth, it was not one so binding that forgiveness necessarily followed, as Lady Leicester learned to her sorrow in 1599 when her son Essex was in fatal disfavor. Whyte then reported to Robert Sidney that the lady had "in Hand a Gown she will send to the Queen, which will cost her 100 £. at lest" (Collins 2:172), but she was in effect made what Elizabeth herself called in her personal discourse, an answer answerless. On behalf of Lady Leicester,

Lady Scudamore presented the "most curious fine Gown. . . . Her Majestie liked yt well, but did not accept it, nor refuse yt, only answered, that Things standing as they did, yt was not fitt for her to desire what she did; which was to come her Majesties Presence, to kiss her Hands, vpon her now going to her poore Home" (2:174). The queen rejected a personal gift from Essex, and although she did accept gifts from his sister Penelope Rich, she was likewise denied favor on behalf of her brother (Devereux, ed., *Lives* 2:93). For Elizabeth, as for Lady Anne (*Richard III* 1.2.202), "To take is not to give."

If the fictively spontaneous occasion for reconciliation in fact operated within rather formal although unwritten constraints dictated by time, place, and circumstance, genuinely spontaneous gestures were more at risk of traversing the bounds of an uncharted protocol. The queen was most indulgent toward such gestures when motivated by flirtatious courtship. She was reportedly charmed when Simier stole one of her nightcaps from her chamber as a love token to be given his master Alençon during his courtship of the queen, a daringly impulsive act that might have risked severe censure outside the context of the suit in Alençon's behalf (Somerset, *Elizabeth I* 308). Other cases of unanticipated encounters tested one's decorum, tried one's civility; in extreme challenges to her perception of social order, the queen would personally intervene. Then as now, the playing field was often the setting for such trials, and then as now, the trials ignited hot tempers. Under the guise of the freedom of play, games essentially challenge the player's ingenuity at testing the limits of rules, formal and informal. Dudley, heated one day in play at tennis with Thomas Howard, impulsively borrowed the queen's handkerchief to mop his sweating brow, an action that outraged his opponent and habitual enemy Norfolk, who vowed to lay his racket across Dudley's face for his presumption, a threat that in turn angered the queen (Derek Wilson, *Sweet Robin* 176). More grave was the contretemps at the tennis court between Oxford and Philip Sidney regarding precedence in order of play, a dispute that led to exchange of hot words, including Oxford's insulting address to Sidney as "puppy" and Sidney's precisionist rejoinder regarding literal predication of the term.[21] Oxford's behavior was graceless: James Cleland might have had the incident in mind when he advised young nobles not always to insist upon precedence because "that prerogatiue which yee had before, by antiquitie of race, by vaine glorie contrarie to al honour is changed into an iniurie: which oftentimes cannot be satisfied but by the law of arms" (*Hero-Paideia* Z4^r). The queen reminded Sidney, however, that his lower rank dictated the need for apology to his superior, thus forestalling a likely duel.

Apology indeed often followed upon impulsive action, and the formula for apology embedded recognition that the presumed offender had violated the decorous imperatives of social hierarchy—whether the apology was delivered at the time of offense, as in the case of the *Faerie Queene*'s Sir Calidore, who had sought to know divine mysteries beyond human ken when he happened upon the dance of the Graces; or at the moment of punishment, as in the case of the amputation of the ghoulishly eponymous John Stubbs for his having published opposition to the queen's marriage plans; or from the scaffold as in the cases of countless offenders, Essex among them. Apology was the occasion to articulate the rightness of things as they were conventionally expected to be, although Stubbs managed a small vindication by thereafter signing himself Scaeva, identifying himself with the legendary Roman hero *Scaevola* (left-handed), who burned his right hand as testimony to his indifference to death. To stage one's apology—however lengthy, however formally constructed, however rhetorically contrived—as a spontaneous overflow of feeling from the scaffold was to earn a place in chronicle or legend.

The queen's impulsive actions were, of course, the most observed by all observers, her slightest movement subject to scrutiny and speculation. The subject who received a favorable conciliatory gesture from the queen in public considered himself blessed, like Sir John Harington, who confided to his memoirs, "The Queene stoode up, and bade me reache forthe my arme to reste her thereon. Oh, what swete burden to my nexte songe!—Petrarcke shall eke out good matter for this businesse" (*Nugae Antiquae* 1:167). Dudley's seizing of the queen's handkerchief provoked enmity; her offering of a handkerchief to wipe a smudge from Ralegh's face provoked wonder. Lupold von Wedel entered the event in his journal, juxtaposing his account with the notation that there was much gossip regarding her great love for him, "this one may easily credit, for but a year ago he could scarcely keep one servant, whereas now owing to her bounty he can afford to keep five hundred" (Klarwill 338–39).

Conversely, signs of queenly disfavor also figure large in private communication. The Spanish ambassador reported that when Dudley presented his patent of nobility to the queen, she published his current disfavor by slashing it in half with a knife (Perry, *Word* 164). De Maisse recalled that after an interview with Elizabeth, he presented another ambassador who elicited another playful moment: "He was on his knees and she began to take him by the hair and made him rise and pretended to give him a box on the ears" (60–61). Such accounts are hard to trace, let alone to verify, but their currency in private letters and memoirs bespeaks the significance accorded to the queen's impulsive actions. Many stories circulated regarding Elizabeth's violent expressions of displeasure with her servants, especially regarding their sexual behavior. She reputedly beat Mary Shelton, lady of the Privy Chamber, breaking her finger with a candlestick when she learned of her marriage to John Scudamore.[22] Elizabeth considered it necessary to surround herself only with courtiers who met her standards of decorum, and these extended even to their private lives. Not only did illicit relationships and secret marriages offend her: she was particularly anxious to prevent marriage between parties of unequal social status. Sometimes her spite extended even to decorous petition for her permission to marry. For various reasons, Leicester, Hertford, Sidney, Perrot, Essex, Carey, Ralegh, and Southampton all felt her fury over their marriages.[23]

No less than the queen, courtiers and other more private parties were jealous of their sense of place, a jealousy that often manifested itself in scuffles regarding their physical position in public spaces. *The Covrt of ciuill Courtesie*, a work that was several times reprinted and attributed to various authors, goes to lengthy pains in prescribing reproaches to be employed by the young gentleman who in the home of another is seated inappropriately, the responses ranging from pleasant jests to do-it-oneself seating.[24] Among the humiliations that faced Essex upon his return from his failure in the expedition to Ireland was his demotion in order of procession to Parliament, behind his enemy, the newly created earl of Nottingham and lord steward of Parliament, just as exaltation followed later upon Essex's appointment as earl marshal, an honor that ranked him above Nottingham in order of precedence (Devereux, *Essex* 1:466–72). A letter from Frances Cooke to Lord Burghley, earl marshal, uses the literal and metaphorical senses of place with an explicitness that shows how the two significations implode in Elizabethan usage. Mrs. Cooke complains of the efforts of Lady Cheke, "a woman of no greater byrthe," to put her down. She begs that the greatness of her house be honored even in its present misfortune, "wherof it semeth my Lady Cheke, to whome I neuer gaue cause of just offence, takethe great aduantage, for she dothe not only offer me all the wronge and disgrace that she can in Courte, in takinge place a fore me, wher it becometh not me in modesty to striue for it, but she oppenly publisheth to euery body that I haue no place at all."[25] Sir William Pickering, fancied by some, most ostentatiously by himself, as a suitor to Elizabeth, met a similar check to his premature arrogation of the dignity of place belonging to more noble contenders such as the earl of Arundel, when he encountered Arundel as they passed through the chapel within the apartments of the queen. Arundel chided Pickering for trespassing: the proper place for an underling of his rank was in the presence chamber, a dressing down to which upstart Pickering responded with verbal abuse (Neale 73–74).

Contests for precedence among courtly rivals were also fought through nonverbal means. How better to display one's wealth and power than by maintaining a magnificent style of life, for was not magnificence a virtue proper to nobility? The Venetian ambassador reported to his senate in 1554 that the English nobility resided habitually in their country houses "where they keep up very grand establishments, both with regard to the great abundance of eatables consumed by them, as also by reason of their numerous attendants, in which they exceed all other nations, so that the Earl of Pembroke has upwards of 1000 clad in his own livery." He also computed the cost of maintaining the tables to feed the royal household as exceeding the country's entire military budget by more than 30 percent (*CSPV* 5:544; 553). Sumptuary laws prescribed the exact numbers of messes to be served each social rank, but consumers often violated the most precise efforts to regulate diet. The queen herself exceeded twofold the amount allotted her by the book of diet and supplemented it with expensive delicacies served in as many as forty silver dishes (Klarwill 336). Another Italian visitor recorded the degree of obeisance expected from the servants, who always removed their caps in the presence of their masters. "Moreover, because gentlemen go about on horseback, followed by eight or ten servants in livery, if the horses stop suddenly to urinate, the servants remove their caps and hold them in their hands until the horse has finished" (Magno, *Journal* 146). Stow noted that when Leicester rode into London in 1566 to meet the queen, his train numbered seven hundred (*Three Chronicles* 137). To begin to rival this scale of expenditure indebted many a gentle and lord, Leicester among them, so it is no surprise that the lord keeper should have chided "gentlemen that leave hospitality and housekeeping, and hide in cities and borough towns," according to John Chamberlain's letter to Dudley Carleton on June 13, 1600.[26] The average number of household servants was more than one hundred, a constant and enormous expense to which one must add the supercharges of maintaining tables for daily guests, including many unexpected—a service to be maintained even in the absence of the lord of the house.[27] Shakespeare's Lear embodies the paradox of needless need for display of magnificence when Goneril deprives him of it, "O, reason not the need!" (2.4.264). Ostentatious display may have been downscaled since the fifteenth century, but neither official efforts at sumptuary control nor gentlemanly agreement could effectively legislate restraint. Extravagance continued to serve as a mode of expressing individual desire to be associated with the boundless magnificence of the cynosure. Thus Rowland Whyte wrote to Sir Robert Sidney in May 1597 that four new knights were to be installed, and participants in the ceremony had agreed upon no more than fifty men apiece, but nonetheless the lord chamberlain would have three hundred and Sir Henry Lee two hundred (Collins, *Letters* 2:51).

Not all departures from ceremonial convention involved nobility or court activities. In Herefordshire, Thomas Coningsby reinforced his scuttling up the social ladder en famille by retaining a bunch of liveried followers whom the local residents called the "redcoats." Battle with the more established Croft family resulted in the death of one Croft supporter and the wounding of Coningsby. When Herbert Croft, heir to the family estate, appeared to serve as a magistrate at the Lenten assizes carrying a pistol, followed by fifty armed men, and with three hundred tenants, he insisted upon taking his place on the courthouse bench above Coningsby, thereby fueling a contest that Coningsby carried to the Star Chamber.[28] Even churches offered no sanctuary from disputes regarding hierarchical order. Distinctions were maintained regarding the order of offerings, the grade of communion wine (claret for the lower classes; muscatel for the gentry).[29] Parishioners jealously, even violently, defended their putative rank in the order of seating. The "great disorder" of seating became a concern of the courts in Wakes Colne in 1594 because of the mixing of "the rich with the poor and not according to their calling." Contention for place could generate physical scuffle: one wife landed a punch with her elbow on an intruder who took a seat "above" her; elsewhere, offended parties retaliated against perceived degradations by crowding, shouldering, or grabbing the offender; others vented their resentments by the breaking of stools. A dispute in Northerden, Cheshire, exemplifies many aspects of dispute involving place and position. In contest for part of the lordship of the township, William Tatton and Edward Vawdrey fought each other through infringements upon each other's claimed space through enclosure, hedge cutting, and barriers to highway access and water rights. The worst insult, however, was Tatton's destruction of the Vawdrey family pew in the parish church.[30]

The potentiality even within the church for violent protest necessitated official regulation and restraint. Quite forgotten was Cranmer's rationalization for church ceremony as outlined in his letter to Henry VIII in 1536: like secular laws, "even so were the laws and ceremonies first instituted in the church for a good order."[31] In a letter dated January 25, 1564, regarding clerical controversy, Elizabeth deplored "how Diversity, Variety, Contention, vain Love of Singularity either in the Ministers or the People, must needs provoke Almighty God, and was to her discomfortable, and brought danger of ruine upon her People and Country," indicting the church hierarchy for "suffering of sundry Varieties and Novelties both in Opinions, and especially exterior Ceremonies" as cause for open disorder (Strype, *Annals* 1:417). Within the context of the same religious disputes early in Elizabeth's reign, Cecil used similar language to chide the "certain fond singularities of some men" who deviated from prescribed orders. Cecil's observation that "the question is not of doctrine, but of rites and ceremonies" was a distinction not to be observed in the rebellious disruptions of ceremonies by opponents of the square cap and surplice who saw papist influence in the costume. So hot was the resistance that conforming clerics were pulled from the pulpit and physically attacked, a funeral service was disrupted, and one rebel stole the consecrated bread and wine lest they be distributed in communion by a surpliced minister. When the vice chancellor enjoined Oxford students to restrain their protests against classmates wearing the prescribed garb, he found his horse tonsured and wearing a priest's hat.[32] These singular inversions of ceremony expressed anxiety that prescribed ritual was indeed a question of infringement upon doctrine.

For those who broke the bonds of community, and for those who seemed only to weaken them, a silent lexicon of ceremonial inversions advertised their disgrace. Sometimes gossip circulated news of less serious violations by those whose honor hung on reputation, as when the cleaners reported that at a feast for ambassadors given by the duchess of Suffolk, the house was left "mervelowsly by pyste and by spewyd to the great shame of thos banquettars" (Stow, *Three Chronicles* 142). As a grim reversal for more serious offenses, the heads of noblemen who fell from grace were elevated among other high and mighty skulls on the Tower of London. Thomas Platter counted more than thirty on the top of the tower, commenting that their descendants boasted of this, pointing out the ancestral heads as a mark of high distinction and nearness to the Crown; "thus they make an honour for themselves of what was set up to be a disgrace and an example." Platter also observed that the traitor would first have known his fate through another extraverbal sign, the reversal of the blade of the ax carried before the judge at the trial when he was about to announce sentence so that it turned toward the condemned man, a reversal that Shakespeare and Fletcher use to dramatic effect in *King Henry VIII* (*Platter's Travels* 155; 163). The manner of torture and execution that today seems inhumane signaled in its time a dramatic nonverbal externalization of inward criminal intent. Castration killed the seed for further treasonous acts; drawing and burning the inner organs rendered visible the treasonous heart and stomach; quartering and scattering the evildoing body mimicked and ended its vagrant behavior.[33]

From ancient times, the ceremony for degrading a knight involved a series of reversals of the ceremony for installation. Segar describes the example of the earl of Carlisle, convicted of treason in 1322. Appareled in all of the robes of his estate, he was disrobed by a knave who hewed his spurs from his heels, broke his sword over his head, and removed all of his fine garments, after which he was hanged. For graft, the degradation was no less ceremonious. The miscreant was disarmed on a high stage, each piece of his armor named as party to the offence as it was removed one piece at a time following a funeral psalm: the helmet secreted the traitorous eyes, the

gauntlets right and left committed the crime on the one hand and consented to it on the other, and so on. He was then rebaptized as though
anew, renamed Traitor. The degraded knight was then removed from the
stage by the king and twelve knights in mourning robes, "not by the stayers
hee mounted vp when he was made Knight, but threwe him downe tyed
vnto a rope. Then with great ignominy hee was brought vnto the Altar, and
there layd groueling on the ground, and ouer him was read a Psalme full of
curses."[34] The symmetry is reflected through the looking glass of ceremony
of honor.

Punishment of commoners also employed visualization and parodic
variation or inversion: a processional banner picturing a woman flaying her
servant with a carding tool, while the guilty mistress was compelled to wear
the offending implement around her neck; the severing of the right hand of
John Stubbs, printer; a fish seller collared with a ring of smelts for his
dishonest deal with fish designated for the queen's purveyance (Machyn,
Diary 17; 189). The rough justice of vigilante guardians of sexual mores
particularly enjoyed parodic mimesis of the supposed crimes or offences
of those who transgressed conventional sexual borders or gender-specific
roles. Stow's memoranda include notice of a minister caught in adultery,
who "was caryed to Brydwell thrughe all the stretes, his breche hangynge
aboute his knes, his gowne and his . . . [knave's] hatt borne afftar hym with
myche honor," although the marchers were later chided for their display
(*Three Chronicles* 127).

Neighbors of scolding wives took it upon themselves to enforce customary sexual and gender roles by publicly humiliating the supposed offenders
through disorderly, often mimetic processions. A carved relief on the north
wall of the hall at Montacute House represents a cautionary image of a
henpecked husband being punished in this way for having suffered his wife
so to dominate him. In 1604, a drunken tanner was beaten out of his house
by his wife: disguised as a woman, a neighbor rode upon a staff in order to
shame the wife's abuse of the drunk. This rough ride was known as a
"skimmington," a term that may have derived from the kitchen utensil
used for skimming. Often the victim, his effigy, or his mimetic double
would ride backwards, as symbol of the offending reversal of socially acceptable roles. Invasion of privacy and disregard for lawful order sometimes
led to a mob breaking into a home to beat or to duck the wife.[35] Stow notes
that in 1565 a man was carried on two staves borne on four men's shoulders
"for that his next neybor sofferyd his [that is, his neighbor's] wyffe to beat
hym. There went with hym ny iijc. men with handgunes and pikes well
armyd in cowrsllytts" (132).

More harsh still were the punishments meted out to vagrants, as explained in chapter 6, and indeed to anyone who migrated from what Barry

Taylor calls "the geography of order."[36] The humiliating public procession from the vagrant's door to the pillory was another parodic inversion of honorific triumph—the pillory being a manner of tethering to a fixed site of degradation those who would transgress their proper place in society by straying from it. Repeat offenders could be permanently put in place through execution.

Elizabethans so highly prized ceremony that Shakespeare's Henry V refers to it as "idol Ceremony" (4.1.240). An enormous literature and material witness show the investment in ceremony—whether in the punctiliousness of coronation of a monarch, the stateliness of procession to Parliament or the prose describing that procession, in the presentation of a gift or the procession of food to the table, in the seating of nobility before a cloth of state of appropriate length or of a citizen in the proper pew in the parish church. Respect for position was thus physically demonstrated through material order and bodily decorum. Harington's metaphor for failed ambition was grounded in physical reality: "Goode caution never comethe better, than when a man is climbinge; it is a pityfull thing to sett a wronge foote, and, insteade of raisinge ones heade, to falle to the grounde and showe ones baser partes" (Letter to Thomas Howard [April] 1603, *Nugae Antiquae* 1:339). Punishment for violation of ceremonial decorum was parodically ceremonial, and, like its prototype, the parody was manifested bodily.[37] Whether by spiking the head of a noble on London Bridge, riding a uxorious husband on a pole, or locking the head of a vagrant beside a pillory post, Elizabethan justice enacted social hierarchy by putting everyone bodily in his or her place. The procession to that place of execution of justice traced or reversed the malefactor's metaphoric path to higher position, a ceremonious inversion of ceremony for those who would indeed have found their pursuit of singularity in vain. Their bodies or their body parts were metonymic witness to the constraints of Elizabethan justice. Other forms of sanction were also enacted through the body—even in its absence, as we shall see in the next chapter.

CHAPTER EIGHT

ABSENT/PRESENCE, PRESENT/ABSENCE, GESTURE, SILENCE, AND THE USES OF INDETERMINACY

By being seldom seen, I could not stir
But like a comet I was wond'rd at,
That men would tell their children, "This is he"
Henry IV, part 1 3.2.46–48

There's language in her eye, her cheek, her lip,
Nay, her foot speaks.
Troilus and Cressida 4.5.55–57

THE CALENDARS OF CHURCH and state, the timing of seasonal change, institutionalized procedures, popular expectations shaped through repeated observances—these were the principal determinants of Elizabethan ceremony: where, when, and under what physical circumstances it took place. To an age in which many speak without irony of an instant tradition or a new classic, these constraints may seem rigid and closed to innovation, but firm as these Elzabethan categories were, they did allow for variations that Elizabeth often improvised. Less explicitly formulated than codified observance, and more insidious than direct verbal deviation, but no less important, were nonverbal qualifiers of the meaning of ceremonial occasions: the decorum of bodily presence or absence, and, more subtly, the indeterminate uses of present/absence and absent/presence, of gesture, of silence. In his *Annals of the First Four Years of the Reign of Queen Elizabeth*, John Hayward analyzes the queen's manipulations of these media through a "more felt than seene manner of proceeding." As soon as her title was proclaimed, she immediately moved from Hatfield to London "for that the presence of the Prince is of greatest moment to establish affayres" (5–6). Elizabeth's movements thereafter consistently demonstrate what Kenneth Burke has called the "synecdochic relation" between person and place (*Grammar* 7).

Absence was an ever-present condition of Elizabethan daily life. The structure of the family and of life at court prescribed separations sometimes lengthening to years of absence from lovers, family, home, and country: the education of a courtier took place elsewhere, and his service at court necessitated continual long absences. In today's world, perhaps only the conditions of boarding school, college, corporate transiency, or service abroad in the Peace Corps or the military approximate the conditions usual to Elizabethan courtly life, and then only on a shorter scale. So difficult and even unusual was physical presence that contemporary discourse often concerns the appropriate decorum of presentation of the self. The rigors of courtly behavior governed the queen's presence chamber—even in her absence. When at home or at play, gentlemen were to convey a dignified image of their commanding presence.

Geography engendered the conditions of absence: increasing urbanization and national centralization around London and the court required frequent and long separations, even for heads of families, particularly when these courtiers invested their fortunes in distant prodigy houses and country homes.[1] Roads were difficult in good weather, impassable in bad, and modes of transport were torturously slow and uncomfortable. For instance, even in the month of August, Elizabeth Cavendish's hurried flight from Chatsworth to London (a distance of about two hundred miles) in order to join her dying husband in 1557 took her four days and three nights (Williams, *Bess of Hardwick* 35). When the queen traveled on progress during the summer, her retinue averaged only ten miles a day.[2] At the end of the century, William Kemp danced the morris from London to Norwich in only nine days, and his account of this performance describes nearly impenetrable roadways, overgrown and full of waist-deep holes. His marathon was indeed a feat, as his title indicates and his account testifies (*Kemps Nine Daies Wonder* [8]).

Impediments to physical presence created the need for a decorum governing absence and for compensatory modes of expression for the absent party. Rules and conventions governing absence are occasionally specified in extant documents, such as the regulations for official Garter observances, and the conventions sometimes become subject for explicit comment, as in the courtesy books and in the third book of Puttenham's *Arte of English Poesie*, which has much to do with the decorum of behavior as well as poetry—specifically, the decorum of presence (Whigham, *Ambition and Privilege* 66). More often, the decorum of absence must be inferred from the disappointed, outraged, or surprised speculations to be found in contemporary comment and letters.

Among the primary media for expressing the interests of the physically absent were the letter, the sonnet, and the visual image on portrait, coin, or effigy.[3] The use of such artifacts as reminders of the physical presence of another is their essential function, as young Elizabeth reminded her brother Edward VI in 1547 when he asked for her portrait, begging him to recall when he looked upon it, "you wil witsafe to thinke that as you have but the outwarde shadow of the body afore you, so my inwarde minde wischeth that the body it selfe were oftener in your presence."[4] Pictorial representations could also serve to simulate attributes that were absent from the subject, such as ambitious Leicester's role as the queen's doggedly faithful subject in his representation of himself on the series of coins related to the campaign in the Low Countries, whereon he appears as the queen's good servant, the faithful sheepdog reluctantly leaving his flock (Hawkins, *Medallic Illustrations* 1: no. 100).

From the earliest moments of her reign, Elizabeth dramatized her appearances so as to render them both politically useful and historically memorable. Her public appearances have been subject to much scrutiny, especially her coronation ceremony. Although neither her contemporary observers nor modern scholars are entirely agreed about whether she did indeed withdraw her presence from the elevation of the host at her coronation mass in order to signify her displeasure with the Roman Mass, the interpretation that she did is strengthened by clearer indications that Elizabeth indeed withdrew to her traverse at another mass on Christmas Day.[5]

In the December preceding her January coronation, Elizabeth attended mass in her domestic chapel. In a letter to William More, Sir William Fitzwylliams describes her behavior:

And ffor newes yo^u shall ondyrstand that yestyrdaye beyng Chrystemas day the quene's ma^{tie} repayrd to hyr great closet w'th hyr nobles and ladyes, as hath ben acustomyd yn ssuch high feasts. And she parseving a bysshope p'paring himselfe to masse all in the olde ffowrme, she taryyd there on'till the gospelle was done, and when all the people lokyd ffor hir to have offryde according the olde ffaccon, she w'th hyr nobles reeturnyd agayn ffrom the closet and the masse, on to hir p'veye chamb'r, w'ch was strange on' to dyv's. &c blessid be God in all his gifts, &c. (*The Loseley Manuscripts* 183–84)

The speculation is based on recognition of present/absence as a vehicle of expression, the withdrawal of her visible presence here signifying the queen's displeasure with the religious observance. The gesture was a rhetorical figure in action.

Contemporary rhetoric spells out the significance of silent withdrawal. The queen's abrupt and partial disappearance enacted the trope aposiopesis, the uncompleted sentence broken off as though the speaker were afraid, ashamed, or angry, with the rhetorical effect described in Peacham's *Garden of Eloquence*; that is to say, the gesture raised a "great suspition . . . yet nothing playnly tolde" (N.iᵛ). Proleptically, Quintilian had said of the figure that it may also give an impression of anxiety or quasi-religious scruple ("vel sollicitudinis et quasi religionis").[6] Ironically, one of the most popular Elizabethan rhetorics, Thomas Wilson's *Arte of Rhetorique*, repeats the age-old prescription of silence as the chief virtue in woman, but earlier commends the advantage of *occupatio* as the device whereby "in saiyng we will not speake, we speake our mynde after a sort, notwithstandyng," thus glancing at the expressive power of withdrawal into silence—whether expressing anger, reservation, uncertainty, or what contemporaries called *politique* (400–401). It is particularly telling that the queen did not leave the chapel altogether: her continued presence within the chapel preserved her communion with the essential service. In this way, Elizabeth simultaneously enjoyed the benefits of absence and presence. During the marriage negotiations in 1581, a similar compromise was proposed in behalf of Anjou's religious scruples: after he and Elizabeth exchanged vows before two bishops representing the religion of each, she, under the proposal, would withdraw for prayer in her chapel while he would retreat to another, separate space for his Romanist devotions (Doran, *Monarchy and Matrimony* 182–83). The paradoxes thus engendered by absence or silence fall under the umbrella figure for amplification called *synoeciosis,* or in Puttenham's homely translation, *cross-couple,* so called because "it takes me two contrary words, and tieth them as it were in a paire of couples, and so makes them agree like good fellowes, as I saw once in Fraunce a wolfe coupled with a mastiffe, and a foxe with a hounde" (*Arte of Poesie* 206). When John Hoskins described this figure in *Directions for Speech and Style,* he quoted the example from Sidney's *New Arcadia,* "absented presence," a key phrase in this chapter, and, indeed in the work of Sidney, with his heavy use of the absent presence of characters in disguise, of eavesdropping, of rhetorical devices that figure absent presence poetically, such as occupatio, metonymy, and synecdoche (36). While verbally sparring with Benedick, Shakespeare's Beatrice unhappily employs the figure, "I am gone, though I am here" (*Much Ado about Nothing* 4.1.292).

The presence of any queen generates a strict decorum generally taken for granted. The loud affront of the Polish ambassador who used the occasion of presentation to the queen as a forum for vociferous attack upon her policy was recognized as a violation of the ordinary constraints upon an ambassador's visit. In another notorious example of violation of the decorum of presence, only the physical interposition of Nottingham by placing himself in the queen's line of sight toward Essex saved him from the fatal consequences of first angrily turning his back upon the queen when she boxed his ear for his contemptuous manner and then, worse, moving toward his sword (Birch, *Memoirs* 2:384). Curiously, though, she might also choose to overlook an outrageous violation, as when she affected not to see two courtiers engaged in fisticuffs and a beard-pulling tussle.[7] Her erratic reactions to such outbursts kept her courtiers off-guard, as Robert Markham observed in a letter to Harington in 1598/99 with reference to Essex's threatening gesture, for "tho' the Queene hathe graunted forgivenesse for his late demeanor, in her presence, we know not what to think hereof. . . . [W]e do sometime thinke one way, and sometime another" (*Nugae Antiquae* 1:241–42).

Beyond the ordinary constraints of any royal presence, Elizabeth imposed uniquely exacting standards that were no less consequential than unpredictable. Thus she might parody the gorgeousness of a courtier's plume of bird of paradise by affecting one upon her elbow or her shoe, vent her disapproval of a courtier's waistcoat by spitting upon it, or express her admiration for the magnificent gown of a lady-in-waiting by confiscating it for herself. The handsome presence of a new courtier might single him out for years of favor, or the unapproved marriage of a long-standing favorite might mark him for exile from court, even to the Tower. On the other hand, every publicly extravagant queenly gesture was cynosure for gossip, especially during periods of courtship, as when Elizabeth kissed Anjou on the mouth and presented him with a ring from her own finger.

Contemporary discourse indicates the discomfort of attendance in the presence, the physical discomfort a reminder of the courtier's subservience. Thus George Carey complains to his wife Elizabeth in a letter written on November 13, 1593, that an obligatory meeting with the queen involved much "weeresum kneelinge."[8] There are signs of some relaxation toward the end of Elizabeth's reign, as when John Harington in his *Treatise on Playe* makes amusing analogy to seating and anticipates greater concern for comfort, arguing for greater ease in the presence chamber and for the admission of card playing as pastime for those in attendance, who had often to spend long hours without occupation while awaiting official summons or duty. Harington argues that people who forbid card playing as indecorous in the presence chamber are like those who would argue that "it would not as well become the state of the chamber to have easye quilted and lyned forms and stools for the lords and ladyes to sit on, (which fashyon is now taken up in every marchawnts hall,) as great plank forms that two yeomen can scant remove out of their places, and waynscot stooles so hard, that, since great breeches were layd asyde, men can skant indewr to sitt on" (*Nugae Antiquae* 1:202).

Nor was the physical presence of the queen an unmixed blessing in recreational moments. One assumes the physical discomfort of appropriate costume and bodily carriage for court, but Thomas Platter noted moreover that even when men played cards with the queen, they did so while kneeling (*Travels* 193). Puttenham laid it down as an axiom that "in gaming with a Prince it is decent to let him sometimes win of purpose, to keepe him pleasant," as Elizabeth's courtiers knew to their sorrow (*Arte* 295). The presence of the ruler overruled the rules of the game. Losses to the queen and to other courtiers were sometimes heavy. Lord North often lost as much as £70, and when he lost this sum in December 1576, it was seven times the amount he spent for the queen's New Year's gift in that same month; moreover, he had already lost £60 earlier in the same six-month period. Still, North's loss was only a fraction of the £800 that Robert Cecil reputedly suffered at one sitting for higher stakes in 1602. Gambling losses figure large in the books of Henry Percy, too. Upon his succession in 1585, the earl of Northumberland's expenses became enormous, partly due to normal costs of service at court, but also, according to his own report, because of his profligacy. In his first audit period, he lost £729. Although he regained some of this so that his net loss was £154, one may note for comparison that in 1585, the net value of the five Percy estates in Northumberland was only £826.[9]

Elizabeth had suffered first-hand some of the psychological and political manipulations of presence. The radical change in her sister Mary's accessibility once Mary became queen initiated Elizabeth to the remoteness of power. Indeed, ambassador Giacomo Soranzo reported to the Venetian senate on August 18, 1554, a perceptible difference after Mary's coronation in her treatment of Elizabeth (*CSPV* 5:538). Elizabeth became so uneasy with the political uncertainty and humiliation of her position at court that she was granted permission to absent herself, only later to be summoned peremptorily to return in spite of a prostrating illness. After her own accession, she, too, played the game of approach and withdrawal. Her early relationship with Mary Stuart was characterized by plans for three aborted meetings within a short period (Neale 34–36; 132). Always, politics shaped policy regarding access between royal personages.

Politics also shaped the configuration of meetings with persons in her service. Both the formal structure of the privy chamber and conventional spatial arrangements in the life of the queen preserved traditional signs of the significance of the body of the sovereign. Tradition provided models for the daily presence or absence of the queen and for the subtle nuances of present/absence, that is, the physical presence of one who signals personal separation from foregrounded action, and of absent/presence, that is, the felt presence of one physically absent. Elizabeth's coronation ritual, for example, enacted the historic ceremonial structure of power within a space delineated to manifest a series of increasingly intimate divisions between the monarch and the world acknowledged but withheld outside. The coronation was the most ancient and the most rigorously systemized model of the presentation of the royal person. The first ritual during the initiation of the new monarch emphasized a seriated process of seclusion of her person: from public streets to the interior of the Abbey, thence to the "theatre" of the coronation within the sanctuary, to the more secluded space of Saint Edward's shrine behind the altar, to the shelter of her private traverse. Each of these successive withdrawals was witnessed by a correspondingly smaller number of select participants and spectators: first the public at large, then the nobility, then the religious hierarchy. The most sacred ceremony took place within the most isolated place of all: the anointing of the queen while secreted from the view of even the most powerful few assembled in the Abbey.[10] At this moment, the person of the queen was a present absence; hers was the most felt presence in the body of the congregation although absent from their view. Conversely, the public outside the Abbey, absent from the scene altogether, were nonetheless a felt presence in that the coronation ritual within included a ceremonial acknowledgment of their power: two earls led Elizabeth to the symbolic four corners of the stage where, to the acclamation of the kingdom, the bishop proclaimed her queen.

Elizabeth adapted to her own purposes what she found useful from such older structures of distance and intimacy, reducing the political significance of usual daily attendance upon her person, enhancing the political implications of intimacy outside conventional structures. Upon occasion, her movements would imitate conventional form, modified to suit nonce purposes. For example, she enacted a demonstration of her goodwill toward Mary Stuart at one point by leading James Melville, the Scottish ambassador, through a sequence of increasingly private spaces to her bedchamber in order to show him a miniature of Mary. When she opened a little cabinet that held her miniatures, wrapped in paper and identified in her own hand, the first was labeled "My Lord's picture," which Melville discovered to be a portrait of Leicester. Melville was flattered by this initiation into the privacy of the queen's space and her secret affections; Leicester, present at the end of the chamber, were he aware of the drama at the opposite end, would have been flattered even more.[11] Another incident confirms that the queen used intimate proximity to selected parties for more private communication within the public view of others in her chamber, yet another show of her facility in simultaneously gaining the advantages of absence and presence, privacy and display. The Spanish ambassador Mendoza recounted an amusing impediment in 1579 to one such private conversation with Elizabeth until she lifted her enormous French farthingale so that he could make nearer approach (Somerset, *Elizabeth I* 359). The story leaves one wondering whether an implicit purpose of the design of this costume was to distance women from others through an unspoken proscription. In any case, Elizabeth, as she did so often, side-stepped conventional constraints upon women.

Access to the queen depended upon one's position and/or the queen's current favor. As a physical entity, the court was the royal household, numbering about seventeen hundred, of whom about eighty to one hundred were customarily allowed entrance to the privy apartments, with another five hundred to six hundred being permitted access to the public rooms, the remainder being the servants "below stairs," those who supplied the daily physical needs of the household such as cooking and laundry. Politically, the most important constant in the definition of the court, however, was who was in attendance at the time in question.[12] Elizabeth firmly expected regular attendance from her peers without any excuse, so about two-thirds of them were present during the early and middle years of her reign (Loades, *The Tudor Court* 86). Elizabeth was an equally hard taskmaster of her ladies of the court, refusing permission, for instance, for Lady Knollys to join her husband when he was posted north to guard Mary Queen of Scots so that he was absent when Lady Knollys sickened and died (Somerset, *Elizabeth I* 346). Daily contingencies continually altered the makeup of the court, and absence was as significant as presence; often, in fact, it was more portentous.

The servants in the privy chambers had most frequent and most intimate contact with the queen, but their political influence was closely circumscribed. With the coronation of Elizabeth, the personnel in this most private service changed automatically. Immediately, ladies displaced gentlemen in a three-tiered organization of the privy chamber: ladies of the bedchamber, gentlewomen of the privy chamber, and chamberers, all of whom were waged servants, numbering only sixteen at most, and supplemented by a small number of unwaged women, with others available as needed. By occasional appointments, the queen was able to piece together an adequate staff without her commitment to a formal verbal reorganization of the privy chamber. Those women selected for the first tier of service had nearest access to the queen, but their power faded in contrast to that of Elizabeth's closest male courtiers, the most powerful being those very few who served both at court and on the Privy Council.[13] The women's influence, often secured through bribery, was restricted to individual suits for such cases as pardon or lower office. The queen made it plain, on the other hand, that they were not to approach her in the interest of political factions. At the same time, the official neutrality of the privy chamber gave Elizabeth a medium through which she could communicate without penalty of public authorization; the ladies' letters and gossip discreetly served the queen for sounding others' views or broadcasting her own. She used her presence in chamber in this devious fashion, for example, when she wished to maintain flexibility regarding pending marriage negotiations. In the words of Pam Wright, she regarded the privy chamber as "an extension of herself."[14]

Several of the more weighty powers held by members of the privy chamber during previous reigns were transferred from Elizabeth's female privy staff to a few male officers outside: William Cecil, the queen's secretary, gained access to the royal signature and effective control of the privy purse; the lord chamberlain now became administrative head of the privy chamber and the servants above stairs, organizer of the royal progresses, and gatekeeper of lodgings at court. These last two duties meant that the lord chamberlain managed both the presence of the queen on her travels and the absence of those whom he considered to be politically unsuitable residents at court, as in the case of Mary Sidney, to whom Thomas Radcliffe, as lord chamberlain, assigned unsatisfactory quarters at a time when he considered her presence as lending undesirable support for her brother Dudley. The gentleman usher of the chamber also controlled access to the queen even more directly, as Dudley himself learned to his anger when Simon Bowyer exercised his commission to scrutinize all comers, and having found wanting the credentials of a Dudley client (Dudley's absent presence), denied him access to the chamber. The queen did not give way to Leicester's rage, thus advertising where control of access to the chamber lay and underscoring the convention that anyone not on the Ordinary required formal leave to come and go at court (Loades, *The Tudor Court* 85). The gatekeepers had a powerful position, but it was also a difficult one. So numerous were the eager petitioners in 1594 that the masters of requests had special offices outside the gates of court to scrutinize visitors and issue controlled passes for admission.[15]

Although presentation of one's suit before the queen was desirable, not all court favors required personal appearance, and may not have been "commendable."[16] One might also make one's way through intervention by a highly placed officer or one of Elizabeth's favorites. As a long-term and effective court official, Burghley received from sixty to a hundred letters of petition a day, and Leicester was highly successful in mediating patronage for church, diplomatic, and military offices, although less so in matters political.[17] The characters and personal interests of intermediaries affected the suits of those absent parties who petitioned at court. Sir John Harington confides to his "Breefe Notes and Remembraunces" his dissatisfaction with Lord High Treasurer Buckhurst in 1598, in contrast to former days when Burghley's counsel moderated the attitudes of the queen's advisers: "I this daye wente to the new Lord High Treasurer, Lorde Buckhirst; I was not ill receivede; nor, in soothe, so well as I had beene usede to in the daye of Lorde Burleighe. When shall oure realme see suche a man, or when suche a mistresse have suche a servante; well mighte one weepe when the other diede" (*Nugae Antiquae* 1:173).

As opposed to contemporary evidence of the difficulty of access to the queen and the court, in a skit presented to Elizabeth at Theobalds while she was on progress in 1591, John Davies extravagantly flattered the queen's gracious accessibility to messengers. Davies represents the Post in conference with the Gentleman Usher outside the home of Secretary Burghley. Because the Secretary is away, the gentleman urges the messenger to deliver his letter, supposedly from the emperor of China, to the queen in person: "Ah, symple Post, thou art the wilfullest creature that lyveth. Dost thou not knowe that, besides all her perfections, all the earth hath not such a Prince for affability; for all is one; come Gentleman, come Servingeman, come Plowman, come Beggar, the hower is yet to come that ever shee refused petition" (Nichols, *Progresses* 3:78). Burghley's son Robert Cecil may have somewhat benefited from the compliment: he was knighted when Elizabeth departed (although denied the coveted secretaryship), but some petitioners found the queen not at all accommodating.[18]

One's fortunes were never permanently secure and they were unstable even on a daily basis, responsive to the moods of the queen. Thus Harington, the most sensitive of commentators on presence, notes in October 1598: "The Queene seemede troubled to daye; Hatton came out from her presence with ill countenaunce, and pulled me aside by the girdle, and saide, in secrete waie, 'If you have any suite to daie, I praye you put it aside, *The sunne dothe not shine.*' 'Tis this accursede Spanishe businesse; so will not I adventure her Highnesse *choller*, leste she shoulde *collar* me also" (*Nugae Antiquae* 1:175–76). Years later, Harington wrote to his wife a long description of the stress of audience with the queen. He weathered her storms and managed even to evoke a sunny smile, but he adds, "Several menne have been sente to, and when readie at hande, her Highnesse hathe dismissede in anger; but who, dearest Mall, shall saye, that '*youre Highnese hathe forgotten*'" (1:323). Anxiety was heightened by uncertainty whether one was forgotten, which was a frustration, or banished, which was a portent.

Fuller cites an image that captures a repellent aspect of the courtly effort to insinuate oneself into favor: Peregrine Berty, Lord Willoughby, "could not brook the obsequiousness and assiduity of the court, and was wont to say that he was none of the *reptilia*, which could creep on the ground," preferring to thrive in his own element as a great soldier (*Fuller's Worthies* 236). Willoughby's language chimes closely with Spenser's in *Prosopopoia or Mother Hubberds Tale*, which satirizes the follies of the court, contrasting the "brave courtier" who "will not creepe, nor crouche with fained face" with those who fruitlessly give their lives "To fawne, to crowche, to waite, to ride, to ronne, / To spend, to give, to want, to be undonne" (lines 727; 905–6). Like Willoughby, Charles Blount betook himself abroad as a soldier, serving under Sir John Norris, but "having twice or thrice stolen away without the queen's leave or knowledge," he was summoned back to court under the queen's express command. She threatened to disable him for any further running because he would never leave until he was knocked over the head, as that "inconsiderate fellow Sidney was. You shall go, when I send you. In the mean time see, that you lodge in the court, where you may follow your books, read, and discourse of the wars" (Birch 2:190–91). In no uncertain terms, the queen dictated not only the presence of her courtiers, but also the absence of their concerns.

Still, as many a neglected soldier came to realize, in order to be favored, one had to be present in the eye, or at least the consciousness, of the monarch. Personal presence in the favor of the queen was the nearest a courtier could be to the highest power. Fuller figures Essex's dependence upon it as Antaeus recruiting his strength from touching mother Earth (*Fuller's Worthies* 182). The metaphor is appropriate: Essex's repeated failure to secure a position for Francis Bacon was harbinger of his own loss of favor. When Essex-Antaeus lost touch with Earth, he failed ever after to find footing. Other disappointed courtiers did not, like Essex, seek redress through rebellion, but many shared his uncertainty. A long letter from Gilbert Talbot to his father the earl of Shrewsbury conveys a sense of the volatility of the race for favor:

> My Lo. Lecester is very muche w^t her Matie, and she sheweth the same great good affection to him that she was wonte; of late he hath indevored to please hir more then hertofore. . . . [Two women at court are warring for Leicester's affections] and the Queine thinketh not well of them, and not the better of him; by this meanes there is spies over him. My Lo. of Sussex goeth wth the tyde, and helpethe to backe others; but his owne credite is sober, consydering his estate. . . . My Lo. of Oxforth is lately growne into great credite; for the Q. Matie delitithe more in his parsonage, and his daunsinge, and valientnes, then any other: I thinke Sussex doth back him all that he can; if it were not for his fyckle hed he would passe any of them shortly. . . . Hatton is sicke still. . . . Now is there devices (chefely by Lecester, as I suppose, and not without Burghley his knowledge) how to make Mr. Edward Dier as great as ever was Hatton; for now, in this tyme of Hatton's sicknes, the tyme is convenient. (Nichols, *Progresses* 1:328–29)

In summary, the letter sounds like a stock report, and the stock of some fell as others' rose.

The pressure of both the queen's exactions and competition with one's peers often made retreat attractive. Puttenham describes the contrivance of withdrawal in the homology between the artificiality of courtly poetry and the dissimulation of the courtly poet. Having analyzed the figures of poetry, he turns to the figure of the courtier, recalling that he has named allegory "the Courtier or figure of faire semblant," suggesting that the courtier must dissemble not only his countenance, but also his actions,

> as now & then to haue a iourney or sicknesse in his sleeue, thereby to shake of other importunities of greater consequence . . . to faine himselfe sicke to shunne the businesse in Court, to entertaine time and ease at home, to salue offences without discredite, to win purposes by mediation in absence . . . to auoid therby the Princes present reproofe, to coole their chollers by absence, to winne remorse by lamentable reports, and reconciliation by friends intreatie. Finally by sequestring themselues for a time fro the Court, to be able the freelier & cleerer to discerne the factions and state of the Court and of al the world besides, no lesse then doth the looker on or beholder of a game better see into all points of auauntage, then the player himselfe? (*Arte of English Poesie* 299–300)

Traces of the pain and the desire for retreat surface in contemporary discourse. John Harington confides to his private papers in 1584 that the envy and jealousy of "divers menne in high states" have greatly troubled him: "I will bid adieu to good companie, and leave sueing and seeking at cowrte; for if I have no more friends nor better at Heaven's cowrte than at this, I shall beginne to thinke somewhat of breefe damnation" (*Nugae Antiquae* 1:168). As one wit has observed, an impending execution wonderfully concentrates one's attention, an aphorism supported by the condemned like Ralegh and Norfolk, whose attention turned to the folly of courtly ambition. Contemporary poetry also often reflects disgust with the court and a resolve to leave it. The theme may be endemic to pastoral literature, but the Elizabethan historical context renders it particular. George Gascoigne's repeated failures are text for his longer poems. *Gascoignes woodmanship* follows the chronology of his successive careers, including how "he shotte to catch a courtly grace," but because of others' envy and his own "purse of prodigalitie" wasted on elegant clothing and bribery, he failed, having "much mistooke the place" (lines 33–43). Spenser's Colin of *Colin Clouts Come Home Againe* retreated from court to his pastoral existence because he "Some part of those enormities did see / The which in court continually hooved" (lines 665–66). Spenser's *Faerie Queene* also poetically represents Belphoebe (figuring Elizabeth) as exiling the squire

Timias (often read as figuring either Leicester or Ralegh) when she comes upon Timias caressing Amoret: " 'Is this the faith?' she said,—and said no more, / But turnd her face, and fled away for evermore" (*Poetical Works* 4.7.36). The episode allegorizes Elizabeth's well-known jealous proprietary attitude toward her favorites' sexual behavior, for which both Leicester and Ralegh suffered her anger, so the vignette could apply to either, although discovery of Ralegh's offense was much closer to the time of publication of the poem. Leicester was restored to full favor, but Ralegh was banished first to the Tower and, after release, from the queen's presence for five years.[19] Ralegh's poems understandably reflect at first, sorrow ("Farewell to the Covrt," 1593) and later, anger: "Say to the Court it glowes, / and shines like rotten wood" ("The Lie," 1611).

The queen often imposed banishment from court to express extreme displeasure. As noted in chapter 7, she was furious at secret marriages, so if not first banished, offending parties often prudently absented themselves from court, at least temporarily. Major figures in Elizabethan history were absent from court at various times because of other actions. A popular explanation had it that Harington was banished for his translation of a lascivious passage in *Orlando Furioso*—but only until he should have translated the rest of that long poem, which he did. Nearer the end of Elizabeth's reign, on October 9, 1601, Harington wrote from Kelstone to Sir Hugh Portman a letter that amusingly describes his share in the anxiety that permeated the court of an angry queen, and it reveals an interplay between banishment and self-removal that was typical there:

> For six weeks I left my oxen and sheep, and venturd to Court, where I find many lean-kinded beastes, and some not unhorned. Much was my comfort in being well received, notwithstanding it is an ill hour for seeing the Queen. The madcaps are all in riot, and much evil threatend. In good soothe I feard her Majestie more than the rebel Tyrone, and wishd I had never received my Lord of Essex's honor of knighthood. . . . I had a sharp message from her brought by my Lord Buckhurst, namely thus, "Go tell that witty fellow, my godson, to get home: it is no season now to foole it here." I liked this as little as she dothe my knighthood, so tooke to my bootes and returned to the plow in bad weather. . . . [The queen is so furious she stamps her feet] and thrusts her rusty sword at times into the arras in great rage. . . . I obtained a short audience at my first coming to courte, when her Highness told me, "If ill counsel had brought me so far from home, she wish'd Heaven might marr that fortune which she had mended." I made my peace in this point, and will not leave my poor castle of Kelston, for fear of finding a worse elsewhere, as others have done. [He will eat local game] and leave all great matters to those that like them better than myself. (*Letters* 90–91)

If presence in the court generated uneasiness, anxiety, or terror, absence from court—even voluntary absence—carried its own perils. A cat might look at a queen, but when the cat was absent, the mice played politics. The stakes of the game of cat and mouse played out at court, and to have one's opponent removed from the field was to score high points. Master players worked to contrive that their adversaries were posted abroad: Dudley (Norfolk to Scotland), Hatton (Perrot to Ireland), Robert Cecil (Essex to Ireland). In the absence of rivals, players at court were freer to maneuver for favor and position. During Harington's rustication, Robert Markham advised him, "Those whome you feared moste are now bosoming themselves in the Queene's grace" (*Nugae Antiquae* 1:239). The Cecils, father and son, were grand masters. In 1569, their enemies collaborated with Norfolk supporters on the Privy Council to plot Cecil's arrest and imprisonment during the queen's absence only to find themselves unmasked—whereupon they absented themselves from the queen's call for a council meeting. Still, the opposition used the advantage of present/absence to voice their resentment when the duke of Norfolk complained to Northampton that the queen was at that moment at the other end of the room dressing down Leicester for his opposition to Cecil. Norfolk's objection to her treatment of Leicester elicited the audible support of Northampton—this exchange clearly audible to the queen (Neville Williams, *Howard* 148). During the absence of Leicester in the Netherlands, Burghley won places on the Privy Council for three of his supporters, Buckhurst, Cobham, and Whitgift. While Essex was in Cadiz, Burghley managed the appointment of his son Robert as secretary, and in the next year, while Essex was on the Azores expedition, Robert Cecil gained the chancellorship of the duchy of Lancaster.

Essex, too, was a sometime player. In 1589, an informant wrote Francis Bacon that "the earl of Essex had *chased Mr.* Ralegh *from the court, and confined him into Ireland*" (Birch 1:56). Even Cecil, in spite of his father's protection, feared absence from court in 1598 until Cecil in effect bought Essex's assurance that he would not exploit this advantage, a promise only partly kept. Essex, though, was no match for his opponents. With a misplaced confidence in his military skills, he inadvertently cooperated in his own ruin. He was eager for post abroad, ignoring the advice of an anonymous friend, "Let nothing draw thee from the Court; sit in every council."[20] As de Maisse, the French ambassador, put it,

> The Lord Treasurer, the Admiral and Master Cecil are well content to see the Earl of Essex go on a distant and hazardous voyage as he has done again this year [1597]; partly to see him removed from Court, and meanwhile to manage their own affairs; also because he hazards his life in such voyages. If he comes back victorious they take occasion thereby to make him suspected by the

Queen; and if nothing is accomplished then to ruin him. And besides he has indebted himself and risked his own fortune and his friends', and will ruin himself. The Queen being avaricious will never give him means to re-establish himself, so they deem his departure will be happy for them. (6–7).

In the absence of Essex, Burghley prevailed on the court. After 1585, warrants for payment issued by the Privy Council indicate the degree of Burghley's power. Absences from the frequent meetings were numerous, and in a departure from precedent, Lord Treasurer Burghley endorsed warrants as "allowed by the lords and others of the Privy Council . . . signed W. Burghley," without consulting his absent colleagues.[21]

The case of Thomas Howard, fourth duke of Norfolk, dramatizes miscalculation of a wide variety of uses of absence. The richest peer in England and exceedingly powerful, Howard was courting Mary Stuart when he made the fatal error of not only neglecting to consult with Elizabeth, but also failing to inform her of his near-betrothal on the three occasions that she created for him to do so after others, unfriendly to Howard, behind his back had informed her of his plans. His silence allowed Burghley, with whom he disagreed about policy toward Spain, to represent Norfolk to the queen as conspiring with rebellious northern earls to place Mary on the throne of England and restore Roman Catholicism. Norfolk's long enmity with Leicester motivated a succession of absences from 1566 to 1569 that were critically harmful to his defense against suspicion of treason: the Saint George's Day celebrations at Windsor, Elizabeth's visit to Oxford, an early departure from the queen's progress in Southampton. Indecision and panic motivated fatal absences thereafter: withdrawal from court without formal leave (this after observing that no peer would join him at table—an ominous present/absence); failure, on excuse of an ague, to respond to the queen's call for his submission at Windsor; unexplained retreat to his home, Kenninghall. The signature on his last letter, written to his children as he awaited execution, heralds his final absence:

Sometime NORFOLK

now

Thomas HOWARD

Degraded from knighthood, deprived of family, and soon to be decapitated, he signed himself as one bereft of all (Williams, *Howard* 155ff.; 249).

Outside the structure of formal affairs at court, a less explicitly codified protocol governed meetings with the queen, but because the imperatives and prohibitions were generally understood, violations of these unspoken limits were unusual. Such violations often resulted from a miscalculation of proxemics—that is, the maintenance of bodily distance appropriate to person, place, time, and occasion. For instance, Melville was made to feel that he had transgressed the boundaries of decorum when, hearing the queen playing the virginals, he was drawn into the room where she was performing, her back to the door and the tapestry that hung before it. As soon as she was aware of his presence, she stopped playing: "She appeared to be surprised to see me, and came forward, seeming to strike me with her hand; alleging she used not to play before men, but when she was solitary, to shun melancholy." Melville excused himself for his intrusive "homeliness, as being brought up in the Court of France, where such freedom was allowed," and, although he declared himself ready to accept any punishment the queen might inflict, she offered him a cushion to place under his knee as he knelt beside her, Melville's violation of proxemic decorum thus forgiven through the grace of a royal cushion (*Memoirs* 96–97). Melville's tentative terminology ("appeared . . . seeming . . . alleging") conveys his suspicion that the queen was manipulating the conditions of presence. De Maisse gives an account of a somewhat similar interruption, and he, too, insinuates that Elizabeth may have staged the circumstances. She was listening to the spinnet in her chambers, "seeming very attentive to it; and because I surprised her, or at least she feigned surprise, I apologized for diverting her from her pleasure" (*Journal* 55). Because he was expected and because Elizabeth had sent her coach to fetch him, de Maisse's skepticism was well-grounded. Elizabeth's motive is transparent: to begin an interview by accepting the visitor's apology is to be in the superior position of control and power.

Essex, unlike the intrusive ambassadors, had no formal excuse for his invasions of the queen's privacy, but contrived them rather as opportunities to distinguish himself as an intimate favorite of the queen—successfully so at first, as when he flaunted his collar of esses, but some of his other intrusions were less favorably received. In a letter to Robert Sidney dated Michaelmas Day at noon, 1599, Rowland Whyte narrates one such occasion when Essex abandoned his disastrous campaign in Ireland. Rather than having properly petitioned and received a formal summons from the queen, on the morning of Michaelmas Eve he "staied not till he came to the Queens Bed Chamber, where he found the Queen newly up, the Hare about her Face; he kneeled vnto her, kissed her Hands, and had some priuat Speach with her. . . . 'Tis much wondred at here, that he went so boldly to her Majesties Presence, she not being ready, and he soe full of Dirt and Mire, that his very Face was full of yt" (Collins, *Letters* 2:127). Elizabeth seemed not immediately offended with his precipitate appearance, but late that night the queen sent word confining him to his chamber, and when he was summoned before council on the next day among the charges against him were "His rash Manner of coming away from *Ireland*: His ouerbold going Yesterday to her Majesties Presence to her Bedchamber: His making of so many idle Knights" (129). Essex was on an ambitious climb; each intrusion, each indecorous excess, was a rung in his ascent to the height where he would be topped. The scandal aroused by the specific circumstances of invasion of the queen's bedchamber, where she was sighted with her hair about her face, lends weight to the case that Lyly specifically dramatized the episode in Actaeon's view of Diana with its consequences in *Cynthia's Revels.*[22]

By way of contrast, Harington's "Breefe Notes and Remembraunces" for 1594 afford a glimpse of a more sensitively decorous approach when Harington was pursuing his case for his lands in the north:

> I muste go in an earlie hour, before her Highnesse hathe speciale matters broughte up to councel on.—I muste go before the breakfastinge covers are placede, and stande uncovered as her Highnesse comethe forthe her chamber;—then kneel and saie, "God save youre Majestie, I crave youre eare at what houre may suite for youre servante to meete your blessede countenaunce." Thus will I gaine her favoure to followe to the auditorie.
>
> Truste not a friende to doe or saie
> In that yourselfe can sue or praie. (*Nugae Antiquae* 1:169)

That Essex observed no such caution is obvious from Harington's account of the earl's interview in a letter to Robert Markham dated 1606. It is especially relevant because it not only reports the queen's reactions to the presence of both Essex and Harington but also comments on the pragmatic uses of presence and absence by all parties:

> Surely she did plaie well hir tables to gain obedience thus wythout constraint: again, when she coude pute forthe suche alteracions, when obedience was lackinge, as lefte no doubtynges whose daughter she was. I saie thys was plain on the Lorde Deputy's cominge home, when I did come into hir presence; she chaffed muche, walkede fastly to and fro, looked with discomposure in her visage; and, I remember, she catched my girdle when I kneelede to hir, and swore, "By God's Son, I am no Queen; that *man* is above me;—Who gave him commande to come here so soon? I did sende hym on other busynesse." It was longe before more gracious discourse did fall to my hearynge; but I was then put oute of my trouble, and bid "Go home." I did not stay to be bidden twise; if all the Iryshe rebels had been at my heels, I shoude not have had better speede, for I did now flee from one whom I both lovede and fearede too. (1:356–57)

Other courtiers intruded upon the queen unceremoniously, occasionally sharing some of Essex's untimely circumstances, but none with his finally disastrous consequences. Thus Sir Henry Carey similarly appeared in the presence at Hampton Court, all unprepared after a hard ride to Edinburgh and back on a mission ordered by the queen: "Dirty as I was, I came into the presence, where I found the lords and ladies dancing. The Queen was not there. . . . [Carey refuses to entrust his message to an intermediary, even though ordered to do so by the queen.] With much ado I was called for in; and I was left alone with her. Our first encounter was stormy and terrible, which I passed over with silence" (*Memoirs* 30). The tension of the encounter was heightened by the queen's predisposed anger toward Carey for his unapproved marriage and for his having peremptorily left court because of lack of favor, but they made peace during the course of their interview.

To surprise the queen was always risky, and as Essex came to understand, to surprise the queen in dishabille was an especially grave indiscretion. By chance, Gilbert Talbot suffered the queen's displeasure at another such encounter. He wrote to his father the earl of Shrewsbury in 1578 that Elizabeth gave him "a great fillip on the forehead" for having shamed her by surprising her at a window "for that she was unready, and in her night-stuff," a relatively inconsequential reproof for this Elizabethan Actaeon (Lodge, *Illustrations* 2:98). Indeed, Spenser's *Faerie Queene* anticipates the Ovidian overtones of these episodes in an allegorical reprise when Sir Calidore happens upon the dance of the graces, causing them to disappear from his sight. Calidore apologizes to the shepherd who has been piping to the gracious dance, "pardon thou my shame, / Who rashly sought that which I mote not see" (6.10.29).

Neither Calidore nor Elizabeth's courtiers were governed by explicit proscription; the decorum of presence required decoding unwritten preventions and favorable approaches. The queen's extraordinary steps toward a meeting were particularly auspicious. Continental tradition preceded English practice. The *"Libro Cerimoniale"* of the Florentine Republic richly illustrates the nice protocol regarding ceremonial approach. Filarete was watchful of the Ritual of the Stairs, the procedure for escorting visitors to the Signoria. Significant were the point at which a visiting dignitary dismounted, how many stairs and how promptly he descended them from his lodging in order to greet his escort. To dismount too late, to be tardy in descending the steps or to descend too few, to reject the courtesy of accompaniment, was egregiously rude (61–66). Venetian protocol for welcoming pageant guests was likewise excruciatingly precise, and variations signaled the degree of honor accorded, depending on the distance from the Palazzo Ducale, where the doge greeted the guest, and whether he removed his *corno*. So portentous were proxemic signals that the Signoria decided not to invite to a reception on board the Bucintoro those foreign orators from the Continent and England who refused to be seated below the duke as prescribed by Venetian protocol.[23] Montaigne recalls examples of the protocol observed at meetings between kings, the emperor, and the pope, as well as disagreements regarding proper form for greeting, and he disdains when "men proove unmanerly by too much maners, and importunate by overmuch curtesie" (*Essays* 1:60).

Elizabethans may not have adopted such elaborate protocol for greetings, but they nonetheless closely observed the honor given or withheld during greetings on specific occasions. *The Black Book of Warwick* documents how the earls of Warwick and Leicester took offense from a perceived failure on the part of their hosts to greet them generously on a visit in 1571. The burgesses had decided that to come out to greet the visitors at a distance was a welcome appropriate only to the sovereign. Leicester brushed past them, leaving it to his servants to convey his anger. When the men came to apologize to the earl and offer him a gift, they were kept waiting for a long time in a garden "where the said Earle out of the Lord Marques chamber might see them but they could not see him," Leicester thus enacting present absence as a mode of reproof.[24] The elaborate welcomes he received during his mission to the Netherlands on land and on water would better suit his sense of honor, indeed swell it to the vainglory that propelled him to accepting the forbidden governorship.

Citizens were finely attuned to proxemic decorum during the visit of a monarch. The official greeting party acted out an old choreography of approach and withdrawal, both physical and psychic. City magistrates stood with an assembled crowd at a significant point to greet the monarch, stepping forward for the recorder's speech to pledge the city's loyalty and its trust in the reciprocal goodness of the sovereign, and to proffer a sword or scepter that the ruler in turn gave to the mayor as sign of the monarch's spoken trust in the city. The mayor then preceded the monarch in the procession, the welcome and its attendant gestures having affirmed the mutuality of their hierarchical relationships.[25]

Within the thrice protective space of a fiction-within-a-fiction about a deceased monarch, Thomas Deloney daringly subverted the conventional proxemics of approach in *Jack of Newberie*.[26] He represents Henry VIII while on progress as coming upon the weaver Jack and his men playing the part of a colony of ants defending the kingdom against the idle butterflies (i.e., Wolsey's party). Jack and his men are armed and they are impeding the progress of the king. Even more daringly, in an outrageous violation of decorum in the presence of the monarch, Jack refuses to approach the king because he is on foot while the king is on horseback. Only when Henry, participating in the fiction of the pageant within the fiction, approaches his subjects, do they kneel in submission. The entertainment taught as well as delighted, although not perhaps in equal measure of both to all members of the audience.

In a more conventional mode, Elizabeth maintained her own private sense of the refinements of decorum of approach and presence, and she was determined to teach it to Essex. Among his many letters regarding his fruitless efforts on behalf of Francis Bacon, one in particular narrates the queen's imposition of restrictions upon the courtier in her presence, restrictions that effected her present/absence. About 1594, Essex writes Bacon in an undated letter:

> I wrote not to you till I had had a second conference with the queen, because the first was spent only in compliments. She at the beginning excepted all business. This day she hath seen me again. After I had followed her humour in talking of those things, which she would entertain me with . . . [Essex brings up the suit]. Her answer in playing just was, that she came not to me for that. I should talk of those things, when I came to her, and not when she came to me. . . . I would have replied, but she stopped my mouth. To morrow or the next day I will go to her, and then this excuse will be taken away. (Birch 1:171–72)

Duly chastened, Essex's next letter to Bacon begins: "I went yesterday to the queen thro' the galleries, in the morning, afternoon, and at night." After outlining her rebuttal of his case, Essex concludes, "She did in this as she useth in all, went from a denial to a delay" (1:172). By Essex's account, six approaches on the same item of business had profited him only further procrastination.

For Elizabeth to approach a subject spontaneously was, on the other hand, a special sign of grace. Thus Elizabeth sometimes made overtures toward favored courtiers when they were sick, for example, Essex, even when he was already under suspicion of treason; Leicester, even when he was likely feigning illness; and Burghley, whose death would in the end precipitate the queen's own temporary absence from view.[27] Stow's memoranda detail an extraordinary meeting between the queen and Leicester on April 2, 1566, when Leicester rode into London with a company of seven hundred "all in theyr riche cotes" and progressed through the city (tracing much of the route followed by Elizabeth's coronation procession) to London Stone and on to Oxford Place, where it was appointed that he would meet the queen "(who had come frome Grenewytche secretly in to Sothewarke)" by boat. Leicester anticipated her arrival by riding with his train to Southwark, to which the queen returned from Oxford Place. Near the Church of Saint George, Elizabeth "cam owt of her coche in ye highe way, and she imbrased ye earle and kyssed hym thrise, and then they rode to-gythar to Grenewytche" (*Three Fifteenth-Century Chronicles* 137). Queen met courtier more than halfway.

So did she again on the famous occasion of the knighting of her pirati-cal courtier Francis Drake. Maria Perry's narration of the event encapsu-lates it as an outstanding example of the implications of many variations on presence as silent language. Drake returned from his raid upon the Spanish fleet, loaded with treasure from America, in 1580. Burghley and Sussex regarded the plunder as stolen property honor-bound to be restored, but on New Year's Day Elizabeth showed her pleasure in it by wearing Drake's gift of a crown with five dazzling Peruvian emeralds, and she temporized with Mendoza's insistence upon need for audience with her. In April 1581, under pretext of first questioning Drake, Elizabeth spent six hours with him aboard his *Golden Hind* at Deptford while holding dissenting parties at bay.

After a magnificent banquet, the like of which had never been seen since Henry VIII's day, Elizabeth, accompanied by Alençon's envoy, inspected the ship. The King of Spain, she said, had asked for Drake's head, and raising a golden sword of state, she teased as if to strike it off herself. Then, passing the sword to de Marchaumont, she ordered him to knight Francis Drake, thus neatly drawing the French into the proceedings. During the tour of inspec-tion Elizabeth's garter became loose. When de Marchaumont asked for it to add to Alençon's peculiar collection of souvenirs, she pointed out that she had nothing else to hold up her hose, and stooped significantly to re-adjust it. Later she gave it to the envoy for Monsieur. (*The Word of a Prince* 250)

The silent gestural commitment through wearing the confiscated jewels, the forced absence of the Spanish envoy Mendoza, the calculated presence of the French representative, the present/absence of the queen's gesture of knighting through the hand of a surrogate, the present/absent provocative feint of the gift of the garter, to be followed by the absent/present gift of it to the absent suitor—the superficial game of presence and absence covered a wordless subtext of money, power, and sex that was serious play indeed. Stakes were yet higher in the combat with Spain in 1588, when the queen's likely reward for Drake's part in the victory was the gift of her absent/pres-ence on the Hilliard miniature that lies inside the Drake jewel dated 1588, and that Drake sports on the Gheeraerts portrait of 1594.[28]

The queen's annual summer progress provided a more structured ap-proach to her less familiar subjects. A hundred years after her accession, Arch-bishop Laud's former chaplain invidiously compared the political acumen of her public appearances with the self-destructive withdrawal from public view by her successors: "[Elizabeth] did very seldom end any of her summer progresses but she would wheel about to some end of London, to make her passage to Whitehall through . . . the City. . . . By means whereof she did not only preserve that Majesty which did belong to a Queen of England, but kept the Citizens (and consequently all the subjects) in a reverent estimation of her."[29] In this way, she visited herself upon many of her subjects and became a visible presence to many more. Her presence on progress was a vehicle for personal and political gratification. Both satisfactions were hers; for the hosts, the latter may have been uppermost, to judge from the frustration, anxiety, and expense unveiled in their letters.

To be prepared to receive the monarch was a matter of great moment, greater inconvenience, and greatest expense. Numerous letters register the anxiety and implied reluctance of target hosts when they found themselves within range of one of the progresses. Sir Julius Caesar had the unhappiness to prepare for an expected visit from the queen eight times, according to John Chamberlain's report, and to be five times disappointed by her absence (Nichols, *Progresses* 3:428–29). The Loseley manuscripts record how on several occasions the More family was disrupted by their similar misfortune to have a house that the queen favored by her presence. Sir Anthony Wyngfeld writes in about 1567 to warn Sir William More that the queen is planning a visit "and for that ytt shalbe a grete trouboul and a henderanes unto you," and that in spite of his description of Loseley as too small and inconvenient to accommodate the royal entourage, the queen is persevering (*Loseley Manuscripts* 266). Another letter addressed to Sir William More ten years later by Henry Goringe alludes to the queen's recent visit to Loseley. Goringe betrays anxiety verging on panic because the "jestes" or gestes (lists of the stages of the progresses) indicate a stop in Sussex, and "it semethe her gracis meaning is to lye at my howse two nights," and because "I am altogether unacquaynted wth the order," he begs advice regarding how to purvey for the occasion (267). Similarly, Lord Keeper Bacon writes to Burghley from Gorhambury in 1572 for advice regarding an impending royal visit because "in very deede, no man is more rawe in suche a matter then my selfe" (Ellis, *Letters* 1.2.266).

Documents relating to the progress entertainments uncover other inconvenient results of the queen's changing plans. On the one hand, the queen might not be present for the performance of a carefully planned entertainment. She was, for instance, not present in Croydon to view Thomas Nashe's *Summer's Last Will and Testament* in the autumn of 1592. On the other hand, her presence could cause elaborate subterfuge to avoid possible offense, as when Thomas Pound employed the fiction of Elizabeth's present absence in order to be free in his wedding masque to compliment a bride as the fairest of all the party present.[30]

Well might a host worry about provisions for the royal presence. In 1594, for example, the Privy Council ordered the county of Surrey to provide at the court gate one hundred fat, large veals between April and September and fifty fat lambs in May, plus 161 dozen birds of varieties specified to be delivered in London or elsewhere upon a month's notice—all at prices fixed at low rate by the court (*Loseley Manuscripts* 272–73). When the court spent three days in Kirtling, Lord North spent about £642 on food and drink, having served more than twenty species of birds, cartloads of oysters, 2,522 eggs, and 430 pounds of butter (Stevenson 287–90). More than a decade later, when Elizabeth visited Cowdray on progress in 1591, "The proportion of [Sunday] breakefast was three Oxen, and one hundred, and fourtie Geese." When she dined in the garden on Thursday, the table was forty-eight yards long (*Honorable Entertainment* A4ʳ, B3ʳ).

Not only were the quantities gargantuan, but sources of supply were often scarce and inconvenient. A visit from the queen on progress especially strained the local resources of her hosts. In 1561, when she stayed with Sir William Petre at Ingatestone for four days during her first such visitation upon her courtiers, much of the food had to be imported from London and even from the Fenlands, where the indispensable fowl were to be bought (Emmison, *Tudor Food* 90–91). The weight of similar worries prompt a harried letter from Thomas Sackville, Lord Buckhurst, to the earl of Sussex regarding provisions for an impending royal visit in 1577. Buckhurst has found sources of supply in Sussex and adjoining counties already exhausted or bespoke for other noblemen, and he now plans to send to Flanders—if only the earl can "procure her H. to grow to some resolucion both of the time when her Ma. wilbe at Lewis, and how long her H. will tary theare" (Ellis, *Letters* 1.2.271).

As for the costs of such provisions, according to one estimate, Elizabeth's nineteen-day stay at Kenilworth cost Leicester more than £1,000 a day (Langham 16). Braithwait recalls that the "greatest state that ever I did hear of in an Earles house" was the entertainment of Elizabeth at Kenilworth by the earl of Leicester and at New Hall by the lord chamberlain—immediately before the author launches into his cautionary observations on the dire social consequences of overspending on the table. Braithwait's chain of association is reasonable: upon Leicester's death, Elizabeth ended his patents and declared his debts due.[31] Leicester, like many another courtier, spent lavishly to entertain the queen as silent expression of the hope of expanding his fortunes, only to realize to his shame the expense of fortune in a waste of debt.

The royal indecisiveness is a recurrent theme in correspondence regarding the progresses. Goringe chooses his words advisedly in that letter to More in 1577 when he frets over the gestes because it "semethe" he must incur a visitation by the royal household. Two letters from Sir Christopher Hatton to More in 1583 create a veritable cat's cradle of queenly intention. The first announces that "she hath an intention about ten or twelve dayes hence to visite yo' house by Guylforde, and to remayne there some foure or fyve dayes," but twenty days later, another letter explains that the weather is getting too cold, so that the queen "is now pleased to abridge the jorney w'ch first her highnes intended" and so will now arrive in three days for an overnight stay (*Loseley Manuscripts* 268–69). The cat's cradle tightens into a veritable noose in a letter from the earl of Leicester acknowledging an invitation from the earl of Sussex to the queen in 1577. The queen "saith very earnestly that she wil by no means come this time," but "Nevertheles, my Lord, for mine own opinion, I believe she wil hunt, and visit your house, coming so neer. Herein you may use the matter accordingly, since she would have you not to look for her" (Ellis, *Letters* 1.2.273).

Three letters from Henry Maynard to Michael Hickes, secretary to Lord Burghley, speak in the provisional language of the subjunctive regarding progress gestes for 1597. In the second letter Maynard warns Hickes, "you are like to be the Queens first host," and he concludes, "I coulde be glad to be gon heare, but this Progresse much trowbleth mee, for that we knowe not what corse the Queen will take" (1.2.274–75). Earlier, in a letter to Lord Burghley in 1572, the earl of Bedford more explicitly states his unwillingness to accommodate royal impositions: "I trust yo' L. will have in remembraunce to provide and help her Ma'ts tarieng be not above two nights and a daye; for, for so long tyme do I prepare. . . . If I could make them [lodgings] better upon suche a sodeyn, then wold I, be assured" (1.2.267). Lady Anne Askew writes to Sir Christopher Hatton in 1581 in an effort to forestall altogether a royal visit: "Sir, This short warning, and my unfurnished house, do ill agree; for, besides her Majesty's diet, there be many things which I know to be fit for her ease that I want: wherefore, if her Majesty's pleasure would otherwise determine, my shame were the less, and my band to you the greater" (Nicolas, *Memoirs* 223).

Causes for the anxiety are largely self-explanatory; letters and accounts document the enormous difficulty and expense of purveying for a party of hundreds for an indeterminate stay, but other unusual debits also emerge from the records: the obligatory gifts such as jewels and clothing, construction of special accommodations as at Gorhambury, and erection of lakes or earthworks for outdoor entertainment as at Kenilworth and Elvetham. More surprising incidental costs also appear. Ellis reprints a story of how the queen's hunting party so depleted and abused Henry Lord Berkeley's favorite herd of deer during his absence (Berkeley Castle was not on the gestes) that he disparked the grounds (that is, converted them to other uses). A friend advised him from court that the queen had heard that he was "repining" at her coming to his house, and warned that Leicester, whose plot it had been, was also eager to have Berkeley's castle and perhaps his head as well (1.2.277).

Leicester himself had suffered verbal demotion to a lower link of the food chain when Elizabeth tartly put him down with the sharp reminder that the lake was hers on which the Kenilworth pageant was taking place. Even the family home was only provisionally one's own. In Hatton's letter to More revising plans for 1583, not only does he give More short and uncertain notice, but he directs that while awaiting the queen's visit, "you may avoyde yor famely" and make everything ready for the queen (*Loseley Manuscripts* 269). Under advice from the lord chamberlain in 1597, Maynard off-handedly suggests that Hickes need not worry about the added trouble of entertaining the queen's servants, "but onelie to leave the howse to the Quene" and present her with a fine waistcoat (Ellis, *Letters* 1.2.276).

Preparations for the physical presence of the monarch set the stage for perceptible enactment of the social and political hierarchy. Hosts were forcibly reminded of the obligations of prestation and of the contingent nature of ownership; their wives were no doubt even more painfully reminded of woman's place; children were displaced; household servants must have been worked to exhaustion; villagers and countryfolk for miles around were pressed into service, provision, and performance for the sovereign. In the event, all might be undone at the last moment or even during the course of the event should the weather change or the local beer not be to the queen's liking. Yet, the silent rhetoric of protocol was a medium available to both royal visitor and host, as illustrated in an anecdote concerning James Stuart, then king of Scotland and the future king of England. The earl of Gowrie's abrogation of the decorum of seating and dining disturbed his king James on what would shortly emerge as the occasion of the earl's assault upon his life. The earl having failed to observe the usual courtesies in seating and feeding the members of the king's party, James announced that "his Maiestie would drink to him his own welcome," teaching the Scottish fashion, and the earl should take drink forth to the rest of the company in his majesty's name and make them welcome.[32]

Anxiety centered on the procurement, cost, preparation, and service of food according to protocol, but these concerns were not restricted to royal entertainment. More private meals in the great houses were also extravagant, highly formal, and ruled by a protocol that inflected a gestural rhetoric. One infers from early courtesy books the bestial conditions that necessitated their publication to assure observance of the honor due the presence—or absent/presence—of every party. Many books, for instance, specifically proscribe blowing the nose into one's hand or spitting on the floor or walls of the dining room. John Russell's early example of the type,

The Booke of Nurture, admonishes servingmen with a list of forbidden gestures:

> youre hed ne bak ye claw / a fleigh as thaughe ye sought . . .
> pike not youre nose / ne that it be droppynge with no peerlis clere . . .
> put not youre handes in youre hosen youre codware for to clawe . . .
> lik not with thy tonge in a disch, a mote to have owt.
> (Furnivall, *Early English Meals and Manners* 18–19)

The arming of the servants and the ordering of food service were, ideally, the performance of a highly systemized corps disciplined in the defense and the display of honor, and their drill executed many tropes of the language of absence and presence. The military model of a chain of command prevails, but an even more solemn note enters the household books. The "Booke of Orders and Rules" describes procedures for table service for Anthony, Viscount Montague, at Cowdray in 1595, ordering that servants are to bow when they reach the center of the hall, even if it is empty. The usher kisses his hand and places it at the center of the table in order to show his subordinate where the cloth is to be laid. This man in turn kisses the table. Bows accompany the laying of service (Montague 199). The gestural prescriptions are remarkably similar to the ordinance followed by priests and their assistants in the laying of the cloth upon the altar, imparting an aura of solemnity almost sacral.

At great feasts, the emphasis was upon the solemnization of eating rather than upon the mutual sharing of food, and the elaborate provision for majestic service even in the absence of the queen celebrates the concept of banquet rather than its actual consumption. In order to underscore the importance of separation between classes, royalty and nobility were seated apart from the rest of the company, as present absences. Lupold von Wedel describes the queen dining at Christmastide, 1584, in a ceremony that illustrates the deference accorded the royal presence on the only occasion in the year when the queen dined in public. She sat alone at a large table, on which were forty large silver dishes of meat. He remarks on the costly drinking vessels and notes that her cupbearer knelt for as long as the queen drank. The servants bearing food bowed three times, as they had done earlier with the napkins and tableware, even though the queen was not yet present in the room. Five men presented the queen with a covered basin and a towel so that she could wash her hands, remaining on their knees during the procedure, their submissive, reverential attitude a shadow of feudal and religious obeisance. Von Wedel's long passage describing the annual lord mayor's feast in London indicates that the ceremonial protocol of the mayor's formal banquet resembled that of the royal feast. He counted sixty long tables. More long tables were elevated by a few steps, and through a screen and above these was a table on a dais where the dignitaries sat. That a new mayor so recently gifted by the city paid £500 for this feast reveals the reciprocal nature and the cost of prestation, as does his obligation to keep daily open board for all comers (Klarwill 326–37; Platter 158). One foreign visitor to London records in his diary that every fourth year at the beginning of Lent, students at Temple Bar elected the dubious honor of kingship to one who was then obliged to give a banquet for the queen and her whole court, and says the scandalized visitor-observer, "many a one spends all his patrimony on this occasion."[33]

It was the job of the marshal to know the historic dignity appropriate to all of the estates, which Wynkyn de Worde's *Boke of Keruynge* (1513) lists at length, and to assure that everyone received due honor, but no more. He devotes a passage to the proper segregation of diners according to their dignity, beginning with those who must dine alone: "An archebysshop and a duke may not kepe the hall, but eche estate by them selfe in chaumbre or in pauylyon, that neyther se other"; he then lists in descending order of estate how many may share a mess (Furnivall 171). By a similar legerdemain of present absence, the "Breviate" for a nobleman's house of 1605 stipulates the seating arrangements that honor a lord's presence in company. He is to be seated before the appropriate cloth of state "placede in the upper ende thereof [i.e., the great chamber], with chaire, cushinge, and stooles suetable thereunto, and at dinner, or supper, is to have his seate in the midest of the table, a littell above the salte, his face beeinge to the whole vewe of the chamber . . . and in this service it is to bee notede, that the lordes messe is to bee placed above the salte."[34] This passage reveals how segregation of the highest ranks might be effected: the lord is to face the crowd. When the lord and lady dined in company, they were often seated at the end of the hall behind a table on a raised dais, hence the term *high table* (Bailey, *English Manor Houses* 36). Segar schematizes the honors due not only ranking nobility but familial hierarchy, specifying position at table and appropriate degree of "delicacy" of diet (*Honor* [1602] S4ʳ). The whole ceremony of service positioned the social hierarchy of those at table.

The handling of the food was another medium with numerous forms for nonverbal expression of honor due those present. The instructions in the housebooks prescribe a virtual choreography of bows, coverings and uncoverings, and other deferential gestures to attend the service of food. Only the most senior diner would be served drink from a covered cup.[35] The "Breviate" instructs the gentleman usher to oversee the service at table in the great chamber, ensuring that the cupbearers serve drink "with takinge of sayes, on theire knee, in humble and dewetifull sorte," and that the assay of the meat is to be done "at the first course standinge, and the seconde course, kneelinge of one knee" (Banks 322; 324). Wynkyn de Worde's *Boke of Keruynge* (1513) gives directions for laying the cloth, covering the cupboard, covering the lord's bread, and serving his napkin that are as reverently detailed as instructions for a communion service (Furnivall 154), as are the instructions that appear in most of the housebooks for the washing of hands. The difference from the communion service is critical: the dinners in the great houses manifestly emphasized distinction in rank rather than the communion of participants.

The success of a dinner or a feast depended upon the knowledge, discipline, and skill of the servants. Household instructions often imply that service is a performance. The usher of the hall is to ensure that the meat is "hansomly placed on the board," that nothing "vncomly" be seen in the hall.[36] No part of the service is more concerned with decorum of performance than carving, a legacy from the past as glimpsed, for instance, in Chaucer's squire and in its metaphoric role in *Sir Gawain and the Green Knight*. De Worde's *Boke of Keruynge* transmits the old specificity of terminology and process, but *Cyuile and vncyuile life* (1586) more cynically conveys the significance of such exactitude if gracefully observed. Vincent, the country gentleman in the dialogue, rationalizes the need for a large retinue of servants in a country house because "our seruingmen, besides that they al, (or the greatest number) can well and decently weare their garments, and cheefely their lyuery coates, their swordes & bucklers, they can also carue very cumly at your table, as to vnlase a Conny, to raise a Capon, trompe a Crane, and so likewise handle all other dishes, and meates that are set on the board before you: some of them also can wrestle, leape well, run & daunce." Vincent adds that in the absence of better company, some are able also to engage in table talk with the master. Valentine, the city man, is amazed: "But altogeather they make a world," advising dismissal of the superfluity of servants, but Vincent responds that it upsets him "to discharge a lusty fellow, though his conditions bee but skantly commendable. And the reason is because he becommeth a house well." Valentine closes in with the riposte that in that case it were better to hang the servants' pictures in their best array.[37] The servants performed the same function as the elegant tableware: they exhibited the magnificence, and therefore the taste and the *virtù* of the lord of the house. The servants, in short, constituted a present absence.

Sumptuary prescription dictated differences in the number and quality of dishes served to each diner in order to manifest his status to all present. Social status even ruled the type of bread one ate. William Harrison names several grades, beginning with manchet, the finest white bread, and ranging down to miscelin or maslin, bread made of "mingled corn" rather than pure wheat (*Description* 133–35). Not only was the best bread served to the lord's table; when it was sliced, the lord was served the upper crust.[38] The location of the salt on the high table marked it as the most honored table. Salt was graded according to purity and color, and so the quality served to each diner reflected the quality of the guest. A footed salt cellar indicated the high rank of the host; the covering of any utensil did obeisance to status; the placement of the salt marked the position of highest status both physically and metaphorically—that is to say, upon the lord's table, which was up on a dais, where it remained on display throughout the entire meal, while lesser salts at lesser tables were cleared after use.[39]

Entrées also wordlessly singled out those most honored at a feast. The ranking diner traditionally received the gilded head and feet of the peacock.[40] The lords of council were rarely served pork, considered a plebeian dish, but poultry was prized as a dish more expensive than beef, one of the most expensive varieties being gulls, which cost more than capon or goose.[41] You are, it is said, what you eat; but you not only are what you eat, what you eat shows who you are. Both law and custom reserved the best, the most, and the greatest variety of foods for the most honorable members of society, a practice most stringently enforced during time of dearth. During the sixteenth century, this meant an increasingly mean diet for the poor as their fare was ground down to the cheap bread grains, while the tables of the rich groaned ever more luxuriously under mounds of delicacies.[42] Indeed, through a sensible rhetoric, every part of meal service enacted ceremonial hierarchy. The very nomenclature of the procession of some selected guests to the dessert course—that is, the "void"—signals the exclusivity of withdrawal of their presence.[43]

As for the numbers of guests present at meals, in 1600 Thomas Wilson estimated the cost for daily service at the forty-six or forty-seven tables maintained by the queen to be £120,000 a year (a figure that includes the expenses for the stables) and equals, says Thomas Wilson, "a third part of the whole revenue" (*State of England* 30). His editor cautions that the accuracy of the calculation cannot be verified (vii), but Wilson registers a valuable contemporary impression that the queen's expense "for hospitality is much exceedinge all other Princes in Christendome" (29). Nor was the queen's the only dining hall to be filled with guests daily; as we have seen, the lord mayor of London and owners of great houses also maintained hospitable halls. A letter among the *Memorials of the Holles Family* records specific evidence that Sir William used to delay his daily dinner until late in the day in order to include any extra guest who might arrive. For the twelve days of Christmas, he customarily served "a fat oxe every day with sheep and other provision answerable" (Holles 41–42). Twice on Twelfth Day at Ingatestone Hall in 1552, Sir William Petre fed more than a hundred people (Emmison, *Tudor Secretary* 28). Harrison estimates the number of mouths at the tables of the nobility (besides that of the chief table) to be between forty and sixty (*Description* 127). Such statistics were cited as evidence of either magnificent *virtù* or foolish extravagance, the contemporary ambivalent possibilities of interpretation bespeaking the tensions of cultural change.

Even for lesser occasions than a royal visitation, statistics regarding amounts and costs of food are daunting. Star Chamber dinner accounts reveal an allotment of ten pounds of beef for each lord per meal, probably distributed among his attendants (*Star Chamber Accounts* 3). In a period of fifty-one weeks (a period that did not include even a family wedding), about twenty thousand loaves of bread were baked at Petre's Ingatestone Hall (Emmison, *Tudor Secretary* 38). William Smythe records that the lord mayor's inaugural banquet in London in 1575 cost £400, of which the mayor paid half the cost (Sayle, *Lord Mayors' Pageants* 3). The private journal of Grace Sherrington, Lady Mildmay, records her food supplies for Christmas week 1594: "Wheaten bread, 16 dozen loaves [each loaf weighing 40 ozs.]; brown bread, 28 dozen loaves; beere, 8 hogsheads [one hogshead is brewed of 12 pecks of malt]; beef, 50 stone; mutton, 6 carcases 1 joint; pork, 27 joints 8 pigges; blackbirds, 6 dozen; larks, 8 dozen; rabbits, 50; also geese, hennes, and wild game; flour, 9 pottles; candles, 36 lbs.; butter (fresh), 15 lbs.; butter (salt), 35 lbs."[44] Seen in this context, Anthony Mildmay's chronic financial stress becomes understandable, as does the general sense of financial shortfall among Elizabeth's courtiers. The honorifics accorded presence through culinary signifiers often correlated with the absence of the funds and the peace of mind of the host.

Sumptuary laws attempted to calibrate and to control the amount and type of food apportioned to each social class on a graduated scale of power, property, and income; the absence or presence of quantity and quality indicated at a glance the social status of the consumer. A regulation dating from the time of Henry VIII, for example, specifies that a cardinal may have nine dishes at his own mess at one meal, whereas lords temporal under the degree of earl may have only six, and so on, each level of consumption to be reduced according to relative income, so that those who could spend only between £40 and £100 a year were restricted to three dishes. The regulation ends with the decree that persons who "so following their sensual appetite shall violate the same, he or they so doing shall not only be reputed and taken as a man of evil order," but shall be punished as a cautionary example (*Tudor Proclamations* 1:128–29). These very few words convey three of the intentions of the sumptuary laws: to restrain human indulgence, to manifest social distinction, and to reinforce the economic basis of privilege. Consumers, however, often violated the most precise efforts to regulate diet. The queen herself exceeded twofold the amount allotted her by the book of diet and supplemented it with expensive delicacies: forty silver dishes, not only at Christmastide, but also at a luncheon, as foreigners noted. Some of her officers pilfered her huge supplies, and only periodic efforts at reform kept the court solvent.[45]

Granted the astronomical expense and trouble of maintaining hospitality on this scale, it is only to be expected that many would absent themselves in order to evade such a responsibility. For many a moralist, the good old days were a time when English hospitality was more generous and more personal, administered by the presence of the host.[46] As early as 1555, the anonymous *Institucion of a Gentleman* was commending the good keepers of the country houses who used to "relieue their neighbours with meate and drynke . . . to seke London seldome. . . . Then stoode the buttery dore without a hatche" (G.ii^v–iii^r). Robert Greene's *Quip for an Vpstart Courtier* (London, 1592) recalls nostalgically the days when "Westminster hall was a dining chamber, not a den of controuersies" and when the great number of smoking chimneys was a sign of the old hospitality, but "now adaies men builde for to please the eye, not to profit the poore, they vse no rost, but for themselues and their houshold, nor no fire but in a little court chimnie in their owne chamber" (E^r; F4^r). In times of "great dearth," the wealthier might need to be reminded "upon pain of her majesty's heavy indignation" to remain in their "hospitalities" as indicated by the royal proclamation of 1596 that "her majesty is particularly informed of some intentions of sundry persons, of ability to keep hospitality in their countries, to leave their said hospitalities and to come to the city of London and other cities and towns corporate, thereby leaving the relief of their poor neighbors as well for food as for good rule, and with covetous minds to live in London and about the city privately and so also in other towns corporate without charge of company." Both the proclamation and a letter from the lord mayor of London to Lord Burghley in 1573 regarding the "meaner sort" who are violating sumptuary regulations explicitly connect the order of consumption with the order of society.[47]

Food substantiated demarcations of class, and it often served liminally to memorialize those permanently absent. It figured in the last thoughts—or rather, the thoughts about last things—of many an Elizabethan; in their wills, bequests of food often serve to recall the absent/present deceased in a secularized communion. The *Memorial Portrait of Sir Henry Unton*, painted about 1596, memorializes the place of food and food service in the life of a busy Elizabethan diplomat (fig. 22). The painting represents highlights from the life of the deceased. About one half of the ten or eleven vignettes from the career of Unton that are pictured on the right half of the work include feasts or representations of plate. Food paradoxically also served beyond the grave as reciprocal honor to living guests and deceased hosts. When a will specifies funeral arrangements, often a dinner is ordered, or, for the less wealthy, at least a distribution of spiced bread. Typical is the will of Agnes Lewen, widow of Thomas, ironmonger and alderman of London. Henry Machyn records in his *Diary* that after her funeral in 1562, "ther was a grett dener for as mony as wold cum, and after was sent spyse bred to evere howse and about the cette unto worshephulle men and women" (295). During the early modern period, food service and the language in which it is described coexpress through word and gesture the adaptation of religious and chivalric ritual to more secular contexts in order to honor or to memorialize the presence of those deemed worthy of respect.

Nor are associations between food, social order, and religious ritual unique to funeral arrangements. A similar aura of solemnity permeates descriptions of two feasts within the career of Robert Dudley, earl of Leicester, for example. In 1571, Dudley signaled his acceptance of apologies from the burgesses of Warwick through a mutuality of present/absent ceremony when, according to John Fisher, recorder of the Black Book of Warwick, the town folk were permitted to watch Dudley, a companion of the Order of Saint Michael, as he ate alone in celebration of the Feast of Saint Michael. His apparel and his movements are reverently described.[48] A second feast from Dudley's career bears some resemblance to the first in its solemnization of the act of eating.

The regulations of the knights of the Garter prescribed the celebration of the Feast of Saint George by all of the knights of the order, and the stringency of these requirements once again recalls the military model for the regulation of food service. That the knights were required to follow these instructions even when ill or abroad introduces the note of inexorable religious ritual, a comparison that is strengthened by the details of the service at Leicester's Garter banquet in Utrecht in 1586. The dinner took place in a hall hung with tapestries. At the upper end was a sumptuous cloth and a vacant chair of estate for the earl's absent queen. The service, presented to the sound of trumpets, was, according to John Stow, "most Prince-like and aboundant, serued on the knee, carued and tasted to her Maiesties trencher" (*Annales* 717). A foreign visitor to London also described how at Garter feasts, the queen's meat was carved "with the same ceremoniousness in her absence as when she is present. This is done even when no one sits and dines there [the Presence Chamber]." On the occasion of the visitor's report, Lord Cobham, sitting alone, attended as representative of the absent queen. "He was also served and waited upon exactly as if Her Majesty had been present in person" (Klarwill 378–79).

Garter ceremonies occasioned a number of variations upon absent/presence. If unable to attend as required by regulations of the order and enforced by fines, the absent knight was represented by his escutcheon of arms at his own charge and expense in the chapel of Windsor Castle (Beltz,

Memorials xcv). According to Ashmole, the absent knight was also required to set up both a capital stall with cloth of state, cushions, carpet, and the arms of the order within the Garter in honor of the sovereign in the church or chapel where he heard a service, and a second stall bearing his own arms in the same relative location prescribed by the protocol of the order in a highly schematized application of the synecdochic relationship between person and place. The knight, dressed in the whole habit of the order, was to hear service, and whenever coming, going, or passing the sovereign's arms, to do reverence toward first the altar and then the absent sovereign's stall. Thus simultaneously in two locations, absent presence was a cere-monial condition: the absent presence of the knight at Windsor and of the monarch at the place of the knight's observance, a cross-coupling of cross-couplings. Not even illness relieved the knight of the obligation to observe Saint George's Feast. The two stalls, again properly accoutred and located, were to be set up in the sick knight's chamber, where he would attend divine offices. If the knight was bedridden, the burden of the whole habit was to lie on his bed (*Institution* Gggg3ᵛ–4ᵛ).

Ashmole tallied Elizabeth's absences from Garter ceremonies, noting that in three years of her reign, she appeared wearing the prescribed collar and habit "to grace the *Grand Procession* it self with her own presence." But, he adds, "this *Queen* (and only she, of all the *Soveraigns* of this most noble *Order*) did sometimes publickly proceed to the *Chappel* (aswell [*sic*] as to the great *Closet*) and also passed in the *Grand Procession*, without wearing the whole *Habit* of the *Order*" (Bbbb2ʳ). He also calculates five other occa-sions when the queen either absented herself from attendance at chapel for Garter observances or, although physically present, remained in the "closet" of the chapel before proceeding thence to the presence chamber "with all usual state, though in her ordinary Apparel, and without the *Robes* of the *Order*," deputizing her lieutenant to take her place in the procession and in the choir of the chapel (Sssᵛ–Sss2ʳ).

Paradoxically, by appointing a lieutenant, Elizabeth was able to create an oppressive sense of her power: the presence of a subordinate emissary is always a reminder that the absent power may have weighed the occasion and found it short of full measure of importance. The resultant anxiety can be detected in Ashmole's rationalizations regarding her behavior: "But this may admit of some excuse; first, as a Woman, she thought her self not so strictly typed, to the exact observation of the Rules of so martial an *Order* . . . [and, he adds, the heaviness of the habit may have impeded her health]. Howbeit, her other Apparel, splendid attire, and the Lustre of her Jewels, (at those Solemnities) exceeded both in richness and glory, all that she wore at other times" (Bbbb2ʳ). In light of the lavish costumes to be seen on Elizabeth's portraits, the rationalization has the appearance of partial truth, but one wonders whether Garter robes could have been heavier than those jewel-encrusted gowns. In short, through the absence of either her person or the conventional accoutrements of presence at Garter ceremonies, Elizabeth may have been resisting assimilation into the masculine model of princedom—as Ashmole implies.

As for the masculine model of the uses—and miscalculations—of presence and absence, it is exemplified in the behavior of the earl of Essex. Countless observers note his frequent absences at critical times. Chief among his critics was the queen herself; on April 15, 1589, she harshly reprimanded him for having disobeyed her orders and joined the Portuguese expedition: "Your sudden and undutiful departure from our presence and your place of attendance, you may easily conceive how offensive it is, and ought to be, unto us . . . having so special office of attendance and charge near our person. We do therefore charge and command you forthwith . . . all excuses and delays set apart, to make your present and immediate repair unto us. . . . [You] will answer for the contrary at your uttermost peril" (Devereux, *Essex* 1:204–5). Anthony Standen wrote to Francis Bacon in 1593 of how his efforts to communicate with the elusive earl were frustrated by the "starts of his in stealing manner," fleeing town or remaining incommunicado (Birch 1:134–35). In 1596, Bacon advised the earl to seem always to have business afoot when in the presence of the queen and to pretend imminent absence on an unimportant journey such as to his estate in Wales as a decoy negotiable for his real cause (2:160). A year later, having absented himself from the view of the court for some time under pretext of illness while he and the queen exchanged private visits, the earl emerged, only to take to his quarters again for two weeks, emerging once again with plans to visit his estate, "on account of health, but more probably from discontent," according to court gossip (2:282; de Maisse 33).

When Essex, angry at his humiliation at the hands of the queen, absented himself from court, even from her Accession Day celebration, numerous friends, advisers, and relations wrote to urge his return. An anonymous writer cautioned him, "the greatest subject that ever is or was greatest in the prince's favor, in his absence is not missed" (Devereux, *Essex* 1:468). To the lord keeper's avuncular counsel that he yield, Essex responded that he had found his enemies at court "absolute and therefore I had rather they should triumph alone, than they should have me attendant on their chariots" (Birch, *Memoirs* 2:386–87). John Chamberlain described to Dudley Carleton more specifically an example of the behavior of Essex and the queen's reprisal: "presently after dinner he [Essex] retired to Wansted where they say he meanes to settle, seing he cannot be receved in court, though he have relented much and sought by divers meanes to recover his hold: but the Quene says he hath playde long enough upon her, and that she meanes to play a while upon him, and to stand as much upon her greatnes as he hath don upon stomacke" ([August 30, 1598], *Letters* 1:41).

So dangerous was Essex's volatility that Robert Markham, hearing that Sir John Harington was to serve in Ireland with Essex in 1599, wrote him a long letter cautioning silence (*Nugae Antiquae* 1:239–44). Francis Bacon advised the queen, on the other hand, "if you had my lord of Essex here with a white staff in his hand, as my lord of Leicester had, and continued him still about you, for society to yourself, and for an honour and ornament to your attendance and court, in the eyes of your people, and in the eyes of foreign embassadors, then were he in his right element" (Birch 2:432). Queen and courtier opposed "greatnes" versus "stomacke" in the play of absent presence, as John Chamberlain put it.

Essex relented, as he was strategically required to do in any game of greatness versus stomach, having disobeyed orders by abandoning his command in Ireland in September 1599 and then intruding upon the queen in dishabille. The queen shortly committed him to house arrest, preparatory to proceedings against him. Elizabeth, surprisingly, visited him when he was ill, but she refused his New Year's gift, and he found himself banished from her presence (Devereux, *Essex* 2:92–93). The body language of the presence of the commissioners at York House during the inquiry into his conduct in Ireland was ominous: all eighteen sat in chairs at a long table, neither uncovering nor extending him any courtesy, while Essex was compelled to kneel for a long time, although later permitted a cushion and, finally, a stool (Birch, *Memoirs* 2:447). Although cleared of the most serious charge of disloyalty, he was convicted of contempt, stripped of his military offices, and continued under house arrest. On September 6, 1600, he wrote the queen in a melodramatic vein: "Haste paper to that happy presence, whence only unhappy I am banished! Kiss that fair correcting hand which lays now plaisters to my lighter hurts, but to my greatest wound applieth nothing. Say thou camest from shaming, languishing, despairing ESSEX" (*CSPD 1598–1601* 465). Just three days later, he assured the queen, "my uttermost ambition is to be a mute person in that presence where joy and wonder would bar speech" (466). A flurry of similar letters became a blizzard as Michaelmas approached and his license for profits from sweet wines customs revenue would fall due, but renewal was denied as well as his continual petition to appear before the queen mute, as a present absence. Facing financial ruin, humiliation, and loss of honor, Essex rallied his supporters and embarked upon the rebellion that cost his life.

Like his earlier behavior, the final trial and execution of Essex were marked by dramatic instances of absence and presence. Robert Cecil found himself primarily responsible for the arrangements for the trial, other members of the council having absented themselves. At the arraignment,

Essex was unnerved by confessions read from his absent former supporters, and these absent presences precipitated desperate accusations on his part. His attempt to impugn the loyalty of Robert Cecil was thwarted by the secretary's sudden appearance from behind a tapestry in order to beg opportunity to defend himself immediately (Handover, *Cecil* 224–25). Having been found guilty, Essex confessed and made a last request that the queen "would be pleased to suffer him to die privately in the Tower," which request was granted (*CSPD 1598–1601* 588). In the event, privacy meant the presence of about a hundred observers in the absence of the public at large, and among the observers was his enemy Ralegh, who, in response to objections that he was present only to gloat, watched instead from an armory window, a present absence (Harrison, *Essex* 322).

Elizabeth felt keenly the absence of Essex. Almost two years after the execution of the former favorite, Sir John Harington wrote to his wife that when bidden to the queen's presence, he found her "in moste pitiable state." When conversation about Ireland recalled the absent presence of Essex, the queen "droppede a teare, and smote her bosome." She confessed that she felt "creepinge tyme" at the gate (*Nugae Antiquae* 1:322–23). When, in her last days, she fell into melancholy silence, one popular report attributed it to sadness over the death of Essex, but John Clapham would recall shortly after her death her efforts to offset public impressions of such disability: "And she would often show herself abroad at public spectacles, even against her own liking, to no other end but that the people might the better perceive her ability of body and good disposition, which otherwise in respect of her years they might perhaps have doubted; so jealous was she to have her natural defects discovered for diminishing her reputation."[49] Nonetheless her own presence was fading into impotent absence, and attendance of others at her jousts, progresses, and revels was diminishing.[50] In the end, she withdrew from company, food, and speech altogether, her last vital gesture of presence being a nonverbal signal that James Stuart was to be her successor.[51]

Her ultimate absent presence/present absence was manifest as the effigy that was mounted upon her casket as it progressed through the streets of London toward Westminster. Arabella Stuart had the last word as a wilfull absent presence: "The Lady Arbella Stuart, being of the royal blood, was especially required to have honored the funeral with her presence, which she refused, saying that, sith her access to the Queen in her lifetime might not be permitted, she would not after her death be brought upon the stage for a public spectacle" (Clapham 114). The bitter epitaph of Arabella, like Elizabeth herself, still an absent presence, bespeaks the power of absent presence to speak beyond silence.

NOTES

INTRODUCTION

1. "Prohibiting Portraits of the Queen [draft]," in *Tudor Proclamations* vol. 2, no. 516, dated December 1563. The editors Hughes and Larkin note official efforts as late as 1596 to destroy all "unseemly portraits of the Queen" (240). Strong has written extensively about the portraits of Elizabeth; see in particular *Gloriana*; see also Hazard, "Case" for more specific attention to the portraits as medium for silent language.

2. All references to Shakespeare's plays will be indicated, as here, by Arabic numerals signifying act, scene, and lines. Unless otherwise stated, all references are to the Riverside edition. Bevington has taken a phrase from this passage as title of his study of Shakespearean stage direction, *Action Is Eloquence*, a book that locates countless references to gesture in Shakespeare. See also Slater, *Shakespeare the Director*, and Fisch, "Language of Gesture," which schematizes the types, including the gesture opposing verbal communication.

3. Marlowe, *Hero and Leander*, in Donno, *Minor Epics* 53.

4. Transcribed from BM Add.MS 41499A (f. 6) by Chambers, *Sir Henry Lee* app. D, 271.

5. Bulwer, *Chirologia* 49.

6. Yates, *Astraea* 56–58.

7. Camden, *Remains concerning Britain* 190.

8. Elton, *England under the Tudors* 374–76; Palliser, *Age of Elizabeth* 26; Collins,

"Progress of Queen Elizabeth" 166; more recently, Frye, "Myth" calls into question whether Elizabeth really appeared in armor or ever delivered her famous speech.

9. Greene uses this term for the "signifying universe" accessible to each member of a culture (*Light in Troy* 20).

10. For example, Bevington's chapter on "The Language of Theatrical Space" analyzes Shakespeare's use of "spatial vocabulary," "spatial metaphor" (*Action* 118, 109). Bath's heuristic reminder that impresa portraits are necessarily "circumstantial" is an essential guideline for understanding the larger context of silent language (*Speaking Pictures* 12).

11. Elizabeth I, *Public Speaking* 116.

12. Folger Shakespeare Library MSS V.b.232, 184^v. A reproduction of the *Ermine* portrait appears as fig. 5, together with reproductions of other relevant portraits of the queen as examples of the silent language of portraits, in Hazard, "Case."

13. Stone, *Family and Fortune* 71.

14. Hanawalt, *Medieval London* 127–28.

15. All references to Shakespeare's sonnets refer to Shakespeare, *Art of Shakespeare's Sonnets*, the edition by Helen Vendler.

1. DRAWING THE LINE

1. Pliny, *Natural History* 9:35.36.84.

2. This woodcut is reproduced in Osley, *Scribes and Sources* fig. 1. Goldberg, *Writing Matter* is a book that might have saved me from much slogging had it been available when I was writing this chapter, although his approach is both more contentiously theoretical and more elaborately detailed in its treatment of graphology.

3. It may be that the privileging of line over picture in the early development of the northern Renaissance recapitulates earlier history in Italy where, for instance, the scribal signatures in manuscript books are bolder than those of the illuminators, but this is a question not to be pursued here.

4. Harold F. Brooks's editorial note in the Arden edition neatly summarizes other Tudor uses of mispointing for rhetorical or dramatic effect; see also, for this passage, Montrose, *Purpose of Playing* 194–96.

5. Erasmus, *Speaking Latin and Greek* 399. The translator, Maurice Pope, notes (597) that Erasmus reverses the roles of the principals in the anecdote according to his source in Pliny, wherein Apelles accuses Protogenes of excessive perfectionism.

6. Panofsky, *Albrecht Dürer* 44–45; also "Erasmus and the Visual Arts." On the relations between Erasmus and Dürer, and on linear emphasis, see Bialostocki, "Dürer and the Humanists"; Hayum, "Dürer's Portrait of Erasmus"; Kuspit, *Northern Critics*. Evett also begins his study of Tudor aesthetics by considering linear and planar elements. The coincidence is inevitable, and so at many places our works complement each other, although *Literature and the Visual Arts in Tudor England* is dedicated to aesthetics and is not all concerned with my interest in silent language.

7. Haydocke, trans. *Tracte* 2. For a lucid discussion of the matrix of the "polemic of *disegno* (drawing, design) against *colore*" in the history of Italian art, where the

terminology and outcome differed somewhat from the English experience, see Gage, *Color and Culture* ch. 7.

8. More, *Complete Works* vol. 6, pt. 1, pp. 40, 46. A lecture by J. B. Trapp first called my attention to these passages from More's refutation (Victoria and Albert Museum: "Sir Thomas More and the Visual Arts" [August 21, 1983]).

9. Franko, *Dance as Text* 5. See Franko's fig. 1 for an illustration of Giovanni Braccelli's "Figured Alphabet."

10. See, in particular, Gent, *Picture and Poetry*, from which I draw her examples of Hoby (15–16) and Haydocke (9). Baxandall also addresses the shortcomings of contemporary English translation of "*designo*" ("English *Disegno*" 203–14).

11. As Gent pointed out in a lecture entitled " 'Viewing with the Eye of Persons Accustomed to Drawing,' " delivered at the Victoria and Albert Museum on October 22, 1983.

12. Strype, *Annals* vol. 1, pt. 1, p. 409.

13. Davidson, *Guild Chapel Wall Paintings* 10; Howard, *Early Tudor Country House* 114; Strong, *Gloriana* fig. 21.

14. Aston, *England's Iconoclasts* 1:312.

15. Pliny, *Pliny's "Natural History,"* ed. Newsome, 281.

16. Dee, preface to *Elements of Geometrie* d.iiij^r.

17. Strong analyzes this miniature in great detail in *Cult of Elizabeth* (56–83), where he summarizes earlier scholarship regarding the inscription, the iconography, and the various identifications proposed for the sitter.

18. Strong, *Artists* 135.

19. Strong reproduces another of Cumberland's suits of armor and its appearance on another miniature by Hilliard and a contemporary drawing (*Cult of Elizabeth* figs. 65–67). On this suit, flowers also appear, linked by lover's knots.

20. Hazard, "Anatomy of 'Liveliness' " 407–18.

21. Rebuses are italicized in my transcription, guided by the label on the *Buss* at the Victoria and Albert Museum and the transcription in the early and groundbreaking study by Nevinson ("Domestic Embroidery Patterns"); for more detailed technical analysis of the embroidery, see Edwards, *Black Work*; for the iconography see Strong, *Cult of Elizabeth* 76–77. Note that Camden scornfully describes more rustic application of courtly rebus, a painted cloth whereon a lover "mystically" figures that he loves well Rose Hill by representing an eye, a loaf, a well, a rose, and a hill (*Remains* 140).

22. Marston, Satire III: *uaedam et sunt, et videntur* lines 61–62, *Works* 3:278.

23. Nevinson, "Embroidery Patterns of Thomas Trevelyon" 19 and plates 18A and 18B. For other uses of the knot in contemporary costume, see Baines, *Fashion Revivals* 66–67.

24. Hawkins, *Medallic Illustrations* 1: fig. 11.5.

25. Vasari, *Lives* 4:192–93; *Le vite* 6:74.

26. Yoch's stimulating article ("Renaissance Gardening and Pastoral Scenery") led me to the passage from Vasari; Strong (*Renaissance Garden* 40–41) conveniently reproduces designs for knots, and Girouard (*Robert Smythson and Architecture* 26)

demonstrates their relevance to architectural plans; several illustrations in Scho-field, *Medieval London Houses* show the similarities of pattern in gardens and ceilings of early modern properties: cf. figs. 57, 218 for gardens; figs. 137–42 for ceilings. Less often remarked are the similarities between knot patterns and archi-tectural facades as on the lawyer's town house of 1603, now the Feather Inn, a photo of which appears in Mowl, *Style* 56; additionally, leaded glass designs are similar linear patterns, for which see the many figures in Castle's chapter on the Tudor window (*Domestic Gothic* 64–78).

27. Plat[t], *Garden of Eden* B^r–B^v.

28. Peele, *Works* 2:310. Strong's third chapter ("The Emblematic Garden," *Renaissance Garden* 45–71) discusses Theobalds among other contemporary examples of the type, generously illustrated.

29. For a brief discussion of historical controversy over chrysography (i.e., "golden inscription on paper") generated precisely because of its sumptuous char-acter, see Shell, *Money, Language, and Thought* app. 1.

30. Dawson and Kennedy-Skipton, *Elizabethan Handwriting*, reproduces the signatures of Cavendish (no. 7), Leicester and Burghley (no. 12), and Essex (no. 13); Lodge, ed., *Illustrations*, has those of Anne Warwick and Elizabeth in vol. 3, at plate 9.

31. Thomson, *Shakespeare's Professional Career* 124.

32. Wright, "Change in Direction" 152–53.

33. As quoted by Nevinson from the Penrose copy of the manuscript in his richly illustrated study of Trevelyon ("Embroidery Patterns of Thomas Trevelyon" 2). This article led me to several of the handbooks cited.

34. For etymological analysis of the word-cluster, see Spitzer, *Classical and Christian Ideas* 18–19, 84, 148–52n. I am grateful to Elizabeth McCutcheon for having reminded me of Guazzo's allusion.

35. Bevington, *Tudor Drama* 8–9. On the frequency of use of cipher, see Haynes, *Invisible Power*; a photograph of a letter in cipher by Elizabeth appears with a translation on pp. 20–21.

36. Davies, *Devices* nos. 240, 242.

37. King, *Tudor Iconography* 264–65, fig. 87.

38. Sisson, "Marks as Signatures" 20–23; Dawson and Kennedy-Skipton, *Elizabethan Handwriting* 9–11; Cressy, *Literacy* 59. These sources are generously illustrated.

39. "Enfin, il ne faut pas oublier que l'écriture possible aussi est un geste, à une époque où il n'y a pas d'autre écriture possible que celle de la main (elle aussi riche d'un symbolisme très fort) courant sur le parchemin" (Schmitt, *La Raison des Gestes* 15). Goldberg even goes so far as to construe writing as violence, a terminus for the gradations of intensity and literalism of metaphor that seems to me to be both excessive and overgeneralized. He makes a nice case for the carnality of letter, however (*Writing Matter* esp. 226–28).

40. Bowle, "Singultientes lusus" 1:15. (Note that this is my only reference to

Nichols's edition of Jacobean progresses in this text; all others refer to Elizabeth's and are usually documented parenthetically.)

41. As pointed out by Marotti, *Manuscript, Print, Lyric* (28).

42. Gombrich, "Revival" 93–110. Note that Aldus emphasizes the invention and impress of the human hand in the description of his Aldine type, "a Latin chancery and cursive letter of surpassing beauty which seems as written by the very hand" (Barolini, *Dream Book* 80).

43. Howard-Hill, "Evolution" 112–45.

44. Parkes, *Cursive* xiii–xviii; Clanchy, *Memory to Record* 97ff.

45. On the question of attitudes toward publication in print, see Saunders, "Stigma" 139–64, and the rejoinder by May, "Tudor Aristocrats" 11–18.

46. Salesbury's *Dictionary in Englysh and Welshe,* for instance, prints English definitions in formal Gothic letters, whereas Welsh is in less formal bastarda. On the question of type as social distinction, see Mish, "Black Letter" 627–30, but also Howard-Hill's cautionary note ("Evolution" 138). For a carefully researched and closely argued case of use of type as fictive construct, see the study by Luborsky ("Allusive Presentation"); also, McCanles ("Document and Monument" esp. p. 13).

47. As pointed out by Saunders, "Stigma" 156. Facsimiles of these title pages are reproduced in Drayton, *Works,* corrected ed., vol. 2.

2. LINE AS INTERSECTION

1. Ferry, *Art of Naming* 19.

2. Salusbury, *Poems by Salusbury and Chester,* ed. Brown, xlv–xlvi.

3. [William Kemp], *Kemps Nine Daies Wonder* 16; Thomas Kemp, *Book of John Fisher* 92; for a broader view of concern with the physicality of letters, see Elsky, *Authorizing Words.*

4. On the religious iconography associated with Elizabeth, see King, "The 'Godly' Queens," in *Tudor Iconography* 182–266; for an earlier, comprehensive, and indispensable study of her mythological associations as well, see Wilson, *England's Eliza.*

5. For background and references on figured texts, see *Elizabethan Critical Essays* 2:416n., and Higgins, *Pattern Poetry* ch. 1.

6. Sylvester, *Divine Weeks* 2: app., 892–93; plate 2. In a good summary of the practice, Cook uses the example of William Gager's visible pyramid of words to illustrate how some poets took literally Horace's *Exegi monumentum* theme, shaping writing into the forms of stony monuments ("Figured Poetry").

7. Note that Strong attributes the *Sieve Portrait* to Cornelius Ketel (*Gloriana* 101). For review of the imperialistic intentions of the iconography, see Yates, "Charles V and the Idea of Empire," in *Astraea* 1–28 also, Rosenthal, "Columnar Device,"; more recently, Sider, "Transcendent Symbols."

8. Watson, *Poems* LXXX–LXXXII; Higgins, *Pattern Poetry* figs. 2.82–83 and gloss. 230.

9. I was led to these poems by Wilson's exhaustive early study of iconography of the queen (*England's Eliza* 379–82).

10. Painter, *"Hypnerotomachia Poliphili"* 20. The work has, however, also been attributed to Fra Eliseo.

11. Frere, *Newe Booke of Cokerye*, reproduced on page facing clxiv.

12. The frontispiece is reproduced in the facsimile edition of Spenser, *Faerie Queene* vol. 1.

13. John Milsom, "Music" in Ford, *Sixteenth-Century Britain* 184.

14. Foster, *Patterns of Thought* ch. 5. Foster locates the Platonic image of the sphere in *Timaeus* 320–38. For Renaissance adaptations of ancient philosophical figural concepts of the universe, see the lavishly documented and illustrated study by Heninger, *Touches of Sweet Harmony*.

15. Jennifer Stead, "Bowers of Bliss: The Banquet Setting," in Wilson, *"Banqueting Stuffe"* 136.

16. Franko, *Dance as Text* 60. Dance could figure complex ideas: Skiles Howard analyzes the case of dance as representation of the provisional nature of rank and gender in *A Midsummer Night's Dream* ("Hands, Feet, and Bottoms,") and more recently he concludes that in *Orchestra*, John Davies "choreographs a nation" ("Rival Discourses" 50).

17. For other kinds of verbal imitations of circular figure, see Ferry, *Art of Naming* 33–35.

18. See the pioneering study of this scheme by Hieatt, *Endless Monument*.

19. Hazard, " 'Ornament.' " This topic will be developed more fully in subsequent chapters.

20. The woodcut illustrations are reproduced in the facsimile edition, Spenser, *Shepheardes Calendar*, from which I quote. For more detailed analysis, see the studies by Luborsky ("Allusive Presentation" and "Illustrations").

21. Fumerton, "Exchanging Gifts" 266.

22. Ribner, " 'Compasse' "; Smarr, "Pyramid and Circle."

23. Strong, *Gloriana* 133; Barber, "England II" 77.

24. Reproduced in Edgerton, *Heritage of Giotto's Geometry* fig. 6.4.

25. As Greenblatt reminds us, "possession in Roman law was based largely upon the principle of bodily occupation: 'possession is so styled,' the Digest of Justinian explains, 'from "seat," as it were "position" [*a sedibus quasi positio*], because there is a natural holding, which the Greeks call *katoche* by the person who stands on a thing' " (*Marvelous Possessions* 27).

26. Strong, *Gloriana* 134–41; Hazard, "Case" 79–80.

27. For a thorough review of the subject, see in particular Barber, "England II" 57–98.

28. Read, *Mr. Secretary Walsingham* 1:428 app.

29. Tyacke and Huddy, *Christopher Saxton* 31–43, passim.

30. Robinson and Petchenik, *Nature of Maps* 44, 56; Blakemore and Harley, "Early Maps as Language" 87, 104; Head, "The Map as Natural Language," in *Cartographica* 21, no. 1 (1984): 1–32. Schlictmann's rejoinder (33–36) makes essen-

tially the same objections as Robinson and Petchenik. Gillies (*Geography of Difference* 54) provides the quoted, last, succinct definition.

31. Schulz, "Barbari's View of Venice" 447–68.

32. Schulz, "Barbari's View of Venice" 447–48; BL Add. MS 28681, f. 9.

33. Williams, *Thomas Howard* 44.

34. Barber, "England II" 96n., 180.

35. Frutaz, *Le Piante di Roma* 1: plate III, 44–46; 2: table 13; van der Heijden traces other uses of the image of Europe as a virgin in his "Heinrich Bünting's *Itinerarium Sacrae Scripturae.*"

36. Beresford, *History on the Ground* 55–60; Tyacke and Huddy, *Christopher Saxton* 16–18, 50–51, figs. 14 and 15, 66.

37. Overall, *Civitas Londinum* 20; Hurst, *Oxford Topography* 4–8.

38. Tyacke and Huddy, *Christopher Saxton* 48–49; they quote Norden on 33.

39. As quoted by Lawrence, "Permission to Survey" 17–18.

40. N[orden], *Surveyors Dialogue* B 7^r; I was led to consult this text by Tyacke and Huddy, who quote the 1607 edition (58); for a searching analysis of the (literally) instrumental role of mathematically based surveying in the maintenance of unequal distribution of property, see Crystal Bartolovich, "*The Surveyor* and the Politics of Transition," in Vos, *Place and Displacement* 255–83.

41. Batho, "Finances" 441.

42. Buisseret, *Rural Images* 3–4.

43. Lane quoted from SP 63/200/78 by Skelton, "Maps of a Tudor Statesman," Skelton and Summerson, *Description of Maps* 3–4; Harvey, *Maps in Tudor England* 47–52. Thomas notes Burghley's incongruous failure to hire surveyors for the royal estate, doubtful perhaps of their new science ("Elizabethan Crown Lands" 66–67).

44. Evans and Lawrence, *Christopher Saxton* 20–25, front., plate 1; Orgel, "Gendering the Crown," in de Grazia, Quilligan, and Stallybrass, *Subject and Object* 133–65. I have greatly condensed Orgel's case, omitting here his evidence based upon historical iconography of the personifications and contemporary attitudes toward female chastity.

45. Hazard, " 'Ornament.' "

46. Summerson, "Book of Architecture of John Thorpe" 1.

47. Reproduced in Ravenhill and Rowe, "Decorated Screen Map" 1–12.

48. Tyacke and Huddy, *Christopher Saxton* 41; Buxton, *Elizabethan Taste* 114. Victor Morgan discusses not only the tapestry maps, but also other ornamental uses of maps, including images reproduced on playing cards ("Cartographic Image" 149–54). As Streitberger points out, Edmond Tyllney's "Topographical Descriptions, Regiments and Policies" (Folger Shakespeare Library MS v.b.182) contains details of the map of England cut from the earliest known set of geographical playing cards ("Tyllney Manuscript at the Folger Shakespeare Library," *Papers* 452).

49. Harley nicely reviews the symbolic values of Tudor maps in "Meaning and Ambiguity" (22–45). For especially suggestive readings of symbolic uses of maps in Elizabethan theater, see Gillies and Vaughan, *Playing the Globe*. Richard Helgerson

chronologically develops the concept of maps as political assertions beyond the time at which this chapter must leave it, and he corroborates many of the observations made above in the chapter "The Land Speaks" in his *Forms of Nationhood*. See also Manley, "From Matron to Monster" for an imaginative analysis of the iconographic representation of London on maps and urban views.

3. SURFACE, COLOR, TEXTURE

1. Laird, "*Vt figura poesis*," *Art and Text* 295; textum (L): that which is woven; figuratively, of a written composition, texture, style.

2. Reproduced in Philippa Glanville, "The Crafts and Decorative Arts," in Ford, *Sixteenth-Century Britain* 3:268. The poster displays a towering arrangement of grotesque plate, bags and chests of gold, ewers, and so forth. Curiously, perhaps as a pictorial juxtaposition of gold like King Solomon's with an image of his wisdom, he is pictured on the inset tapestry below rendering his most famous judgment. One is left to infer a legitimation of desire for worldly goods.

3. Banks, " 'Breviate' " 321.

4. Klein, "Your Humble Handmaid." This article nicely places these gifts within the anthropological context of gifts as negotiations and the empowerment of women.

5. Swain, "New Year's Gift" 266; Barber, *Textile* 5, plates 7 and 8; Jourdain, *Secular Embroidery* 56.

6. Swain, *Needlework* 78; see also 106.

7. Swain, *Needlework* 75, plate 42; Williams, *Thomas Howard* 236. Summit indicates the association between Mary's embroideries and Elizabeth's verse "The Doubt of Future Foes" as a possible exchange of the "poetics of queenship" (" 'Arte of a Ladies Penne' " 418–21; reproduction of the Oxburgh hanging "*Virescit Vulnere Virtus*" opp. 416).

8. Gunn and Lindley, *Cardinal Wolsey* 44–45.

9. Starkey, "Legacy" 8; CSPV 7:16.

10. Jourdain, *Secular Embroidery* 36; Williams, *Howard* 45; Robinson, *Dukes of Norfolk* 55; Girouard, *Hardwick Hall* 77; Williams, *Bess of Hardwick* 204.

11. *Elizabethan Midlands* (catalog) 6; Brodhurst, "Sir William Cavendish" 86.

12. Swain, *Needlework* 51, 82; Leader, *Mary Queen of Scots* 372. Swain notes that perhaps this skirt and certainly another belonging to Elizabeth were later converted into altar frontals (82); apparently churchly and courtly elegance were indeed interchangeable value.

13. Erler, "Davies and the Rainbow Portrait" 370. Fischlin makes a strong case for the primacy of political allegory on the portrait ("Political Allegory" 175–206).

14. Swain, *Needlework* 75, plate 41.

15. Roethlisberger, "Ulysses Tapestries" iii, 118, fig. 12.

16. Girouard, *Hardwick Hall* 77, 93.

17. Boynton and Thornton, "Hardwick Hall Inventory" 26–27.

18. In a wide-ranging but closely reasoned article, Ann Rosalind Jones argues

that Spenser's rhetoric in this poem and in Sonnet 71 of his *Amoretti* dematerializes the gender-specific act of feminine embroidering in order to subordinate it to the masculine creation of text ("Dematerializations," in de Grazia, Quilligan, and Stallybrass, *Subject and Object* 200–204); for moral and aesthetic implications of several of the examples discussed in this chapter, see Hazard, "Anatomy of 'Liveliness.'"

19. Boorde's picture is reproduced in Boorde, *Fyrst Boke of the Introduction of Knowledge* 116. For de Heere's version, see Croft-Murray and Hulton, *Catalogue of British Drawings* 1:28.

20. Cressy, "Gender Trouble."

21. According to Donaldson, Mary loved male costume and sports, traveling the streets icognito in male dress, entertaining the French ambassador in male costume together with her four Maries, and entering the battlefield dressed as a man (*All the Queen's Men* 68).

22. For more detailed discussion of other examples of Amazonian iconography associated with Elizabeth, see Schleiner, "*Divina virago*"; also, Marcus, "Shakespeare's Comic Heroines" 135–53.

23. For this and other examples in the history of the terminology since antiquity, see the comprehensive study of color by Gage, *Color and Culture* 82 and all of ch. 7.

24. Sands attributes eternity to green and purity to white (*Gardens of Hampton Court* 46).

25. For a well-researched summary of Elizabethan use of color, see Arnold, *Elizabeth's Wardrobe* 90–91.

26. "An Account of the Expences of Robert Sidney," in *Antiquarian Repertory* 1: 275–77, 288–90.

27. Stallybrass, "Worn Worlds," in de Grazia, Quilligan, and Stallybrass, *Subject and Object* 292.

28. Batho, "Finances," 436.

29. Evans and Lawrence, *Christopher Saxton* 11.

30. Palliser, *Age of Elizabeth* 203, table 7.1.

31. Manley, "Of Sites and Rites," in Smith, Strier, and Bevington, *Theatrical City* 45–46.

32. Stallybrass also comments on the ambiguity of *livery,* from a slightly different perspective—that is, the wearer's freedom to wear the livery that signals the protection of the house as well as his service to it ("Worn Worlds" in de Grazia, Quilligan, and Stallybrass, *Subject and Object* 289–90).

33. McCracken, "Dress Colour." I have summarized and paraphrased those parts of this analysis that pertain to color-as-language, without, I trust, distorting the main point of McCracken's study of color as an "operator" in Elizabethan culture that both structured opposition and, through doubled evaluation of color, provided the framework that permitted social change, a concept that lies too far afield from present purposes, although contiguous.

34. Jones, *Birth* 104; for several references to hatbands, see Smith, *Homosexual Desire* 290, n.13.

35. As quoted by Neale, *Queen Elizabeth I* 290.

36. Whigham's discussion of this and of several specific cases contextualizes the sumptuary discourse within the larger social and political rivalries and supplies further bibliographic references (*Ambition and Privilege* 159); see his figs. 1–2 for a convenient graphic representation of the strictures of the proclamation of 1577/80, and his useful table of the English Renaissance editions of "basic" courtesy books (199). Youngs summarizes the history of the sumptuary regulations and futile efforts to enforce them (*Proclamations* 161–70).

37. Hooper, "Tudor Sumptuary Laws" 447.

38. Baldwin, *Sumptuary Legislation* 230–38; for earlier Italian sumptuary regulations, see Lawner, *Courtesans* 22.

4. SHAPE AND SUBSTANCE

1. Strong reproduces large, clear details of the queen's sleeve on this portrait in *Gloriana* color plate 4.

2. Batho, "Finances" 447.

3. *Illustrations of Ancient State* app. 130.

4. Literary use of gems has been comprehensively researched by Hansen, "Sermons in Stones."

5. Baldwin, *Sumptuary Legislation* 231–33.

6. For examples of some of these less familiar uses of rings, see the portraits of Elizabeth as a princess, attributed to William Scrots (Strong, *Gloriana* fig. 28), as well as Lady Chandos (my fig. 10), and Sir Henry Lee (my fig. 12), whereon he wears one suspended from his neck and another tied to his elbow, as well as finger rings.

7. For the complicated question whether the queen actually displayed her ring or was only reported to have done so, see King, "Queen Elizabeth I" 36–38.

8. Kunz, *Rings* 56; Douce, "Runic Jasper Ring" 124; Jones, *Finger-Ring Lore* 290–93.

9. Burgon, *Thomas Gresham* 1:51–52; Scarisbrick, *Rings* 51.

10. Ellis, *Original Letters* 2nd ser. 2:288–90.

11. Bruster discusses the ring in *Cymbeline*, for example, within the context of an analysis of theatrical props as commodities that encode the body (*Drama and the Market* 86–96).

12. Hemp, "Grasshopper Rings" 403–8; Scarisbrick, "Gresham" 300–301, with a clear color photo on 301.

13. Inderwick, *Calendar of Inner Temple Records* lxii–lxiii, 217; Wilson, *Sweet Robin* 131.

14. Aubrey, *Memoires of Naturall Remarques* 260–61; Devereux, *Lives and Letters* 2:180–84; Kunz, *Rings* 186–88; Oman, *British Rings* 66–67.

15. Williams, *Howard* 161; Kunz, *Rings* 184.

16. On the "semantic duality" of *gift* and related words, see Starobinski, *Largesse* 62.

17. Stone, *Crisis* 452–53. Trexler notes in the Florence of the Medici the transition from the old practice of bringing tribute to the ruler to the offering of gifts (*Dependence in Context* 45n.).

18. Rushton, "Testament" 25–31.

19. Whigham, *Ambition and Privilege* 69; Loades, *Tudor Court* 144–47; on the records of New Year's gifts as indication of social status, see May, *Elizabethan Courtier Poets* 22–26.

20. Kingsford, "Essex House" 9, 48; for more detail regarding Leicester's extravagance, see Hazard, "Magnificent Lord."

21. Girouard, "Elizabethan Holdenby" 1401.

22. Guy, *Tudor England* 395; Gunn and Lindley, *Cardinal Wolsey* 44.

23. Von Bülow, "Diary," in *Transactions* 17; Klarwill, *Queen Elizabeth and Some Foreigners* 325. For an illustration of the lord mayor's chain, see Jackson, *An Illustrated History of English Plate* 2:1056, fig. 1497.

24. Nichols 3:24; Outhwaite, "Dearth," *The European Crisis of the 1590s*, ed. Clark 27.

25. [Gough], *Sepulchral Monuments* vol. 1, pt. 2, 215; *Tudor Proclamations* 2:384–85.

26. *Entertainments* 102; Churchyard, *A Discourse* Biiiʳ.

27. Glanville, "The Crafts and Decorative Arts," in Ford, *Sixteenth-Century Britain* 3:289.

28. Lancashire, "Orders for Twelfth Day," *English Literary Renaissance* 32.

29. *John Russell's Boke of Nurture*, in Furnivall, *Early English Meals* 15.

30. Dewar, *Sir Thomas Smith* 90; *CSPF* 1562 no. 872, 1564–65 no. 523.

31. Jackson, *English Plate* 1:173–75 and figs. 193, 194.

32. Honour, "Silver" 1:72–73, plate 38b.

33. Holmes, *Elizabethan London* 116; Duffy, *Stripping of the Altars* 133ff., 328ff., 585–88.

34. A. R. Humphreys observes that the earl of Shrewsbury found himself similarly constrained (*Henry IV, part 2*, Arden, ed., 45–46 n. 141). Note that the Hostess also contemplates pawning her tapestry.

35. *Calendar of Letters and State Papers . . . Simancas* 2:606–7.

36. Palliser's discussion of Elizabethan currency provides a useful overview with pertinent data: *Age of Elizabeth* 134–39; see also Brown, "Notes on Coinage" tables 5, 6.

37. Heth, "The goulden arte" (BL MS Stowe 1071) 15ʳ.

38. *Gesta Grayorum* 49; Trexler again supplies fascinating precedent in Italian use of coinage as political counter and as insult (*Dependence in Context* 127–28).

39. Starkey, "Ightham Mote" 154–58.

40. For a history of the political portent of the closed imperial crown that Elizabeth wears on the First Seal as well as on many graphic images, see Hoak, "The Iconography of the Crown Imperial," in Hoak, *Tudor Political Culture* 54–103; for the history of its religious and political significance in Tudor use, see King, *Tudor Iconography* ch. 3.

41. Strong, *Artists* nos. 44, 193.

42. On the connections between decor and decorum, ornament and ethics, see Hazard, " 'Ornament.' "

43. Fig. 30; also, Hawkins 1: no. 129. There is a two-page color reproduction of this pendant medal in *Currency of Fame* (no. 164).

44. See, for example, Rodríguez-Salgado, *Armada.*

45. Tenison, *Elizabethan England* 6:59; Strong and Van Dorsten quote this passage within the context of a detailed description of the triumphal festivities (*Leicester's Triumph* 41).

46. Peter Brears, "Rare Conceites and Strange Delights," in Wilson, "*Banquetting Stuffe*" 61.

47. Fumerton describes in some detail the practice of breaking up the sugar works after a banquet, a custom that later occasionally became violent (*Cultural Aesthetics* 112–15). As will become apparent in succeeding chapters, Fumerton's interests closely parallel my own, and she often pursues arguments with the support of evidence that complements mine.

48. Scodel *(English Poetic Epitaph)* cites several examples of the funeral-epitaph-as-monument, and although his work is mainly concerned with later epitaphs, it is valuable in situating the English tradition.

49. Vincent, "Precedents," College of Arms MS 151, 2:325; for a photo of the tomb, see Mann, "English Church Monuments" plate 20a.

50. Panofsky, *Tomb Sculpture* 66; Gittings, *Death, Burial, and the Individual* plate 9. Gittings's study is a rich source of comprehensive, generously illustrated data re funeral practice.

51. Llewellyn, "Claims to Status" 145–60. This piece also usefully pinpoints the shift in definition of chivalric honor from (sometimes fictive) family lineage to service to the state. See also Llewellyn's *Art of Death.*

52. Llewellyn, "John Weever" 1:28–49.

53. Friedman, "Patronage" pt. 2: 396–97; for a well-illustrated study of changing fashions in tomb sculpture, see Mann, "English Church Monuments."

54. Chatwin, "Monumental Effigies" 158–65.

55. Norris, *Monumental Brasses: The Craft* 93, plates 74 and 75.

56. Mann, "Instances of Antiquarian Feeling" 267–71.

57. Norris, *Monumental Brasses: The Portfolio Plates* plate 360.

58. Hurtig, "Shroud Tombs" 217–39.

59. Llewellyn, "The Royal Body," in Gent and Llewellyn, *Renaissance Bodies* 226, with photo. Although James's treatment of Elizabeth's tomb lies beyond the chronological limits of my study, his contrivance regarding its making, placement, and inscription so as to diminish her status and to emphasize his own dynastic claim is a case that calls for notice; see Walker, "Reading the Tombs" 510–30.

60. According to Thompson, *Kenilworth Castle, Warwickshire* 26–27. Both Thompson (18, 26) and Renn (*Kenilworth Castle* 24) reproduce photos of the gatehouse and porch. The latter also reproduces on the title page a large, clear

illustration of the fireplace. The clearest photo of the entrance to the gatehouse, showing the initials R. D., is in Mowl, *Style* 75.

61. Hussey, "Hardwick Hall 1" 809; Stallybrass, "Bess of Hardwick's Buildings" 371–72.

62. Summerson, "Three Elizabethan Architects" 218–19.

63. Jourdain, "Sir Thomas" 129–43; [Isham], *Lyveden New Bield* 12; Mowl reproduces a photo of the emblems of the Passion used in place of conventional metopes on Lyveden (*Style* 107). Kaushick speculates that the provocation of the overtly Roman Catholic symbolism of his building may have partly motivated anti-enclosure riots directed at Tresham ("Resistance" 49).

64. [Isham], *Rushton Triangular Lodge* 11; Isham's note on this page comments on the significance of the nine chicks, and Lomas describes that number in the planning of the lodge (HMC, *Manuscripts of Clarke-Thornhill* xlv), but only two are visible on modern photos of the facade. See Mowl (*Style* 188–89) for photos of other angles of the lodge.

65. For a color plate of Longford, see Mowl, *Style* 111.

66. Airs discusses these several examples at greater length in his article "The English Country House" 15–18.

67. De Maisse, *Journal* 30; for a reproduction of a woodcut illustrating the seating arrangements for Elizabeth's presence in the House of Lords, see Perry, *Word of a Prince* 227.

5. PLACE, BOUNDARY, POSITION

1. Manley, "Of Sites and Rites," in Smith, Strier, and Bevington, *Theatrical City* 45–46. For the symbolic significance of mayoral midsummer riding as proprietary gesture, see Sheila Lindenbaum, "Ceremony and Oligarchy," in Hanawalt and Reyerson, *City and Spectacle* 171–88.

2. Anglo, *Spectacle, Pageantry, and Policy* 156, 158; Hill, *Arte of the Interpretacion of Dreames* Evii^v. For medieval precedents, see both Koziol, *Begging Pardon* 305–6, and Bialostocki's historical overview, "Dichotomy" 23–40. Levin quotes Knyght's claim in her "*Heart and Stomach of a King*" 117.

3. Stock, *Implications of Literacy* 48. Enactment of appropriation of territories in the New World similarly involved physical gesture, such as the cutting down of tree boughs, the movement of sand from place to place—a symbolic act known as "turf and twig" when exercised by Drake in South America (Keller, Lissitizyn, and Mann, *Creation of Rights* 40–41, 56–57); more recently, Seed has contrasted national differences in *Ceremonies of Possession*, with English claims based upon house building, as opposed, for example, to French procession or Spanish proclamation.

4. Beresford, *History on the Ground* 28–30. Seed names such "perambulation" as an ancient British rite of possession as early as 600 AD, detailed descriptions as if observed on a walk of boundary markers: trees and hedges (*Ceremonies of Possession* 19).

5. On the iconography of Truth the Daughter of Time, see Saxl, "*Veritas filia*

temporis" 204–6; on the device, see Giovio, *Worthy Tract* 71. For Italian precedents in manipulation of ceremony, see Trexler, *Dependence in Context*: "[O]ne of the ways in which the Medici showed authority was by effecting a shift in ritual spaces, times, and objects" (45).

6. *Breefe Discourse, declaring and approuing the necessarie and inuiolable mainte-nance of the laudable Customes of London* Aviii^v–B^r. I was led to this pertinent source by Manley, "From Matron to Monster" 349. This piece, together with the work of Steven Mullaney (*Place of the Stage*, especially the chapter reprinted as "Civic Rites, City Sites: The Place of the Stage" in *Staging the Renaissance* 17–26) and that of Marcus (*Puzzling Shakespeare*) have helped me to situate my own work on Elizabethan uses of space. This last led me to the dispute recorded in the *Remembrancia* mentioned below.

7. [Overall and Overall], *Analytical Index* 426–34; for other disputes between the Tower, the City, and the monarch, see Manning, *Village Revolts* 200ff.; Manley, *Literature and Culture* 271.

8. Starkey, "Legacy" 8; Aston, "English Ruins and English History" 242.

9. Airs, *English Country House* 18; Stone and Stone, *Open Elite?* 361; for other specific cases of what they call "lay ascendancy" as result of the Dissolution, see Heal and Holmes, *Gentry* 326–35. Prokter and Taylor enlarge details from Eliz-abethan maps and point out the evidence of these changes in their *A to Z of Elizabethan London* vii.

10. The factual data regarding Ingatestone are from Emmison, *Tudor Secretary* 20–35.

11. Pevsner, "Old Somerset House" 163–67.

12. Hussey, "Burghley House" 1962; Pevsner, *Bedfordshire* 219–21.

13. Stow, *Three Chronicles* 134–35; Emery, "England *circa* 1600" 300; Bindoff, *Fame* 18.

14. *Fuller's Worthies* 252; Berlin, "Civic Ceremony" 21.

15. Stone and Stone, *Open Elite?* 298ff.; Tittler, *Architecture and Power* 112–33.

16. Maurice Howard speaks aptly of "Self-Fashioning and the Classical Moment in Mid-Sixteenth-Century English Architecture" in Gent and Llewellyn, *Renais-sance Bodies* 198–217.

17. Pevsner reproduces Dolman's motto in *Berkshire* 214; Palliser quotes the Newbury rhyme in *Age of Elizabeth* 91.

18. For instance, Knecht observes that traditionally no one outside the royal family was allowed to reside above the king of France ("New Light on Francis I" 3). Palmer speaks of how the elevated status of one's sleeping rooms "encoded" one's degree of authority (*Hospitable Performances* 12–13).

19. Girouard admits that his hypothesis that Willoughby's prospect room may express even higher aspirations—imitation of the Temple of Solomon—is beyond proof, but he offers fascinating data (*Town and Country* 187–96). The location of the prospect room is on the uppermost level of the central tower between the two bartizans.

20. For a summary of such difficulties, see Hazard, "Absent Presence and Present

Absence" *TSLL* 13–16; for an example of the specific logistical problems posed by a queen's visit, see also *Entertainments* 52–57.

21. Sladen, "Kirby Hall," 144–45; Beresford, *History on the Ground* 211–14. Mowl reproduces a photo of the imposing giant order on the facade of the north side of the courtyard at Kirby (*Style* 95). Platt recalls that many large country houses profited from enclosure (*Great Rebuildings* 10–15), and Taylor reproduces plans and photos for the garden sites in *Archaeology of Gardens* (41–48).

22. White, "Tudor Classicism" 56; Brooke and Highfield, *Oxford and Cambridge* 158–61.

23. I here adapt a term from Bruster, *Drama and the Market* xii.

24. HMC, *Report on the Manuscripts of Lord Middleton, Preserved at Wollaton Hall* 538–40.

25. Inderwick, *Calendar of Inner Temple Records* 1:xxxv.

26. Banks," 'Breviate' " 317, 332.

27. The photographs of the Burton Agnes screen in Mowl, *Style* (132, 137) are splendid.

28. N[orden], *Speculi Britanniae* 49–50. For illustrations of Holdenby, including some imaginative and carefully reasoned reconstructions, see Girouard, "Elizabethan Holdenby" 1286–89, 1398–1401.

29. Girouard, *Robert Smythson and the Elizabethan Country House* 90; Mowl reproduces views of the ceiling (*Style* 102, 233).

30. Pevsner, *Nottinghamshire* 275. For clear photos of the exterior roof interest at Wollaton, see Mowl, *Style* 97. The single most important study of Wollaton is by Friedman, *House and Household*; it is generously illustrated with photographs of the house, plans, interiors, and architectural details. For corroborative evidence of Willoughby's pride in his humanistic learning and his commitment to display of family achievements, see also Friedman, "Patronage" 390–401.

31. Friedman, *House and Household* 49, 149–51.

32. Girouard, *Robert Smythson and the Elizabethan Country House* 153. See also Girouard, *Hardwick Hall* figs. on 31, 53, 55. Girouard's works comprise a comprehensive and lavishly illustrated study of Hardwick. Mowl, *Style* reproduces a dramatic photo of the stairway (115).

33. Strong, *English Icon* 44; Girouard, *Hardwick Hall* 77; Boynton and Thornton, "Hardwick Hall Inventory" 29.

34. Von Bülow, "Diary" in *Transactions* 31.

35. Quoted in Pevsner, "Somerset" 163. Whetstone's translation of the *Heptameron* may locate both the prototype for the hierarchical arrangement of Tudor galleries and the motive for moralists' objections to their magnificence when a fictive gallery is compared to the "Popes *Micrcosmos* at *Latteran,* which hath beene this sixteene yeares a making" (Whetstone, *A Critical Edition* 115).

36. *Works* vol. 6: *Literary and Professional Works* 1:482–85.

37. As noted by Hard in his editorial comments prefacing Wotton's *Elements of Architecture* lxv.

38. Evelyn B. Tribble, " 'We Will Do No Harm with our Swords': Royal Repre-

sentation, Civic Pageantry, and the Displacement of Popular Protest in Thomas Deloney's *Jack of Newberie*," in Vos, *Place and Displacement*, 150–54. In a diachronic study Greene positions Sidney's particularly dangerous use of the safe haven of pageantry to oppose Elizabeth's possible marriage to Alençon in "The Fortresse of Perfect Beautie" and subsequent representations of the queen's inaccessibility during tilting by the Foster Children of Desire ("Besieging the Castle" 34).

39. On Henry as a Worthy, see Anglo, *Great Tournament Roll* 1; on the Elizabethan spoons, see Moore, "Wall-paintings Recently Discovered" 287.

40. Marshall, *Queen of Scots* 102 and fig. 96.

41. Kastan, "Proud Majesty" 468.

42. On the Arthurian myth in Tudor history, see Young, "Tudor Arthurianism" 176–89.

43. *Henry IV, part 2*, Arden Edition, 156 n.

44. For an analysis of Sidney's adaptation of the unfolding of meaning as a function of sequential movements through space, see Farmer, *Poets and Visual Arts* 1–18.

45. William Fleetwood to Lord Burghley, June 18, 1584 (Wright, *Queen Elizabeth* 2:226–31). Manning also cites this letter in his analysis of the role of boundary changes in economic and political change (*Village Revolts* 202). He discusses the "significant increase in the number of enclosure riots" in the 1590s (65).

46. A number of scholars have analyzed the feminist implications of representations of the female body with particular reference to the significance of spatial metaphor, and I have drawn upon their research: Fumerton considers in greater detail the viewing of miniatures in private spaces (*Cultural Aesthetics* 70–72); Ziegler explores the invasion of women's space as metaphorical rape ("My Lady's Chamber" 73–90); Chirelstein considers the metaphorical relationships between the female body and heraldry in portraiture in "Lady Elizabeth Pope: The Heraldic Body," in Gent and Llewellyn, *Renaissance Bodies* 36–59. Woodbridge's wide-ranging analysis of political implications of metaphorical concepts of the female body is especially relevant to the study of Elizabethan liminality ("Palisading" 327–54).

47. Strong (*Portraits of Queen Elizabeth I*, no. W.2) catalogs later uses of the cut in John Dee's *General and Rare Memorials pertayning to the perfect Arte of Navigation* (1577) and Gabriel Harvey's *Gratulationem Valdeninsium Libri Quatuor* (1578). Yates (*Astraea* 42–51, fig. 4a) discusses in detail the imperial implications of the use of the initial in the different editions of Foxe and in Dee; Hoak summarizes more recent work on the cut ("The Iconography of the Crown Imperial," in Hoak, *Tudor Political Culture* 90–94, plates 20–21).

48. Yates, *Astraea* 54–56; Thomas Floyd, *Picture of a perfit Common wealth* A6ʳ.

49. Strong, *Gloriana* 64–69, fig. 53.

50. On earlier iconography of the myth that "neatly anticipates" the painting, see Kipling, " 'He That Saw It' " 39; Hazard, "Case" (61–88) analyzes at greater length the points glanced at above and reproduces photos of all of the portraits here mentioned. See also the subtle, cogent analysis of modes of portraying female subjects by Simons, "Portraiture, Portrayal, and Idealization" 262–311.

6. MOTION, MEASURE, MEANING

1. Because several key terms in this and the next chapter are subject of debate that cannot be pursued here, let alone settled, a provisional heuristic definition may be in order. *Protocol* refers to the forms, rules, and conventions, whether explicit or understood, that govern political intercourse. *Ceremony* is here taken to mean any solemn event signifying the ostensible sharing of communal values. *Ritual*, along the same continuum of solemnization, refers more specifically to observances of sacred import, often signifying initiation or change in the principals, and it implies a greater degree of constraint under traditionally prescribed form. Although all three kinds of prescription are resistant to change, ritual offers less occasion for variation and improvisation and is less tolerant of spontaneous expression than protocol or ceremony. It is the nature of all three to be concerned with power—whether deference to superior power, affirmation of one's own power or recognition of its limitations, or aspiration to increased power. *Political power* is here construed with the broad connotation of influencing and potentially controlling the lives of others.

The discursive introduction to Muir, *Civic Ritual in Renaissance Venice*, is a useful prolegomenon to discussion of the terminology as it applies to Renaissance practice. Koziol, in *Begging Pardon*, has also diagnosed the difficulties caused by the terminology, and Hutton, like me, concluded in face of these problems that his subject, too, required provisional terminology (*Rise and Fall* 1–2).

2. See, for example, "Time and Space," the first chapter in Hale, *Renaissance Europe*; Sarton, *History of Science* 716–22.

3. Clay, *Liturgies* 548–61; Cressy, *Bonfires and Bells,* led me to this reference as well as offering much careful detail on the observance (30, 50–57). An early study of relevant Elizabethan sermons, with extensive bibliography, appears in Wilson, *England's Eliza*, especially 221–23. For additional discussion and relevant examples, see Strong, *Cult of Elizabeth* 117–28. For a crisp summary of Elizabethan calendrical adjustments, see also Cressy, "Protestant Calendar" 31–36. Levin briefly summarizes Elizabethan political-religious calendrical observances ("Power, Politics, and Sexuality" 98–99). For a more comprehensive analysis, see McClure and Wells, "Second Virgin Mary" 38–70.

4. Holland, *[Panyguris] D. Elizabethae* N4^r. Norbrook's dissertation ("Panegyric of the Monarch") led me to this useful source.

5. My summary of Roman practice depends upon the stimulating analysis by Price, *Rituals and Power*.

6. Wright, *Passions of the Minde* 167.

7. I here would disagree with McCracken's implication ("Pre-coronation Passage" 47–61) that the people retained "an essential freedom" in their hearts and their tongues, granted that Elizabeth had the power to mutilate, draw, quarter, and disembowel those who freely expressed a dissenting heart with a ready tongue. This article is nonetheless a valuable, stimulating anthropological approach to the precoronation pageantry and a concise review of earlier literature on the subject.

8. On the Roman *adventus*, see MacCormack, *Art and Ceremony* 19–22; for Elizabeth's demonstration of interest, see Bergeron, "Elizabeth's Coronation Entry" 3–8.

9. [Overall and Overall], *Remembrancia* 407. In an especially astute analysis of the coronation entry, Frye points out that the Merchant Adventurers largely funded the event and the publication of the pamphlet, contriving an economically mutual benefit between their capitalist interests (to be underwritten by a stabilized Protestantism) and Elizabeth's need for support for her succession and her financial transactions (*Elizabeth I* 43–55).

10. Hayward, *Annals* 15. Machiavelli recommended the use of pageantry as a vehicle for diverting the people's attention from political problems: "To do away with idleness then, and to give men something to think about that would remove their thoughts from the government," festivals were held in 1466 in Florence (Machiavelli, *The History of Florence*, in *Machiavelli: The Chief Works* 3:1352).

11. Elizabeth is pictured with her apron on a Maundy Thursday occasion on a miniature attributed to Lavina Teerlinc (Strong, *Gloriana* plate 35). Levin records that reminders of the age of the monarch became institutionalized by the start of the reign of Henry VIII and that Elizabeth continued this practice (" 'Would I Could Give You Help and Succour,' " *Albion* 194); Brian Robinson recalls the earlier practice of Edward III (*Royal Maundy* 25), as does Hutton (*Rise and Fall* 57).

12. In 1579, Elizabeth ordered forty-five sets of clothing for poor women on Maundy. It appears that on this occasion too she emended her age by again dropping a year from the count (Nichols, ed., *Illustrations* 2); Arnold points out that Elizabeth also altered her age from fifty-four to fifty-three on the warrant for the thirtieth year of her reign (*Elizabeth's Wardrobe* 68).

13. Williams, *Tudor Regime* 201. Stow's account captures the horrible specificity of parliamentary prescription in 1572 against first offenders, "that all persons aboue the age of fourteene yeares, being taken begging, vagrant, & wandring misorderly, should be apprehended, whipped, and brent through the gristle of the right eare, with a hot yron of one inch compasse for the first time so taken" (*Annales* [1615] Kkk5ʳ).

14. Beier, "Social Problems in Elizabethan London," *Journal of Interdisciplinary History* 204.

15. Summary chronology and statistics from Schoenherr, "The Pageant of the People," diss., Yale U, 1973, 145. For clear maps of Elizabeth's progress landmarks, see the endpapers in Johnson, *Elizabeth I*.

16. Carnicelli's well-illustrated edition of *Lord Morley's* Tryumphes of Fraunces Petrarcke contains a valuable introduction which reviews the history and iconography of the triumph, particularly in England, from which I draw the factual data.

17. I have considered the triumphs in greater detail with reference to one Shakespearean play in " 'Order' " 95–103; the Triumph of Time over Fame appears there as fig. 5 among the illustrations.

18. For a broader and more complete treatment of Lee's tournaments, and

especially for comparison and contrast with Sidney's tilts, see the sixth chapter of Alan Young's valuable study, *Tudor and Jacobean Tournaments.*

19. Transcription by Yates, "Elizabethan Chivalry," *Astraea* 100. This seminal study, first presented in 1954, traces the thematic development of the imagery used in Sir Henry Lee's entertainments and its influence on Elizabethan writers. It should be read in conjunction with Chambers's analytical description of the contents of the Ditchley manuscript and his edition of the complete text of the Ditchley entertainment in his *Sir Henry Lee* (app. D, E). I quote from this edition, and I depend upon these two indispensable sources for my summary account of Lee's entertainments. Wilson's notes and commentary to her edition of the text of the Ditchley entertainment of 1592 *(Entertainments for Elizabeth I)* reconstruct the complicated narrative line. The fourth and fifth chapters of Strong's *Cult of Elizabeth* include a great deal of related material on the entertainments and the arts.

20. [Dowland], *Douland's "Musical Banquet"* 14.

21. Elton, *England under the Tudors,* 374–76; Palliser, *The Age of Elizabeth* 26; A. J. Collins, "The Progress of Queen Elizabeth to the Camp at Tilbury, 1588," *British Museum Quarterly* 166. A map by Robert Adams now in the British Museum (Add. MS 44839) pricks out the route followed by the queen from London to Tilbury.

22. Whiting, *The Enterprise of England* reproduces two of the playing cards (148); a reproduction of the painting appears (fig. 16.31) in Rodríguez-Salgado, *Armada*; fig 14.35 reproduces a photo of BM Add. MS 44839. Frye examines the evidence for the legendary status of the reports in "Myth" 95–114. Teague thoroughly reviews the doubtful deliverance of Elizabeth's speech at Tilbury ("Elizabeth in Her Speeches" 66–69).

23. Hind, *Engraving* 1: front., 263.

24. Young has sorted out the confusion of fragmentary texts and proposes the outlines of the reading on which I here depend (*Tudor* 172–76). For the larger political context, see also McCoy, *Rites of Knighthood* ch. 4.

25. In the introduction to the Arden edition of *King Richard II* (lvii–lxii), Peter Ure concisely reviews the case against Essex in this affair.

26. *Summer's Last Will,* in Nashe, *Unfortunate Traveller* 150. Geller reads the entertainment as a veiled complaint against what Nashe regarded as inadequate patronage ("Commentary as Cover-Up" 148–78).

27. Nichols, *Progresses* 3:588–90. For a discussion of the connections between the queen's entertainment and the *Rainbow Portrait,* see Erler, "Davies and the Rainbow Portrait" 359–71; for the attributions of the text for the Harefield entertainment, see Erler's note (362).

28. Nichols, *Progresses* 1:192–97. The city annals record a much reduced text (Ingram, *Coventry* 232–33). Colthorpe corrects Nichols's misdating and supplements with a more detailed description and quotations from the De L'Isle manuscript in Kent (MS U 1475 L 2/1) ("Pageants" 458–60).

29. Goodman, *Court of James* 1:18.

30. The locus classicus for the theory of the legal fiction is Kantorowicz, *King's Two Bodies*; for application to Elizabeth's case, see Axton, *Queen's Two Bodies* 30; Loomis reprints "Elizabeth Southwell's Manuscript Account" together with a thorough historical analysis (26, 482–509).

31. For an analysis of how Shakespeare manipulates time and space in his last plays, a subject that falls outside the chronological limits of this chapter but is highly relevant to it, see Berry, "Word and Picture" 81–101.

7. CEREMONIAL DEPARTURES

1. Brackett, "Florentine Onestà" 273–300.

2. For the martyrs, see Hill, *World Turned Upside Down* 246–47. The report of the Gowrie conspiracy is especially pertinent: the conspirator bowed his head below the king's knee "(althogh he was neuer wont to make so low courtesy)," and the king became alarmed when confronted with the would-be assassin's dagger because he was "standing so irreuerently, couered with his hat on; which forme of rigorous behauior, could prognisticat no thing to his Majestie, but present extremitie" (*Gowrie's Conspiracy*, in *Harleian Miscelleny* 2:335, 342). For Essex's contemptuous refusal to uncover, see Harrison, *Devereux* 285–86.

3. Wriothesley, *Chronicle* 1:19.

4. Ridley, *Elizabeth I* 21–28; Loades narrates in detail Mary's aggrieved responses to her humiliating reductions in status (*Mary Tudor* 73ff.).

5. Many wills and inventories of farmers' furnishings in the mid-sixteenth century indicate possession of a single chair, at most two. See Fussell, *English Labourer* 14–24; Jourdain, *English Decoration* 241–42; also, Eames, *Furniture in England* xxi, 181–82. Bedingfield's insulting behavior was also reported earlier, in 1584, by Anthony Munday (*Watch-woord to Englande* [London, 1584] H.ij^r).

6. For a review and summary of scholarship on the vexed question of who celebrated the coronation mass, whether the host was elevated, and whether Elizabeth withdrew to her traverse on this occasion, too, as sign of disapproval, see Haugaard, "Coronation" 161–70. The pertinent documents are reprinted in the pioneering article by Bayne, "Coronation of Elizabeth" 650–73. McCoy's review of some of these events makes greater allowance than I for ambiguity in Elizabeth's actions, but he omits some of the evidence that Bayne includes in his notes regarding such telling details as the order of homaging and the distribution of cloth to the bishops. In any case, the contemporary records are indeed sketchy and confusing. McCoy, happily, includes reproductions from the College of Arms MS M 6. ("'Thou Idol Ceremony'" 240–66), which manuscript I, too, have found useful in my research. McCoy again covers some of the pertinent material in "'Wonderfull Spectacle,'" in Bak, *Coronations* 217–27. In this same volume, see also David J. Sturdy, "'Continuity' versus 'Change': Historians and English Coronations of the Medieval and Early Modern Periods" (240).

7. BL Egerton MS 3320 fol. 12^v. The catalog for *The Renaissance at Sutton Place* describes a similar drawing of Henry dining alone on a dais under a canopy (#34).

8. Dean, "Image and Ritual in the Tudor Parliaments," in Hoak, *Tudor Political Culture* 262.

9. A London haberdasher's manuscript description of the lord mayor's procession in 1575 is characterized by a similar circumstantiality and rhythmic sequential narrative (Sayle, *Lord Mayors' Pageants* 2–3). This is true also of the account of a lord mayor's procession in the travel diary of the visiting German nobleman Lupold von Wedel (Klarwill, *Queen Elizabeth and Some Foreigners* 324ff.).

10. Devereux, *Lives and Letters* 2:481–83.

11. The list of expenses for cloth alone comprises nine pages of the accounts for the funeral of Sir Nicholas Bacon, the lord keeper (*Bacon Papers* 2 [1578–1585]:47–57).

12. Bos, Lange-Meyers, and Six, "Sidney's Funeral Portrayed" 51–52. This study thoroughly reviews the context, history, and implications of the ceremonies as well as the Lant roll, plates from which it lavishly reproduces. Strickland ingeniously argues that Sidney's ambiguous status between aristocrats and the general populace is expressed in the unorthodox composition and marching order of the classes of mourners and the presentation of the Lant roll in letterpress script, in both Latin and English ("Pageantry" 19–36).

13. *Proceedings* 1:167. Lupold von Wedel also described the seating arrangements in Parliament, differing in some details from de Maisse, but also commenting upon the woolsacks (Klarwill, *Queen Elizabeth and Some Foreigners* 334). Generic sketches of the monarch sitting in Parliament appear in Glover, *Nobilitas Politica vel Civilis* (erratic pagination and signatures); [Milles], *Catalogve of Honor* G5^r. Dean ("Image and Ritual," in Hoak, *Tudor Political Culture* 243–71) reproduces Glover's illustration as well as other pertinent illustrations together with well-researched documentation.

14. BL Add. MS 6297 fol. 3^r–3^v. J. P. Cooper provides an overview of efforts to define and to monitor the concept of gentility in *Land, Men and Beliefs* chapters 3 and 4.

15. Trexler's introduction to the *Libro Cerimoniale* clearly and concisely summarizes, contextualizes, and indexes the contents. See also the rich examples published in the papers collected in *"All the world's a stage."*

16. Wright, *Queen Elizabeth* 1:59. For the delicate calculus of gifts to ambassadors, see Gentili, *De legationibus libri tres* 2:138–40.

17. From the transcription of a manuscript formerly in the possession of Peter Le Neve, Norroy king at arms (signed May 13, 1726), printed in *Antiquarian Repertory* 1:329–30, with minor variations from BL Add. MS 6297 and Harl. 69.

18. Harington, *Nugae Antiquae* 1:118–19. For the sensitive balance between gift and commodity exchange, see Sharp, "Gift Exchange" 250–65. The distinction between the two is less firm, however, in the economy of queenly exchange.

19. Frye analyzes this episode in the coronation entry in her *Elizabeth I* 43ff.

20. *Relation* 24ff., 75–77. For a fine analysis of literary implications of the practice, see Fumerton, "Exchanging Gifts."

21. Duncan-Jones's narration of the affair traces many of its social and political nuances (*Sir Philip Sidney* 163–67).

22. Arnold traces this anecdote, with some reservation, in *"Lost from Her Majesties Back"* 15n.2).

23. Somerset, *Elizabeth I* 346; Stone, *Crisis* 606; Haigh, *Elizabeth I* 96.

24. *The Covrt of ciuill Courtesie. Fitlie furnished with a pleasant port of stately phrases and pithy precepts: assembled in the behalfe of all young Gentlemen, and others, that are desirous to frame their behauior according to their estates, at all times, and in all companies. Therby to purchase worthy praise of their inferiours: and estimation and credite among their betters,* trans. from the Italian by S. R. [but also now attributed to other, English authors] (London, 1591) A3ʳ–4ᵛ. The complete title conveys the depth and range of jealousy of place.

25. Ellis, *Original Letters,* 3rd ser., 4:96.

26. CSPD (1598–1601) 441. Archer, commenting upon the typical lament about the passing of the good old days of charitable household maintenance, notes that charitable giving actually increased during the sixteenth century ("The Nostalgia of John Stow,"in Smith, Strier, and Bevington, *Theatrical City* 27).

27. Batho, *Household Papers of Henry Percy* xxii–xxiii; Montague, " 'A Booke of Orders and Rules' " 182–84. The number of household servants had greatly increased over those prescribed according to hierarchical rank by the *Black Book* of Edward IV, whereby an earl would have been the lowest rank permitted to have exceeded one hundred (Starkey, "Age of the Household" 244.) Adams observes the correspondence between Dudley's growing number of servants and his increase in rank as being in keeping with that of his peers (*Household Accounts* 29–30). See also Cooper, *Land,* ch. 4, on official efforts to restrict the number of legally permissible retainers.

28. Fletcher, "Honour, Reputation and Local Officeholding," in Fletcher and Stevenson, *Order and Disorder* 102; Heal and Holmes allude to this fracas as one among many regarding precedence among justices, one of whom erased another's name in order to place his own higher on the list (170–71).

29. Hill, *Society and Puritanism* 427.

30. Emmison, *Elizabethan Life* vol. 2: *Morals and the Church Courts* 130–35; Manning, *Village Revolts* 65. This work is a valuable analysis of the larger question of the political and social consequences of enclosure.

31. Cranmer, *Works* vol. 2: *Miscellaneous Writings and Letters of Thomas Cranmer* 326; also, Strype, *Memorials* 1:43.

32. Stow, *Three Chronicles* 138–40; Norman Jones, *Birth* 35, 58–61.

33. Maus, "Proof and Consequences" 157–80.

34. Segar, *Honor Military and Ciuill* (1602) G2ʳ, E3ᵛ–4ʳ. For a fuller discussion, see Ranald, "The Degradation of Richard II" 170–96. Ranald quotes Segar from the 1590, slightly variant, edition. She points out the parallel ceremonies of military and ecclesiastical degradations, which also inverted ceremonies of installation.

35. Newman, *Fashioning Femininity* 27, 35; Newman's fig. 5 reproduces a contemporary illustration of a skimmington. Chambers discusses the tradition in *Mediaeval Stage* 1:152–56.

36. Taylor, *Vagrant Writing* 12. Taylor's introduction includes many pertinent

comments on the role of geographical place in locating Elizabethan social position: he makes the point about the pillory that I paraphrase below. Patricia Fumerton commented in a paper ("Not Home: Alehouses, Vagrancy, and Broadside Ballads") delivered at the Folger Shakespeare Library conference in 1995 on "Material London ca. 1600," "To be a Londoner was to be vagrant" because nearly half of London's labor force was in service, leading lives unattached to their own families, "a lifestyle of adolescence" in a permanent search for identity.

37. Bevington discusses how Shakespeare uses ceremonial decorum and its inversion in *Action Is Eloquence* (see especially 159ff.).

8. ABSENT/PRESENCE, PRESENT/ABSENCE

1. Stone and Stone, *Open Elite?* 298ff.

2. Christy, *Progresses* 3.

3. My immediate concern is the use of silent language; I have discussed briefly some literary examples in "Absent Presence and Present Absence," TSLL 1–27. For a fine analysis of another literary medium of absence, see Whigham, "Rhetoric."

4. Quoted by Arnold, " 'Pictur' " 303.

5. For the sequence of events and different interpretations, see chapter 7 above, n. 6.

6. Quintilian, *Institutio Oratoria* vol. 3, pt. 9.2.54.

7. Bishop Quadra to the duchess of Parma, Feb. 7, 1560, *Calendar of Letters . . . Simancas* 1:126.

8. As quoted by Duncan-Jones from the holograph letter among the Berkeley Castle muniments ("Nashe in Newgate" 15).

9. Somerset, *Elizabeth I* 367; Nichols, *Progresses* 2:241; for more specific data on North's losses, see, for example, entries in Stevenson, "Extracts" 292; Batho, "Finances" 435, 449.

10. Egerton MS 3320 is an unbound collection of sketches of the coronation ceremony. Fols. 20ᵛ–22ʳ diagram the coronation setting within the Abbey. These are reproduced in Collins, "Ordering of the Coronation" (figs. 2, 6). The upper half of fig. 2 shows the location of Saint Edward's shrine and Elizabeth's traverse behind the altar. More recently, McCoy has reproduced this illustration (" 'Thou Idol Ceremony' " fig. 1), but not the picture of the throne setting. For an anthropological analysis of the ceremonial spaces, see Hayden, *Symbol and Privilege* 148–57.

11. Melville 94; Fumerton, on a similar point about Elizabethan uses of space, traces in detail the route that would have been followed into the bedchamber on this occasion (*Cultural Aesthetics* 71–72).

12. Guy thus classifies and defines the constitution of the Elizabethan court in his introduction to *Reign of Elizabeth* 1–2.

13. Starkey's assessment of the political implications of the male servant's intimacy with the person of the king, the most influential being the Groom of the Stool, contrasts with the relatively ineffectual roles of Elizabeth's female attendants ("Representation" 187–224).

14. Wright, "Change In Direction" 168. My discussion of the constitution of Elizabeth's privy chamber is a highly compressed summary of Wright's remarkably well-researched chapter.

15. As discussed by Williams in "Court and Polity" 263. Williams usefully notes Essex's own distinction between "access" to the queen (which he was granted although excluded from the queen's presence) and *"near access,"* which he was denied. Williams lists the few families at the end of her reign with near access: "the Cecils; Essex until 1599; the Howards; Ralegh; the Careys; the Knollys; and the Stanhopes" (270).

16. Simon Adams, "The Patronage of the Crown in Elizabethan Politics: The 1590s in Perspective," in Guy, *Reign of Elizabeth* 37.

17. Haigh, *Elizabeth I* 90. Haigh summarizes Talbot's letter that I quote below.

18. Natalie Mears, *"Regnum Cecilianum?* A Cecilian Perspective of the Court," in Guy, *Reign of Elizabeth* 50.

19. Ralegh, *Poems* (Latham, ed.) xvi–xvii. Quotations from Ralegh will be from this edition.

20. Mears, *"Regnum Cecilianum?"* in Guy, *Reign of Elizabeth* 56–57; Haigh, *Elizabeth I* 89.

21. Guy, introduction to *Reign of Elizabeth* 14.

22. Barry Taylor, *Vagrant Writing* 188–89.

23. Patricia Fortini Brown, "Measured Friendship, Calculated Pomp: The Ceremonial Welcomes of the Venetian Republic," in *"All the world's a stage"* pt. 1: *Triumphal Celebrations and the Rituals of Statecraft* 142.

24. Kemp, *Book of John Fisher* 34.

25. Smuts, "Public Ceremony" 72–73.

26. I here summarize the analysis of proxemics in this work by Evelyn B. Tribble, " 'We Will Do No Harm with our Swords': Royal Representation, Civic Pageantry, and the Displacement of Popular Protest in Thomas Deloney's *Jacke of Newberie,"* in Vos, *Place and Displacement* 147–57.

27. Birch, *Memoirs* 2:441, 390; Williams, *Howard* 159; Harington, *Nugae Antiquae* 1:314.

28. Color illustrations of the jewel and the portrait appear in *Princely Magnificence* nos. 40, P15.

29. Peter Heylin, *A Short View of the Life and Reign of King Charles* (London, 1658) 228, as quoted by Smuts, "Public Ceremony" 90.

30. Marie Axton, *"Summer's Last Will and Testament:* Revel's End," in Guy, *Reign of Elizabeth* 265; Axton transcribes part of the masque in *Queen's Two Bodies* (51–52), analyzing the embarrassment occasioned by the presence of the queen; Bliss ("Some Account of a Manuscript" 609–18) describes the manuscript (Rawl. Poet 108, 33ʳ) in detail and transcribes a few longer passages from it; I discuss the Pound manuscript and related literature in "Presence" 17–18.

31. Braithwait, *Rules and Orders* 20–21; Kingsford, "Essex House" 9, 48; Adams in Guy, *Reign of Elizabeth* 40.

32. *Gowrie's Conspiracy: A Discourse of the Vnnatvrall and Vyle Conspiracie, At-*

tempted against the Kings Maiesties Person, At Sanct-Iohnstovn, vpon Twysday the Fifth of August, 1600, rpt. in *Harleian Miscellany* 2:340.

33. Von Bülow, "Diary," in *Transactions* 9.

34. Banks " 'Breviate' " 321.

35. Philippa Glanville, "The Courtier as Consumer," in *Renaissance at Sutton Place* 41.

36. Fitzherbert, *Booke of Husbandrie* T2ᵛ–3ʳ.

37. Hazlitt, ed., *Cyuile and vncyuile life,* in Hazlitt, *Inedited Tracts* 40–41.

38. Henisch, *Fast and Feast* 157–59; Furnivall, *Early English Meals* 157.

39. Henisch, *Fast and Feast* 161–64; Eames, "Documentary Evidence" 42, 51.

40. Wheaton, *Savoring the Past* 16; this is a rich source for details regarding extravagant meals and service.

41. *Star Chamber Dinner Accounts* 5–6.

42. Appleby, "Diet" 115.

43. Fumerton here again is helpful on the significant nomenclature and uses of space (*Cultural Aesthetics* 111–16).

44. Notations by Weigall, ed., "Elizabethan Gentlewoman" 134.

45. Platter, *Travels* 194; Woodworth, "Purveyance" 12–13, 16–17.

46. The classic treatment of the concept of English hospitality is Heal, "Idea of Hospitality" 66–93.

47. *Tudor Proclamations* 3:171–72; Ellis, *Original Letters* 2.3.37.

48. Kemp, *Book of John Fisher* 36–38.

49. As in a communication in French attributed to Dudley Carleton and quoted by Devereux, *Essex* 2:206–7; Clapham, *Observations* 90.

50. As summarized by McCoy, " 'Thou Idol Ceremony' " 260.

51. Handover, *Cecil* 295–96; Clapham, *Observations* 99.

WORKS CITED

MANUSCRIPT SOURCES

Bodley MS Rawlinson Poet 108.

BL Add. MS 5408.

BL Add. MS 6297.

BL Add. MS 28681.

BL Add. MS 36991. Joseph Lawson. " 'Pennarum Nitor' or The Pens Excellency." 1609.

BL Add. MS 44839. Robert Adams. Tilbury Route.

BL Cotton MS Claudius D.vi. f.12. Matthew Paris. Map of Great Britain.

BL Egerton MS 3320.

BL Harl. MS 69.

BL MS Stowe 1071. William Heth. "The goulden arte or The Jewell house of gemes." 1603.

College of Arms MS 8 temp. Hen. 8.

College of Arms MS 151. Augustine Vincent. Precedents: The marshalling of all Estates and degrees at publique assemblies and funeralls, together with their seuerall priuiledges and institutions, habits, robes and their fashions, herses, modells, proportions and allowances for the same. 2 vols.

Folger Shakespeare Library MSS v.b.232. Thomas Trevelyon. "A Commonplace Book."

Folger Shakespeare Library MS v.b.182.mond Tyllney. "Topographical Descriptions, Regiments and Policies."

PUBLISHED SOURCES

Acts of the Privy Council of England. Ed. John Roche Dasent. N.s. vol. 30: 1599–1600. London: HMSO, 1905.

Adams, Simon, ed. *Household Accounts and Disbursement Books of Robert Dudley, Earl of Leicester, 1558–61, 1584–86.* Camden Fifth Series 6. New York: Cambridge UP, 1995.

Agnew, Jean-Christophe. *Worlds Apart: The Market and the Theater in Anglo-American Thought, 1550–1750.* New York: Cambridge UP, 1986.

Airs, Malcolm. "The English Country House in the Sixteenth Century." *Oxford Art Journal* 2 (April 1979): 15–18.

——. *The Making of the English Country House, 1500–1640.* London: Architectural P, 1975.

"All the world's a stage . . .": Art and Pageantry in the Renaissance and Baroque. Ed. Barbara Wisch and Susan Scott Munshower. 2 vols. Papers in Art History, Pennsylvania State University, vol. 6. University Park: Department of Art History, Pennsylvania State U, 1990.

Anglo, Sydney. "An Early Tudor Programme for Plays and Other Demonstrations against the Pope." *Journal of the Warburg and Courtauld Institutes* 20 (1957): 176–79.

——. *The Great Tournament Roll of Westminster: A Collotype Reproduction of the Manuscript.* Oxford: Clarendon, 1968.

——. *Spectacle, Pageantry, and Early Tudor Policy.* Oxford-Warburg Studies. Oxford: Clarendon, 1969.

The Antiquarian Repertory. Ed. Edward Jeffery et al. 4 vols. London, 1807–9.

Apple, Thomas T. "'And Attend that in Person which you cannot Execute by Deputy': Elizabeth I at Revels." In *Ceremony and Text in the Renaissance*, ed. Douglas F. Rutledge. Cranbury, N.J.: Associated UP, 1996. 123–36.

Appleby, Andrew B. "Diet in Sixteenth-Century England: Sources, Problems, Possibilities." In *Health, Medicine and Mortality in the Sixteenth Century*, ed. Charles Webster. Cambridge Monographs on the History of Medicine. Cambridge: Cambridge UP, 1979. 97–116.

Aristotle. *The Basic Works of Aristotle.* Ed. Richard McKeon. New York: Random, 1941.

Arnold, Janet. "The 'Pictur' of Elizabeth I when Princess." *Burlington Magazine* 113 (1981): 303–4.

——, ed. *Queen Elizabeth's Wardrobe Unlock'd.* Leeds: Maney, 1988.

——. *"Lost from Her Majesties Back."* Costume Society Extra Series 7. Wisbech, Cambridgeshire, U.K.: Daedalus, 1980.

Ascham, Roger. *The Schoolmaster (1570).* Ed. Lawrence V. Ryan. Charlottesville: UP of Virginia, 1967.

Ashmole, Elias. *The Institution, Laws & Ceremonies of the Most Noble Order of the Garter.* London, 1672.

Aske, James. *Elizabetha Trivmphans.* The English Experience: Its Record in Early Printed Books, Published in Facsimile 78. 1588. New York: Da Capo, 1969.

Aston, Margaret. *England's Iconoclasts.* Vol. 1: *Laws against Images.* Oxford: Clarendon, 1988.

———. "English Ruins and English History: The Dissolution and the Sense of the Past." *Journal of the Warburg and the Courtauld Institutes* 36 (1973): 231–55.

Aubery, Louis [Benjamin], Seigneur du Maurier. *Mémoires pour servir à l'Histoire de Hollande, et des autres provinces unies.* Paris, 1680.

Aubrey, John. *Memoires of Naturall Remarques in the County of Wilts.* 1847. London: Wiltshire Topographical Society, 1969.

Axton, Marie. *The Queen's Two Bodies: Drama and the Elizabethan Succession.* London: Royal Historical Society, 1977.

Bacon, Francis. *The Works of Francis Bacon.* Ed. James Spedding, Robert Leslie Ellis, and Douglas Denon Heath. 15 vols. 1857–74. New York: Garrett, 1968.

Bacon, Nathaniel. *The Papers of Nathaniel Bacon of Stiffkey.* Ed. A. Hassell Smith and Gillian M. Baker. 3 vols. Norwich: Centre of East Anglian Studies and Norfolk Record Society (vols 46, 49, 53), 1979–88.

Bailey, Brian. *English Manor Houses.* London: Hale, 1983.

Baines, Barbara Burnham. *Fashion Revivals from the Elizabethan Age to the Present Day.* London: Batsford, 1981.

Bak, János M., ed. *Coronations: Medieval and Early Modern Monarchic Ritual.* Berkeley: U of California P, 1990.

Baldwin, Frances Elizabeth. *Sumptuary Legislation and Personal Regulation in England.* Johns Hopkins University Studies in Historical and Political Science. Series 44, no. 1. Baltimore: Johns Hopkins UP, 1926.

Banks, Joseph, ed. "Copy of an Original Manuscript, entitled, 'A Breviate touching the Order and Governmente of a Nobleman's House, &.'" *Archaeologia* 13 (1800): 315–89.

Barber, Giles. *Textile and Embroidered Bindings in the Bodleian Library.* Bodleian Picture Books. Special Series 2. Oxford: Bodleian Library, 1971.

Barber, Peter. "England I: Pageantry, Defense, and Government: Maps at Court. England II: Monarchs, Ministers, and Maps, 1550–1625." In *Monarchs, Ministers, and Maps: The Emergence of Cartography as a Tool of Government in Early Modern Europe,* ed. David Buisseret. Kenneth Nebenzahl Jr. Lectures in the History of Cartography. Chicago: U of Chicago P, 1992. 26–56; 57–98.

Barley, William. *Lute Music of Shakespeare's Time, William Barley: A new Booke of Tabliture, 1596.* Edited and transcribed for keyboard with the original tablature by Wilburn W. Newcomb. University Park: Pennsylvania State UP, 1966.

Barnes, Barnabe. *Fovre Bookes of Offices: Enabling Privat persons for the speciall service of all good Princes and Policies.* London, 1606.

Barolini, Helen. *Aldus and His Dream Book: An Illustrated Essay.* New York: Italica, 1992.

Barrow, Henry. *The Writings of Henry Barrow, 1587–90.* Ed. Leland H. Carson. Elizabethan Nonconformist Texts 3. London: Allen & Unwin, 1962.

Bates, Catherine. *The Rhetoric of Courtship in Elizabethan Language and Literature.* Cambridge: Cambridge UP, 1992.

Bath, Michael. *Speaking Pictures: English Emblem Books and Renaissance Culture.* Longman Medieval and Renaissance Library. Gen. eds. Charlotte Brewer and N. H. Keeble. New York: Longman, 1994.

Batho, Gordon R. "The Finances of an Elizabethan Nobleman: Henry Percy, Ninth Earl of Northumberland (1564–1632)." *Economic History Review* 2nd ser. 9 (1957): 433–50.

——, ed. *Household Papers of Henry Percy, Ninth Earl of Northumberland.* Camden 3rd Series 93. London: Royal Historical Society, 1962.

Baxandall, Michael. "English *Disegno.*" In *England and the Continental Renaissance: Essays in Honour of J. B. Trapp,* ed. Edward Chaney and Peter Mack. Rochester: Boydell, 1990. 203–14.

Bayne, G. C. "The Coronation of Queen Elizabeth." *English Historical Review* 22 (1907): 650–73.

Beauchesne, Jean de. *A booke containing divers sortes of hands.* London, 1571.

Beier, A. L. *Masterless Men: The Vagrancy Problem in England, 1560–1640.* New York: Methuen, 1985.

——. "Social Problems in Elizabethan London." *Journal of Interdisciplinary History* 9 (1978): 203–21.

Beltz, George Frederick. *Memorials of the Order of the Garter.* London, 1841.

Bentley, Thomas. *The Monvment of Matrones.* London [1582].

Bercher, William. *The Nobility of Women.* (1559). Ed. R. Warwick Bond. London: Roxburghe, 1904.

Beresford, Maurice. *History on the Ground.* 1957; rev. edn. 1971. London: Sutton, 1984.

Bergeron, David M. "Elizabeth's Coronation Entry (1559): New Manuscript Evidence." *English Literary Renaissance* 8 (1978): 3–8.

The Berkeley Manuscripts. Ed. John Maclean. 3 vols. Gloucester, 1883–85.

Berlin, Michael. "Civic Ceremony in Early Modern London." In *Urban History Yearbook 1986,* ed. David Reeder. Leicester: Leicester UP, 1986. 15–27.

Berry, Francis. "Word and Picture in the Final Plays." In *Later Shakespeare.* Stratford-upon-Avon Studies 8. London: Arnold, 1966. 81–101.

Bevington, David. *Action Is Eloquence: Shakespeare's Language of Gesture.* Cambridge: Harvard UP, 1984.

——. *Tudor Drama and Politics: A Critical Approach to Topical Meaning.* Cambridge: Harvard UP, 1968.

Bialostocki, Jan. "The Dichotomy of Good and Evil in the Visual Arts: Remarks on Some Aspects." In *The Verbal and the Visual: Essays in Honor of William Sebastian Heckscher,* ed. Karl-Ludwig Selig and Elizabeth Sears. New York: Italica, 1990. 23–40.

——. "Dürer and the Humanists," *Bulletin of the Society for Renaissance Studies* 4 (Oct. 1986–Jun. 1987): 18–21.

Bindoff, S. T. *The Fame of Sir Thomas Gresham.* Neale Lecture in English History 4. London: Cape, 1973.

Birch, Thomas, ed. *Memoirs of the Reign of Queen Elizabeth.* 2. vols. 1754. New York: AMS, 1970.

The Bishops' Bible. *The holie bible.* [London], 1568.

Blakemore, M. J., and J. B. Harley. "Concepts in the History of Cartography: A Review and a Perspective: Early Maps as Language." *Cartographica* 17, no. 4 (1980): 87–106.

Blenerhasset, Thomas. *A Revelation of the True Minerva.* Intro. Josephine Waters Bennett. 1582. New York: Scholars' Facsimiles, 1941.

B[liss], P[hilip]. "Some Account of a Manuscript in Dr. Rawlinson's Collection in the Bodleian Library." In *The British Bibliographer,* ed. Egerton Brydges and Joseph Haslewood. 4 vols. 1810–14. New York: AMS, 1968. 2: 609–18.

Bloom, J. Harvey. *English Seals.* London: Methuen, 1906.

Bohun, Edmund [trans.]. *The Character of Queen Elizabeth.* London, 1693.

Bonifaccio, Giovanni. *L'arte de' cenni con la qvale formandosi favella visibile, si tratta della mvta eloqvenza, che non l' altro che vn facondo silentio.* Vicenza, 1616.

The Booke of Curious and Strange Inuentions . . . Called . . . Needlework. 1596. BL shelflist C.31.h.31.

"A Booke of Orders and Rules, established by me Anthony Viscount Mountague . . . 1595." Ed. Sibbald David Scott. *Sussex Archaeological Collections* 7 (1854): 173–212.

Boorde, Andrew. *The Fyrst Boke of the Introduction of Knowledge made by Andrew Borde of Physycke Doctor.* Ed. F. J. Furnivall. EETS es 10. London, 1870.

Bos, Sander, Marianne Lange-Meyers, and Jeanine Six, "Sidney's Funeral Portrayed." In *Sir Philip Sidney: 1586 and the Creation of a Legend,* ed. Jan Van Dorsten, Dominic Baker-Smith, and Arthur F. Kinney. Publications of the Sir Thomas Browne Institute, n.s. 9. Leiden: Brill/Leiden UP, 1986. 38–61.

Bowle, I. "Singultientes lusus" from *Sorrowes ioy,* in *The Progresses, Processions, and Magnificent Festivities of King James the First.* Ed. John Nichols. 4 vols. 1828. New York: AMS, n.d.

Boynton, Lindsay, and Peter Thornton, eds. "The Hardwick Hall Inventory of 1601." *Furniture History* 7 (1971): 1–40.

Brackett, John K. "The Florentine Onestà and the Control of Prostitution, 1403–1680." *Sixteenth Century Journal* 24 (1993): 273–300.

Braithwaite, Richard. *Some Rules and Orders for the Government of the House of an Earle.* 1630. London, 1821.

A Breefe Discourse, declaring and approuing the necessarie and inuiolable maintenance of the laudable Customes of London. The English Experience: Its Record in Early Printed Books, Published in Facsimile 538. 1584. New York: Da Capo, 1973.

Briant, Sir Fancis, trans. *A Dispraise of the life of a Courtier and an commendation of the life of the labouring man.* London, 1548.

Bristol, Michael D. *Carnival and Theater: Plebeian Culture and the Structure of Authority in Renaissance England.* New York: Methuen, 1985.

Brodhurst, F. "Sir William Cavendish—1557." *Journal of the Derbyshire Archaeological and Natural History Society* 29 (January 1907): 81–102.

Brooke, Christopher, and Roger Highfield. *Oxford and Cambridge.* New York: Cambridge UP, 1988.

Brown, I. D. "Some Notes on the Coinage of Elizabeth I with Special Reference to Her Hammered Silver." *British Numismatic Journal* 28 (1957): 568–603.

Bruster, Douglas. *Drama and the Market in the Age of Shakespeare.* Cambridge Studies in Renaissance Literature and Culture 1. Ed. Stephen Orgel. New York: Cambridge UP, 1992.

Bry, Theodore de. "The Funeral Roll of Sir Philip Sidney." Engraved after Thomas Lant. 1587. College of Arms.

Buisseret, David, ed. *Rural Images: The Estate Plan in the Old and New Worlds.* A Cartographic Exhibit at the Newberry Library on the Occasion of the Ninth Series of Kenneth Nebenzahl Jr., Lectures in the History of Cartography. Chicago: Newberry Library, 1988.

Bülow, Gottfried von, ed. "Diary of the Journey of Philip Julius, Duke of Stettin-Pomerania, through England in the Year 1602." *Transactions of the Royal Historical Society* n.s. 6 (1892): 1–67.

Bulwer, John. *Chirologia: or the Natural Language of the Hand and Chironomia: or the Art of Manual Rhetoric.* Ed. James W. Cleary. Carbondale: Southern Illinois UP, 1974.

Burgon, John William. *The Life and Times of Sir Thomas Gresham.* 2 vols. London, 1839.

Burke, Kenneth. *A Grammar of Motives and A Rhetoric of Motives.* Cleveland: Meridian-World, 1962.

Buxton, John. *Elizabethan Taste.* London: Macmillan, 1963.

Calendar of Letters and State Papers Relating to English Affairs, Preserved Principally in the Archives of Simancas. Ed. Martin A. S. Hume. 4 vols. London, 1892–99.

Calendar of State Papers and Manuscripts relating to English Affairs, Existing in the Archives and Collections of Venice, and in Other Libraries of Northern Italy. Vol. 7: 1558–80. Ed. Rawdon Brown and G. Cavendish Bentinck. 10 vols. in 12. London, 1864–90.

Calendar of State Papers, Domestic Series, of the Reign of Elizabeth, 1581–1590. Ed. Robert Lemon. 1865. Nendeln, Liechtenstein: Kraus, 1967.

Calendar of State Papers, Domestic Series, of the Reign of Elizabeth, 1598–1601. Ed. Mary Anne Everett Green. 1869. Nendeln, Liechtenstein: Kraus, 1967.

Calendar of State Papers, Foreign Series, of the Reign of Elizabeth. 23 vols. in 26. 1863–1950. Nendeln, Liechtenstein: Kraus, 1966–69.

Camden, William. *The History of the Most Renowned and Victorious Princess Elizabeth Late Queen of England: Selected Chapters.* Ed. Wallace T. MacCaffrey.

Classics of British Historical Literature. Ed. John Clive. Chicago: U of Chicago P, 1970.

——. *Remains Concerning Britain.* Ed. R. D. Dunn. Toronto: U of Toronto P, 1984.

Carey, Robert. *The Memoirs of Robert Carey.* Ed F. H. Mares. Oxford: Clarendon, 1972.

Casa, John Della. *Treatise of the Maners and Behauiors.* Trans. Robert Peterson. The English Experience: The Record in Early Printed Books Published in Facsimile 120. 1576. New York: Da Capo, 1969.

Case, John. *Sphaera civitatis.* Oxford, 1588.

Castiglione, Baldesar. *Il libro del Cortegiano con una scelta delle Opere minori.* Ed. Bruno Maier. 2nd edn. Torino: UTET, 1964.

Castle, Sydney E. *Domestic Gothic of the Tudor Period.* Jamestown, N.Y.: International Casement, 1927.

The Catalogve of Honor or Treasvry of Trve Nobility. [By Robert Glover. Trans. Thomas Milles. Ed. William Camden et al.]. London, 1610.

Cavendish, George. *The Life and Death of Cardinal Wolsey.* In *Two Early Tudor Lives: "The Life and Death of Cardinal Wolsey" by George Cavendish and "The Life of Sir Thomas More" by William Roper,* ed. Richard S. Sylvester and Davis P. Harding. New Haven: Yale UP, 1962.

Chamberlain, John. *The Letters of John Chamberlain.* Ed. Norman Egbert McClure. 2 vols. Memoirs 12, pt. 1. Philadelphia: American Philosophical Society, 1939.

Chambers, E. K. *The Mediaeval Stage.* 2 vols. Oxford: Clarendon, 1903.

——. *Sir Henry Lee: An Elizabethan Portrait.* Oxford: Clarendon, 1936.

Chapman, George. *Hero and Leander: Completed by George Chapman.* In *Elizabethan Minor Epics,* ed. Elizabeth Story Donno. London: Routledge, 1963. 85–126.

Chatwin, Philip B. "Monumental Effigies of the County of Warwick: pt. 3: 'Knights,' 'Laymen,' and 'Ladies' of the Sixteenth Century." *Birmingham Archaeological Society Transactions* 48 (1922): 136–68.

Chettle, G. H. *Kirby Hall, Northamptonshire.* 2nd. edn. 1947. London: HMSO, 1975.

[Chettle, Henry]. *Englandes Mourning Garment.* London, [1603].

Christy, Miller. *The Progresses of Queen Elizabeth through Essex, and the Houses in Which She Stayed.* Colchester: n.p., 1917; rpt. from *The Essex Review* 26 (1917): pt. 1, 115–29; pt. 2, 17–33.

——. "Queen Elizabeth's Visit to Tilbury in 1588." *English Historical Review* 34 (1919): 43–61.

Churchyard, Thomas. *Chvrchyards Challenge.* London, 1593.

——. *A Discovrse of The Queenes Maiesties entertainement in Suffolk and Norffolk.* London, 1578.

——. *A light Bondell of liuly discourses called* Churchyardes Charge. London, 1580.

Clanchy, M. T. *From Memory to Record: England, 1066–1307.* London: Arnold; Cambridge: Harvard UP, 1979.

Clapham, John. *Elizabeth of England: Certain Observations concerning the Life and*

Reign of Queen Elizabeth. 1603. Ed. Evelyn Plummer and Conyers Read. University of Pennsylvania Department of History: Translations and Reprints from the Original Sources of History. Ed. William C. McDermott. 3rd ser. Vol. 6. Philadelphia: U of Pennsylvania P, 1951.

Clay, William Keatinge, ed. *Liturgies and Occasional Forms of Prayer Set Forth in the Reign of Queen Elizabeth.* Cambridge, 1847.

Cleland, James. *Hero-Paideia: or the Institvtion of a Yovng Noble Man.* Oxford, 1607.

A Collection of Ordinances and Regulations for the Government of the Royal Household. London, 1790.

A Collection of Seventy-Nine Black-Letter Ballads and Broadsides, Printed in the Reign of Queen Elizabeth, between the Years 1559 and 1597. Ed. [Joseph Lilly]. London, 1867.

Collins, A. J. "The Ordering of the Coronation of Elizabeth I: Drawings and Descriptions from a Contemporary Official Manuscript." *Illustrated London News,* 30 May 1953, 880–83.

——. "The Progress of Queen Elizabeth to the Camp at Tilbury, 1588." *British Museum Quarterly* 10 (1936): 164–67.

Collins, Arthur, ed. *Letters and Memorials of State . . . Written and collected by Sir Henry Sydney.* 2 vols. London, 1746.

Colonna, Francesco. *Hypnerotomachia Poliphili.* Venice, 1499.

——. *Hypnerotomachia: The Strife of Love in a Dream.* The Renaissance and the Gods 15. 1592. Facsimile. New York: Garland, 1976.

Colthorpe, Marion. "Pageants before Queen Elizabeth I at Coventry in 1566." *Notes and Queries* 32 (1985): 458–60.

Constable, Henry. *The Poems of Henry Constable.* Ed. Joan Grundy. Liverpool: Liverpool UP, 1960.

Cook, Elizabeth. "Figured Poetry." *Journal of the Warburg and Courtauld Institutes* 42 (1979): 1–15.

Cooper, J. P. *Land, Men and Beliefs: Studies in Early-Modern History.* Ed. G. E. Aylmer and J. S. Morrill. London: Hambledon, 1983.

Cornwallis, Sir William. *Essayes.* 2 vols. in 1. London, 1606, 1601 [*sic*].

The Covrt of ciuill Courtesie. Trans. from the Italian by S. R. [but also now attributed to other, English authors]. London, 1591.

Cranmer, Thomas. *The Works of Thomas Cranmer.* Ed. John Edmund Cox. 2 vols. Cambridge, 1846.

Cressy, David. *Bonfires and Bells: National Memory and the Protestant Calendar in Elizabethan and Stuart England.* London: Weidenfeld, 1989.

——. *Birth, Marriage and Death: Ritual, Religion, and the Life-Cycle in Tudor and Stuart England.* New York: Oxford UP, 1997.

——. "Gender Trouble and Cross-Dressing in Early Modern England." *Journal of British Studies* 35 (1996): 438–65.

——. *Literacy and the Social Order: Reading and Writing in Tudor and Stuart England.* Cambridge: Cambridge UP, 1980.

——. "The Protestant Calendar and the Vocabulary of Celebration in Early Modern England." *Journal of British Studies* 29 (1990): 31–52.

Croft-Murray, Edward. *Decorative Painting in England, 1537–1837*. 2 vols. Vol. 1: Early Tudor to Sir James Thornhill. London: Country Life, 1962.

Croft-Murray, Edward, and Paul Hulton. *Catalogue of British Drawings: XVI & XVII Centuries*. Vol. 1 in 2 vols. London: British Museum, 1960.

The Currency of Fame: Portrait Medals of the Renaissance. Ed. Stephen K. Scher and John Bigelow Taylor. New York: Abrams, 1994.

Cutwode, T. *Caltha "Poetarum": Or The Bumble Bee*. London, 1599. Facsimile, n.p.: n.d.

Dallington, Sir Robert. *View of Fraunce*. London, 1604.

Daniel, Samuel. *"Poems" and "A Defence of Ryme."* Ed. Arthur Colby Sprague. 1930. Chicago: U of Chicago P, 1965.

Davidson, Clifford. *The Guild Chapel Wall Paintings at Stratford-upon-Avon*. AMS Studies in the Renaissance. New York: AMS, 1988.

Davies, Hugh William. *Devices of the Early Printers, 1475–1560: Their History and Development*. 1935. London: Grafton, 1974.

Davies, John. *The Poems of John Davies*. Ed. Robert Krueger. Oxford: Clarendon, 1975.

Dawson, Giles E., and Laetitia Kennedy-Skipton, eds. *Elizabethan Handwriting, 1500–1650: A Guide to the Reading of Documents and Manuscripts*. 1966. London: Faber, 1968.

Dee, John. Preface to *The Elements of Geometrie of the most auncient Philosopher Evclide of Megara, Faithfully (now first) translated into the English toung, by H. Billingsley, Citizen of London. . . With a very fruitfull Praeface made by M. I. Dee*. London, 1570.

Dekker, Thomas. *The Non-Dramatic Works of Thomas Dekker*. Ed. Alexander B. Grosart. 5 vols. London, 1884–86.

——. *Thomas Dekker: "The Wonderful Year, The Gull's Horn-Book, Penny-Wise, Pound-Foolish, English Villanies Discovered by Lantern and Candlelight" and Selected Writings*. Ed. E. D. Pendry. Stratford-upon-Avon Library 4. Cambridge: Harvard UP, 1968.

Devereux, Walter Bourchier. *Lives and Letters of the Devereux, Earls of Essex, in the Reigns of Elizabeth, James I, and Charles I, 1540–1646*. 2 vols. London, 1853.

Dewar, Mary. *Sir Thomas Smith: A Tudor Intellectual in Office*. London: U of London, Athlone, 1964.

Donaldson, Gordon. *All the Queen's Men: Power and Politics in Mary Stewart's Scotland*. London: Batsford, 1983.

Donno, Elizabeth Story, ed. *Elizabethan Minor Epics*. London: Routledge, 1963.

Doran, Susan. *Monarchy and Matrimony: The Courtships of Elizabeth*. New York: Routledge, 1996.

Douce, Francis. "Dissertation on the Runic Jasper Ring belonging to George Cumberland, Esq. of Bristol." *Archaeologia* 21, no. 1 (1826): 119–37.

[Dowland, John]. *Douland's "Musical Banquet".* N.p.: Chiswick Press by Charles Whittingham, 1817.

Drayton, Michael. *The Works of Michael Drayton.* Ed. J. William Hebel, Bernard H. Newdigate, and Kathleen Tillotson. 5 vols. Corrected edn. Oxford: Blackwell for Shakespeare Head P, 1961.

Dudley, Robert. *Correspondence of Robert Dudley, Earl of Leicester, during His Government of the Low Countries, in the Years 1585 and 1586.* Ed. John Bruce. London, 1844.

Duffy, Eamon. *The Stripping of the Altars: Traditional Religion in England, c. 1400–c. 1580.* New Haven: Yale UP, 1992.

Dugdale, Sir William. *The Antiquities of Warwickshire.* 2nd edn. 2 vols. Rev. by William Thomas. London, 1730.

Duncan-Jones, Katherine. "Nashe in Newgate," *Times Literary Supplement* March 22, 1996: 15.

———. *Sir Philip Sidney: Courtier Poet.* New Haven: Yale UP, 1991.

Eames, Penelope. "Documentary Evidence concerning the Character and Use of Domestic Furnishings in England in the Fourteenth and Fifteenth Centuries." *Furniture History* 7 (1971): 41–60.

———. *Furniture in England, France and the Netherlands from the Twelfth to the Fifteenth Century.* London: Furniture History Society, 1977.

Eco, Umberto. *A Theory of Semiotics.* Advances in Semiotics. Ed. Thomas A. Sebeok. Bloomington: Indiana UP, 1976.

Edgerton, Samuel Y., Jr. *The Heritage of Giotto's Geometry: Art and Science on the Eve of the Scientific Revolution.* Ithaca: Cornell UP, 1991.

Edmondson, Joseph. *A Complete Book of Heraldry.* 2 vols. London, 1780.

Edwards, Joan. *Black Work.* Joan Edwards' Small Books on the History of Embroidery 2. Dorking, Surrey: Bayford, 1980.

The Egerton Papers. Ed. J. Payne Collier. 1840. New York: AMS (Ser. I. 12), 1968.

Elizabeth I. *The Public Speaking of Queen Elizabeth: Selections from Her Official Addresses.* Ed. George P. Rice Jr. New York: Columbia UP, 1951.

Elizabethan Critical Essays. Ed. G. Gregory Smith. 2 vols. 1904. London: Oxford UP, 1964.

The Elizabethan Midlands. Catalog, Exhibition of Later Sixteenth Century Art Objects with a Midlands Provenance and in Midland Collections. Birmingham: Birmingham City Museum and Art Gallery [1979].

Elizabethan Sonnet-Cycles: "Idea" by Michael Drayton; "Fidessa" by Bartholomew Griffin, "Chloris" by William Smith. Ed. Martha Foote-Crow. Chicago, 1897.

"Eliza Trivmphans." London, 1597. Broadside. British Library. Shelflist C.121.g.6 (14).

Ellis, Henry, ed. *Original Letters Illustrative of English History.* 11 vols. 1824; 2nd ser, 1827; 3rd. ser. 1846; rpt. New York: AMS, 1970.

Elsky, Martin. *Authorizing Words: Speech, Writing, and Print in the English Renaissance.* Ithaca: Cornell UP, 1989.

Elton, G. R. *England under the Tudors.* A History of England in Eight Volumes. Ed. Sir Charles Oman. Vol. 4. 2nd edn. London: Methuen, 1974.

Elyot, Sir Thomas. *The Boke named "the Gouernour."* Ed. Henry Herbert S. Croft. 2 vols. London, 1883.

Emery, F. V. "England *circa* 1600." In *A New Historical Geography of England before 1600,* ed. H. C. Darby. Cambridge: Cambridge UP, 1976. 248–301.

Emmison, F. J. *Elizabethan Life.* 5 vols. Essex Record Office Publications 56, 63, 69, 71, 75. Chelmsford: Essex County Council, 1970–80.

——. *Elizabethan Wills of South-West Essex.* Waddeston, Bucks., U.K.: Kylin, 1983.

——. *Essex Wills (England).* 2 vols. Vol. 1 (1558–65). Washington, D.C.: National Genealogical Society, 1982. Vol. 2 (1565–71). Special Publications of the New England Historic Genealogical Society 51. Boston: New England Historic Genealogical Society, 1983.

——. *Tudor Food and Pastimes.* London: Benn, 1964.

——. *Tudor Secretary, Sir William Petre at Court and Home.* London: Longmans, 1961.

Entertainments for Elizabeth I. Ed. Jean Wilson. Studies in Elizabethan and Renaissance Culture 2. Totowa, N.J.: Rowman, 1980.

Erasmus, Desiderius. *On Good Manners for Boys: De civilitate morum puerilium.* Trans. Brian McGregror. *Literary and Educational Writings* 3: *De conscribendis epistolis formula; De civilitate.* Ed. J. K. Sowards. Vol. 25. 1985. *Collected Works of Erasmus.* Ed. James K. McConica, et al. 86 vols. to date. Toronto: U of Toronto P, 1974–.

——. *The Right Way of Speaking Latin and Greek: A Dialogue: De recta latini graecique sermonis pronuntiatione dialogus.* Trans. Maurice Pope. *Literary and Educational Writings* 4: *De pueris instituendes; De recta pronunciatione.* Ed. J. K. Sowards. Vol. 26. 1985. *Collected Works of Erasmus.* Ed. James K. McConica, et al. 86 vols. to date. Toronto: U of Toronto P, 1974–.

Erler, Mary C. "Sir John Davies and the *Rainbow Portrait* of Queen Elizabeth." *Modern Philology* 84 (1987): 359–71.

Esdaile, Katharine A. *English Church Monuments, 1510 to 1840.* New York: Oxford UP [1946].

Evans, Ifor M., and Heather Lawrence. *Christopher Saxton: Elizabethan Map Maker.* Wakefield, U.K.: Wakefield Historical Publications, 1979.

Evans, Joan. *A History of Jewellry, 1100–1870.* 2nd edn. Boston: Boston Book, 1970.

Evelyn, John. *Tyrannus or The Mode.* Ed. J. L. Nevinson. Luttrell Reprints 11. 1661. Oxford: Blackwell, 195l.

Evett, David. *Literature and the Visual Arts in Tudor England.* Athens: U of Georgia P, 1990.

Farmer, Norman K., Jr. *Poets and the Visual Arts in Renaissance England.* Austin: U of Texas P, 1984.

Ferne, Sir John. *The Blazon of Gentrie.* London, 1586.

Ferry, Anne. *The Art of Naming.* Chicago: U of Chicago P, 1988.

Fisch, Harold. "Shakespeare and the Language of Gesture." *Shakespeare Studies* 19 [1987]: 239–52.

Fischlin, Daniel. "Political Allegory, Absolutist Ideology, and the 'Rainbow Portrait.'" *Renaissance Quarterly* 50 (1997): 175–206.

Fitzherbert, John. *Booke of Husbandrie.* The English Experience: Its Record in Early Printed Books Published in Facsimile 926. 1598. Amsterdam: Theatrum Orbis Terrarum, 1979.

Fletcher, Anthony, and John Stevenson, eds. *Order and Disorder in Early Modern England.* New York: Cambridge UP, 1985.

Floyd, Thomas. *The Picture of a perfit Common wealth.* 1600. The English Experience: The Record in Early Printed Books, Published in Facsimile 518. New York: Da Capo, 1973.

Ford, Boris, ed. *Sixteenth-Century Britain.* Vol. 3 of *The Cambridge Cultural History of Britain,* in 9 vols. 1988. Cambridge: Cambridge UP, 1992.

Foster, Richard. *Patterns of Thought: The Hidden Meaning of the Great Pavement of Westminster Abbey.* London: Cape, 1991.

Foxe, John. *The Acts and Monuments of John Foxe: A New and Complete Edition with a Preliminary Dissertation by the Rev. George Townsend.* Ed. Stephen Reed Cattley. 8 vols. London, 1837–41.

Franko, Mark. *Dance as Text: Ideologies of the Baroque Body.* RES Monographs on Anthropology and Aesthetics. New York: Cambridge UP, 1993.

Fraunce, Abraham. *The Arcadian Rhetoric [1588].* English Linguistics 1500–1800: A Collection of Facsimile Reprints 176. Menston, Yorkshire: Scolar P, 1969.

Frere, Catherine Frances, ed. *A Proper Newe Booke of Cokerye.* Cambridge: Heffer, 1913.

Friedman, Alice T. *House and Household in Elizabethan England: Wollaton Hall and the Willoughby Family.* Chicago: U of Chicago P, 1989.

——. "Patronage and the Production of Tombs in London and the Provinces: The Willoughby Monument of 1591." *Antiquaries Journal* 65 (1985) pt. 2: 390–401.

Frutaz, Amato Pietro. *Le Piante di Roma.* 3 vols. Roma: Istituto di studi romani, 1962.

Frye, Susan. *Elizabeth I: The Competition for Representation.* New York: Oxford UP, 1993.

——. "The Myth of Elizabeth at Tilbury." *Sixteenth Century Journal* 23 (1992): 95–114.

Fuller, Thomas. *Fuller's Worthies: Selected from "The Worthies of England" by Thomas Fuller.* Ed. Richard Barber. London: Folio Society, 1987.

——. *The Holy State.* Cambridge, 1642.

Fumerton, Patricia. *Cultural Aesthetics: Renaissance Literature and the Practice of Social Ornament.* Chicago: U of Chicago P, 1991.

——. "Exchanging Gifts: The Elizabethan Currency of Children and Poetry." ELH 53 (1986): 241–78.

Furnivall, Frederick J., ed. *Early English Meals and Manners.* EETS 32. 1868. London: Trübner, 1904.

Fussell, G. E. *The English Labourer: His Home, Furniture, Clothing & Food from Tudor to Victorian Times.* London: Batchworth, 1949.

Gage, John. *Color and Culture: Practice and Meaning from Antiquity to Abstraction.* Boston: Little, Brown-Bullfinch, 1993.

Gardiner, Stephen. *The Letters of Stephen Gardiner.* Ed. James Arthur Muller. Cambridge: Cambridge UP, 1933.

Gascoigne, George. *Gascoignes woodmanship* and *The Steele Glas.* In *The Anchor Anthology of Sixteenth-Century Verse,* ed. Richard S. Sylvester. Garden City, N.Y.: Anchor-Doubleday, 1974. 268–273; 275–317.

Gawdy, Philip. *The Letters of Philip Gawdy.* Ed. Isaac Herbert Jeayes. Roxburghe Club 148. London: Nichols, 1906.

Gedde. W. *A Booke of sundry Draughtes, Prinicipaly Serving for Glasiers: And Not Impertinent for Plasterers, and Gardiners: Besides Sundry Other Professions.* 1615. Facsimile. London, 1898.

Geller, Sherry. "Commentary as Cover-Up: Criticizing Illiberal Patronage in Thomas Nashe's *Summer's Last Will and Testament.*" *English Literary Renaissance* 25 (1995): 148–78.

Gent, Lucy. *Picture and Poetry, 1560–1620: Relations between Literature and the Visual Arts in the English Renaissance.* Leamington Spa: Hall, 1981.

——. " 'Viewing with the Eye of Persons Accustomed to Drawing,' " lecture delivered at the Victoria and Albert Museum on October 22, 1983.

Gent, Lucy, and Nigel Llewellyn, eds. *Renaissance Bodies: The Human Figure in English Culture, c. 1540–1600.* Critical Views. London: Reaktion, 1990.

Gentili, Alberico. *De legationibus libri tres.* Trans. Gordon J. Laing. Classics of International Law. 2 vols. New York: Oxford UP, 1924.

Gesta Grayorum or the History of the High and Mighty Prince Henry Prince of Purpoole Anno Domini 1594. Ed. Desmond Bland. English Reprints Series 22. Liverpool: Liverpool UP, 1968.

Gillies, John. *Shakespeare and the Geography of Difference.* Cambridge Studies in Renaissance Literature and Culture 4. New York: Cambridge UP, 1994.

Gillies, John, and Virginia Mason Vaughan, eds. *Playing the Globe: Genre and Geography in English Renaissance Drama.* Madison, N.J.: Fairleigh Dickinson UP, 1998.

Giovio, Paolo. *The Worthy Tract of Paulus Iovius (1585), Translated by Samuel Daniel, Together with Giovio's "Dialogo dell'Imprese Militari et Amorose."* Ed. Norman K. Farmer Jr. Delmar, N.Y.: Scholars' Facsimiles, 1976.

Girouard, Mark. "Elizabethan Holdenby." *Country Life* 150 (Oct. 18, 25, 1979): 1286–89, 1398–1401.

——. *Hardwick Hall, Derbyshire: A History and a Guide.* London: National Trust, 1976.

——. *Robert Smythson and the Architecture of the Elizabethan Era.* London: Country Life, 1966.

——. *Robert Smythson and the Elizabethan Country House.* New Haven: Yale UP, 1983.

———. *Town and Country: Essays on Buildings, Places, and People*. New Haven: Yale UP, 1992.

Gittings, Clare. *Death, Burial, and the Individual in Early Modern England*. London: Routledge, 1984.

Glover, Robert. *Nobilitas Politica vel Civilis*. London, 1608.

Goffman, Erving. *Interaction Ritual: Essays in Face-to-Face Behavior*. Chicago: Aldine, 1967.

Goldberg, Jonathan. *Writing Matter: From the Hands of the English Renaissance*. Stanford: Stanford UP, 1990.

Gombrich, E. H. "From the Revival of Letters to the Reform of the Arts: Niccolò Niccoli and Flippo Brunelleschi." In *The Heritage of Apelles: Studies in the Art of the Renaissance*. Oxford: Phaidon, 1976. 93–110.

Goodman, Dr. Godfrey. *The Court of King James the First*. Ed. John S. Brewer. 2 vols. London, 1839.

Gotch, John Alfred. *A Complete Account, Illustrated by Measured Drawings, of the Buildings Erected in Northamptonshire by Sir Thomas Tresham between the Years 1575 and 1605*. London, 1883.

[Gough, Richard]. *Sepulchral Monuments in Great Britain*. 2 vols. in 4. London, 1786–96.

Grazia, Margreta de, Maureen Quilligan, and Peter Stallybrass, eds. *Subject and Object in Renaissance Culture*. Cambridge Studies in Renaissance Literature and Culture 8. New York: Cambridge UP, 1996.

Greenblatt, Stephen. *Marvelous Possessions: The Wonder of the New World*. Chicago: U of Chicago P, 1991.

[Greene, Robert]. *A Quip for an Vpstart Courtier: Or, A quaint dispute between Veluet breeches and Clothbreeches. Wherein is plainely set downe the disorders in all Estates and Trades*. London, 1592.

Greene, Thomas M. *Besieging the Castle of Ladies*. Center for Medieval and Early Renaissance Studies Occasional Papers 4. Binghamton, N.Y.: Medieval and Renaissance Texts and Studies, 1995.

———. *The Light in Troy: Imitation and Discovery in Renaissance Poetry*. New Haven: Yale UP, 1982.

Guazzo, M. Steven. *"The civile conuersation" of M. Steeuen Guazzo, written first in Italian, and nowe translated out of French by George Pettie, deuided into foure bookes*. London, 1581. Copy preserved in the Newberry Library, Chicago.

Gunn, S. J., and P. G. Lindley. *Cardinal Wolsey: Church, State, and Art*. New York: Cambridge UP, 1991.

Guy, John. *Tudor England*. New York: Oxford UP, 1988.

———, ed. *The Reign of Elizabeth I: Court and Culture in the Last Decade*. Cambridge: Cambridge UP, 1995.

Haddon, Walter. *Poemata*. Ed. Thomas Hatcher. London, 1567.

Haigh, Christopher. *Elizabeth I*. Profiles in Power. Ed. Keith Robbins. New York: Longman, 1988.

Hale, J. R. *Renaissance Europe: Individual and Society, 1480–1520.* 1971. New York: Harper, 1973.

Hanawalt, Barbara A. *Growing Up in Medieval London: The Experience of Childhood in History.* New York: Oxford UP, 1993.

Hanawalt, Barbara A., and Kathryn L. Reyerson, eds. *City and Spectacle in Medieval Europe.* Medieval Studies at Minnesota 6. Minneapolis: U of Minnesota, 1994.

Handover, P. M. *The Second Cecil: The Rise to Power, 1563–1604, of Sir Robert Cecil, Later First Earl of Salisbury.* London: Eyre, 1959.

Hansen, Abby Jane Dubman. "Sermons in Stones: The Symbolism of Gems in English Renaissance Literature." Diss., Harvard University, 1977.

Harington, Sir. John. *The Letters and Epigrams of Sir John Harington together with "The Prayse of Private Life."* Ed. Norman Egbert McClure. Philadelphia: U of Pennsylvania P, 1930.

——. *Ludovico Ariosto's "Orlando furioso," Translated into English Heroical Verse by Sir John Harington (1591).* Ed. Robert McNulty. Oxford: Clarendon, 1972.

——. *Nugae Antiquae.* Ed. Henry Harington. Newly arranged by Thomas Park. 2 vols. 1804. New York: AMS, 1966.

The Harleian Miscellany. 12 vols. London, 1808–11.

Harley, J. B. "Meaning and Ambiguity in Tudor Cartography." In *English Map-Making, 1500–1650,* ed. Sarah Tyacke. London: British Library, 1983. 22–45.

Harrison, G. B. *The Life and Death of Robert Devereux Earl of Essex.* New York: Holt, 1937.

Harrison, William. *The Description of England.* Ed. Georges Edelen. Ithaca: Cornell UP, 1968.

Hart, John. *John Hart's Works on English Orthography and Pronunciation (1551, 1569, 1570).* Ed. Bror Danielsson. Stockholm Studies in English 5. Stockholm: Almqvist, 1955.

Harvey, Gabriel. *Letter-book of Gabriel Harvey, A.D. 1573–1580.* Ed. Edward John Long Scott. Camden Society Publications n.s. 33. London, 1884.

Harvey, P. D. A. "Estate Surveyors and the Spread of the Scale-Map in England, 1550–80." *Landscape History* 15 (1993): 37–49.

——. *The History of Topographical Maps: Symbols, Pictures, and Surveys.* London: Thames, 1980.

——. *Maps in Tudor England.* Chicago: U of Chicago P, 1993.

Haugaard, William P. "The Coronation of Elizabeth I." *Journal of Ecclesiastical History* 19 (1968): 161–70.

Hawes, Stephen. *The Pastime of Pleasure.* Ed. William Edward Mead. Os 173. London: EETS, 1928 (for 1927).

Hawkins, Edward. *Medallic Illustrations of the History of Great Britain and Ireland to the Death of George II.* Ed. Augustus W. Franks and Herbert Grueber. 2 vols. London: British Museum, 1885–1904.

Hayden, Ilse. *Symbol and Privilege: The Ritual Context of British Royalty.* The Anthropology of Form and Meaning. Tucson: U of Arizona P, 1987.

H[aydocke], R[ichard], trans. *A Tracte Containing the Artes of curious Paintinge Caruinge & Buildinge.* By Paolo Giovanni Lomazzo. The English Experience: The Record in Early Printed Books, Published in Facsimile 171. 1598. New York: Da Capo, 1969.

Haynes, Alan. *Invisible Power: The Elizabethan Secret Services, 1570–1603.* Wolfeboro Falls, N.H.: Alan Sutton, 1992.

Hayum, Andrée. "Dürer's Portrait of Erasmus and the *Ars Typographorum.*" *Renaissance Quarterly* 38 (1985): 650–87.

Hayward, Sir John. *Annals of the First Four Years of the Reign of Queen Elizabeth.* Ed. John Bruce. Camden Society Series 7. London, 1840.

Hazard, Mary E. "Absent Presence and Present Absence: Cross-Couple Convention in Elizabethan Culture." *TSLL* 29 (1987): 1–27.

——. "The Anatomy of 'Liveliness' as a Concept in Renaissance Aesthetics." *Journal of Aesthetics and Art Criticism* 33 (1975): 407–18.

——. "The Case for 'Case' in Reading Elizabethan Portraits." *Mosaic* 23 (1990): 61–88.

——. "An Essay to Amplify 'Ornament': Some Renaissance Theory and Practice." *SEL* 16 (1976): 15–32.

——. "A Magnificent Lord: Leicester, Kenilworth, and Transformations in the Idea of Magnificence." *Cahiers Élisabethains* 31 (1987): 11–35.

——. " 'Order gave each thing view': 'shows, pageants and sights of honour' in *King Henry VIII.*" *Word and Image* 3 (1987): 95–103.

Hazlitt, W. C., ed. *Inedited Tracts.* 1868. Burt Franklin Research and Source Works Series 49. New York: Franklin, [1963].

Head, C. Grant. "The Map as Natural Language: A Paradigm for Understanding." In *New Insights in Cartographic Communication,* ed. Christopher Board. Monograph 31. *Cartographica* 21, no. 1 (1984): 1–32. Rejoinder, Hansgeorg Schlictmann 33–36.

Heal, Felicity. "The Idea of Hospitality in Early Modern England." *Past and Present* 102 (1984): 66–93.

Heal, Felicity, and Clive Holmes. *The Gentry in England and Wales, 1500–1700.* Stanford: Stanford UP, 1994.

Heijden, van der, H. A. M. "Heinrich Bünting's *Itinerarium Sacrae Scripturae,* 1581: A Chapter in the Geography of the Bible." *Quaerendo* 28 (winter 1998): 49–71.

Helgerson, Richard. *Forms of Nationhood: The Elizabethan Writing of England.* Chicago: U of Chicago P, 1992.

——. "The Land Speaks: Cartography, Chorography, and Subversion in Renaissance England." *Representations* 16 (fall, 1986): 50–85.

Hemp, W. J. "The Goodman and Other Grasshopper Rings." *Antiquaries Journal* 5 (1925): 403–8.

Heninger, S. K., Jr. *Touches of Sweet Harmony: Pythagorean Cosmology and Renaissance Poetics.* San Marino, CA: Huntington Library, 1974.

Henisch, Bridget Ann. *Fast and Feast: Food in Medieval Society.* University Park: Pennsylvania State UP, 1976.

Heywood, Thomas. *Englands Elizabeth. The English Experience: The Record in Early Printed Books, Published in Facsimile 128*. 1631. New York: Da Capo, 1973.

———. *If You Know Not Me You Know Nobody*. 2 pts. Ed. Madeleine Doran. N.p.: Malone Society Reprints, 1934 (1935).

Hic Mulier: Or, The Man-Woman and Haec-Vir: Or, The Womanish Man. 1620. Facsimile. Ilkley, Yorkshire: Scolar P, 1973.

Hieatt, A. Kent. *Short Time's Endless Monument: The Symbolism of Numbers in Edmund Spenser's "Epithalamion."* New York: Columbia UP, 1960.

Higgins, Dick. *Pattern Poetry: Guide to an Unknown Literature*. Albany: State U of New York P, 1987.

Hill, Christopher. *Society and Puritanism in Pre-Revolutionary England*. New York: Schocken, 1964.

———. *The World Turned Upside Down: Radical Ideas during the English Revolution*. 1972. Harmondsworth: Penguin, 1975.

Hill, Thomas. *The moste pleasaunte Arte of the Interpretacion of Dreames*. London, 1576.

Hilliard, Nicholas. *Nicholas Hilliard's "Art of Limning": A New Edition of "A Treatise Concerning the Arte of Limning Writ by N. Hilliard."* Ed. Arthur F. Kinney and Linda Bradley-Salamon. Boston: Northeastern UP, 1983.

Hind, Arthur M. *Engraving in England in the Sixteenth and Seventeenth Centuries: A Descriptive Catalogue with Introductions*. 2 vols. Cambridge: Cambridge UP, 1952.

Histrio-mastix. The School of Shakespere. Ed. Richard Simpson. 2 vols. New York, 1878. Vol. 1.

HMC. *Report on Manuscripts in Various Collections*. 11 vols. London, 1901–14. Vol. 3: *The Manuscripts of T. B. Clarke-Thornhill, Sir T. Barrett-Lennard, Pelham R. Papillon, and W. Cleverly Alexander*. Ed. M. C. Lomas. London: HMSO, 1904.

———. *Report on the Manuscripts of Lord Middleton, Preserved at Wollaton Hall, Nottinghamshire*. London: HMSO, 1911.

———. *Report on the Manuscripts of the Lord L'Isle and Dudley Preserved at Penshurst Place*. Ed. C. L. Kingsford. 6 vols. London: HMSO, 1925–42.

Hoak, Dale, ed. *Tudor Political Culture*. New York: Cambridge UP, 1995.

Hoby, Thomas, trans. *Castiglione, "The Courtier."* In *Three Renaissance Classics: Machiavelli, "The Prince"; More, "Utopia"; Castiglione, "The Courtier."* Ed. Burton A. Milligan. New York: Scribner's, 1953.

Hogenberg, Franz. *Leo Belgicus*. 1582.

Holinshed, Raphael. *Holinshed's "Chronicles of England, Scotland, and Ireland."* 6 vols. London, 1807–08.

Holland, Thomas. *[Panyguris] D. Elizabethae, Dei gratiâ Angliae, Franciae, & Hiberniae Reginae. A Sermon Preached at Pavls in London the 17. of November Ann. Dom. 1599*. Oxford, 1601.

Holles, Gervase. *Memorials of the Holles Family, 1493–1656*. Ed. A. C. Wood. Camden 3rd ser. 55. London: Offices of the Society, 1937.

Holmes, Martin. *Elizabethan London.* London: Cassell, 1969.

The Honorable Entertainment giuen to the Queenes Maiestie in Progresse, at Cowdrey in Sussex, by the Right Honorable the Lord Montecute, 1591. London, 1591.

Honour, Hugh. "Silver." In *The Tudor Period, 1500–1603,* 6 vols, ed. Ralph Edwards and L. G. G. Ramsey. Connoisseur Period Guides. London: Connoisseur, 1956. 1: 65–78.

Hooper, Wilfrid. "The Tudor Sumptuary Laws." *English Historical Review* 30 (1915): 433–49.

Hoskins, John. *Directions for Speech and Style.* Ed. Hoyt H. Hudson. Princeton Studies in English 12. Princeton: Princeton UP, 1935.

Howard-Hill, T. H. "The Evolution of the Form of Plays in English during the Renaissance." *Renaissance Quarterly* 43 (1990): 112–45.

Howard, Maurice. *The Early Tudor Country House: Architecture and Politics, 1490–1550.* London: George Philip, 1987.

Howard, Skiles. "Hands, Feet, and Bottoms: Decentering the Cosmic Dance in *A Midsummer Night's Dream.*" *Shakespeare Quarterly* 44 (1993): 325–42.

———. "Rival Discourses of Dancing in Early Modern England." *SEL* 36 (1996): 31–56.

Howson, John. *A Sermon Preached at St. Maries in Oxford the 17, Day of November, 1602. in defence of the Festivities of the Church of England, and namely that of her Maiesties Coronation Day of November, 1602.* Oxford, 1602.

Hulse, Clark. *The Rule of Art: Literature and Painting in the Renaissance.* Chicago: U of Chicago P, 1990.

Humfrey, Lawrence. *The Nobles or of Nobilitye.* London, 1563.

Hunter, Joseph. *Hallamshire.* Rev. edn. Ed. Alfred Getty. London, 1869.

Hurst, Herbert. *Oxford Topography: An Essay.* For *Oxford Historical Society,* vol. 39. Oxford: Clarendon, 1899.

Hurtig, Judith. "Seventeenth-Century Shroud Tombs: Classical Revival and Anglican Context." *Art Bulletin* 64 (1982): 217–39.

Hussey, Christopher. "Burghley House, Northamptonshire." *Country Life* 114 (Dec. 3, 10, 17, 24, 31, 1953): 1828–32; 1962–65; 2038–41; 2104–7; 2164–67.

———. "Hardwick Hall." *Country Life* 64 (Dec. 8, 15, 22, and 29, 1928): 806–14; 870–78; 904–11; 934–42.

Hutton, Ronald. *The Rise and Fall of Merry England: The Ritual Year, 1400–1700.* New York: Oxford UP, 1994.

Illustrations of Ancient State and Chivalry from Manuscripts Preserved in the Ashmolean Museum. Ed. William Henry Black. Roxburghe Club 56. London, 1840.

Inderwick, F. A., ed. *Calendar of Inner Temple Records.* 1 vol. in 2 pts. London: Masters of the Bench. 1896–1901.

Ingram, R. W., ed. *Coventry.* Records of Early English Drama. Buffalo: U of Toronto P, 1981.

The Institucion of a Gentleman. The English Experience: Its Record in Early Printed Books, Published in Facsimile 672. 1555. Norwood, N.J.: Johnson, 1974.

Isham, Gyles. "Sir Thomas Tresham and His Buildings." *Reports and Papers of the Northamptonshire Antiquarian Society* 65, pt. 2 (1966): 1–37.

[Isham, Gyles]. *Lyveden New Bield, Northamptonshire.* 1973. London: National Trust, 1981.

——. *Rushton Triangular Lodge, Northamptonshire.* Department of the Environment Ancient Monuments and Historic Buildings. 1970. London: HMSO, 1975.

Jackson, Charles. *An Illustrated History of English Plate.* 2 vols. 1911. London: Holland, 1967.

Jewels and Plate of Queen Elizabeth I: The Inventory of 1574, Edited from Harley MS 1650 and Stowe MS 555 in the British Museum by A. Jeffries Collins. London: Trustees of the British Museum, 1955.

Johnson, Paul. *Elizabeth I: A Study in Power and Intellect.* London: Weidenfeld, 1974.

Jones, Norman. *The Birth of the Elizabethan Age: England in the 1560s.* A History of Early Modern England. Cambridge, Mass.: Blackwell, 1993.

Jones, William. *Finger-Ring Lore: Historical, Legendary, Anecdotal.* 2nd, rev. and enlarged edn. 1890. Detroit: Singing Tree, 1968.

Jonson, Ben. *Ben Jonson.* Ed. C. H. Herford and Percy Simpson. 11 vols. Oxford: Clarendon, 1925–52.

Jourdain, M[argaret]. *English Decoration and Furniture of the Early Renaissance (1500–1650).* London: Batsford, 1924.

——. *The History of English Secular Embroidery.* London: Kegan Paul, 1910.

——. "Needlework at Hardwick Hall." *Country Life* 61 (1927): 328–30.

——. "Sir Thomas and His Symbolic Buildings." In *Memorials of Old Northamptonshire,* ed. Alice Dryden. London: Bemrose, 1903. 129–43.

——. "Some Tapestries at Hardwick Hall." *Country Life* 61 (1927): 499–501.

Kantorowicz, Ernst K. *The King's Two Bodies: A Study in Mediaeval Political Theology.* Princeton: Princeton UP, 1957.

Kastan, David Scott. "Proud Majesty Made a Subject: Shakespeare and the Spectacle of Rule." *Shakespeare Quarterly* 37 (winter 1986): 459–75.

Kaushick, Sandeep. "Resistance, Loyalty and Recusant Politics: Sir Thomas Tresham and the Elizabethan State." *Midland History* 21 (1996): 37–72.

Keller, Arthur S., Oliver J. Lissitizyn, and Frederick J. Mann. *Creation of Rights of Sovereignty through Symbolic Acts, 1400–1800.* 1938. New York: AMS, 1967.

Kemp, Thomas, ed. *The Book of John Fisher.* Warwick [1898].

[Kemp, William]. *Kemps Nine Daies Wonder: Performed in a Daunce from London to Norwich.* Ed. Alexander Dyce. Camden Society Publications 11. London, 1840.

King, John N. "The Godly Woman in Elizabethan Iconography." *Renaissance Quarterly* 38 (spring 1985): 41–84.

——. "Queen Elizabeth I: Representations of the Virgin Queen." *Renaissance Quarterly* 43 (spring 1990): 30–74.

——. *Tudor Royal Iconography: Literature and Art in an Age of Religious Crisis.* Princeton Essays on the Arts. Princeton: Princeton UP, 1989.

Kingsford, Charles Lethbridge. "Essex House, formerly Leicester House and Exeter Inn." *Archaeologia* 73 (1923): 1–54.

Kipling, Gordon. " 'He That Saw It Would Not Believe It': Anne Boleyn's Royal Entry into London." In *Civic Ritual and Drama,* ed. Alexandra F. Johnston and Wim Hüsken. Ludus: Medieval and Early Renaissance Theatre and Drama 2. Atlanta: Rodopi, 1997. 39–79.

Klarwill, Victor von, ed. *Queen Elizabeth and Some Foreigners.* Trans. T. H. Nash. New York: Brentano's, 1928.

Klein, Lisa M. "Your Humble Handmaid: Elizabethan Gifts of Needlework." *Renaissance Quarterly* 50 (1997): 459–93.

Knecht, Robert J. "New Light on Francis I." *Bulletin of the Society for Renaissance Studies* 11 (May 1994): 1–7.

Koziol, Geoffrey. *Begging Pardon and Favor: Ritual and Political Order in Early Medieval France.* Ithaca: Cornell UP, 1992.

Kunz, George Frederick. *Rings for the Finger.* Philadelphia: Lippincott, 1917.

Kuspit, Donald Burton. "Dürer and the Northern Critics." Diss., University of Michigan, 1971.

Kyffin, Maurice. *The Blessednes of Brytaine, or A Celebration of the Queenes Holyday.* London, 1588.

Laird, Andrew. "*Vt figura poesis*: Writing Art and the Art of Writing in Augustan Poetry." In *Art and Text in Roman Culture,* ed. Jas Elsner. Cambridge: Cambridge UP, 1996. 75–102.

Lancashire, Ian. "Orders for Twelfth Day and Night circa 1515 in the Second Northumberland Household Book." *English Literary Renaissance* 10 (1980): 7–45.

Langham, Robert. *Robert Langham: A Letter.* Ed. R. J. P. Kuin. Medieval and Renaissance Texts 2. Leiden: Brill, 1983.

Lawner, Lynne. *Lives of the Courtesans: Portraits of the Renaissance.* New York: Rizzoli, 1987.

Lawrence, Heather. "Permission to Survey." *Map Collector* 19 (June 1982): 16–18.

Leader, John Daniel. *Mary Queen of Scots in Captivity.* London, 1880.

Lefebvre, Henri. *The Production of Space.* Trans. Donald Nicholson-Smith. Cambridge, Mass.: Blackwell, 1991.

Legh, Gerard. *The Accedens of Armory.* London, 1568.

Levin, Carole. *"The Heart and Stomach of a King": Elizabeth I and the Politics of Sex and Power.* University of Pennsylvania Press New Cultural Studies. Philadelphia: U of Pennsylvania P, 1994.

——. "Power, Politics, and Sexuality: Images of Elizabeth I." In *The Politics of Gender in Early Modern Europe,* ed. Jean R. Brink, Allison P. Coudert, and Maryanne C. Horowitz. Sixteenth Century Essays and Studies 12. Kirksville, Mo.: Sixteenth Century Journal Publishers, 1989. 95–110.

——. " 'Would I Could Give You Help and Succour': Elizabeth I and the Politics of Touch." *Albion* 21 (1989): 191–205.

Leycesters Common-wealth. 1641. Ed. Frank J. Burgoyne. New York: Longmans, 1904.

The "Libro Cerimoniale" of the Florentine Republic by Francesco Filarete and Angelo Manfidi. Ed. Richard C. Trexler. Travaux d'Humanisme et Renaissance 165. Geneva: Droz, 1978.

Llewellyn, Nigel. *The Art of Death: Visual Culture in the English Death Ritual, c. 1500–c. 1800.* London: Reaktion, 1991.

——. "Claims to Status through Visual Codes: Heraldry on post-Reformation Funeral Monuments." In *Chivalry in the Renaissance*, ed. Sydney Anglo. Rochester, N.Y.: Boydell, 1990. 145–60.

——. "John Weever and English Funeral Monuments of the Sixteenth and Seventeenth Centuries." Diss. School of Combined Historical Studies. London: U of London and the Warburg Institute, 1983.

Lloyd, Lodowick. *The Order, Solemnitie, and Pompe, of the Feastes, Sacrifices, Vowes, Games, and Triumphes.* London, 1610.

——. *The Triplicitie of Triumphes.* London, 1591.

Loades, David. *Mary Tudor: A Life.* Cambridge, Mass.: Blackwell, 1989.

——. *The Tudor Court.* Totowa, N.J.: Barnes, 1987.

Lodge, Edmund, ed. *Illustrations of British History, Biography, and Manners, in the Reigns of Henry VIII, Mary, Elizabeth, and James I.* 3 vols. 2nd. edn. London, 1838.

Loomis, Catherine. "Elizabeth Southwell's Manuscript Account of the Death of Queen Elizabeth [with text]." *English Literary Renaissance* 26 (1996): 482–509.

The Loseley Manuscripts. Ed. Alfred John Kempe. London, 1836.

Luborsky, Ruth Samson. "The Allusive Presentation of *The Shepheardes Calender.*" In *Spenser Studies: A Renaissance Poetry Annual*, ed. Patrick Cullen and Thomas P. Roche Jr. Pittsburgh: U of Pittsburgh P, 1980. 1: 29–67.

——. "The Illustrations to *The Sheapherdes Calender.*" In *Spenser Studies: A Renaissance Poetry Annual*, ed. Patrick Cullen and Thomas P. Roche Jr. Pittsburgh: U of Pittsburgh P, 1981. 2: 3–53.

Lyly, John. *The Complete Works of John Lyly.* Ed. R. Warwick Bond. 3 vols. 1902. Oxford: Clarendon, 1967.

McCanles, Michael. "*The Shepheardes Calender* as Document and Monument." *SEL* 22 (1982): 5–19.

Machiavelli, Niccolò. *Machiavelli: The Chief Works and Others.* Trans. Allan Gilbert. 3 vols. 1958. Durham, N.C.: Duke UP, 1965.

Machyn, Henry. *The Diary of Henry Machyn.* Ed. John Gough Nichols. London, 1847.

McClure, Peter, and Robin Headlam Wells. "Elizabeth I As a Second Virgin Mary." *Renaissance Studies* 4 (1990): 38–70.

MacCormack, Sabine G. *Art and Ceremony in Late Antiquity*. Berkeley: U of California P, 1981.

Mccoy, Richard C. *The Rites of Knighthood: The Literature and Politics of Elizabethan Chivalry*. The New Historicism: Studies in Cultural Poetics 7. Berkeley: U of California P, 1989.

——. "'Thou Idol Ceremony': Elizabeth I, *The Henriad*, and the Rites of the English Monarch." In *Urban Life in the Renaissance*, ed. Susan Zimmerman and Ronald F. E. Weissman. Newark: U of Delaware P, 1989. 240–66.

McCracken, Grant. "Dress Colour at the Court of Elizabeth I: An Essay in Historical Anthropology." *Canadian Review of Sociology and Anthropology* 22 (1985): 515–33.

——. "The Pre-coronation Passage of Elizabeth I: Political Theatre or the Rehearsal of Politics?" *Canadian Review of Sociology and Anthropology* 21 (1984): 47–61.

Magno, Alessandro. "The London Journal of Alessandro Magno, 1562." Ed. Caroline Barron, Christopher Coleman, and Claire Gobbi. *London Journal* 9 (1983): 136–52.

Maisse, de, André Hurault. *De Maisse: A Journal of All That Was Accomplished by Monsieur de Maisse Ambassador in England from Henri IV to Queen Elizabeth Anno Domini 1597*. Trans. and ed. G. B. Harrison and R. A. Jones. London: Nonesuch, 1931.

Manley, Lawrence. "From Matron to Monster: Tudor Stuart London and the Languages of Urban Description." In *The Historical Renaissance: New Essays on Tudor and Stuart Literature and Culture*, ed. Heather Dubrow and Richard Strier. Chicago: U of Chicago P, 1988. 347–74.

——. *Literature and Culture in Early Modern London*. Cambridge: Cambridge UP, 1995.

Mann, J. G. "English Church Monuments, 1536–1625." *Walpole Society* 21 (1932–33): 1–22.

——. "Instances of Antiquarian Feeling in Medieval and Renaissance Art." *Archaeological Journal* 89 (1933): 254–74.

Manning, Roger B. *Village Revolts: Social Protest and Popular Disturbances in England, 1509–1640*. Oxford: Clarendon, 1988.

Manningham, John. *The Diary of John Manningham of the Middle Temple, 1602–03*. Ed. Robert Parker Sorlien. Hanover, N.H.: U of New England P, 1976

Marcus, Leah S. *Puzzling Shakespeare: Local Reading and Its Discontents*. The New Historicism: Studies in Cultural Poetics 6. Berkeley: U of California P, 1988.

——. "Shakespeare's Comic Heroines, Elizabeth I, and the Political Uses of Androgyny." In *Women in the Middle Ages and the Renaissance: Literary and Historical Perspectives*, ed. Mary Beth Rose. Syracuse, N.Y.: Syracuse UP, 1986. 135–53.

Markham, Gervase. *The English Housewife*. Ed. Michael R. Best. 1615. Montreal: McGill-Queen's UP, 1986.

[Markham, Gervase ?]. *Excellent and new invented knots and mazes*. The English

Experience: The Record in Early Printed Books, Published in Facsimile 611. 1623. New York: Da Capo, 1973.

Marotti, Arthur F. *Manuscript, Print, and the English Renaissance Lyric.* Ithaca: Cornell UP, 1995.

Marshall, Rosalind K. *Queen of Scots.* Edinburgh: HMSO, 1986.

Marston, John. *The Works of John Marston.* Ed. A. H. Bullen. 3 vols. London, 1887.

Maus, Katharine Eisaman. "Proof and Consequences: Inwardness and Its Exposure in the English Renaissance." In *Materialist Shakespeare: A History,* ed. Ivo Kamps. New York: Verso, 1995. 157–80.

May, Steven W. *The Elizabethan Courtier Poets: The Poems and Their Contexts.* Columbia: U of Missouri P, 1991.

——. "Tudor Aristocrats and the Mythical 'Stigma of Print.'" In *Renaissance Papers 1980,* ed. A. Leigh Deneef and M. Thomas Hester. Valencia: Southern Renaissance Conference, 1981. 11–18.

Melville, James. *Memoirs of Sir James Melville of Halhill, 1535–1617.* Ed. A. Francis Steuart. New York: Dutton, 1930.

Meres, Francis. *Palladis Tamia.* Ed. Don Cameron Allen. 1598. New York: Scholars' Facsimiles, 1938.

[Milles, Thomas]. *The Catalogve of Honor.* London, 1610.

Mish, Charles C. "Black Letter as a Social Discriminant in the Sixteenth Century." *PMLA* 68 (1953): 627–30.

Montague, Anthony. "'A Booke of Orders and Rules' of Anthony Viscount Montague in 1595." Ed. Sibbald David Scott. *Sussex Archaeological Collections* 7 (1854): 173–212.

Montaigne, Michel de. *The Essays.* Trans. John Florio. 3 vols. 1910. London: Dent; New York: Dutton, 1973.

Montrose, Louis. *The Purpose of Playing: Shakespeare and the Cultural Politics of the Elizabethan Theatre.* Chicago: U of Chicago P, 1996.

Moore, Elsie Matley. "Wall-paintings Recently Discovered in Worcestershire." *Archaeologia* 2nd ser. 88 (1940): 281–88.

More, Thomas. *The Complete Works of St. Thomas More.* Ed. Thomas M. C. Lawler, Germain Marc'hadour, and Richard C. Marius. New Haven and London: Yale UP, 1963–.

——. *The English Works of Sir Thomas More.* Ed. W. E. Campbell et al. 2 vols. New York: Macveagh-Dial, 1931.

Morgan, Victor. "The Cartographic Image of 'The Country' in Early Modern England." *Transactions of the Royal Historical Society* 5th ser. 29 (1979): 129–54.

Morley, Thomas. *A Plain and Easy Introduction to Practical Music.* Ed. R. Alec Harman. London: Dent, 1952.

Mowl, Timothy. *Elizabethan and Jacobean Style.* London: Phaidon, 1993.

Muir, Edward. *Civic Ritual in Renaissance Venice.* Princeton: Princeton UP, 1981.

Muir, Miri. *Corpus Christi: The Eucharist in Late Medieval Culture.* New York: Cambridge UP, 1991.

Mullaney, Steven. "Civic Rites, City Sites: The Place of the Stage." In *Staging the Renaissance: Reinterpretations of Elizabethan and Jacobean Drama,* ed. David Scott Kastan and Peter Stallybrass. New York: Routledge, 1991. 17–26.

——. *The Place of the Stage: License, Play, and Power in Renaissance England.* Chicago: U of Chicago P, 1988.

[Munday, Anthony]. *A Watch-woord to Englande.* London, 1584.

Nashe, Thomas. *The Unfortunate Traveller and Other Works.* Ed. J. B. Steane. New York: Penguin, 1972.

Naunton, Sir Robert. *Fragmenta Regalia or Observations on Queen Elizabeth, Her Times & Favorites.* Ed. John S. Cerovski. Washington, D.C.: Folger Shakespeare Library, 1985.

Neale, J. E. *Queen Elizabeth I.* 1934. Chicago: Academy, 1992.

The Necessarie, Fit and Convenient Education of a Yong Gentlewoman. Trans. W. P. The English Experience: The Record in Early Printed Books, Published in Facsimile 168. 1598. New York: Da Capo, 1969.

Nevinson, J. L. "The Embroidery Patterns of Thomas Trevelyon." *Walpole Society* 41 (1966–68): 1–77.

——. "English Domestic Embroidery Patterns of the Sixteenth and Seventeenth Centuries." *Walpole Society* 28 (1939–40): 1–13.

Newman, Karen. *Fashioning Femininity and English Renaissance Drama.* Women in Culture and Society. Ed. Catherine R. Stimpson. Chicago: U of Chicago P, 1991.

Niccols, Richard. *England's Eliza.* London, 1610.

Nichols, John, ed. *Illustrations of the Manners and Expences of Antient Times in England in the Fifteenth, Sixteenth, and Seventeenth Centuries.* 1797. New York: AMS, 1973.

——. *The Progresses and Public Processions of Queen Elizabeth.* 2nd edn. 3 vols. 1823. New York: AMS, n.d.

Nicolas, Harris. *Memoirs of the Life and Times of Sir Christopher Hatton.* London, 1847.

Norbrook, David. "Panegyric of the Monarch and Its Social Context under Elizabeth I and James I." Diss. Magdalen College, Oxford. 1978.

N[orden], I[ohn]. *Speculi Britanniae, Pars Altera: or, a Delineation of Northamptonshire.* 1610. London, 1723.

——. *The Surveyors Dialogue.* London, 1618.

Norris, Malcolm. *Monumental Brasses: The Craft.* Boston: Faber, 1978.

——. *Monumental Brasses: The Portfolio Plates of the Monumental Brass Society, 1894–1984.* Bury St. Edmunds: St. Edmundsbury P for the Monumental Brass Society, 1988.

Northumberland, Henry Percy. *Household Papers.* Ed. G. R. Batho. Camden 3rd Series 93. London: Royal Historical Society, 1962.

Norton, Thomas. "Instructions to the Lord Mayor of London, 1574–75: Whereby he is to govern himself and the City." In *Illustrations of Old English Literature,* ed. J. Payne Collier. 3 vols. London, 1866. 3: 1–17.

——. *Warning against the dangerous practises of Papistes, and specially the parteners of the late Rebellion.* London [1569].

Oman, Charles C. *British Rings, 800–1914.* London: Batsford, 1974.

Osley, A. S. *Scribes and Sources: Handbooks of the Chancery Hand in the Sixteenth Century, Texts from the Masters Selected, Introduced and Translated by A. S. Osley.* Boston: Godine, 1980.

Outhwaite, R. B. "Dearth, the English Crown and the 'Crisis of the 1590s.' " In *The European Crisis of the 1590s: Essays in Comparative History,* ed. Peter Clark. London: Allen, 1985. 23–43.

Overall, William Henry. *Civitas Londinum, Ralph Agas . . . The Fac-simile by Edward J. Francis.* London: 1874.

——. "On the Early Maps of London and More Especially as to the Map Attributed to Ralph Agas." *Proceedings of the Society of Antiquaries* 2nd ser. 6 (Dec. 11, 1873): 81–99.

[Overall, William Henry, and H. C. Overall, eds.]. *Analytical Index to the Series of Records Known as the "Remembrancia."* London, 1878.

Painter, George D. *The "Hypnerotomachia Poliphili of 1499": An Introduction on [sic] the Dream, the Dreamer, the Artist, and the Printer.* London: Eugrammia, 1963.

Palliser, D. M. *The Age of Elizabeth: England under the Later Tudors, 1547–1603.* Social and Economic History of England. Ed. Asa Briggs. New York: Longman, 1983.

Palmer, Daryl W. *Hospitable Performances: Dramatic Genre and Cultural Practices in Early Modern England.* West Lafayette, Ind.: Purdue UP, 1992.

Panofsky, Erwin. "Erasmus and the Visual Arts." *Journal of the Warburg and Courtauld Institutes* 32 (1969): 200–27.

——. *The Life and Art of Albrecht Dürer.* Rev. edn., 1945. Princeton: Princeton UP, 1971.

——. *Tomb Sculpture: Four Lectures on Its Changing Aspects from Ancient Egypt to Bernini.* Ed. H. W. Janson. New York: Abrams, 1964.

Parker, Henry, Lord Morley. *Lord Morley's "Tryumphes of Fraunces Petrarcke": The First English Translation of the "Trionfi."* Ed. D. D. Carnicelli. Cambridge, Mass.: Harvard UP, 1971.

Parkes, M. B. *English Cursive Book Hands, 1250–1500.* Oxford Paleographical Handbooks. Ed. R. W. Hunt, C. H. Roberts, and F. Wormald. Oxford: Clarendon, 1969.

Peacham, Henry. *The Garden of Eloquence.* 1577. Facsimile. Menston, Yorkshire: Scolar, 1971.

Peele, George. *The Life and Minor Works of George Peele.* Ed. David H. Horne. 3 vols. Ed. Charles Taylor Prouty. New Haven: Yale UP, 1952.

——. *The Works of George Peele.* Ed. A. H. Bullen. 2 vols. London, 1888.

Perlin, Stephen. "A Description of England and Scotland (1558)." In *The Pleasures of London.* By James Beeverell. Trans. and ed. W. H. Quarrell. 1727. [London]: Witherby, 1940. 57–70.

Perry, Maria. *The Word of a Prince: A Life of Elizabeth I from Contemporary Documents*. Rochester, N.Y.: Boydell, 1990.

Pevsner, Nikolaus. *Bedfordshire and the County of Huntingdon and Peterborough*. The Buildings of England. 1968. Harmondsworth: [Penguin], 1974.

———. *Berkshire*. The Buildings of England. Harmondsworth: Penguin, 1966.

———. *Nottinghamshire*. The Buildings of England. Rev. Elizabeth Williamson. 1951. New York: Penguin, 1979.

———. "Old Somerset House." *Architectural Review* 116 (1954): 163–67.

Phillips, John. *The Reformation of Images: Destruction of Art in England, 1535–1660*. Berkeley: U of California P, 1973.

Platt, Colin. *The Great Rebuildings of Tudor and Stuart England: Revolutions in Architectural Taste*. London: University College London, 1994.

Plat[t], Hugh. *Delightes for Ladies, to adorne their Persons, Tables, closets and distillatories with Beauties, banquets, perfumes and waters*. London, 1603.

———. *Floraes Paradise*. London, 1608.

———. *The Garden of Eden*. London, 1653.

Platter, Thomas. *Thomas Platter's Travels in England, 1599*. Trans. Clare Williams. London: Cape, 1937.

A Pleasaunt Dialogne [sic] or disputation betweene the Cap, and the Head. London, 1565.

Pliny. *Natural History*. Trans. H. Rackham. 10 vols. Cambridge, Mass.: Harvard UP, 1938–62.

———. *Pliny's "Natural History": A Selection from Philemon Holland's Translation*. Ed. J. Newsome. Oxford: Clarendon, 1964.

Polydore Vergil. *Polydori Virgili, De Rerum Inventoribus*. Trans. John Langley. Ed. William A. Hammond. 1867. New York: Franklin, 1971.

Price, S. R. F. *Rituals and Power: The Roman Imperial Cult in Asia Minor*. New York: Cambridge UP, 1984.

Princely Magnificence: Court Jewels of the Renaissance, 1500–1630. [Ed. A. G. Somers Cocks]. London: Debrett's Peerage for the Victoria and Albert Museum, 1980.

Proceedings in the Parliaments of Elizabeth I. Ed. T. E. Hartley. 3 vols. Wilmington, Del.: Glazier, 1981.

Prokter, Adrian, and Robert Taylor, eds. *The A to Z of Elizabethan London*. London Topographical Society Publication 122. London: London Typographical Society, 1979.

Puttenham, George. *The Arte of English Poesie*. Ed. Gladys Doidge Willcock and Alice Walker. 1936. Folcroft, Pa.: Folcroft, 1969.

The Queenes Maiesties Entertainement at Woodstock. London, 1585.

Quintilian. *The "Institutio Oratoria" of Quintilian*. Trans. H. E. Butler. 4 vols. 1921–22. Cambridge, Mass.: Harvard UP, 1943.

Ralegh, Sir Walter. *The Poems of Sir Walter Ralegh*. Ed. Agnes Latham. London: Routledge, 1951.

Ranald, Margaret Loftus. "The Degradation of Richard II: An Inquiry into the Ritual Backgrounds." *English Literary Renaissance* 7 (1977): 170–96.

Ravenhill, William, and Margery Rowe. "A Decorated Screen Map of Exeter Based on John Hooker's Map of 1587." In *Tudor and Stuart Devon: The Common Estate and Government: Essays Presented to Joyce Youings*, ed. Todd Gray, Margery Rowe, and Audrey Erskine. Exeter: U of Exeter P, 1992. 1–12.

Ravenshaw, Thomas F. *Antiente Epitaphes from AD 1250 to AD 1800*, Collected and sett forth in Chronologicall order. London, 1878.

Read, Conyers. *Mr. Secretary Walsingham and the Policy of Queen Elizabeth*. 3 vols. Oxford: Clarendon, 1925.

A Relation, or Rather a True Account, of the Island of England; with Sundry Particulars of the Customs of These People, and of the Royal Revenues under King Henry the Seventh, about the Year 1500. Trans. Charlotte Augusta Sneyd. Camden Society Ser. 1, no. 37. 1847. New York: AMS, 1968.

The Renaissance at Sutton Place: An Exhibition to Mark the 450th Anniversary of the Visit of King Henry VIII to Sutton Place. May 18–September 15, 1983. N.p.: Sutton Place Heritage Trust, 1983.

Renn, D. F. *Kenilworth Castle*. Department of the Environment Souvenir Guidebook. London: HMSO, 1973.

Ribner, Rhoda M. " 'The Compasse of This Curious Frame': Chapman's *Ovids Banquet of Sence* and the Emblematic Tradition." *Studies in the Renaissance* 17 (1970): 233–58.

Riche, Barnabe. *His Farewell to Military Profession*. Ed. Donald Beecher. Publications of the Barnabe Riche Society 1. Binghamton, N.Y.: Medieval and Renaissance Texts and Studies vol. 91, 1992.

Ridley, Jasper. *Elizabeth I: The Shrewdness of Virtue*. New York: Viking, 1988.

Robinson, Arthur H., and Barbara Bartz Petchenik. *The Nature of Maps: Essays toward Understanding Maps and Mapping*. Chicago: U of Chicago P, 1976.

Robinson, Brian. *The Royal Maundy*. London: Kaye, 1977.

Robinson, John Martin. *The Dukes of Norfolk: A Quincentennial History*. New York: Oxford UP, 1982.

Rodríguez-Salgado, M. J., and Staff of National Maritime Museum. *Armada: 1588–1988. An International Exhibition to Commemorate the Spanish Armada: The Official Catalogue*. New York: Penguin, 1988.

Roethlisberger, Marcel. "The Ulysses Tapestries at Hardwick Hall." *Gazette des Beaux-Arts* 79 (1972): 111–25.

Rosenberg, Eleanor. *Leicester: Patron of Letters*. New York: Columbia UP, 1955.

Rosenthal, Earl. "The Invention of the Columnar Device of Emperor Charles V at the Court of Burgundy in Flanders in 1516." *Journal of the Warburg and Courtauld Institutes* 36 (1973): 198–230.

Rubin, Miri. *Corpus Christi: The Eucharist in Late Medieval Culture*. Cambridge: Cambridge UP, 1991.

Rushton, Peter. "The Testament of Gifts: Marriage Tokens and Disputed Contracts in North-East England, 1560–1630." *Folk Life* 24 (1985/86): 25–31.

Salesbury, William. *Dictionary in Englysh and Welshe*. London, 1547.

Salter, Thomas. *A Critical Edition of Thomas Salter's "The mirrhor of modestie."* Ed.

Janis Butler Holm. The Renaissance Imagination: Important Literary and Theatrical Texts from the Late Middle Ages through the Seventeenth Century 32. New York: Garland, 1987.

Salusbury, Sir John. *Poems by Sir John Salusbury and Robert Chester.* Ed. Carleton Brown. EETS es 113. London: Oxford UP, 1914.

Sands, Mollie. *The Gardens of Hampton Court: Four Centuries of English History and Gardening.* London: Evans, 1950.

Sarton, George. *Introduction to the History of Science.* Vol. 3: *Science and Learning in the Fourteenth Century,* pt. 1. Baltimore: Williams, 1947. 716–22.

Saunders, J. W. "The Stigma of Print: A Note on the Social Bases of Tudor Poetry." *Essays in Criticism* 1 (1951): 139–64.

Saxl, Fritz. *"Veritas filia temporis."* In *Philosophy and History: Essays Presented to Ernst Cassirer,* ed. Raymond Klibansky and H. J. Paton. 1936; 1963. Gloucester, Mass.: Peter Smith, 1975. 197–222.

Sayle, R[obert] T. *Lord Mayors' Pageants of the Merchant Taylors' Company in the 16th, 17th, & 18th Centuries.* London: Eastern, 1931.

Scarisbrick, Diana. *Rings: Symbols of Wealth, Power, and Affection.* New York: Abrams, 1993.

——. "Sir Thomas Gresham and the Grasshopper Rings." In *Christie's Review of the Season, 1978,* ed. John Herbert. London: Studio Vista, 1978. 300–301.

Schleiner, Winfried. *"Divina virago*: Queen Elizabeth as an Amazon." *Studies in Philology* 75 (1978): 163–80.

Schmitt, Jean Claude. *La Raison des Gestes dans l'Occident Médiéval.* Paris, Gallimard, 1990.

Schoenherr, Douglas E. "The Pageant of the People: A Study of Queen Elizabeth I's Royal Entries." Diss. Yale U, 1973.

Schofield, John. *Medieval London Houses.* New Haven: Yale UP, 1994.

Schulz, Juergen. "Jacopo di Barbari's View of Venice: Map Making, City Views, and Moralized Geography before the Year 1500." *Art Bulletin* 60 (1978): 425–74.

Scodel, Joshua. *The English Poetic Epitaph Commemoration and Conflict from Jonson to Wordsworth.* Ithaca: Cornell UP, 1991.

Seed, Patricia. *Ceremonies of Possession in Europe's Conquest of the New World, 1492–1640.* Cambridge: Cambridge UP, 1995.

Segar, William. *The Book of Honor and Armes (1590) and Honor Military and Civil (1602).* Facsimile. Delmar, N.Y.: Scholars, 1975.

Shakespeare, William. *The Art of Shakespeare's Sonnets.* Ed. Helen Vendler. Cambridge, Mass.: Belknap P, 1997.

——. *King Henry IV, part 2.* Ed. A. R. Humphreys. Arden edn. Cambridge: Harvard UP, 1966.

——. *King Richard II.* Ed. Peter Ure. 4th, rev. edn. Arden edn. Cambridge, Mass.: Harvard UP, 1956.

——. *Midsummer Night's Dream.* Ed. Harold F. Brooks. Arden edn. London: Methuen, 1979.

———. *The Riverside Shakespeare.* Ed. G. Blakemore Evans et al. 2nd edn. New York: Houghton Mifflin, 1997.

Sharp, Ronald A. "Gift Exchange and the Economies of Spirit in *The Merchant of Venice.*" *Modern Philology* 83 (1986): 250–65.

Shell, Marc. *Money, Language, and Thought: Literary and Philosophical Economies from the Medieval to the Modern Era.* Berkeley: U of California P, 1982.

Shute, John. *The First & Chief Groundes of Architecture.* 1563. Facsimile. London: Marshe, 1912.

Sider, Sandra. "Transcendent Symbols for the Hapsburgs: *Plus Ultra* and the Columns of Hercules." *Emblematica* 4 (1989): 257–72.

Sidney, Sir Philip. *The Countesse of Pembrokes Arcadia* (1590). Ed. Albert A. Feuillerat. Vol. 1. *The Prose Works of Sir Philip Sidney.* 4 vols. 1912. Cambridge: Cambridge UP, 1965.

———. *The Poems of Sir Philip Sidney.* Ed. William A. Ringler, Jr. Oxford: Clarendon, 1962.

———. *Sidney: A Defence of Poetry.* Ed. J. A. Van Dorsten. London: Oxford UP, 1966.

Simonds, Peggy Muñoz. *Myth, Emblem, and Music in Shakespeare's* Cymbeline: *An Iconographic Reconstruction.* Newark: U of Delaware P, 1992.

Simons, Patricia. "Portraiture, Portrayal, and Idealization: Ambiguous Individualism in Representations of Renaissance Women." In *Language and Images of Renaissance Italy,* ed. Alison Brown. Oxford: Clarendon, 1995. 262–311.

Sisson, Charles. "Marks as Signatures." *Library* 4th ser. 9 (1928): 1–37.

Skelton, R. A., and John Summerson. *A Description of Maps and Architectural Drawings in the Collection Made by William Cecil, First Baron Burghley, Now at Hatfield House.* 234 [for 235]. Oxford: Roxburghe Club, 1971.

Sladen, Teresa. "The Garden at Kirby Hall 1570–1700." *Journal of Garden History* 4 (April–June 1984): 139–56.

Slater, Ann Pasternak. *Shakespeare the Director.* Totowa, N.J.: Barnes, 1982.

Smarr, Janet Levarie. "The Pyramid and the Circle: 'Ovid's Banquet of Sense.'" *Philological Quarterly* 63 (1984): 369–86.

Smith, Bruce R. *Homosexual Desire in Shakespeare's England: A Cultural Poetics.* Chicago: U of Chicago P, 1991.

Smith, David L., Richard Strier, and David Bevington, eds. *The Theatrical City: Culture, Theatre and Politics in London, 1576–1649.* New York: Cambridge UP, 1995.

Smith, Henry. *A Preparatiue to Marriage; Of the Lords Supper; Of Usurie.* 1591. Facsimile. Norwood, N.J.: Johnson, 1975.

Smuts, R. Malcolm. "Public Ceremony and Royal Charisma: The English Royal Entry in London, 1485–1642." In *The First Modern Society: Essays in Honour of Lawrence Stone,* ed. A. L. Beier, David Cannadine, and James M. Rosenheim. New York: Cambridge UP, 1989. 65–93.

Somerset, Anne. *Elizabeth I.* New York: St. Martin's, 1991.

Spenser, Edmund. *The Complete Poetical Works of Spenser.* Ed. R. E. Dodge. Cambridge edn. 1908. Boston: Houghton, 1936.

——. *The Faerie Queene*. 2 vols. 1596. Facsimile. New York: Scolar P, 1976.

——. *The Shepheardes Calender*. 1579. Facsimile. Menston, Yorkshire: Scolar P, 1968.

Spitzer, Leo. *Classical and Christian Ideas of World Harmony: Prolegomena to an Interpretation of the Word "Stimmung."* Ed. Anna Granville Hatcher. Baltimore: Johns Hopkins UP, 1963.

Staley, Vernon, ed. *Hierurgia Anglicana: Documents and Extracts Illustrative of the Ceremonial of the Anglican Church after the Reformation*. 3 vols. 1848. New edn. London: De La More, 1902–04.

Stallybrass, Basil. "Bess of Hardwick's Buildings and Building Accounts." *Archaeologia* 2nd ser. 64 (1913): 347–98.

The Star Chamber Dinner Accounts. Ed. André L. Simon. London: Rainbird, 1959.

Starkey, David. "The Age of the Household: Politics, Society and the Arts." In *The Later Middle Ages*, ed. Stephen Medcalf. The Context of English Literature. London: Methuen, 1981. 255–90.

——. "Ightham Mote: Politics and Architecture in Early Tudor England." *Archaeologia* 107 (1982): 153–64.

——. "The Legacy of Henry VIII." In *Henry VIII: A European Court in England*, ed. David Starkey. London: Collins, 1991. 8–13.

——. "Representation through Intimacy: A Study in the Symbolism of Monarchy and Court Office in Early-Modern England." In *Symbols and Sentiments: Cross-cultural Studies in Symbolism*, ed. Ioan Lewis. New York: Academic, 1977. 187–224.

Starobinski, Jean. *Largesse*. Trans. Jane Marie Todd. Chicago: U of Chicago P, 1997.

Stevenson, William. "Extracts from 'The Booke of howshold Charges and other Paiments laid out by the L. North and his commandement: beginning the first day of January 1575, and the 18th yere of' [*sic*] Queen Elizabeth." *Archaeologia* 19 (1821): 283–301.

Stock, Brian. *The Implications of Literacy: Written Language and Models of Interpretation in the Eleventh and Twelfth Centuries*. Princeton: Princeton UP, 1983.

Stone, Lawrence. *The Crisis of the Aristocracy, 1558–1641*. Oxford: Clarendon, 1965.

——. *Family and Fortune: Studies in Aristocratic Finance in the Sixteenth and Seventeenth Centuries*. Oxford: Clarendon, 1973.

Stone, Lawrence, and Jeanne C. Fawtier Stone. *An Open Elite?: England, 1540–1880*. Oxford: Clarendon, 1984.

Stow, John. *The Annales, or Generall Chronicle of England*. London, 1615.

——. *Three Fifteenth-Century Chronicles*. Ed. James Gairdner. Camden Society Publications n.s. 28. Westminster, 1880.

Streitberger, W. R. "The Armada Victory Procession and Tudor Precedence." *Notes and Queries* 27 (1980): 310–12.

——. *Edmond Tyllney: Master of the Revels and Censor of Plays: A Descriptive Index to His Diplomatic Manual on Europe*. AMS Studies in the Renaissance 15. New York: AMS, 1986.

——. "On Edmund Tyllney's Biography." *Review of English Studies* 29 (1978): 11–35.

——. "The Tyllney Manuscript at the Folger Library." *Papers of the Bibliographical Society of America* 69 (1975): 449–64.

Strickland, Ronald. "Pageantry and Poetry as Discourse: The Production of Subjectivity in Sir Philip Sidney's Funeral." *ELH* 57 [1990]: 19–36.

Strong, Roy. *Artists of the Tudor Court: The Portrait Miniature Rediscovered, 1520–1620.* London: Victoria and Albert Museum, 1983.

——. *The Cult of Elizabeth: Elizabethan Portraiture and Pageantry.* Berkeley: U of California P, 1977.

——. *The English Icon: Elizabethan and Jacobean Portraiture.* Studies in British Art. New Haven: Yale UP, 1969.

——. *Gloriana: The Portraits of Queen Elizabeth I.* New York: Thames, 1987.

——. *Portraits of Queen Elizabeth I.* Oxford: Clarendon, 1963.

——. *The Renaissance Garden in England.* London: Thames, 1979.

Strong, Roy, and J. A. Van Dorsten. *Leicester's Triumph.* London: Oxford UP, 1964.

Strype, John. *The Life of the Learned Sir Thomas Smith.* 1698. Oxford, 1820.

——. *Memorials of the Reverend Father in God Thomas Cranmer.* Rev edn. 3 vols. Oxford, 1812.

——, ed. *Annals of the Reformation and Establishment of Religion.* 4 vols. in 7 pts. Oxford, 1824.

Stuart, Mary. *The Letters of Mary, Queen of Scots and Documents Connected with Her Personal History.* Ed. Agnes Strickland. 2 vols. London, 1844.

Stubbes [or Stubbs], Philip. *Phillip Stubbes's "Anatomy of the Abuses" in England in Shakespeare's Youth,* A.D. 1583. Ed. Frederick J. Furnivall. New Shakespere Publications ser. 6, nos. 4, 6, 12. 1877–79. Vaduz, Liechtenstein: Kraus, 1965.

Summerson, John. "The Book of Architecture of John Thorpe." *Walpole Society* 40 (1966): 1–119.

——. "Three Elizabethan Architects." *Bulletin of the John Rylands Library* 40 (1957): 202–28.

Summit, Jennifer. " 'The Arte of a Ladies Penne': Elizabeth I and the Poetics of Queenship." *English Literary Renaissance* 26 (1996): 395–422.

Swain, Margaret. *The Needlework of Mary Queen of Scots.* New York: Van Nostrand, 1973.

——. "A New Year's Gift from the Princess Elizabeth." *Connoisseur* 183 (1973): 258–66.

Sylvester, Josuah, trans. *The Divine Weeks and Works of Guillaume de Saluste, Sieur du Bartas.* Ed. Susan Snyder. 2 vols. New York: Oxford UP, 1979.

Taylor, Barry. *Vagrant Writing: Social and Semiotic Disorders in the English Renaissance.* Theory/Culture. Ed. Linda Hutcheon and Paul Perron. Buffalo: U of Toronto P, 1991.

Taylor, Christopher. *The Archaeology of Gardens.* Shire Archaeology. Ed. James Dyer. 1983. Aylesbury: Shire, 1988.

Taylor, E[va] G[ermaine] R[emington]. *Tudor Geography, 1485–1583*. London: Methuen, 1930.

Taylor, John. Preface. "The Praise of the Needle." *The Needle's Excellency*. By James Boler. London, 1631.

Teague, Frances. "Queen Elizabeth in Her Speeches." In *Gloriana's Face: Women, Public and Private, in the English Renaissance*, ed. S. P. Cerasano and Marion Wynne-Davies. New York: Harvester-Wheatsheaf, 1992. 61–78.

Tenison, E. M., ed. *Elizabethan England*. 10 vols. Leamington Spa: Sign of the Dove with the Griffin, 1937.

Thomas, David. "The Elizabethan Crown Lands: Their Purposes and Problems." In *The Estates of the English Crown, 1558–1640*, ed. R. W. Hoyle. New York: Cambridge UP, 1992. 58–87.

Thompson, M. W. *Kenilworth Castle, Warwickshire*. English Heritage Handbook. 1977. London: Historic Buildings and Monuments Commission for England, 1990.

Thomson, Peter. *Shakespeare's Professional Career*. Cambridge: Cambridge U P, 1992.

Tilney, Edmond. *A brief and pleasant discourse of duties in marriage, called the Flower of Friendshippe*. London, 1568.

Tittler, Robert. *Architecture and Power: The Town Hall and the English Urban Community, c. 1500–1640*. Oxford: Clarendon, 1991.

Trapp, J. B. Lecture. "Sir Thomas More and the Visual Arts." Victoria and Albert Museum. August 21, 1983.

Trexler, Richard C. *Dependence in Context in Renaissance Florence*. Medieval and Renaissance Texts and Studies 111. Binghamton, N.Y.: Medieval and Renaissance Texts and Studies, 1994.

Tudor Royal Proclamations. Ed. Paul L. Hughes and James F. Larkin. 3 vols. New Haven: Yale UP, 1964–69.

Turner, William. *A new booke of spirituall Physik for dyuerse diseases of the nobilitie and gentlemen of Englande*. London, 1555.

Tyacke, Sarah, and John Huddy. *Christopher Saxton and Tudor Map-Making*. British Library Ser. 2. London: British Library, 1980.

Vasari, Giorgio. *Le vite de' più eccellenti pittori scultori ed architettori*. Ed. Gaetano Milanesi. 9 vols. Florence, 1878–85.

———. *Lives of the Most Eminent Painters, Sculptors, and Architects*. Trans. Mrs. Jonathan Foster. 5 vols. London, 1894–98.

V[erstegan], R[ichard]. *A Restitvtion of Decayed Intelligence*. Antwerp, 1605.

Vos, Alvin, ed. *Place and Displacement in the Renaissance*. Medieval and Renaissance Texts and Studies 132. Binghamton, N.Y.: Medieval and Renaissance Texts and Studies, 1995.

Waldstein, Baron. *The Diary of Baron Waldstein: A Traveller in Elizabethan England*. Trans. and ed. G. W. Groos. New York: Thames, 1981.

Walker, Julia M. "Reading the Tombs of Elizabeth I." *English Literary Renaissance* 26 (1996): 510–30.

Wallis, Helen M. "Globes in England up to 1600." *Geographical Magazine* 35 (1962): 267–79.

Watson, Thomas. *Poems*. Ed. Edward Arber. English Reprints 21. London, 1870.

Weever, John. *Ancient Fvnerall Monvments*. London, 1631.

Weigall, Rachel, ed. "An Elizabethan Gentlewoman: The Diary of Lady Mildmay, 1570–1617." *Quarterly Review* 215 (1911): 119–38.

Wells-Cole, Anthony. "The Elizabethan Sheldon Tapestry Maps." *Burlington Magazine* 132 (1990): 392–401.

Wheaton, Barbara Ketcham. *Savoring the Past: The French Kitchen and Table from 1300 to 1789*. Philadelphia: U of Pennsylvania P, 1983.

Whetstone, George. *A Critical Edition of George Whetstone's 1582 "An Heptameron of Civill Discourses."* Ed. Diana Shklanka. The Renaissance Imagination 35. New York: Garland, 1987.

Whigham, Frank. *Ambition and Privilege: The Social Tropes of Elizabethan Courtesy Theory*. Berkeley: U of California P, 1984.

——. "The Rhetoric of Elizabethan Suitors' Letters." *PMLA* 96 (1981): 864–82.

White, Adam. "Tudor Classicism." *Architectural Review* 171 (1982): 52–58.

Whiting, Roger. *The Enterprise of England: The Spanish Armada*. New York: St. Martin's, 1988.

Whitney, Geffrey. *A Choice of Emblemes*. 1866. New York: Blom, 1967.

Wickham, Glynne. *Early English Stages, 1300–1660*. 2 vols. in 3 pts. New York: Columbia; London: Routledge, 1959–81.

Wight, Jane A. *Brick Building in England from the Middle Ages to 1550*. London: Baker, 1972.

Wilbraham, Sir Roger. *The Journal of Sir Roger Wilbraham*. Ed. Harold Spencer Scott. *Camden Miscellany* 3rd ser. 10 (1902): 1–139.

Willet, Andrew. *Sacrorvm Emblematvm Centuria Vna*. Cambridge [1592–98].

Williams, E. Carleton. *Bess of Hardwick*. London: Longmans, 1959.

Williams, Neville. *Thomas Howard Fourth Duke of Norfolk*. New York: Dutton, 1964.

Williams, Penry. "Court and Polity under Elizabeth I." *Bulletin of the John Rylands University Library of Manchester* 65 (1983): 259–86.

——. *The Tudor Regime*. Oxford: Clarendon, 1979.

Williamson, G. C. *George, Third Earl of Cumberland (1558–1605): His Life and His Voyages: A Study from Original Documents*. Cambridge: Cambridge UP, 1920.

Wilson, C. Anne, ed. *"Banquetting Stuffe": The Fare and Social Background of the Tudor and Stuart Banquet*. Edinburgh: Edinburgh UP, 1991.

Wilson, Derek. *Sweet Robin: A Biography of Robert Dudley, Earl of Leicester, 1533–1588*. London: Hamish Hamilton, 1981.

Wilson, Ezra Calhoun. *England's Eliza*. Harvard Studies in English 20. 1939. New York: Octagon, 1966.

Wilson, Thomas (d. 1581). *The Arte of Rhetorique*. Ed. Thomas J. Derrick. The Renaissance Imagination 1. New York: Garland, 1982.

Wilson, Thomas (d. 1629). *State of England Anno Dom. 1600*. Ed. F. J. Fisher. *Camden Miscellany* 16. Camden 3rd ser. 52. London: Offices of the Society, 1936.

Woodbridge, Linda. "Palisading the Elizabethan Body Politic." *TSLL* 33 (1991): 327–54.

Woodworth, Allegra. "Purveyance for the Royal Household in the Reign of Queen Elizabeth." *Transactions of the American Philosophical Society* n.s. 35 (1945): 1–89.

Wotton, Sir Henry. *The Elements of Architecture*. Ed. Frederick Hard. 1624. Facsimile. Charlottesville: UP of Virginia, 1968.

——. *Reliquiae Wottonianae*. 4th edn. London, 1685.

Wright, Pam. "A Change in Direction: The Ramifications of a Female Household, 1558–1603." In *The English Court: From the Wars of the Roses to the Civil War*, ed. David Starkey et al. London: Longman, 1987. 147–73.

Wright, Thomas. *The Passions of the Minde in Generall*. Ed. Thomas O. Sloan. 1604. Urbana: U of Illinois P, 1971.

Wright, Thomas, ed. *Queen Elizabeth and Her Times*. 2 vols. London, 1838.

Wriothesley, Charles. *A Chronicle of England during the Reigns of the Tudors, from A.D. 1485 to 1559*. Ed. William Douglas Hamilton. Camden n.s. 11, 20. 2 vols. London, 1875, 1877.

Yates, Frances A. *Astraea: The Imperial Theme in the Sixteenth Century*. Boston: Routledge, 1975.

Yoch, James J. "Renaissance Gardening and Pastoral Scenery in Italy and England." *Research Opportunities in Renaissance Drama* 20 (1978, for 1977): 35–43.

Young, Alan R. *Tudor and Jacobean Tournaments*. London: George Philip, 1987.

——. "Tudor Arthurianism and the Earl of Cumberland's Tournament Pageants." *Dalhousie Review* 67 (1987): 176–89.

Youngs, Frederic A., Jr. *The Proclamations of the Tudor Queens*. New York: Cambridge UP, 1976.

Ziegler, Georgianna. "My Lady's Chamber: Female Space, Female Chastity in Shakespeare." *Textual Practice* 4 (1990): 73–90.

INDEX

absent presence, 18, 48, 61–62, 101,
    231–66; decorum governing, 232–
    34; of Elizabeth I, 131, 233–34, 262,
    263–64, 266
Accession Day (annual celebration of),
    7, 101; Armada celebration moved to
    coincide with, 190; entertainments
    on, 99–100, 185–88, 191–92, 220;
    jewels and finery worn on, 115, 120;
    ringing of church bells on, 175–76
acrostics, 47–49, 54, 56
acrotelestic poems, 55
Adams, Robert, 73, 285 n.21
Adams, Simon, 288 n.27
Agas, Ralph, 70, 71, 72–73
Agnew, Jean-Christophe, 19, 146–47
Alberti, Leon Battista, 28
Alciati, Andrea, 120
Aldus Manutius, 271 n.42
Alençon, duc d'. *See* Anjou et d'Alen-
    çon, duc d'

alphabets, 27, 39, 47–48
anagrams, 47, 49
Anjou et d'Alençon, duc d': courtship
    of Elizabeth by, 112, 124, 222, 235,
    251; Elizabeth's religious compro-
    mise with, 234; English hostility to,
    117–18, 282 n.38; representation of,
    on Elizabethan medal, 126–27
Apelles, 23, 24, 29, 52, 268 n.5
architecture: Elizabethan interest in,
    29, 138–39, 160, 164; English forms
    grafted onto Renaissance styles of,
    9–10, 16; figured in other arts, 11, 39,
    51–55, 63, 168–70, 269 n.26, 271 n.6;
    magnificence in, 149–53, 159–60; as
    silent language, 2, 3, 18, 109–10. *See
    also* great houses
Ariosto, 185; *Orlando Furioso*, 30, 94,
    243
Aristotle, 159, 160; *Nicomachean Ethics*,
    91, 98, 135

Armada: artifacts celebrating defeat of, 54, 128–29, 190–91; queen's visit to Tilbury during, 8–9, 49, 73, 166, 188–90, 285 n.21 n.22. *See also* *Armada Portrait*

Armada Portrait (of Elizabeth I), 13, 69, 96, 172, 191

armillary sphere, 32, 36, 65, 71, 110

Arnold, Janet, 103, 275 n.25, 284 n.12

Arte of English Poesie (Puttenham), 24, 49, 214, 234; on courtly decorum, 232, 236, 242; on shaped text, 50–54, 55, 58–61

Arundel, earl of, 97, 224

Ascham, Roger: *Scholemaster*, 49–50, 120–21

Ashmole, Elias, 263, 264

Aske, James: *Elizabetha Trivmphans*, 49, 188–90

Askew, Lady Anne, 254

Aston, Margaret, 148

Aubrey, John: *Memoires*, 114, 120

Augustus (first Roman emperor), 176–77

Axton, Marie, 286 n.30, 290 n.30

Bacon, Sir Francis, 91, 192, 216; Essex's failure to secure position for, 241, 250; interest of, in fortunes of Essex, 98, 244, 264, 265; "Of Building," 164

Bacon, Sir Nicholas, 126, 154, 252, 287 n.11

Bailey, Brian, 257

Barker, Christopher, 80

Barley, William: *Booke of Tabliture*, 48; "Your face / So fair," 58

Barnes, Barnabe: *Fovre Bookes of Offices*, 93–94, 150, 221

Barolini, Helen, 271 n.42

Barrow, Henry, 210

Bartolovich, Crystal, 273 n.40

Bates, Catherine, 136

Bath, Michael, 268 n.10

Bayne, G. C., 286 n.6

Beale, Robert, 66

Beauchesne, Jean de: *A booke containing divers sortes of hands*, 39, 40

Bedford, earl of, 254

Bedingfield, Sir Henry, 204, 205, 286 n.5

Beier, A. L., 125

Beltz, George Frederick, 262–63

Bennett, Josephine Waters, 60

Bentley, Thomas: *Monvment of Matrones*, 48, 49, 212

Bercher, William: *Nobility of Women*, 145

Berkeley, Henry, Lord, 254–55

Berlin, Michael, 151, 201

Berry, Francis, 286 n.31

Bess of Hardwick. *See* Shrewsbury, countess of

Bevington, David, 19, 267 n.2, 268 n.10, 289 n.37

Bindoff, S. T., 114

Biron, Marshal, 99

Bishops' Bible, 55

The Black Book of Warwick, 249, 262, 288 n.27

Blakemore, M. J., 67

Blenerhasset, Thomas: *A Revelation of the True Minerva*, 55, 60

Bliss, Philip, 290 n.30

Bloom, J. Harvey, 126

Blount, Sir Charles, 102, 241

Bohun, Edmund: *Character of Queen Elizabeth*, 179, 181

Boler, James: *The Needle's Excellency*, 34

Boleyn, Anne, 203

Bonifaccio, Giovanni: *L'arte de cenni*, 4–5

Bonner, Edmund, 204, 212

The Booke of Curious and Strange Inuentions . . . Called . . . Needlework, 34

"Booke of Orders and Rules," 256

Book of Common Prayer, 28, 131

Boorde, Andrew, 91, 153

boundaries, 44–45, 47, 143–72; displacement of, 148–52, 282 n.45; disputes about, 69–70; in fashion, 94–96; importance of taking physical possession of, 66, 68–69, 143–48, 178, 272 n.25, 279 n.1 n.3 n.4; movement across, 143–44, 154–56, 170–71, 282 n.46. *See also* proxemics

Bowyer, Simon, 239

Braithwait, Richard: *Some Rules and Orders for the Government of the House of an Earle*, 156, 253

"A Breviate touching the Order and Governmente of a Nobleman's House," 80, 156, 257–58

Briant, Sir Francis, 221

Brodhurst, Frederick, 84

Bromley, Thomas, 126

Bruster, Douglas, 276 n.11

Bruto, Giovanni Michele, 85

Buckhurst, Lord, 239–40, 244, 253

Bülow, Gottfried von, 196

Bulwer, John, 7, 8

Burghley, Lord (William Cecil), 40, 81, 119, 191–92, 251; insistence of, on ceremony, 216, 226; interest of, in maps, 66, 71, 74, 273 n.43; letters to, 214, 224, 252, 254, 261; power of, 39, 239–40, 241, 244, 245, 250, 290 n.15; visit to Holdenby by, 158, 159. *See also* Burghley House; Theobalds

Burghley House, 150, 155

Burke, Kenneth, 232

Burton Agnes, 157–58, 159

Buxton, John, 151

Caesar, Sir Julius (Elizabethan courtier), 252

Caesar, Julius (Roman general), 111, 160, 164

Caius, John, 155, 160

calendars and calendrical observances, 62, 63–64, 174–76, 193, 201, 231, 283 n.3

calligraphy. *See* handwriting and lettering

Calthrop, Sir Philip, 91

Camden, William: Funeral Roll, 209; *Princess Elizabeth*, 112–13, 127; *Remains*, 41–42, 91, 133, 269 n.21

Campion, Edmund, 49

Carew, Sir Francis, 193

Carew, Sir Gawan, 134

Carey, George, 235

Carey, Sir Henry, Lord Hunsdon, 214, 248

Carey, Sir Robert, 115, 220

Carey family, 290 n.15

Carleton, Dudley, 196, 215, 225, 264

Carlisle, earl of, 227–28

Carnicelli, D. D., 284 n.16

cartography. *See* maps

Case, John: *Sphaera civitatis*, 65, 69, 172

Castiglione, Baldesar: *Book of the Courtier*, 27, 133

Castle, Sydney E., 270 n.26

Castle Ashby, 153, 155

The Catalogve of Honor, 111

Catherine of Aragon, 203

Cato, 159

Cavendish, Elizabeth. *See* Shrewsbury, countess of

Cavendish, George, 114

Cavendish, Sir William, 39, 83, 84, 232

Cecil, Sir Robert, 154, 191–92, 213, 236, 240; behavior of, during disgrace and trial of Essex, 215, 265–66; Elizabeth ridicules portrait of, 90; power of, 83, 244, 290 n.15; tomb of, 133

Cecil, William. *See* Burghley, Lord

Cellini, Benvenuto, 122

ceremony, 173–97, 201–29; awareness of boundaries in, 144–48, 279 n.1 n.3 n.4; changes in, 164–65, 201–5, 214–16, 231–32; church, 226–27; civic, 48, 102–3, 120, 201, 249; definition of, 283 n.1; of degradation, 227–29,

ceremony (*continued*)
288 n.34; Elizabethan descriptions
of, 77–78, 178–79, 205–8, 212–13,
287 n.9; of food service, 155–57,
163, 255–62; functions of, 179–80;
funeral, 208–11, 287 n.11 n.12; Garter, 262–64; importance of, to Elizabethans, 229; Italian, 216–17, 248–
49, 280 n.5; Maundy, 180–81; regalia
used in, 122–23. *See also* coronation
(of Elizabeth I); processions
*Certain Observations concerning the Life
and Raigne of Elizabeth*, 116
chains, 70, 83, 134, 197, 216; gold, 119–
20, 184; of sonnets, 63; worn by servants, 125
chairs, 146, 161, 166, 286 n.5; cloths of
state behind, 17, 80, 204, 205, 257
Chamberlain, John, 108, 120, 196, 215,
225, 252, 264–65
Chandos, Lady, 35, 276 n.6
Chantmarle House, 139
Chapman, George: completion of
Marlowe's *Hero and Leander* by, 88;
"Coronet for his Mistresse Philoso-
phie," 63; *Ovids Banquet of Sence*,
64–65
charitable giving, 139, 163, 180–81,
288 n.26
Charles V, 8, 54, 55, 144–45, 172, 186
Chaucer, Geoffrey, 258
Cheke, Lady, 224
Chettle, G. H., 154
Chettle, Henry: *Englandes Mourning
Garment*, 209
chivalry, 278 n.51; concern of Elizabeth
I with, 215; parlay on hands in, 6, 7,
101. *See also* Cumberland, third earl
of; Garter, Order of the; Lee, Sir
Henry; tournaments
Churchyard, Thomas, 102, 120;
Chvrchyards Challenge, 48, 56, 92–
93; *A light Bondell*, 118
Cicero, 5, 120

ciphers, 40–41, 42, 48, 82, 270 n.35
Clapham, John, 266
Cleland, James: *Hero-Paideia*, 98, 144,
157, 222
Clifford, Lady Anne, 139
Clifford, George. *See* Cumberland,
third earl of
Clinton, Evard, Lord, 91
Cobham, Lord, 244, 262
coins, 79, 109, 110, 129, 139, 233;
Maundy, 180; political messages on,
126–27, 165, 277 n.38; stamping of,
124–25
Collins, A. J., 289 n.10
Collins, Arthur, 116, 118, 219, 221, 225,
246
Colonna, Fra Francesco: *Hypneroto-
machia*, 54, 56, 122, 272 n.10
Colt, Maximilian, 135
Colthorpe, Marion, 285 n.28
columns, 35. *See also* pillars
Coningsby, Thomas, 225–26
Constable, Henry, 101
Cook, Elizabeth, 271 n.6
Cooke, Frances, 224
Cooper, J. P., 287 n.14, 288 n.27
Cornwallis, William, 221
coronation (of Elizabeth I): banquet,
122, 205; mass, 205, 233, 286 n.6;
procession, 7, 147, 177–79, 220,
283 n.7, 284 n.9; ring, 112–13,
115; significance of, 146, 236–37,
289 n.10; sumptuousness of, 77–78;
variations on traditional ceremony
during, 204–5. *See also* Accession
Day
coronations, 10, 201, 217, 229; of Anne
Boleyn, 203; of Mary I, 102, 203,
236. *See also* coronation (of Elizabeth I)
costume: color of, 99–101, 104–6; as
gender marker, 94–96, 106, 237–38,
275 n.21; official, 102–3; as silent language, 10–11, 17. *See also* chains;

head coverings; jewels; sumptuary display

Countess of Pembrokes Arcadia. See New Arcadia

courtesy: basis of, 171; Italian codes of, 248–49; reciprocal, 144–45; refusal of, 176, 202–3, 265, 286 n.2. See also courtesy books; decorum; prestation; proxemics

courtesy books, 10; codes governing absence in, 232, 255; codes of female behavior in, 84, 94; rigidity of, 202; sumptuary excess attacked in, 103–4

The Covrt of ciuill Courtesie, 224, 288 n.24

Cranmer, Thomas, 226

Cressy, David, 43, 144, 175, 191, 283 n.3

Croft, Herbert, 226

Cromwell, Thomas, 149

Cumberland, third earl of, 104, 108, 221; portrait of, 13, 32–33, 36, 101, 166–67, 269 n.19

cups, 2, 17, 56–57, 122–23, 126, 194, 256, 257

Custodis, Hieronimo: Frances Clinton, 35

Cutwode T.: Caltha "Poetarum," 58, 111

Cyuile and vncyuile life, 258

Dallington, Robert, 91

dance, 18, 27, 158; in Davies's Orchestra, 37, 272 n.16; Elizabeth's love of, 196–97; harmony figured in, 11, 59, 64; in Spenser's Faerie Queene, 64, 170–71, 223, 248; Will Kemp's morris, 48, 232

Dangers Averted pendant, 128

Daniel, Samuel: Delia sonnets, 62

Dante: Purgatorio, 5

Darnley, Lord, 105, 165

Davies, Sir John, 240; Hymnes of Astraea, 49; Orchestra, 37, 59, 272 n.16

Davies of Hereford, John, 64

Dawson, Giles E., 44, 270 n.30

Daye, John, 132

Dean, David, 208, 287

decorum: assumed value of, 17; decor as, 82, 89–91, 128; Essex's violations of, 105–6, 166, 234–35; funeral, 132–33, 208–11; governing absence, 231–34; governing presence, 234–51; governing room assignment, 153; personal variations on, 18, 164, 179; sexual, 223–24. See also ceremony; meals and banquets; prestation; protocol

Dee, John: The Elements of Geometrie, 28, 68; General and Rare Memorials, 282 n.47

Dekker, Thomas: The Dead Terme, 152; The Wonderful Year, 174

Deloney, Thomas: Jack of Newberie, 249–50, 290 n.26

Derby, earl of, 209

Derby, Lady, 90

Description of England (Harrison): on food and table service, 121, 258–59; on the increased use of glass, 136; on material progress, 78–79, 80; on men's costume, 91, 93; on the reduction of feast days, 175; on women's costume, 94, 97, 103

Dethick, Sir William, 132, 208

Digby, Ann, 134

Dissolution of monasteries, 83, 135, 148–49, 280 n.9. See also Reformation

Ditchley manuscript, 7, 185, 187, 285 n.19

Ditchley Portrait (of Elizabeth I), 30, 96; armillary sphere in, 36; map of England in, 14, 65–66, 68, 172, 188

Dolman, Thomas, 152

Donaldson, Gordon, 275 n.21

Doran, Susan, 112, 118, 234

Dowland, John, 185

Drake, Sir Francis, 101, 221, 279 n.3; knighting of, 251

Drayton, Michael, 44; *Barrons' Wars*, 87

dress. *See* costume

Drummond, William, 81

Du Bartas, Guillaume: *Divine Weeks and Works*, 52, 63, 64

Dudley, Robert. *See* Leicester, earl of

Duffy, Eamon, 123, 148

Dugdale, Sir William: *The Antiquities of Warwickshire*, 113, 136–37, 155

Duncan-Jones, Katherine, 287 n.21

Dürer, Albrecht, 24–25, 268 n.6

Eames, Penelope, 286 n.5

Edward III, 134, 180, 284 n.11

Edward IV, 147, 288 n.27

Edward VI, 26, 130, 233

Egerton, Sir Thomas, 116, 193, 194

Elizabeth I: access to, 220–21, 236–51, 266, 290 n.15; corporal eloquence of, 5; crown imperial of, 191, 277 n.40; death of, 11, 115, 193, 196–97; departures of, from traditional observances, 180–81, 204–5, 211–12, 215–16, 221–24, 231, 234–38, 250–51, 284 n.12; displays of disfavor by, 213, 219; displays of favor by, 250–51; eglantine associated with, 31–32, 33, 125, 161; as Europa, 69; as Fairy Queen, 59, 96, 126, 186, 187–88; funeral of, 209; manipulation of gender by, 13, 17, 95–96, 178, 189–90, 237–38; medal commemorating recovery of, from smallpox, 128; portraits and images of, 1–2, 3, 11, 13–14, 65, 68–69, 71–72, 267 n.1, 276 n.6; privy chamber of, 236–39, 289 n.13, 290 n.14; public appearances by, 176–81, 190–91, 194–97, 233, 251–52, 266; religious independence of, 204–5, 211–12, 233–34; sanctification of, 48–49, 54–57, 123, 128–29, 171–72, 174–76, 186–87, 190; sumptuary displays of, 13, 97, 108, 110–11, 260–

61; as sumptuary monitor, 89–90; tomb of, 135, 278 n.59; two bodies of, 196–97, 236–37; as United Provinces peacemaker, 126–27; views of, on sexual decorum, 223–24, 243–44; "wedding" ring of, 13, 112–13, 276 n.7; writings of, 80, 274 n.7. *See also* Accession Day; coronation (of Elizabeth I); *Ditchley Portrait*; progresses (of Elizabeth I); *Rainbow Portrait*; Virgin Queen

Elizabeth I and the Three Goddesses, 172

"Eliza *Trivmphans*" (broadside poem), 60, 115

Ellis, Henry, 116, 252, 253, 254–55

Elvetham Hall entertainment, 59, 120, 131, 254

Elyot, Sir Thomas, 91; *Gouernour*, 121, 122

embroidery, 33–36, 77, 79–88, 269 n.21, 274 n.7 n.12, 275 n.18; compared with other arts, 38, 39–40; sumptuary restrictions on, 107

Emmison, F. J., 133, 162, 253, 259, 260, 280 n.10

engravings: of Elizabeth, 42–43, 54, 55, 69, 71–72, 172, 191; popularity of, 25; restrictions on circulation of, 171

entertainments, 11–12, 18, 184–97; ambivalence of, 164, 184; civic, 193–95; compliments to the queen in, 38, 59, 85–86, 165–67, 252; humorous, 240, 249–50; stopping of time in, 181–82, 184–88, 192–93, 285 n.19 n.27. *See also* tournaments

entries. *See* processions; progresses

Erasmus, Desiderius, 268 n.6; *De civilitate*, 89; *De recta Latini Graecique sermonis pronuntiatione*, 24–25, 43, 268 n.5

Erler, Mary C., 285 n.27

Ermine portrait (of Elizabeth I): 13

Esdaile, Katharine A., 134

Essex, first earl of, 209

Essex, Lady, 105–6
Essex, second earl of: downfall of, 215, 221–22, 224, 241, 250, 290 n.15; entertainments staged by, 165–66, 191–92; execution of, 114–15, 223, 265–66; as queen's favorite, 102, 116, 167, 188, 196, 213; rash absences of, from court, 244–45, 264–65; signature of, 39, 165; sumptuary displays of, 98, 99–100, 101; violations of courtly decorum by, 105–6, 203, 234–35, 246–48, 286 n.2
Evans, Joan, 119
Evelyn, John: *Tyrannus*, 90
Evett, David, 268 n.6

Faerie Queene (Spenser), 16, 105; allegory of the human body in, 11, 168–71; allusions to Elizabeth I in, 96, 242–43; compared with Ditchley manuscript and *Portrait*, 30, 185, 187–88; dance of the Three Graces in, 64, 170–71, 223, 248; ecphrastic passages in, 86–87; iconoclastic dispute in, 126; image of cup in dedication of 1596 edition to, 56–57
Farmer, Norman K., Jr., 282 n.44
Ferne, Sir John: *Blazon of Gentrie*, 96–97, 119, 121
Field of Cloth of Gold, 144–45, 163, 203
Filarete, Francesco: *The "Libro Cerimoniale" of the Florentine Republic*, 216–17, 248
Fisch, Harold, 267 n.2
Fischlin, Daniel, 274 n.13
Fisher, John, 262
Fitzwylliams, Sir William, 233
Fletcher, John: *King Henry VIII*, 11, 59, 126, 203, 227
Florentine Republic, 216–17, 248, 277 n.17, 280 n.5, 284 n.10
Floyd, Thomas, 172
foodstuffs, 108, 129–32, 253, 258–59, 260–62. *See also* meals and banquets

Foster, Richard, 148, 272 n.14
The Four Foster Children of Desire, 97
Foxe, John: *Acts and Monuments*, 126, 164–65, 172, 282 n.47
Franko, Mark, 59
Fraunce, Abraham: *Arcadian Rhetorike*, 50
Friedman, Alice T., 281 n.30
Frye, Susan, 268 n.8, 284 n.9, 285 n.22
Fuller, Thomas: *History of the Worthies of England*, 12, 38, 151, 154, 240, 241; *The Holy State*, 49, 110–11, 216, 221
Fumerton, Patricia, 19, 64, 278 n.47, 282 n.46, 289 n.11 n.36, 291 n.43
funeral: monuments, 109, 132–35, 278 n.48 n.59; processions, 103, 184, 191, 208–11, 287 n.11 n.12
Fussell, G. E., 286 n.5

Gage, John (Elizabethan), 134
Gage, John (modern), 268 n.7
Gager, William, 271 n.6
gardens, 33, 38–40, 187–88, 269 n.26
Gardiner, Stephen (bishop of Winchester), 26, 125–26, 165
Garter, Order of the, 119, 262–64
Gascoigne, George: *Gascoignes woodmanship*, 98, 242; *The Steele Glas*, 89, 150
Gates of Honour (at Gonville and Caius College, Cambridge), 155
Gawdy, Philip, 106–7
Gedde, W.: *A Booke of sundry Draughtes*, 40
Geller, Sherry, 285 n.26
Gent, Lucy, 19, 27–28, 138
Gentili, Alberico, 287 n.16
Gesner, Conrad, 81
Gesta Grayorum, 120, 188, 220
gesture: Elizabethan allusions to, 4–8, 267 n.2; Elizabeth's employment of, 112–13, 115, 189, 251, 266; handwriting as, 43; prescribed, 10, 123, 208, 209, 256–58; as silent language, 18,

gesture (*continued*)
233–34; spontaneous, 12, 215–16, 222–23, 234–35; territorial, 146, 279 n.1 n.3

Gheeraerts, Marcus, the Younger, 251. See also *Ditchley Portrait*; *Rainbow Portrait*

Gideon tapestries, 82, 84

gifts: of clothing, 98; to Elizabeth on progress, 12, 116–18, 193–95, 254, 277 n.17; of embroidery, 80, 83, 274 n.4 n.7; link between shape and substance in, 36–37, 130; politically motivated, 82, 113, 149, 218–19, 251; protocol governing, 202, 216–22, 249, 265, 287 n.16; of rings and jewels, 109–10, 114–16; as silent language, 64. See also prestation

Gillies, John, 273 n.49

Girouard, Mark, 19, 159, 160, 161, 269 n.26, 280 n.19

Glanville, Philippa, 124

glass, 41, 121, 122, 136, 137, 149, 270 n.26

gloves, 32, 33, 83, 101–2, 104, 167. See also hands

Glynne Cup, 123

gold: chains, 119–20, 184; coin, 125; Elizabethan love of, 79, 139, 207, 274 n.2; Elizabeth as a bird of, 48; garments of, 77, 97–98, 134; given to Elizabeth, 37, 117–19, 165, 194; lettering, 39, 270 n.29; medals, 127–28; plate, 121, 124; sumptuary restrictions on, 89–92, 107, 111. See also Field of Cloth of Gold; jewels; rings

Goldberg, Jonathan, 268 n.2, 270 n.39

Gombrich, E. H., 43

Gonville and Caius College (Cambridge), 155

Gorhambury, 154, 252, 254

Goringe, Henry, 252, 253

Gotch, John Alfred, 138

Gower, George. See *Armada Portrait*

Gowrie conspiracy, 203, 255, 286 n.2

great houses, 135–40, 148–64; elevated dining rooms in, 163, 208; elevated sleeping rooms in, 280 n.18; facades of, 51, 138–39, 154–55, 270 n.26, 279 n.64, 281 n.21; galleries in, 162–63, 281 n.35; halls in, 160–61; huge retinues kept in, 225, 258; inconvenient locations of, 232; prospect rooms in, 153, 280 n.19; screens in, 155–56, 157, 160, 161; sculptural reliefs in, 132; sumptuous furnishings of, 78–79; values embodied in, 110, 135–39, 157–64, 168–71. See also architecture; meals and banquets; tapestry

Great Seal, 124, 125–26, 215, 277 n.40

Greenblatt, Stephen, 19, 272 n.25

Greene, Robert: *A Quip for an Vpstart Courtier*, 92, 93, 261

Greene, Thomas M., 268 n.9, 282 n.38

Gresham, Sir Thomas, 8, 9, 113, 114, 124, 150–51, 154

Grey, Catherine, 114

Grey, Lady Jane, 159

Grindal, Edmund (archbishop of Canterbury), 175

Guazzo, M. Steven: *Civile Conuersation*, 4

Guevara, Antonio de: *Menosprecio*, 221

Guy, John, 289 n.12

Hamilton, John, 115

Hampton Court, 82, 119, 159, 183

Handover, P. M., 120, 165

hands: feminine, 34, 131; kissing of the queen's, 204, 216, 222, 246; moralization on, 194, 195; in portraits of Elizabeth, 13–14, 69, 172; right versus left, 144–45, 163, 223; silent language of, 6–8; washing of, 256, 258. See also gloves; rings

handwriting and lettering, 25, 39, 40, 43–45, 47–49, 270 n.39, 271 n.42

Hardwick Hall: rooftop banqueting room at, 153, 208; soaring height of, 51, 137, 159, 160–62; tapestries at, 82, 83–84, 86

Harefield entertainment, 193

Harington, Sir John, 15, 243; translation of *Orlando Furioso*, 30, 94, 243; *Treatise on Playe*, 90–91, 235. See also *Nugae Antiquae*

Harley, J. B., 67, 273 n.49

Harrison, Richard, 41

Harrison, William. See *Description of England*

Hart, John, 27

Harvey, Gabriel, 4, 50; *Gratulationem Valdeninsium*, 282 n.47; *Letter-book*, 48

hats. *See* head coverings

Hatton, Sir Christopher, 69, 102, 118, 240, 244; appointment of, as lord chancellor, 126; Elizabeth's gift of plate to, 119; extravagant devotion of, to Elizabeth, 115–16; fondness of, for knots, 37, 42, 117; Gideon tapestries of, 82, 84; magnificent homes of, 153–54, 155, 158–59; magnificent tomb of, 133–34; as manager of Elizabeth's progresses, 179, 254, 255

Haugaard, William P., 286 n.6

Hawes, Stephen: *Pastime of Pleasure*, 183

Hawkins, Edward, 127, 128, 190, 233

Hayden, Ilse, 146

Haydocke, Richard: *A Tracte Containing the Artes of curious Paintinge Caruinge & Buildinge*, 25, 28, 29, 45, 81, 268 n.7

Haynes, Alan, 270 n.35

Hayward, Sir John, 192; *Annals of the First Four Years of the Reign of Queen Elizabeth*, 5, 7, 179, 231

head coverings, 104, 202–3, 212, 286 n.2

Heal, Felicity, 280 n.9, 288 n.28

Heere, Lucas de, 91

Heijden, van der, H. A. M., 273 n.35

Helgerson, Richard, 273 n.49

Heneage, Thomas, 37, 115, 154

Heninger, S. K., 272 n.14

Henry IV, 192

Henry VII, 119, 217

Henry VIII, 82, 114, 180, 203, 286 n.7; in Deloney's *Jack of Newberie*, 249–50; at Field of Cloth of Gold, 144–45, 163, 203; institutionalized age of, 284 n.11; portraits of, 13, 164–65; sumptuary laws of, 119, 260. *See also* Dissolution of monasteries

heraldry: ceremonies held under auspices of, 206–8, 209; common people's, 43; female body and, 282 n.46; importance of line in, 40; order and status guarded by, 125, 144; perceived decline of, 214–15; significance of color in, 96–97, 103, 106

Herbert of Cherbury, Lord, 216

Hertford, earl of, 114, 120, 224

Heth, William: "The goulden arte," 112, 115, 124–25

Heywood, Thomas: *Englands Elizabeth*, 203–4; *If You Know Not Me, You Know Nobody*, 151, 152, 204

Hickes, Michael, 254, 255

Hic Mulier: Or, the Man-Woman, 94, 106

Hill, Thomas: *Interpretation of Dreames*, 145

Hill Hall, 155

Hilliard, Nicholas, 16, 124, 251, 269 n.19; ornate inscriptions of, 39, 79. Works: *Art of Limning*, 29–30; *George Clifford, Third Earl of Cumberland as the Knight of Pendragon Castle*, 13, 32, 36, 101; *Young Man among Roses*, 30–32, 269 n.17

Hind, Arthur M., 191, 209

Histrio-mastix, 99

Hoak, Dale, 277 n.40

Hoby, Sir Thomas, 133; translation of Castiglione's *Courtier* by, 27–28

Hogenberg, Franz: *Leo Belgicus*, 69
Holdenby, 154, 155, 158–59, 160
Holinshed, Raphael: *Chronicles*, 203
Holland, Philemon, 29
Holland, Thomas, 175
Holles, Sir William, 259
Holmes, Clive, 280 n.9, 288 n.28
Homer, 59
Honor Military and Civil (Segar): on
    ceremonies of degradation, 227–28,
    288 n.34; on color, 100; on funeral
    ceremony, 210–11; on the honor due
    to rank, 204, 214, 257; on magnifi-
    cence, 78; on spatial decorum, 144,
    145, 213; specification for garter col-
    lar in, 119
Horace, 271 n.6
Horshey, Sir John, 134
Hoskins, John, 234
Howard, Charles L., 214
Howard, Henry, 23, 31, 37, 176
Howard, Lady Mary, 89–90, 108
Howard, Skiles, 272 n.16
Howard, Thomas. *See* Norfolk, fourth
    duke of
Howard, Lord Thomas (lord high
    admiral), 39, 165
Howard family, 290 n.15
Howard-Hill, T. H., 271 n.46
Howson, John, 175
Huddy, John, 70, 273 n.40
Hugh of Saint Victor, 68
Hulse, Clark, 19, 157
Humphrey, Laurence, 99, 135
Humphreys, A. R., 277 n.34
Hunsdon, Lord. *See* Carey, Sir Henry
Hunter, Joseph, 209, 219
Hurst, Herbert, 70
Hutton, Ronald, 283 n.1

iconoclasm, 25–27, 28, 125–26
impresas, 32, 36, 41–42, 72, 81, 83,
    268 n.10
Ingatestone Hall, 149, 162, 253, 259–60

Institucion of a Gentleman, 261
Isham, Gyles, 279 n.64

James I, 63, 115, 255, 266; completion
    of Elizabeth's tomb by, 135, 278 n.59
Jerusalem, 68, 167
jewels, 109–20; Elizabeth's, 110–11, 115,
    212, 263–64; gifts of, to Elizabeth,
    37, 80, 115–18, 218–19, 221, 251; por-
    traits of Elizabeth wearing, 36, 72,
    102, 110; as silent language, 109–10
Johnson, Gerard, 134
Jones, Ann Rosalind, 274 n.18
Jonson, Ben, 31, 81; "To Penshurst," 98
Jourdain, Margaret, 286 n.5

Kantorowicz, Ernst K., 286 n.30
Kaushick, Sandeep, 279 n.63
Keller, Arthur S., 279 n.3
Kemp, Will: *Kemps Nine Daies Won-
    der*, 48, 232
Kenilworth Castle: architecture of, 135–
    37, 149, 154–55; entertainment at, 12,
    117, 166, 181–82, 186, 253, 254, 255;
    imported fabrics at, 83; maps at, 74
Kennedy-Skipton, Laetitia, 44,
    270 n.30
Ketel, Cornelius, 271 n.7
King, John N., 19, 42–43, 271 n.4,
    276 n.7, 277 n.40
King Arthur, 166, 213
Kingsmill, Richard, 133
Kirby Hall, 154, 155, 281 n.21
Klarwill, Victor von, 121, 124, 196, 223,
    225, 257, 262, 287 n.9 n.13
Klein, Lisa M., 274 n.4
Knecht, Robert J., 280 n.18
Knollys, Lady, 238
Knollys, Sir Francis, 119, 290 n.15
knots: collars of, 119, 124; Elizabethan
    fondness for, 36–40, 51, 80,
    269 n.26; lover's, 41, 83, 114,
    269 n.19; personal devices of, 42, 117,
    189, 218

Knox, John, 163
Knyght, Nicholas, 145
Koziol, Geoffrey, 283 n.1
Kyffin, Maurice: *Blessednes of Brytaine*, 125

Lambarde, William, 180, 192
Lane, Sir Ralph, 71
Langham, Robert: "Letter," 136, 181–82, 253
Lant, Thomas, 209, 210, 287 n.12
Lawson, Joseph: "Pennarum Nitor, or The Pens Excellency," 39
Lee, Sir Henry, 117, 225; Ditchley entertainment of, 14, 55, 68, 172, 185–88, 196, 284 n.18, 285 n.19; portrait of, 36, 276 n.6
Lefebvre, Henri, 148
Legh, Gerard: *Accedens of Armory*, 101, 210, 214
Leicester, earl of (Robert Dudley), 114, 119, 131, 153, 239; concern of, with protocol, 10, 249, 262; debts of, 118, 225, 253; elevation of, to peerage, 215–16, 223, 288 n.27; gifts to the queen from, 116–17, 194, 218, 219–20; hopes vested in estate of, 8, 42, 113; military ambitions of, 13, 122, 127, 166, 233; as queen's favorite, 188, 216, 224, 237, 241, 243, 250–51, 265; rivalry of, with Thomas Howard, duke of Norfolk, 99, 222, 244, 245. *See also* Kenilworth Castle
Leicester, Lady, 221
Leonardo da Vinci, 174
Levin, Carole, 19, 284 n.11
Lewen, Agnes, 262
Leycesters Common-wealth, 153, 219
line, 23–45, 47–74; cartographic, 65–74; circular, 58–65; in embroidery, 33–36, 80, 83; in figured texts, 49–58; in handwriting and lettering, 43–45, 47–49; influence of music on, 57–58; knots and, 36–40,

270 n.26; northern Renaissance privileging of, 16, 23–33, 268 n.3 n.6; in personal devices, 40–43; as ritual language, 202; as silent language, 18, 77. *See also* boundaries
Lissitizyn, Oliver J., 279 n.3
Llewellyn, Nigel, 133, 135, 278 n.51
Lloyd, Lodowick, 209–10; *Triplicitie of Triumphes*, 175–76
Loades, David, 238, 239, 286 n.4
Lomazzo, Paolo Giovanni, 25, 28, 29, 45, 81
London: Agas's map of, 72–73; boundaries of, 147–48, 171; drawbacks of, compared with countryside, 152; Elizabeth's coronation procession through, 177–79, 220; Elizabeth's funeral procession through, 266; Elizabeth's meeting with Leicester in, 250–51; Elizabeth's removal to, 231; flight to, from countryside, 232, 261; objections to fashions of, 92–93, 94; obligatory gifts from City of, 217; public appearances of Elizabeth in, 252; as stage for Essex's rebellion, 166; vagrant population of, 181, 289 n.36. *See also* lord mayor (of London); Royal Exchange; Saint Paul's Cathedral; Westminster Abbey
Longford Castle, 139, 168–69
Longleat House, 153
lord mayor (of London): annual ceremonial banquet of, 256–57, 260; attendance of, at Sidney's funeral, 210; gift to newly elected, from the City, 217; gold chains of, 119, 120; hospitality of, 259; processions of, 287 n.9; role of, at coronation banquet, 122; special status of, 211; sumptuary directives of, 111, 261; Thomas Norton's advice to, 171
Lorenzetti, Ambrogio, 40
Loseley Manuscripts, 130, 233, 252, 253, 254, 255

Luborsky, Ruth Samson, 271 n.46
Lucan, 31
Lucy, Sir Thomas, 133
Lumley, John, Lord, 134
Lyly, John, 43; *Cynthia's Revels*, 247; *Midas*, 79
Lyveden New Bield, 51, 138–39, 279 n.63

Machiavelli, Niccolò: *The History of Florence*, 284 n.10
Machyn, Henry: *Diary*, 102, 212, 262
magnificence: aesthetic value of, 16, 17, 53; of costume, 97–98; duration as a dimension of, 206–8; of foodstuffs, 129, 131; great houses as secular setting for, 135–37, 149, 150, 152–53, 158–63, 224–25; harmonizing qualities of, 123; high cost of, 119; of jewels, 110–11; moralists' objections to, 260, 281 n.35; of servants and followers, 77, 98, 99, 103, 225, 258, 275 n.32; superiority of modern to ancient, 175; of Sidney's funeral, 209–10; texture as a dimension of, 78; of tombs and monuments, 132, 134; visibility as a dimension of, 125. *See also* sumptuary display
Magno, Alessandro, 225
Maisse, André Hurault de: on audiences with the queen, 223, 246; on the custom of giving gifts to the queen, 116, 218; on Essex's absences from court, 244–45, 264; on the woolsack in Parliament, 140, 211, 287 n.13
Manley, Lawrence, 19, 148, 153, 274 n.49, 280 n.6
Mann, Frederick J., 279 n.3
Manning, Roger B., 188 n.30, 282 n.45
Manningham, John, 115
maps, 65–74, 272 n.30, 273 n.40 n.43 n.48 n.49; tapestry, 73–74, 82
Marcus, Leah S., 19, 280 n.6

Marian martyrs, 203
Markham, Gervase: *English Hus-wife*, 130, 156–57; *Excellent and new invented knots and mazes*, 38; *A Health to the Gentlemanly profession of Seruing-men*, 103–4
Markham, Robert, 89, 235, 244, 247, 265
Marlowe, Christopher, 35; *Hero and Leander*, 6, 88
Marnix, Philip de, 126
Marston, John, 36, 38
Mary I: ceremonies and rituals followed by, 126, 164, 175, 204–5; demotion and promotion of, 203–4, 236, 286 n.4
Mary Queen of Scots, 9, 245; Elizabeth's show of goodwill toward, 236, 237; embroidery by, 35, 80–82, 83, 274 n.7 n.12; execution of, 100, 105, 114, 115, 128; male garb of, 95, 275 n.21; marriage of, to earl of Darnley, 104–5, 165
Maynard, Henry, 254, 255
McCoy, Richard C., 286 n.6
McCracken, Grant, 275 n.33, 283 n.7
meals and banquets: cost of, 259–61; decorum of seating at, 166, 204, 262; distinction of rank at, 17, 80, 205, 258–59, 286 n.7; food service at, 155–57, 163, 255–62; location of the salt at, 122, 259; rooftop rooms for, 153, 208; roundelays sung at, 59; sugarwork showpieces at, 131–32, 278 n.47; tableware for, 121–22
medals and medallions, 37, 55, 79, 96, 109, 125–29, 190, 233
Medici, Cosimo di, 38
Medici family, 277 n.17, 280 n.5
Melville, Sir James, 108, 196, 216; visits to queen's private quarters by, 171, 237, 246
Memorial Portrait of Sir Henry Unton, 73, 133, 135, 183–84, 261

Mendoza, Bernardino de, 123–24, 237–38, 251
Merchant Adventurers, 284 n.9
Meres, Francis: *Palladis Tamia*, 85
metals. *See* precious metals
Michelangelo, 54
Mildmay, Lady, 260
Milsom, John, 57–58
Milton, John: *Paradise Lost*, 30
miniatures, 29–33, 35, 39, 90, 251, 284 n.11; Elizabeth's, 171, 237, 282 n.46
Mish, Charles C., 271 n.46
Montacute House, 51, 153, 155, 228
Montague, Anthony, "A Booke of Orders and Rules," 256
Montaigne, Michel de, 249
Montrose, Louis, 19
Mor, Antonio: *Sir Henry Lee*, 36
More, Sir George, 130
More, Sir Thomas, 120, 182; *Dialogue Concerning Heresies*, 25–26
More, Sir William, 233, 252
Morgan, Victor, 273 n.48
Morley, Thomas: *Plain and Easy Introduction to Practical Music*, 58
movement and motion, 173–97; importance of, to Elizabethans, 60, 187; royal, 5, 231–32, 237; as silent language, 18, 143–44, 160, 163–64, 167–71, 173–74, 282 n.44. *See also* dance; processions; progresses
Mowl, Timothy, 270 n.26, 279 n.60 n.63, 281 n.21
Muir, Edward, 19, 283 n.1
Mullaney, Steven, 19, 147, 280 n.6
Munday, Anthony: *Watch-woord to Englande*, 113, 286 n.5

Nashe, Thomas, 191; *Summer's Last Will and Testament*, 192–93, 252, 285 n.26, 290 n.30
Naunton, Sir Robert: 195–96
Neale, J. E., 203, 216, 224, 236

The Necessarie, Fit and Convenient Education of a Yong Gentlewoman, 85
needlework. *See* embroidery
Nevinson, J. L., 36, 40, 269 n.21, 270 n.33
New Arcadia (Sidney), 96, 105, 153, 186, 214; absent presence in, 234; ecphrasis in, 87–88; inset vernacular tales in, 16; passage through space in, 168, 282 n.44; silent language in, 6, 11
Niccols, Richard: *Englands Eliza*, 174–75, 190
Nichols, John, 36, 285 n.28
Nicolas, Harris, 32
nonverbal communication. *See* silent language
Norden, John: *Speculi Britanniae*, 70–71, 153, 158–59; *Surveyor's Dialogue*, 71, 72, 273 n.40
Norfolk, fourth duke of (Thomas Howard): downfall of, 68, 81–82, 89, 143, 242, 245; large household of, 98; rivalry of, with earl of Leicester, 99, 222, 244
Norris, Sir Henry, 145
Norris, Sir John, 241
Norris family, 117
North, Lord, 116, 124, 236, 253
Northumberland, ninth earl of (Henry Percy): early use of surveying by, 71; extravagance of, 98–99, 110, 121, 236
Norton, Thomas: "Instructions to the Lord Mayor," 171; *Warning*, 151
Norwich entertainment, 7–8, 12, 48, 102, 194–95
Nottingham, earl of, 224, 234
Nugae Antiquae (Harington): on Elizabeth's attention to costume, 89–91; on failed ambition, 229; on Harington's career as a courtier, 215, 218, 223, 239–40, 242, 244, 247; on nonverbal language at court, 8; on the queen's relationship with Essex, 235, 265, 266

obelisks, 52, 54, 135, 155
Ogelthorpe, Bishop, 204–5, 212
Old Byland, 69–70, 148
Oliver, Isaac, 42; *Unknown Melancholy Young Man*, 33–34
Oman, Charles C., 115
Orgel, Stephen, 72, 273 n.44
Ortelius, 66
Osterley House, 154
Oxford, earl of, 166, 222
Oxinden, Henry, 139

pageants and pageantry. *See* entertainments; processions; progresses; tournaments
Palmer, Daryl W., 280 n.18
Panofsky, Erwin, 25
Paradin, Claude: *Devises*, 34
Paris, Matthew, 73
Parker, Henry, Lord Morley: "Tryumphe of Tyme," 183
Parker, Matthew, 56, 74
Parliament: Elizabeth's speech to, defending her unmarried state, 95–96, 112–13, 115; harsh poor law enacted by, 181, 284 n.13; processions to, 205–8, 212, 224, 229; seating arrangements in, 140, 211, 287 n.13; sumptuary rulings of, 107–8, 111
Parr, Catherine, 80
The Passage of our most drad Soveraigne Lady Quene Elyzabeth, 177
Passe, Crispin van de, I: *Queen Elizabeth*, 42–43, 55, 172
Peacham, Henry, *Garden of Eloquence*
Peele, George, 38; *Polyhymnia*, 191
Pembroke, earl of, 84–85, 130, 225
Percy, Henry. *See* Northumberland, ninth earl of
Perlin, Stephen, 78
Perrière, Guillaume de: *Le Théâtre des Bons Engins*, 31
Perrot, Sir John, 224, 244

Perry, Maria, 223, 251
Petchenik, Barbara Bartz, 67
Petrarch, 54; *Trionfi*, 182–83
Petre, Sir William, 149, 162, 253, 259–60
Pettie, George, 40
Pevsner, Nikolaus, 150, 159
Peyto, Humphrey, 134, 135
Philip II, 127, 164, 165
Phillips, John, 27, 112, 152
Phoenix Badge, 128
Pickering, Sir William, 224
pillars, 11, 51, 53–55, 57, 122, 187; of Hercules, 8, 9, 54, 172, 186
plate: importance of, to Elizabethans, 10, 79, 120–24, 261, 274 n.2, 277 n.34; role of, in system of prestation, 80, 118, 119, 216, 218, 219
Plato, 159, 160; *Timaeus*, 272 n.14
Platt, Colin, 281 n.21
Platt, Sir Hugh: *Delightes for Ladies*, 131–32; *Floraes Paradise*, 193; *Garden of Eden*, 38
Platter, Thomas, 107, 217, 227, 236, 257
A Pleasant Dialogn[sic]e or disputation betweene the Cap, and the Head, 104, 120
Pliny, 8, 23, 29, 160, 268 n.5
Pope, Maurice, 268 n.5
Portman, Sir Hugh, 215, 243
portraits, 1–2, 3, 11, 13–14, 267 n.1, 276 n.6. *See also* Ditchley Portrait; engravings; miniatures; Rainbow Portrait; Sieve Portrait
Pound, Thomas, 252
Poyntz, Sir Gabriel, 134
precious metals, 79, 111–12, 121, 124–25, 127, 129. *See also* gold; plate; silver
precious stones. *See* jewels
prestation: definition of, 110; high cost of, 116–17, 167, 257, 276 n.16, 287 n.18; queen's part in, 118–20; as

reinforcement of hierarchy, 10, 120, 171, 217–18, 255, 277 n.19

processions: civic, 102, 103, 120, 249; coronation, 7, 102, 147, 177–79, 203, 220, 283 n.7, 284 n.9; detailed circumstantial records of, 205–8, 287 n.9; disorderly mimetic punitive, 228–29; funeral, 103, 184, 191, 208–11, 287 n.11 n.12; Garter, 263; through great houses, 163; to Parliament, 212, 224; Rogation Day, 146, 148; thanksgiving, 78, 128, 190–91; traditional substructure of, 144

prodigy houses, 137, 139, 232. *See also* architecture; great houses

progresses (of Elizabeth I): civil welcomes for, 7–8, 102, 193–95, 249; cost and inconvenience of, 116–17, 131, 218, 252–55; influence of, on Elizabethan architecture, 153–54; management of, 239; purpose of, 179–80, 181, 196–97, 251–52; Roman influence on, 176–78; slow pace of, 232; to Tilbury, 8–9, 49, 73, 166, 188–90, 285 n.21 n.22. *See also* processions

Prokter, Adrian, 280 n.9

protocol: definition of, 283 n.1; inherent value of, 205; Italian, 216–17, 248; of seating, 144, 204, 211, 224, 226, 235, 255, 279 n.67, 287 n.13; violation of, 202–3, 222, 245–48, 249. *See also* ceremony; courtesy; decorum; meals and banquets; prestation; proxemics

proxemics: definition of, 246; violations of, 213, 245–51

Puckering, Sir John, 116, 150

punishment, 89, 181, 227–29, 284 n.13

puns, 54, 132, 157, 168, 194; phonographic, 41; visual, 40, 55, 100

Puttenham, George. See *Arte of English Poesie*

pyramids, 51–52, 54, 65, 271 n.6

Queen Elizabeth as Europa, 69

The Queenes Maiesties Entertainement at Woodstock, 153

Quintilian, 5, 234

Radcliffe, Thomas, 239

Rainbow Portrait (of Elizabeth I): connection of, with Harefield entertainment, 285 n.27; display of jewels in, 110; gifts from courtiers in, 83, 193; images of domination in, 36, 102, 172; as political allegory, 274 n.13

Ralegh, Sir Walter, 61, 110; fall of, 224, 242, 243; intimacy of, with the queen, 218, 223, 290 n.15; portrait of, 13; rivalry of, with Essex, 244, 266

Ranald, Margaret Loftus, 288 n.34

Randolph, Thomas, 105

Ravenshaw, Thomas F., 132

rebuses, 34, 40–41, 269 n.21

Reformation, 112, 123, 151–52, 174–75, 201. *See also* Dissolution of monasteries; iconoclasm

Renaissance, 12, 16; architecture, 133, 136, 138, 149–50, 152, 155, 269 n.26; ceremony, 216–17, 248–49, 280 n.5; circular form in, 59, 113, 169, 174, 272 n.14; concepts of silent language, 4–5; new concepts of time in, 174, 182–84; privileging of line over picture in northern, 23–28, 268 n.3 n.5 n.6 n.7, 269 n.10; revival of antique lettering in, 43–44

The Renaissance at Sutton Place, 286 n.7

rhetorical tropes and figures: *amphibologia*, 24; *aposiopesis*, 233–34; *correctio*, 61–62; *ecphrasis*, 86–88, 186; *occupatio*, 194; *repetition*, 61; *synoeciosis*, 234; *technopaignia*, 49–58

Richard II, 192, 288 n.34

Riche, Barnabe: *His Farewell to Military Profession*, 94, 159

Ridley, Nicholas, 26

rings, 48, 83, 112–16, 134, 276 n.6; in art and literature, 64, 276 n.11; Elizabeth's strategic use of, 13, 112–13, 235, 276 n.7; gimmal, 113–14

ritual, 175–76, 179–81, 201–2; coronation, 146, 205, 236–37; definition of, 283 n.1; Garter, 262–63. *See also* ceremony

Robinson, Arthur H., 67

Robinson, Brian, 284 n.11

Rogers, William: *Eliza Trivmphans*, 54, 191

Rothwell Market House, 51, 138

roundel, 51, 58–60, 61, 159, 272 n.14

Royal Exchange, 8, 114, 124, 150–51, 152, 154

Rubin, Miri, 202

Rushton Triangular Lodge, 8, 139, 168–69, 279 n.63 n.64

Russell, Lady, 132, 208

Russell, John: *The Booke of Nurture*, 121, 255–56

Russell family, 85–86

Rutland, earl of, 209

Saint Paul's Cathedral: Armada procession to, 78, 128, 190; changing use of, 150, 151–52, 164, 165; civic ceremony at, 102–3

Salesbury, William: *Dictionary in Englysh and Welshe*, 271 n.46

Salisbury House, 154

Salter, Thomas: *The mirrhor of modestie*, 85

Salusbury, Sir John, 48

Sands, Mollie, 275 n.24

Saxton, Christopher, 66–67, 69–70, 71–72, 74

Schedel, Hartmann: *Weltchronik*, 65

Schifanoya (Italian diplomat), 77–78, 82, 174, 179, 212

Schmitt, Jean Claude, 43

Schofield, John, 154, 270 n.26

Scodel, Joshua, 278 n.48

Scrope, Lady, 115

Scrots, William, 276 n.6

Scudamore, Lady, 222, 223–24

seals. *See* Great Seal

Seckford family, 101

Seed, Patricia, 279 n.3

Segar, William: *Ermine* portrait (of Elizabeth I), 13. See also *Honor Military and Civil*

Serlio, Sebastiano, 138

servants: chains and badges of, 125; growing number of, 225, 288 n.27; magnificence of, 77, 98, 99, 103, 258, 275 n.32; obeisances expected from, 155–57, 225, 256, 257–58

The Servingman's Comfort, 104

Shakespeare, John, 28

Shakespeare, William, 16, 35, 111; ceremony in plays of, 229, 289 n.37; norm of youth in plays of, 14, 15; silent language of, 5–6, 267 n.2; spatial vocabulary of, 167–68, 268 n.10, 286 n.31. Works: *As You Like It*, 185–86; *Coriolanus*, 6, 40; *Cymbeline*, 276 n.11; *Hamlet*, 11, 12, 44, 94, 211; *Henry IV, part 1*, 102; *Henry IV, part 2*, 123, 167, 277 n.34; *Henry V*, 229; *Henry VI, part 2*, 44; *King Henry VIII*, 11, 59, 126, 203, 227; *King Lear*, 105, 225; *Love's Labor's Lost*, 6; *Macbeth*, 7, 168; *Measure for Measure*, 5–6; *A Midsummer Night's Dream*, 24, 272 n.16; *Much Ado about Nothing*, 93, 234; *Othello*, 24; *Rape of Lucrece*, 171, 186; *Richard II*, 166, 192; *Richard III*, 222; *Romeo and Juliet*, 6–7; *Sonnets*, 11, 15, 61–62; *Troilus and Cressida*, 6; *Twelfth Night*, 100; *The Two Gentlemen of Verona*, 118

shaped text, 11, 47–65, 271 n.6

Sharp, Ronald A., 287 n.18

Shaw House, 152

Sheldon, Ralph, 73–74, 82

Sheldon Tapestry Maps, 73–74, 82

Shell, Marc, 270 n.29

The Shepheard Buss, 34; 35

Shrewsbury, countess of (Bess of Hardwick), 35, 219, 232; as mistress of Hardwick Hall, 82–84, 137, 160–62, 204

Shrewsbury, sixth earl of, 36, 81, 123, 209, 215, 277 n.34

Shute, John: *First & Chief Groundes of Architecture*, 160, 164

Sidney, Mary, 239

Sidney, Sir Philip, 14, 15, 35, 111; death of, 191; encomium on, 52; funeral of, 209–10, 287 n.12; quarrel of, with earl of Oxford, 222; queen's displeasure with, 117, 218, 224; tilts of, 282 n.38, 285 n.18; tournament device of, 8, 9, 42. Works: *Arcadia*, 100–101; *Astrophil and Stella*, 6; *Defence of Poetry*, 11, 12. See also *New Arcadia*

Sidney, Sir Robert, 98, 218, 246

Sieve Portrait (of Elizabeth I), 55, 68–69, 96, 271 n.7

signatures, 39, 40, 42, 43, 165, 268 n.3

silent language, 1–20, 202; ambiguity of, 7–8, 13–14, 24, 32, 100–101, 114, 116, 126, 184; close association of, with literary language, 1, 4, 11; dynamism of, 17–18, 109–10, 174–76; Elizabethan allusions to, 4–6, 11, 43, 185, 209–10; Italian influence on, 4–5; materiality of, 79–80, 139–40; social changes concretized in, 124, 149–50, 274 n.12. *See also* rhetorical tropes and figures

silver: coin, 124–25, 165; Elizabethan love of, 77, 78, 207–8; garments, 83, 98; gifts of, 117, 118; plate, 120–24, 256, 261; sumptuary restrictions on, 107, 111; virtues ascribed to, 112

Simonds, Peggy Muñoz, 120

Sir Gawain and the Green Knight, 258

Smith, Henry: *Preparatiue to Marriage*, 112

Smith, Sir Thomas, 10, 122, 145–46, 155

Smith, William: *Chloris*, 101

Smythe, William, 260

Somerset, duke of (Lord Protector): in debate on iconoclasm, 26–27, 125–26; grand London home of, 149–50, 163

Somerset, Anne, 222, 238

Somerset House, 149–50, 163

sonnets, 6, 7, 14, 36, 61–63, 66, 188, 233

Soranzo, Giacomo, 236

Spenser, Edmund, 14, 35, 111; *Amoretti*, 6, 61, 62, 275 n.18; *Colin Clouts Come Home Againe*, 99, 153, 242; *Epithalamion*, 6, 62–63; *Muiopotmos*, 86, 275 n.18; *Prosopopoia*, 240–41; *Shepheards Calendar*, 63–64. See also *Faerie Queene*

Stallybrass, Peter, 19, 98, 275 n.32

Standen, Sir Anthony, 97–98, 264

Stanhope family, 290 n.15

Star Chamber, 65, 260

Starkey, David, 148, 288 n.27, 289 n.13

Starobinski, Jean, 276 n.16

Stead, Jennifer, 59

Stettin, duke of, 162, 196

Stickells, Robert, 138

St. Loe, Sir William, 219

Stone, Lawrence, 116, 209

Stow, John, 104, 151, 153, 288 n.26; *Annales*, 131, 166, 204, 262, 284 n.13; *Three Chronicles*, 225, 227, 228, 250–51

Streitberger, W. R., 273 n.48

Strode, John, 139

Strong, Roy, 19, 128; *Cult of Elizabeth*, 269 n.21, 285 n.19; *Gloriana*, 36, 69, 188, 191, 267 n.1, 271 n.7, 276 n.1, 284 n.11; *Portraits of Queen Elizabeth I*, 282 n.47

Strype, John, 145, 146, 226

Stuart, Arabella, 137, 266

Stuart, Mary. See Mary Queen of Scots

Stubbes, Philip: *Anatomy*, 93, 94

Stubbs, John, 223, 228

Summerson, John, 138

Summit, Jennifer, 274 n.7

sumptuary display, 77–108, 119–20, 134; Elizabeth's, 13, 96, 97, 108, 212, 263–64; hostility to, 89–90, 91–95, 103–4, 150, 270 n.29; as silent language, 74, 80, 106. *See also* great houses; magnificence; sumptuary regulations

sumptuary regulations: governing dress, 106–8, 128; governing food, 225, 258–61; governing precious metals, 111–12, 119; ineffectiveness of, 10–11, 107–8, 202, 276 n.36. *See also* sumptuary display

surveyors and surveying, 66–67, 69–71, 72–73, 273 n.40

Sussex, earl of, 124, 241, 251, 253, 254

Sutton Place, 286 n.7

Swain, Margaret, 274 n.12

Sylvester, Josuah, 11, 52, 63, 64

Talbot, Gilbert, 241, 248

tapestry, 18, 277 n.34; compared with gardening, 38; Elizabethan love of, 77–79, 82, 84, 161; as emblem of worldliness, 87, 183, 274 n.2; maps, 73–74

Tasso, Torquato, 5

Tatton, William, 226

Taylor, Barry, 228–29, 288 n.36

Taylor, Christopher, 281 n.21

Taylor, John: "The Praise of the Needle," 34, 35

Taylor, Robert, 280 n.9

Teerlinc, Lavina, 284 n.11

textiles, 77–108. *See also* tapestry

Theobalds, 74, 158; design of, 162–63; royal entertainment at, 38, 240, 270 n.28

Thomas, David, 273 n.43

Thorpe, John, 73

Throgmorton, Sir Nicholas, 119, 217

Thynne, Sir John, 116

Tilney, Edmond (also Tyllney): *A brief and pleasant discourse of duties in marriage*, 85; "Topographical Descriptions," 273 n.48

tilts. *See* tournaments

time, 173–97; cyclical, 61–63; Elizabeth as Truth, daughter of, 12, 147, 177, 178, 180; Elizabeth's supposed triumph over, 174–76, 181–82, 193, 196–97; manipulation of, in Elizabeth's processions and progresses, 176–79, 190–91; manipulation of, in royal entertainments, 184–90, 191–93; new Renaissance concepts of, 173–74; as silent language, 4

tournaments: fantastic costumes worn at, 32–33, 97–98, 99–100; silent language of, 8, 9, 101–2, 164, 191–92, 201, 282 n.38. *See also* entertainments

Tower of London: boundary dispute between City and, 147–48; execution of Essex at, 266; exhibition of plate at, 124; impaled heads on, 227

Trapp, J. B., 269 n.8

Tresham, Sir Thomas, 8, 138–39, 168–69, 279 n.63 n.64

Trevelyon, Thomas, 13, 32, 38, 40

Trexler, Richard C., 19, 277 n.17 n.38, 280 n.5

Tribble, Evelyn B., 290 n.26

Turner, William: *A new booke of spirituall Physik*, 91, 155–56

Tyacke, Sarah, 70, 273 n.40

typography, 11, 42–43, 44, 48, 57, 271 n.42 n.46

Unton, Sir Henry: *Memorial Portrait* of, 73, 133, 135, 183–84, 261

Ure, Peter, 285 n.25

vagrants, 181, 228–29, 284 n.13, 288 n.36

Vasari, Giorgio, 38

Vaughan, Virginia Mason, 273 n.49
Vawdrey, Edward, 226
Vergil, Polydore, 28–29
Verstegan, Richard: *A Restitvtion of Decayed Intelligence*, 129
Vesalius, Andreas, 174
Virgil, 159; *Aeneid*, 55, 83
Virgin Queen, 180, 196; at banquets and entertainments, 85–86, 131; on medals and pendants, 128; in poetry, 174–75, 189–90; in portraits and engravings, 13, 55, 69, 72, 96; on tapestries, 161; veiled attack on, by Mary Queen of Scots, 82

Waldstein, Baron, 179
Walker, Julia M., 278 n.59
Walsingham, Francis, 100, 134
Watson, Thomas: *'Ekatompathia*, 43, 55
Webbe, William: *Discourse of English Poetrie*, 50
Wedel, Lupold von, 124, 223, 256–57, 287 n.9 n.13
Weever, John: *Ancient Fvnerall Monvments*, 133, 211
Westminster Abbey, 32, 41, 59, 82, 148, 167
Whetstone, George: *Heptameron of Civill Discourses*, 217, 281 n.35
Whigham, Frank, 118, 232, 276 n.36, 289 n.3
White, Nicholas, 81
Whitney, Geffrey: *A Choice of Emblemes*, 31
Whyte, Rowland, 225; on the fall of Essex, 105, 246–47; on gifts from courtiers, 218–19, 221–22
Wight, Jane A., 160
Wilbraham, Sir Roger, 150
Willet, Andrew: *Sacrorvm Emblematvm*, 55
Williams, E. Carleton, 232

Williams, Neville, 98, 99, 244, 245
Williams, Penry, 290 n.15
Williamson, G. C., 101, 167
Willoughby, Elizabeth, 134
Willoughby, Sir Francis, 134, 155, 159–60, 280 n.18, 281 n.30
Willoughby, Peregrine Lord, 123, 240–41
Wilson, Derek, 122, 222
Wilson, Ezra Calhoun, 271 n.4
Wilson, Jean, 285 n.19
Wilson, Thomas (d.1581): *Arte of Rhetorique*, 4, 234
Wilson, Thomas (d.1629): *State of England*, 89, 259
Wollaton Hall, 134; display of family connections at, 161, 281 n.30; meal service at, 155; soaring height of, 51, 153, 159–60, 280 n.19
Wolsey, Thomas, 114, 119, 126, 144, 249; tapestries of, 82, 183
Woodbridge, Linda, 282 n.46
Woodstock, 38, 204; entertainments at, 153, 185
Worde, Wynkyn de: *Boke of Keruynge*, 257, 258
Worsop, Edward: *A Discoverie of sundrie errors and faults daily committed by Landemeaters*, 70
Wotton, Sir Edward, 41
Wotton, Sir Henry, 153, 166, 191
Wright, Pam, 239, 290 n.14
Wright, Thomas (d.1624): *The Passions of the Minde in Generall*, 4, 178
Wright, Thomas (1810–77), 81, 105, 120, 143, 213
Wyngfeld, Sir Anthony, 252

Yates, Frances A., 185, 271 n.7, 285 n.19
Young, Alan, 191, 285 n.18 n.24
Youngs, Frederic A., Jr., 276 n.36

Ziegler, Georgianna, 282 n.46